CompTIA

A+

STUDY GUIDE

220-1201 Core 1
220-1202 Core 2

Hopperfield
EDUCATION

TABLE OF CONTENTS

Part I – Core 1 (220-1201)

Hardware, Networking, Mobile Devices, and Troubleshooting

CHAPTER 1
Mobile Devices

1.1 Monitoring & Replacing Mobile Hardware Components

If you strip away the sleek glass and marketing buzzwords, a smartphone or tablet is just a compact, sealed computer. Inside the housing you have a system-on-a-chip, memory, storage, radios, power circuitry, and a surprising number of tiny, specialized components all working together. For an entry-level IT technician, you are not expected to become a microsoldering wizard, but you are expected to recognize these parts, interpret symptoms that point to them, and know when a situation calls for a quick field fix, a controlled component replacement, or an escalation to a manufacturer or depot service. That mindset—observing carefully, validating with tools, then acting within your scope—is exactly what the CompTIA A+ exams are probing when they ask about mobile hardware.

A useful way to think about mobile hardware support is in terms of service tiers. At the most basic level are the actions an end user can safely perform: restarting the device, removing and reinserting a SIM card, cleaning a charging port with a non-metallic tool, swapping a protective case, or applying a new screen protector. Above that sits the tier where a field technician operates, often in a corporate or repair-shop environment. This level might include replacing a screen assembly, battery, or camera module on supported models, or performing a more detailed inspection of ports and buttons. At the top is the manufacturer or depot level, where entire logic boards are swapped, chips are reflowed or replaced, and calibration tools you will never see in a typical office are used. In many organizations, any work beyond very basic component replacement is outsourced to that top tier, and the best decision you can make is to recognize, early, that the device should not be opened on your bench at all.

Inside a Smartphone or Tablet: Components and Everyday Symptoms

It's much easier to reason about symptoms when you can picture the parts behind them. Start with the front of the device, where you see the **screen assembly**. On most modern phones and tablets this assembly is actually several layers bonded together: the glass you touch, the **digitizer** that senses your finger position, and the **display panel** underneath, which might be LCD or OLED. In older or cheaper devices, those layers might be more separable; in many current models, they are treated as a single replaceable unit. When a user reports "the screen is cracked but I can still tap things," you can infer that the glass is damaged but the digitizer is at least partially alive. When they say certain parts of the screen do not respond to touch, you suspect the digitizer layer rather than the display panel. If the image looks discolored, full of vertical lines, or has a large black blotch where pixels are clearly dead, that points more to the display itself. And if the device makes notification sounds and vibrates but shows nothing at all, that suggests the main system is running but the display assembly, its backlight, or its connector to the board has failed.

Under or behind that screen is a flat, **lithium-ion or lithium-polymer battery**. Unlike the AA or AAA cells you might see in remotes, this is a slim pouch or pack, usually glued or taped in place. These batteries are rated for a limited number of charge cycles and gradually lose capacity over time. That's why a two-year-old phone might drain from 100% to 20% far more quickly than it did when new. Typical battery-related complaints sound like "my phone dies at 30%," "it only stays on when plugged in," or "it gets hot doing simple things." In more serious cases, you might actually see the battery pushing outward: the screen starts to lift away from the frame, or the back panel bows. That swelling is a red-flag safety issue rather than just an inconvenience, and your response should be much more cautious.

Distributed around the top and bottom edges are islands of **cameras, speakers, microphones, and a vibration motor**. The front and rear cameras sit as small modules attached by thin ribbon cables to the main board.

When someone says the camera app opens but the preview is completely black, even in good lighting, or the device throws an error when trying to access the camera, you connect that to the camera module or its connection. Persistent blur that is not improved by cleaning the lens cover, or obvious failure to focus, can also indicate a camera hardware problem. Speakers and microphones are similarly modular. A user who reports "I get sound through headphones but my ringer is silent" is likely dealing with a failed speaker module or a misdirected audio setting. If callers hear nothing from the other end unless the phone is on speakerphone, you suspect that one of several microphones has failed or is blocked. The vibration motor reveals itself through a different path: if vibration is enabled in settings but the device stays completely still during calls and notifications, or it emits a strange buzzing without proper vibration, the motor or its mount may be damaged.

On the sides you'll find **buttons and switches**—power, volume up and down, perhaps a home or mute switch depending on the device. Inside, each of these is a small mechanical or membrane switch on a tiny board or flex cable. Users describe these failures as "the power button is stuck," "I have to press the volume key really hard," or "the home button works only every other time." These issues might be mechanical wear, contamination from dust or liquid, or damage from drops. At the bottom edge sits the **charging and data port**, typically USB-C on modern Android devices and recent iPads, or Lightning on many iPhones. If a device charges only when the cable is held at a certain angle, disconnects frequently from a PC, or shows "USB device not recognized" on a known-good computer, you're looking at either a bad cable/adapter, debris in the port, or a failing port module itself. Many "my phone won't charge" cases end up being a compacted mass of pocket lint inside the port that prevents full contact, which is why inspection and cleaning come before replacement.

Less visible but just as important are the **wireless radios and antennas**. Wi-Fi, Bluetooth, cellular, NFC, and GPS signals all depend on properly placed antenna traces, often printed onto plastic frames or back covers, connected by tiny coax cables. When only one user's phone has consistently weak Wi-Fi in an area where everyone else is fine, and software misconfigurations like airplane mode have been ruled out, it's reasonable to suspect a damaged Wi-Fi antenna or radio. A bent frame from a drop, or an improperly reinstalled back cover after a previous repair, can easily break or misalign an antenna. NFC failures often surface when contactless payments stop working despite good cellular or Wi-Fi performance; a metal case or damaged NFC coil near the back of the device is a common culprit.

Near the edges you will also encounter the **SIM and SD card slots or trays**. The SIM is the small chip card that identifies the device to the cellular network; the SD card, when present, provides additional user storage. If a user complains that their phone constantly says "No SIM," "Emergency calls only," or randomly drops to no service while others around them have a strong signal on the same carrier, you consider whether the SIM is loose, dirty, damaged, or the tray or slot is failing. Storage-related complaints—apps refusing to install, the camera refusing to take new photos, or warnings that storage is full—point you toward internal storage utilization or a failing SD card, depending on the model and configuration. Confusing SIM and SD roles is a frequent exam trap; always anchor SIM to connectivity and SD to storage.

At the heart of the device sits the **main board or logic board**, where the system-on-a-chip, RAM, and often the primary flash storage are permanently soldered. These components are not field-replaceable in any realistic sense for an A+ technician. Symptoms like a device that never powers on even with a known-good battery and charger, or one that crashes immediately and consistently after boot with no pattern that points to a specific app, can indicate a failed logic board. Physical trauma like severe bending, crushing, or liquid ingress often damages this board. In many corporate environments, the correct action in these cases is to declare the device non-repairable on-site and arrange a replacement or manufacturer service, rather than attempt any disassembly beyond retrieving the SIM and externally accessible data.

Monitoring Mobile Hardware Health Before You Open Anything

Before you even think about disassembling a mobile device, you should exhaust the monitoring and diagnostic options offered by the operating system and by simple physical inspection. This is both a matter of efficiency and of safety. When a user says, "My phone doesn't last through lunch anymore," your first move should not be to reach for a toolkit. Instead, you open the system settings and check what the phone itself reports about its battery behavior.

On iOS, the Battery section in Settings shows you recent power usage, which apps are consuming the most energy, and on many models, an estimate of **battery health**, expressed as a maximum capacity percentage relative to when the device was new. If you see that the battery health has dropped significantly and the phone is shutting down unexpectedly under moderate load, that aligns strongly with a hardware battery problem. If, on the other hand, one social media app is responsible for the lion's share of power drain and the battery is still at 95% of its original capacity, you are dealing more with software and configuration than hardware. Many Android devices offer something similar in their Battery or Device Care sections, breaking down consumption by app and occasionally exposing battery health statistics. When not available natively, simple third-party diagnostic apps can give you an approximate picture.

Storage monitoring follows a similar pattern. In both Android and iOS you can navigate to a Storage or similar section in Settings to see how much capacity is used and what's consuming it—apps, photos, media, system data. When a phone is down to only a small amount of free space, the system may struggle to install updates, cache application data, or even save photos. This can also make the device feel sluggish, as flash storage performs best with some free space available. As a technician, you might guide the user through offloading large videos to cloud storage, uninstalling unused apps, or clearing cache data where appropriate. Only when space is clearly available yet the system still cannot reliably read or write data do you begin to think in terms of storage hardware failure or SD card issues.

Temperature and performance also go hand in hand. Modern devices include temperature sensors and will deliberately **throttle** CPU and GPU performance if they get too hot, sometimes dimming the display and throwing a warning message that the device needs to cool down. A user might reinterpret this as "my tablet suddenly got very slow" or "my screen got darker and I can't brighten it." Part of your job is to translate that experience into the underlying reality that the device is protecting itself, likely due to a combination of heavy usage and ambient conditions. Leaving a phone in direct sunlight on a car dashboard, gaming while charging with the device wrapped in a blanket, or operating in a hot warehouse are all factors you need to consider before blaming a failing battery or processor.

Beyond these general settings screens, many manufacturers and carriers include dedicated diagnostics tools. These can take the form of a Support or Device Care app that can run tests on the display (checking for dead zones in the touchscreen), speakers and microphones (playing and recording test sounds), cameras, vibration, and sensors like the accelerometer. Some devices hide such tools behind special dialer codes or service menus that only authorized technicians routinely use. For exam purposes you do not need to memorize secret codes, but you do need to understand that running hardware diagnostics to confirm a fault is a standard step before you replace anything. If a user claims their microphone is broken but the diagnostic microphone test passes and recordings sound clear, you redirect your attention to call settings, app permissions, or the possibility that a particular case is blocking a specific mic port during calls.

Finally, you should never underestimate the value of a careful visual and physical inspection. With the device powered down, you can check for cracked or separating glass, subtle bends in the chassis, gaps between the screen and frame that might indicate a swollen battery, corrosion or discoloration around ports that could suggest liquid contact, or missing and mismatched screws that hint at prior unauthorized repairs. Lightly wiggling a connector while observing the charging icon, or gently pressing along the screen edges to see if it moves, can provide additional clues. These observations not only guide your technical decisions but also support documentation and warranty discussions later.

1.2 Mobile Accessories & Connections

If you think about how people actually use their smartphones and tablets at work, very few of those devices operate on their own. A sales rep wants to present slides from a phone to a projector. A manager wants to join a video call with a Bluetooth headset while their device charges on a wireless pad. A field technician wants to connect a tablet to a keyboard and mouse back at the office to finish a report. From the help desk point of view, all of these are "my phone won't connect to..." tickets, and the difference between solving them quickly and getting stuck usually comes down to how well you understand mobile accessories and the ways they connect.

A good way to approach this topic is to start by asking what the user is trying to accomplish. Are they trying to hear something, show something, type something, charge something, or share something? Once you can name the goal, you can narrow down the accessory category and the likely connection method—wired, wireless, or some mix of both. The CompTIA A+ exam often hides this logic inside short scenarios, so in this section we will not only describe the accessories and ports by name, but also practice thinking through which technology fits which situation and what to check when things don't work as expected.

Accessory types in everyday support

Audio accessories are one of the most visible and heavily used categories. Many users still carry **wired headsets or earbuds**, especially in business environments where they jump between conference calls and in-person conversations. On older devices and some budget phones, these plug into a 3.5 mm audio jack, usually a **TRRS** connector that handles left and right audio plus a microphone channel. Newer phones increasingly skip this jack entirely and rely on USB-C or Apple's Lightning port for wired audio. That's why you'll often see a short USB-C-to-3.5 mm or Lightning-to-3.5 mm "dongle" attached to someone's old favorite headphones. When a user says, "My wired headset doesn't work with my new phone," the first thing to check is whether their new device actually has a compatible port or whether they now need an adapter or a Bluetooth option instead.

Wireless audio has become the default for many users, especially in the form of **Bluetooth headsets and earbuds**. These trade the reliability of a physical cable for the flexibility to move around freely and connect to multiple devices. From a support perspective, the key concept is pairing. Both the phone and the headset need Bluetooth turned on, the headset must be in pairing or discoverable mode, and the phone must select that device from its Bluetooth list. When things fail, you often discover that the headset is already connected to someone's other phone, the battery is nearly dead, or Bluetooth was disabled by airplane mode. Car integration works on the same principles: **car kits and hands-free systems** use Bluetooth to sync contacts, route calls through the car's microphone and speakers, and stream music. The first time a phone pairs with a vehicle, the user must often grant permissions to share contacts and call logs, and confusion arises when users accidentally deny that request and then wonder why names do not show up on the dashboard screen.

Moving from audio to productivity, you will see a lot of users who want their tablet or even phone to behave more like a traditional computer. **Bluetooth keyboards and mice** are the easiest way to give a tablet laptop-like input without needing a special connector. These devices pair much like headsets: enable Bluetooth, put the accessory in pairing mode, and select it. On some tablets and high-end phones with USB-C, you may also encounter wired USB keyboards and mice, often connected through a dock or a USB-C hub. This is where understanding which device can act as a USB host and whether it supports USB On-The-Go becomes important, a point we will return to when we look at ports and adapters.

Another important productivity accessory is the **stylus or digital pen**. At the simple end, there are passive capacitive styli that mimic a finger and work with almost any touchscreen. More advanced "active" pens support pressure sensitivity, palm rejection, and programmable buttons, but only if the device's digitizer and operating system were designed for that specific pen technology. Many of these pens also use Bluetooth for extra features, which means that if a user's pen "suddenly stopped working," you need to distinguish between a physical screen problem, a dead pen battery, or a lost Bluetooth connection. Some business environments also use **docking stations and keyboard cases** that physically attach to the device, often providing a keyboard, additional ports such as HDMI and USB-A, and sometimes even wired Ethernet. These can be proprietary to a specific tablet model, or they can be generic USB-C docks that rely on industry standards like USB-C Alt Mode for video.

Power accessories form another major category that you will handle constantly. Nearly every user has at least one **wired charger**, which really consists of two parts: an AC adapter ("the brick") that plugs into the wall and converts AC to low-voltage DC, and a **cable** that runs from that adapter to the phone or tablet. At the device end, you will most commonly see USB-C, Apple Lightning, or legacy micro-USB. At the adapter end, you often see USB-A or USB-C. Understanding that voltage and amp ratings matter will keep you from recommending low-power chargers that cannot keep up with a tablet's draw or from ignoring fast-charging capabilities that users expect. Matching a fast-charging phone to a low-power adapter means slower charging; mismatching cheap, poorly made chargers can mean overheating and safety risks, so in business settings many organizations standardize on vendor-certified or quality third-party chargers.

For users on the move, **power banks**—external battery packs—are a common request. Capacity is measured in milliamp-hours (mAh), and larger capacities can recharge a phone several times. Some power banks add features like multiple output ports, USB-C Power Delivery, or wireless charging. Here again, compatibility matters: a bank can supply power to almost any device via USB, but fast charging or laptop charging can require specific voltage profiles and appropriate cabling. Wireless charging pads and stands introduce a different technology entirely: **inductive charging**, most commonly using the Qi standard. To work properly, both the phone and the pad must support Qi, the phone must be positioned correctly over the charging coils, and certain cases—especially metal cases or very thick covers—can interfere. When a user insists "the wireless charger is broken," it is often a matter of misalignment, insufficient power to the pad, or a case that blocks the induction field.

Storage and media accessories show up frequently any time someone needs to move large files without relying on cloud services. Some mobile devices support **external flash drives and storage** that plug directly into USB-C or Lightning ports. Others use dual-interface drives that have USB-C on one end and USB-A on the other, making it easy to move files between a phone and a traditional PC. On mobile platforms, file manager apps and filesystem support can affect whether the drive is recognized. In Android, for example, USB OTG support and file permissions must be in place. In iOS and iPadOS, external storage support depends on OS version and app capabilities. Many Android phones and some tablets also accept **microSD cards** for storage expansion. Technicians should know that not all devices have a card slot, and even when they do, mounting and unmounting the card properly prevents data loss. MicroSD-to-SD adapters can then be used to move those cards into laptops or cameras, which is common in environments where employees capture photos or video in the field.

Protective and mounting accessories may not seem technical at first glance, but they influence troubleshooting more than you might expect. **Cases, covers, and rugged enclosures** are essential for drop protection, particularly in retail, warehouse, and field service roles. However, bulky cases can prevent docks from seating properly, block USB-C or Lightning ports, or reduce contact with wireless charging pads. When a device "won't charge," removing the case briefly to test the bare device is a simple but often overlooked step. **Screen protectors** can also cause issues if installed poorly, trapping dust or bubbles that confuse the touch sensor, or if made from low-quality materials that reduce sensitivity. In vehicles, **mounts and stands** help keep devices visible and within easy reach while complying with hands-free laws. Some mounts integrate Qi charging or use magnetic attachments that require compatible cases or built-in magnets, again adding possible points of failure or misalignment.

You will also see more specialized accessories in business-heavy environments. **Credit card readers and point-of-sale (POS) add-ons** are a classic example: small devices that plug into a phone's headphone jack, Lightning port, or USB-C port, or connect via Bluetooth. These rely on both the physical connection and a companion mobile app, as well as a working network connection for transaction processing. When troubleshooting, you have to think in layers: is the reader physically connected or paired, is the app up to date and allowed to access the accessory, and does the device have adequate network connectivity? Wearables such as smartwatches and fitness bands fall into a similar pattern. They typically use **Bluetooth or Bluetooth Low Energy** to pair with the phone and offload data. If a user complains their wearable stopped syncing, you will check Bluetooth status, pairing state, firmware update prompts, and app permissions for health or notification data.

Physical ports, connectors, and adapters

All of these accessories need a way to attach, and the details of those connections matter a great deal. On mobile hardware, most wired connections revolve around variations of USB and a few proprietary standards. Older and lower-cost Android devices often still use **micro-USB**, a small, trapezoidal connector that only fits one way and is relatively fragile. Many exam questions deliberately contrast micro-USB with the newer **USB-C** connector, which is reversible, more robust, and capable of carrying higher power and faster data. USB-C is appearing on everything from phones and tablets to laptops and docks. A critical point for the exam and real life is that the shape of the connector does not tell you all of its capabilities. One USB-C port might support only basic charging and data, while another on a high-end tablet might support DisplayPort video output, power delivery, and USB OTG for external peripherals. You always have to consider the device's specifications, not just the connector shape.

On the "host" side of charging bricks and computers, you will still see a lot of **USB-A** ports, the traditional rectangular USB connector. Cables often bridge between USB-A on the power adapter or PC and USB-C, micro-USB, or Lightning on the mobile device. Speaking of Lightning, Apple's **Lightning** connector is a proprietary, reversible connector used on many iPhones and some iPads, especially older generations. Like USB-C, it can carry power and data, and with the right adapter, it can output audio and video. With more recent Apple hardware migrating to USB-C, you will need to pay attention to which connector a particular model uses, because that choice drives which cables and adapters apply.

Audio connections are still anchored by the **3.5 mm TRRS jack** on many headphones and some phones, though many premium models have removed that jack altogether. TRRS refers to the four conductors on the plug, which support stereo audio plus a microphone and common ground. If a user reports that only sound, but not microphone, is working, they may be using a TRS (three-conductor) plug with a device expecting TRRS wiring, or vice versa. When that jack is missing from the device, your options shift to USB-C or Lightning audio adapters, or to Bluetooth audio entirely.

For extending displays, you will encounter a variety of **video-out and multi-function adapters**. Many modern phones and tablets with USB-C support display output using technologies such as DisplayPort Alt Mode. In practice, this means you can plug in a USB-C-to-HDMI adapter or connect through a USB-C dock that offers HDMI or DisplayPort ports. Not every USB-C device supports this; lower-cost phones might only provide power and data, so you cannot assume video-out just by looking at the connector. On Apple devices that still use Lightning, you can achieve HDMI output using a **Lightning digital AV adapter**, which converts the Lightning port into an HDMI output plus, usually, a pass-through Lightning port for power. In corporate environments, desktop docks and hubs aggregate these functions, offering a single cable from the mobile device to a dock that then exposes multiple USB ports, a wired network jack, HDMI, audio, and power.

Many scenarios on the exam and in the field center on USB **On-The-Go (OTG)**, which allows a mobile device to act as a USB host for peripherals such as flash drives, keyboards, mice, or card readers. To accomplish this, you use OTG adapters or cables that convert the phone's USB-C or micro-USB port into a full-size USB-A female port. If the hardware and operating system support OTG, plugging in a thumb drive should make it available in the file manager, and plugging in a keyboard should allow text entry. If nothing happens, you have a compatibility or configuration problem: the device might not support OTG at all, or permissions or power limits might be in the way.

Wireless connections: Bluetooth, NFC, tethering, and casting

As important as physical ports are, many mobile accessories connect wirelessly. **Bluetooth** is the workhorse technology here, used by headsets, speakers, car audio systems, keyboards, mice, smartwatches, and more. It is designed for short-range personal area networks—typically up to about 10 meters for most devices, more for some modern versions. Establishing a Bluetooth connection always involves the same pattern: both devices must have Bluetooth enabled, the accessory must enter pairing mode (often indicated by a flashing LED), and the mobile device must select and pair to it, sometimes confirming a PIN or passkey. When troubleshooting, verify pairing mode, check that the accessory is not already paired and actively connected to a different device, ensure that Bluetooth is not disabled by settings or airplane mode, and confirm battery levels. Many intermittent audio problems boil down to low battery on a headset or interference from crowded 2.4 GHz environments.

Near Field Communication (NFC) occupies a different niche. It operates over very short distances—usually just a few centimeters—and requires close physical proximity. You see NFC most often in tap-to-pay systems such as mobile wallets, or in simplified pairing processes where you tap a phone to a speaker to initiate Bluetooth pairing. Some organizations also use NFC tags to store configuration information, such as Wi-Fi credentials, that a user can retrieve by tapping their phone. For troubleshooting, you need to know that NFC must be enabled in the phone's settings, that the NFC antenna's location on the device matters for alignment with the reader, and that NFC itself usually only initiates a transaction or a connection; the actual high-bandwidth data transfer often happens over another channel like Wi-Fi or Bluetooth. Security-wise, NFC's short range and requirement for physical proximity provide some natural protection, but payment applications still enforce PINs or biometric checks.

When users ask, "Can I use my phone as internet for my laptop?" you are dealing with **tethering and mobile hotspot** features. The underlying idea is that a phone with cellular data shares that connection with other devices that lack a cell modem. There are three main methods. With **USB tethering**, you connect the phone to a laptop via a USB cable and enable USB tethering in the phone's settings. The laptop then sees a new network interface and routes traffic through the phone's data plan. This approach is relatively secure and power-efficient because the cable also charges the phone. With a **Wi-Fi hotspot**, also called a personal hotspot, the phone behaves like a small wireless router, broadcasting an SSID and requiring a password. Other devices connect as they would to any Wi-Fi network. This is convenient for multiple clients but drains the battery faster and can be restricted or throttled by the cellular carrier. Finally, **Bluetooth tethering** uses a Bluetooth Personal Area Network (PAN) to share internet access. This method offers lower bandwidth and is less common, but can be a useful option when Wi-Fi is restricted.

Supporting tethering means thinking about both mobile OS settings and carrier policies. If a user cannot find the hotspot option or sees it greyed out, their carrier plan might not allow it, or mobile data might be disabled entirely. If devices see the hotspot but cannot connect, check the SSID and password, encryption type, device limits, and any indicators that the plan's data cap has been exceeded. With USB tethering, ensure that appropriate drivers installed on the laptop, especially on Windows systems that might need a mobile device driver package.

Finally, mobile devices increasingly send video to displays without any cables at all via **wireless display and casting** technologies. Names vary by platform: Miracast, Chromecast, AirPlay, and similar standards all allow a phone or tablet to mirror its screen or cast specific content to a compatible TV, display, or streaming adapter over Wi-Fi. The core requirements are straightforward. Both the sending device and the receiving display or adapter need to support the same protocol or application, they typically need to be on the same Wi-Fi network or otherwise reachable, and the display must be powered on and selected as the active input. When users complain that "casting doesn't work," you will check that the receiving device actually supports the requested protocol, that it is joined to the correct network, and that any required app or feature (such as AirPlay on an Apple TV or casting support on a smart TV) is enabled.

Across all of these technologies, the support mindset stays the same. Start by clarifying what the user is trying to do: output audio, share a display, transfer files, expand storage, or share connectivity. Identify whether a wired or wireless accessory makes the most sense and which connector or radio technology is appropriate. Then verify fundamentals such as power, physical connections, and basic settings like Bluetooth, Wi-Fi, NFC, and airplane mode. Once you are comfortable mapping goals to accessories and connection types, most mobile "won't connect" problems become structured puzzles rather than mysteries, and you will be better prepared for both the exam scenarios and the real tickets that follow.

1.3 Mobile Network Connectivity & App Support

If there is a single theme that runs through almost every mobile support ticket, it is this: the device is only as useful as its connections. A top-of-the-line smartphone with no network access is, practically speaking, an expensive calculator. In a helpdesk role you will constantly be working at two layers: first, making sure the device can talk to the outside world over Wi-Fi, cellular data, and Bluetooth; second, making sure the apps that ride on top of those connections—email, VPN, collaboration tools, storage—are configured and behaving correctly. The CompTIA A+ exam leans heavily on that real-world reality, so in this chapter we will stay close to what you will actually see when users call in and say, "My phone stopped working."

Wi-Fi Connectivity on Mobile Devices

On both Android and iOS, Wi-Fi is usually the preferred way to connect to the internet when you are indoors or anywhere you have a stable wireless network. From the user's point of view, the core concepts are simple. A **Service Set Identifier (SSID)** is just the network's visible name, like "CompanyGuest" or "JonesFamilyWiFi." The "password" is really a **pre-shared key** for security, most commonly using WPA2-Personal or WPA3-Personal in home and small office environments. In corporate environments, that security can get more complex behind the scenes—certificates, RADIUS, 802.1X—but on the device the user still typically taps a network name and enters something.

The basic workflow for joining Wi-Fi is nearly identical across platforms. The user opens the Settings app, finds the Wi-Fi or Network & Internet section, and first verifies that Wi-Fi itself is actually enabled. Then the device scans for nearby SSIDs and presents a list. The user chooses the correct SSID, enters the password if prompted, and waits for the device to show some indicator that it is connected. That indicator might be the Wi-Fi "fan" icon appearing in the status bar, a check mark next to the SSID name, or a simple "Connected" label. Even though the menu labels and icons differ slightly between Android skins and iOS versions, the sequence of "turn on, pick a network, authenticate, confirm connection" is consistent enough that you can comfortably talk a user through it over the phone.

Where things become interesting from a support and exam standpoint is when that simple process does not complete successfully. Consider a user in an office who reports that their phone shows no Wi-Fi networks at all. Your first line of thinking should be toward global radio settings. Is Wi-Fi toggled off in Settings? Has **Airplane mode** been turned on, disabling all radios? If other devices in the same area can see and join the Wi-Fi, it is unlikely to be an access point outage and more likely a device-side setting. On the exam, a scenario describing "no SSIDs visible" in an area where Wi-Fi is known to be present often points to Wi-Fi being disabled or Airplane mode being active.

A more common scenario is that the user sees the network but cannot get connected. They may say the phone "keeps spinning" or "says incorrect password." Here, simple user error is extremely common: mistyped passwords, old passwords saved on the device after the company changed them, or confusion between similarly named SSIDs like "Company" and "CompanyGuest." Your best move is often to have the device "forget this network," which wipes its stored password and settings, and then join again with known-good credentials. If the user is absolutely certain the password is correct, but the device still fails to connect while others can, you start thinking about things like MAC address filtering on the router, limits on the number of connected devices, or, in a corporate environment, the device not being authorized.

There is also the frustrating case where the user connects to Wi-Fi just fine—full signal bars, connected label—but cannot reach any websites. In that case, the wireless connection might be working, but there is a problem beyond the access point. The router could have lost its internet connection, DNS could be failing, or the user could be sitting on a **captive portal** page they have never completed. In hotels, airports, and guest networks, it is very common that the user connects to the SSID but must accept terms or sign in on a web page before real internet access is granted. If the user never opens a browser or dismisses the portal prompt, they believe "Wi-Fi is broken" even though the wireless link itself is fine. As a mobile tech, your practical steps are usually straightforward: confirm other devices on the same Wi-Fi have internet, toggle Wi-Fi off and on, have the user open a browser, and complete any portal requirements.

From a helpdesk perspective, the key habit is to verify the simple and obvious steps before jumping into more invasive procedures. Check whether Wi-Fi is on and Airplane mode is off. Confirm the user is connecting to the intended SSID, not a neighbor's or some random open network. Use "forget network" and reconnect if credentials may be corrupted. The A+ exam will frequently test your ability to choose that modest "next best step" instead of something drastic like resetting network settings or factory-resetting the phone.

Cellular Network Connectivity Basics

When the user walks away from Wi-Fi coverage, the device must fall back on **cellular data** provided by their mobile carrier. This is a completely different path to the internet: instead of a local access point, you have cell towers, a subscriber identity module (**SIM** or **eSIM**), and the user's monthly data plan. Many users blur Wi-Fi and cellular in their minds and will refer to any kind of internet access as "Wi-Fi," so part of your job is silently translating their language into the appropriate technical channel.

On the status bar, the device typically displays two separate elements related to cellular connectivity. One is a set of signal bars indicating radio strength from the nearest tower. The second is a label such as "3G," "4G," "LTE," or "5G" that indicates the data technology in use. In exam scenarios, seeing "LTE" or "5G" with several bars usually implies that cellular data should be performant. Seeing a tiny "E" (for EDGE) or no data label at all suggests extremely slow or nonexistent mobile data, even if there are bars. It is crucial to remember that signal bars alone do not guarantee usable data; a user can have excellent signal for voice calls but still be on a legacy or congested data technology.

On both Android and iOS, there is a master **Mobile Data** toggle. When disabled, the phone will refuse to use cellular data and often displays warnings like "Cellular data is turned off" when trying to access online services away from Wi-Fi. If a user reports that "nothing works unless I'm on Wi-Fi," one of your first checks should be whether that mobile data switch is simply off. Closely related is the concept of data usage limits and throttling. Users with limited plans may hit a monthly cap; at that point, the carrier can block or severely slow data usage. In a corporate environment, especially with company-issued lines, the account may be suspended or restricted for billing reasons. In any of these cases, it is important to distinguish a configuration problem on the device from an account issue that must be escalated to the carrier or administrator.

Another critical setting you will encounter is **data roaming**. When a user travels outside their home carrier's network—especially internationally—the phone may need to roam onto partner networks. To protect users from huge unexpected bills, phones usually ship with data roaming disabled. The result is a classic support story: an employee lands in another country, suddenly cannot use any mobile data, and calls IT. The local bars may be full, but the data indicator is gone or shows an exclamation mark. Your safest first step is to verify whether data roaming is disabled. Depending on policy, the organization may prefer that the user keep roaming off and rely on Wi-Fi, or they may instruct the user to turn roaming on after warning about possible charges.

Underlying the data connection are **Access Point Name (APN)** settings, which tell the phone how to connect to the carrier's data network. For typical consumer devices, these are automatically configured when you insert a SIM, and they rarely need adjustment. However, in bring-your-own-device or specialized scenarios, misconfigured APN values can prevent the device from using cellular data at all. On the exam, if you see a scenario where a phone can make voice calls and send SMS but never gets data, and the user just moved their SIM between carriers or changed plans, APN misconfiguration or an unprovisioned SIM is a reasonable suspect. The usual fix is to restore default APN settings or confirm the correct values with the carrier, rather than trying to guess.

You will also see situations related to SIM activation and carrier locks. A user might insert a new SIM and see "No service" or a prompt that the SIM is not supported. At the A+ level, you are mainly expected to recognize that this can indicate an unactivated SIM or a phone that is locked to a different carrier, rather than something like a Wi-Fi or Bluetooth problem. The correct move is often to verify with the carrier or escalate to whoever manages the mobile fleet.

Bluetooth Connectivity and Accessories

While Wi-Fi and cellular focus on network access, **Bluetooth** is all about short-range device-to-device connections. It is designed for low-power links to peripherals such as headsets, speakers, keyboards, mice, car infotainment systems, and wearable devices like smartwatches. A surprisingly common misconception among nontechnical users—and among exam candidates—is to think of Bluetooth as some kind of internet substitute. It is worth drilling into your own mindset that Bluetooth is essentially a cable replacement, not a path to the internet in ordinary use.

On a smartphone, Bluetooth has its own master toggle in Settings and usually a quick-access icon in the pull-down shade or Control Center. The typical pairing process has two sides. First, you put the accessory into **pairing mode**, which often means holding down a specific button until a light starts flashing. Second, on the phone, you scan for new Bluetooth devices and then select the one that matches the accessory's name. Sometimes you will be prompted to confirm a pairing code; other times it pairs automatically. From then on, the phone stores that pairing and will attempt to reconnect automatically when the accessory is in range and powered on.

From a support angle, a lot of Bluetooth problems track back to that initial pairing step not being done correctly. The user says, "My headphones don't show up on my phone," but when you dig deeper, the headphones are not actually in pairing mode, or they are already paired to a different device nearby. Many Bluetooth devices can only be connected actively to one host at a time. If a user's earbuds are happily connected to their laptop, they may never show as available on the phone until disconnected. Asking the user to fully power-cycle the accessory, clear previous pairings (sometimes by holding a reset button), and then try pairing again from the phone's Bluetooth menu usually resolves these unseen conflicts.

Once paired, users may complain that Bluetooth devices disconnect frequently or seem unreliable. Here you want to think about battery level, range, and interference. A headset with a nearly dead battery may cut in and out. An accessory at the far edge of its nominal range—typically about 10 meters for many consumer devices—will also drop frequently, especially with walls or other obstacles in between. On some phones, aggressive power-saving modes can temporarily suspend Bluetooth connections when the device is idle to conserve battery. Guiding the user to charge their accessory, move closer, or disable an extreme battery-saver mode is often more effective than digging into obscure settings.

There is a subtle but very common issue around audio routing. A user says, "The call is still coming through my phone, not my Bluetooth," even though the headset is paired. Many mobile operating systems allow multiple audio outputs to be connected at once, and merely being paired does not always mean a device is selected as the current output. During a call or while playing media, users can usually tap an audio or speaker icon to choose between "iPhone," "Speaker," "Headset," "Car," and similar options. Part of effective Bluetooth support is calmly explaining that they may have to select the headset as the active output each time, especially with car systems that behave differently depending on the app.

As with Wi-Fi, "forgetting" a problematic Bluetooth pairing and setting it up again from scratch is a safe and often recommended step. You should, however, be cautious about advising users to update firmware on their accessories if the battery on either side is low, as a failed firmware update can permanently brick the device.

Mobile Apps: Sources, Permissions, and Updates

Once the device's radios are behaving, the next layer to understand is the mobile app ecosystem itself. On iOS, the primary trusted source for apps is the **App Store**. On Android, it is the **Google Play Store**, although Android also supports installation from other sources, commonly called side-loading. In corporate environments, you may also see managed app catalogs or "company portal" apps associated with a mobile device management (MDM) system. As an entry-level technician, you do not have to become an expert in MDM yet, but you should recognize that a company device may only be allowed to install approved apps and may receive required apps automatically.

From a support perspective, every app has a basic lifecycle: it is installed, opened and configured, used day-to-day, updated over time, and eventually uninstalled if it is no longer needed. Many frustrating app behaviors—crashing on launch, poor performance, odd display glitches—are rooted in outdated app versions that do not fully support the current operating system. One of the simplest but most important troubleshooting questions you can ask is whether the app has pending updates. In some organizations, policy explicitly requires that a user update certain critical apps before the helpdesk will investigate problems further.

Modern mobile operating systems also apply a strong **permission** model to apps. When an app first needs access to something sensitive—your location, contacts, camera, microphone, storage—it must ask the user to allow or deny that permission. If the user denies a permission that the app genuinely requires, then a major function simply will not work. A maps app without location permission cannot show your current position. A video conferencing app without microphone permission cannot hear you. A QR code or authenticator app without camera permission cannot scan codes. As a technician, you must walk a line between least-privilege (not granting unnecessary access) and functionality. Often, the best practice is to read the app's documentation or corporate guidance and then help the user enable only what is appropriate in Settings under the app's permission list.

1.4 Knowledge Check

Question 1: A user reports their phone's display is completely black, but it still vibrates on incoming calls and plays notification sounds. Based on likely hardware failure, what is the BEST next step for a field technician?

- **A.** Replace the logic board after backing up all user data to a secure external location
- **B.** Suspect a failed screen assembly and arrange screen replacement or authorized manufacturer repair
- **C.** Perform a factory reset from recovery mode to reinstall the OS and restore all user applications
- **D.** Replace the battery with a new pack of the same type and capacity to rule out a power issue

Question 2: A smartphone's battery has started swelling, pushing the screen away from the frame slightly. What should the technician do FIRST?

- **A.** Discharge the battery fully and continue using it as normal until it fails completely
- **B.** Power down the device, isolate it, and follow procedures for safe battery replacement and disposal
- **C.** Press the screen back into place and secure it with tape or clamps until a replacement arrives
- **D.** Puncture the swollen area to release pressure, then recharge the device to test functionality

Question 3: A user says their rear camera app opens, but the preview is always black even in good lighting. Cleaning the lens does not help, and other apps that use the rear camera show the same issue. What is the MOST likely cause?

A. Display backlight failure preventing the image from being visible on the screen
B. Corrupt operating system causing all camera applications to crash silently
C. Low storage space preventing photos from being saved to internal memory
D. Failed or disconnected camera module preventing image data from reaching the system

Question 4: A user's phone only charges when the USB-C cable is held at a specific angle. The technician has verified with multiple known-good chargers and cables. What is the BEST next step, assuming the device is under manufacturer warranty?

A. Document the issue and arrange warranty service for charging port repair or replacement
B. Open the device and re-solder the USB-C connector directly to the system board in the field
C. Perform a factory reset to rule out software issues with the charging controller firmware
D. Disable fast charging in settings and continue using the existing port without service

Question 5: A user complains that only the lower half of their touchscreen responds to taps, while the image looks normal across the entire display. What component is MOST likely at fault?

A. Logic board causing intermittent processing issues for touch input and UI responsiveness
B. Backlight providing uneven illumination to the lower portion of the display panel
C. Digitizer layer that detects touch input and sends coordinates to the operating system
D. Battery providing insufficient power to the lower half of the touchscreen circuitry

Question 6: A user states, "My phone says 'No SIM' and I can't make calls, but Wi-Fi still works." After verifying that Airplane mode is off, what should the technician check FIRST?

A. Whether the SIM card is seated correctly or the tray and contacts are damaged or misaligned
B. If the device has exceeded its storage capacity and is blocking additional network connections
C. If Bluetooth is set to discoverable mode and interfering with the cellular radio functions
D. Whether the SD card is formatted correctly and recognized by the operating system

Question 7: A user reports that their NFC-based tap-to-pay stopped working, but Wi-Fi, Bluetooth, and cellular all function normally. What is the MOST likely issue?

A. The SIM card is failing and preventing secure element access for wireless payments
B. The phone's digitizer is damaged and cannot detect touch input near the NFC area
C. The user's email app is misconfigured and is blocking all NFC-based transactions
D. NFC is disabled in settings or blocked by a case or damaged NFC coil near the antenna

Question 8: On inspection, a technician notices a slight gap forming between the smartphone screen and the frame on one side, with no visible crack in the glass. What potential issue should the technician suspect FIRST?

A. Wi-Fi antenna misalignment causing the frame to separate from the display assembly
B. Swollen lithium battery pushing the screen and lifting it away from the chassis
C. Faulty vibration motor shaking the device and loosening the screen over time
D. Incorrect APN settings causing overheating and warping of the display frame

Question 9: While preparing to open a tablet to replace its internal battery, which of the following safety steps should the technician perform FIRST?

A. Heat the back cover to soften adhesive and make it easier to pry off the housing
B. Remove all screws holding the frame so internal components can be accessed
C. Power down the device completely and disconnect any external power cables
D. Pry directly under the battery with a metal tool to quickly release the adhesive

Question 10: A user's Android phone suddenly becomes very slow and the screen auto-dims, displaying a warning that the device is overheating. What is the BEST interpretation of this behavior?

A. The device is throttling performance and brightness to protect itself from high temperature
B. The battery is at end of life and must be replaced immediately to restore normal function
C. The SIM card is loose and causing the processor to reduce speed to maintain connectivity
D. There is a Wi-Fi antenna failure forcing the device to overheat while searching for networks

Question 11: A user claims their phone will not charge on a Qi wireless charging pad. The technician verifies both devices support Qi, but charging still fails. The wired charger works fine. What should the technician check NEXT?

A. Whether the SIM tray is inserted correctly to allow wireless power negotiation with the pad
B. If Bluetooth is interfering with NFC and preventing the wireless charging handshake
C. Case thickness, case material, and phone alignment on the pad for proper coil contact
D. If the phone's microphone is muted and blocking system sounds during charging

Question 12: A user wants to connect a USB flash drive directly to their Android phone to copy large video files without using the cloud. Which requirement is MOST important for this to work?

A. The phone must support HDMI Alt Mode to mirror the display to an external monitor
B. The phone must have a removable battery to allow safe hot-swapping of USB devices
C. The phone and adapter must support USB On-The-Go (OTG) so it can act as a USB host
D. The phone must be rooted to enable access to external USB mass storage devices

Question 13: A user's new phone does not have a 3.5 mm audio jack, but they want to use an older wired headset with a TRRS plug. What is the BEST solution?

A. Insert the headset plug into the SIM tray slot and twist it to make an audio connection
B. Use a compatible Lightning-to-3.5 mm or USB-C-to-3.5 mm audio adapter for the port
C. Enable Wi-Fi hotspot mode so the headset can connect wirelessly through the phone
D. Replace the headset's plug with a micro-USB connector by cutting and rewiring it

Question 14: A user says, "My Wi-Fi is broken. I don't see any networks at all," while other coworkers nearby see multiple SSIDs and are connected. What is the MOST likely cause on the user's phone?

A. Incorrect email configuration preventing scanning for available wireless networks
B. Wi-Fi is disabled or Airplane mode is enabled, turning off the wireless network radio
C. A swollen battery has disconnected the antennas and damaged the Wi-Fi circuitry
D. The VPN client is misconfigured and blocking the display of all SSID listings

Question 15: A traveler in another country reports, "I have full bars, but mobile data doesn't work unless I'm on hotel Wi-Fi." Which setting is the MOST likely cause?

A. Wi-Fi is disabled, preventing use of local wireless access points for data abroad
B. Bluetooth tethering is enabled, forcing data sharing only with paired devices
C. NFC is turned off, stopping contactless payment and proximity data services
D. Cellular data roaming is disabled, blocking mobile data on the foreign network

Question 16: A user can place voice calls and send SMS messages, but cannot use cellular data at all. They recently moved their SIM card to a new unlocked phone from a different carrier. Wi-Fi works fine. What is the MOST likely cause?

A. Swollen battery causing intermittent power loss to the cellular data radio only
B. Faulty display connector preventing viewing of the cellular data status icon
C. Damaged SIM tray causing the SIM to lose only its data provisioning settings
D. Incorrect or missing APN settings for the current carrier on the new phone

Question 17: A user says, "My phone only works on the internet when I'm on Wi-Fi. As soon as I leave the building, no apps can reach anything." What should the technician check FIRST?

A. Whether VPN is enabled and forcing all traffic through a non-responsive remote tunnel
B. If Mobile Data is turned on in cellular settings and allowed for general app usage
C. The device's HDMI output settings to confirm mirroring is not affecting connectivity
D. The SD card's free space to ensure enough storage for network cache files

Question 18: A user wants to share their phone's cellular internet connection with a laptop while preserving battery as much as possible and keeping the link secure. Which method is MOST appropriate?

A. USB tethering between the phone and laptop for a wired, powered, and encrypted link
B. Bluetooth tethering between two phones to create a short-range wireless bridge
C. Creating an unsecured Wi-Fi hotspot that broadcasts an open SSID for the laptop
D. Using NFC pairing only, without enabling any tethering or hotspot functionality

Question 19: A user reports that their Bluetooth headset "doesn't show up" on their phone when trying to pair. You confirm Bluetooth is enabled on the phone. What is the MOST likely cause?

A. The phone is in Airplane mode, which never affects Bluetooth pairing operations
B. The headset is not in pairing mode or is already connected to another nearby device
C. The phone's SIM card is not activated, preventing new Bluetooth accessories from pairing
D. The Wi-Fi password is incorrect, stopping the headset from appearing in the list

Question 20: A user connects to an office Wi-Fi network and sees full signal strength, but no websites load in the browser. Other users are browsing normally on the same SSID. Which is the BEST next step?

A. Perform a factory reset on the phone to clear all wireless and browser settings
B. Replace the Wi-Fi antenna in the phone to restore full network throughput
C. Disable Bluetooth to reduce interference and then retry loading external sites
D. Forget the network, reconnect, and ensure any captive portal page is completed

ANSWERS

1: Correct Answer: B
Rationale: The device is powered and the OS is running (vibrations and sounds), but the display is black, indicating a likely screen, backlight, or display-connector failure. Arranging screen-level or manufacturer repair is appropriate. Replacing the logic board, factory-resetting, or swapping the battery are unnecessary without evidence.

2: Correct Answer: B
Rationale: A swollen lithium battery is a safety hazard that can lead to fire or explosion. The correct first action is to power down, isolate the device, and follow safe replacement and disposal procedures. Continuing to use it, taping it down, or puncturing it is unsafe and improper.

3: Correct Answer: D
Rationale: The camera app opens and other apps can access the camera, but the preview is always black. This points to a failed or disconnected camera module, not a display issue, OS corruption, or storage problem. A bad module prevents image data from reaching the system.

4: Correct Answer: A
Rationale: Intermittent charging with multiple known-good chargers and cables indicates a failing or loose charging port. Under warranty, the best step is to document the problem and arrange authorized service. Board-level soldering, factory resets, or disabling fast charging do not address a physical port defect.

5: Correct Answer: C
Rationale: A normal image but partial touch response indicates a problem with the digitizer (touch layer), not the LCD/backlight, battery, or logic board. The digitizer detects touch across the screen and passes coordinates to the OS.

6: Correct Answer: A
Rationale: "No SIM" while Wi-Fi works suggests a SIM, tray, or slot problem. The first, least invasive check is to verify that the SIM is properly seated and that the tray and contacts are intact. Storage, Bluetooth, or SD card formatting are unrelated to SIM detection.

7: Correct Answer: D
Rationale: If Wi-Fi, Bluetooth, and cellular radios work but NFC tap-to-pay fails, the most likely causes are NFC being disabled, blocked by a case, or a damaged NFC coil. The SIM, digitizer, or email configuration would not selectively break NFC payments while other radios function.

8: Correct Answer: B
Rationale: A gap between the screen and frame with intact glass commonly indicates a swelling battery pushing the display outward. Wi-Fi antenna alignment, vibration motor issues, or APN settings do not cause physical separation of the screen from the chassis.

9: Correct Answer: C
Rationale: Before opening any device, the first safety step is to power it down completely and disconnect external power to avoid shorts, shocks, or component damage. Heating covers or removing screws comes later, and prying under a battery with a metal tool is unsafe.

10: Correct Answer: A
Rationale: Modern phones throttle CPU/GPU performance and dim the display when overheating to protect internal components. The slowdown and dimming with an overheat warning reflect this protective behavior, not immediate battery failure, a loose SIM, or a Wi-Fi antenna issue.

11: Correct Answer: C
Rationale: Qi wireless charging is sensitive to coil alignment and can be blocked by thick or metal cases. After confirming Qi support, the next step is to check case thickness/material and phone alignment on the pad. SIM tray position, Bluetooth, or microphone mute do not affect wireless charging.

12: Correct Answer: C
Rationale: To connect a USB flash drive directly, the phone must support USB OTG so it can act as a USB host, and the cable/adapter must also support OTG. HDMI Alt Mode, removable batteries, or rooting are not required for basic USB mass storage access.

13: Correct Answer: B
Rationale: Phones without a 3.5 mm jack use their data/charging port (Lightning or USB-C) for wired audio. The correct solution is a compatible Lightning-to-3.5 mm or USB-C-to-3.5 mm adapter. Using the SIM tray, hotspot mode, or rewiring the plug is incorrect and unsafe.

14: Correct Answer: B
Rationale: If only one user's phone sees no SSIDs while others see multiple networks, the most likely cause is that Wi-Fi is disabled or Airplane mode is enabled on that phone. Email settings, swollen batteries, or VPN misconfiguration do not prevent the list of networks from appearing.

15: Correct Answer: D
Rationale: When roaming internationally, having full signal but no mobile data typically means data roaming is disabled. Enabling cellular data roaming (if allowed by policy and plan) restores mobile data. Wi-Fi, Bluetooth tethering, or NFC settings are unrelated to this symptom.

16: Correct Answer: D
Rationale: Voice and SMS working but no cellular data after moving a SIM to a phone from another carrier strongly indicates incorrect or missing APN settings for the current carrier. Battery condition, display connectors, or SIM tray damage would not selectively affect only data services.

17: Correct Answer: B
Rationale: If internet access works on Wi-Fi but not on cellular, the first check should be whether Mobile Data (cellular data) is enabled in settings and allowed for apps. VPN, HDMI output, or SD card space are secondary considerations and do not typically disable all cellular data by themselves.

18: Correct Answer: A
Rationale: USB tethering provides a secure, wired connection that does not broadcast an SSID and simultaneously charges the phone, helping preserve battery life. Bluetooth tethering is slower and less power-efficient, an unsecured hotspot is not safe, and NFC alone does not provide internet sharing.

19: Correct Answer: B
Rationale: If a Bluetooth headset does not appear in the phone's device list, it is usually not in pairing mode or isalready connected to another device. Phone Bluetooth being on is not enough. SIM activation, Wi-Fi passwords, or Airplane mode (with Bluetooth still enabled) are not the primary causes here.

20: Correct Answer: D
Rationale: Full signal but no browsing while others on the same SSID can browse often indicates a connection or captive portal issue. Forgetting and rejoining the network and completing any captive portal page is the best next step. Factory reset, antenna replacement, or disabling Bluetooth are not warranted yet.

CHAPTER 2

Networking

2.1 Common TCP/UDP Ports & Protocol Purposes

When users describe network problems, they almost never say, "Port 443 seems blocked today." They say, "I can't get to my email," or "The shares on the server disappeared," or "Remote Desktop just hangs." Underneath those symptoms are very specific network services that listen on very specific **ports**. To work comfortably in IT support—and to pass the A+ exams—you need to be able to hear the user's description, mentally translate it into "this is probably HTTPS" or "that sounds like SMB," and from there recall the port and behavior of the protocol involved.

It helps to anchor what a port actually is. An IP address gets traffic to the right device, but once packets arrive, the operating system needs a way to tell which application they belong to. A **port** is just a numbered logical endpoint on that device. Think of the IP address as the street address of an office building and ports as the suite numbers inside. You don't need to know all 65,535 possible ports for each transport protocol, but you do need to be fluent with the common "well-known ports" used by everyday services like web browsing, email, file sharing, and remote desktop. You will see these numbers in firewall rules, router configuration pages, and troubleshooting tools constantly.

Beneath these application services sit two main transport protocols: **TCP** and **UDP**. You can think of **TCP (Transmission Control Protocol)** as the careful, reliable courier. It establishes a connection, performs a handshake, numbers and tracks each segment of data, and resends anything that goes missing. If a single piece is lost, TCP knows and asks for it again, making it ideal for things like web pages, file transfers, remote logins, and email, where incomplete or out-of-order data would be a problem. **UDP (User Datagram Protocol)** is the opposite personality: connectionless, "fire and forget," and low overhead. It just sends datagrams without building a session and does not retransmit lost data by itself. That makes UDP great when speed and low latency matter more than perfection, such as streaming, VoIP, and quick DNS lookups. For the exam, many ports are simply "TCP," some are "UDP," and a few use both; when CompTIA names a port, it usually expects you to know which transport is typically associated with that service.

In practice, you rarely start by thinking "TCP 443." You start with what the user is trying to do. It is useful to train your brain to follow the same chain every time: user task, to protocol, to port. For example, "browse securely" -> HTTPS -> TCP 443. "Remote Windows desktop" -> RDP -> TCP 3389. "Windows file share" -> SMB -> TCP 445. Once that pattern becomes automatic, the memorization feels much less like trivia and more like learning a set of tools you can actually use.

Web Services: HTTP and HTTPS

Most day-to-day network usage passes through the web, so it makes sense to start there. When a user enters a URL like http://example.com and the page loads, the browser is using HTTP (Hypertext Transfer Protocol) over TCP port 80. HTTP is a plain-text protocol; the requests and responses are not encrypted. That might be acceptable for a public news site, but it is not acceptable when you are logging in, doing online banking, or doing anything where the content should not be visible to anyone who can intercept the traffic.

That is where HTTPS (HTTP Secure) comes in. With HTTPS, the same HTTP protocol is wrapped in encryption provided by TLS/SSL, and by default it uses **TCP port 443**. In the browser, you see this as URLs that start with https:// and, typically, a padlock icon. From a support point of view, if a user reports that they can reach http://intranet.company.local but not https://intranet.company.local, you immediately think about port 443 and TLS. Perhaps a firewall is blocking 443 while allowing 80, or the web server is misconfigured to only listen on port 80, or there is a certificate issue that the browser is refusing to ignore. The important thing is that you tie the symptom ("secure version of the site fails") to the service (HTTPS) and the port (443).

Captive portals, such as those in hotel or airport Wi-Fi, often make this relationship visible in a different way. Initially, only HTTP/80 traffic may be allowed, and any request is redirected to a login or terms-of-service page. After you authenticate, the network opens up ports like 443 so that secure sites work as expected. Understanding that behavior makes it easier to explain to a user why their browser keeps going to a login page when they first connect.

Remote Access and Management: SSH, Telnet, and RDP

Remote access services are another category where knowing ports and protocols changes guesswork into targeted troubleshooting. On the command-line side, you will meet **Telnet** and **SSH**. **Telnet** runs over **TCP port 23** and provides a remote text-based session, but it is completely unencrypted. Every keystroke, including usernames and passwords, crosses the network in clear text. Because of that, Telnet is considered insecure and is rarely acceptable on modern networks except for legacy devices or isolated lab environments.

The secure replacement is **SSH (Secure Shell)** on **TCP port 22**. SSH provides encrypted remote command-line access and also supports secure tunneling and file transfer mechanisms. When you see a question asking, "Which protocol and port should be used for secure remote command-line access?" the expected combination is SSH on 22, not Telnet on 23. In a real environment, if an administrator says, "I can't SSH to this Linux server," you immediately think about whether the SSH service is running, whether a firewall is blocking TCP 22, or whether the server is only allowing specific source addresses to connect.

For graphical remote access to Windows systems, you will encounter **RDP (Remote Desktop Protocol)**. RDP uses **TCP port 3389** by default. Help desk staff often rely on RDP to see exactly what the user sees, or to manage servers without being physically present. Imagine a user calling in: "I can ping our file server, and I can open our web app on it, but when I try to Remote Desktop into it, the connection never completes." You already know that basic IP connectivity is fine and that at least HTTP/80 to that host is working. That directs your attention straight to port 3389. Either a host-based firewall is blocking inbound RDP, the service is disabled on the server, or a network firewall is blocking that port between you and the target. Again, mapping "Remote Desktop" to "RDP" to "TCP 3389" guides your diagnosis.

File and Printer Sharing: SMB, NetBIOS, AFP, SLP, IPP

File and printer sharing are core services inside many organizations, and here the ports matter a great deal. In Windows environments, the primary protocol is **SMB (Server Message Block)**. Modern SMB typically runs directly over **TCP port 445**. Older Windows systems also used **NetBIOS over TCP/IP**, which relied on ports 137–139 (both TCP and UDP) for name services and session traffic. For CompTIA A+ purposes, when you think "Windows file share," you should strongly associate that with SMB and port 445, and be aware that NetBIOS ports 137–139 may come up as legacy or related pieces.

Consider an office where users suddenly report, "We can browse the internet, but none of the shared folders on the server are opening." You ping the server: replies are fine. You browse to http://fileserver and see a status page: HTTP/80 to that system is fine. But when you type \\fileserver into File Explorer, you see a network path not found error. This combination strongly suggests that something specific to SMB is being blocked. When you inspect the new firewall the company installed that morning and find a rule denying inbound TCP 445 to the file server, you have a smoking gun. Adjusting that rule to allow TCP 445 from the internal LAN restores access immediately.

In macOS-heavy environments, you may run into a few additional protocols. Historically, Macs used **AFP (Apple Filing Protocol)** over **TCP port 548** for file sharing. Modern macOS versions can use SMB by default, but

AFP remains a legacy option and is still tested on the exam. Mac services are often discovered automatically thanks to **SLP (Service Location Protocol)**, which uses **port 427** over TCP and UDP. When a Mac user opens the network browser and sees shared resources appear without manually entering addresses, SLP or other discovery protocols are usually at work.

Printing can also involve standardized network ports. **IPP (Internet Printing Protocol)** commonly runs over **TCP port 631**. With IPP, a print server or printer accepts print jobs using a well-defined, HTTP-like protocol, which many operating systems support natively. A scenario you may see is a user reporting, "I can open the printer's web configuration page, but my computer says it can't send print jobs." If you can reach the printer via HTTP/80 for management, but printing fails, the problem might be that IPP on 631 is blocked or disabled, or that the printer is expecting a different print protocol altogether.

DNS and DHCP: Names and Addresses

Two other services that underpin almost everything on the network are DNS and DHCP. DNS (Domain Name System) is responsible for translating human-friendly names such as www.example.com into IP addresses. Most client queries to DNS servers use UDP port 53 because queries and responses are small and need to be fast. When DNS servers exchange larger data sets, such as zone transfers between primary and secondary servers, they typically use TCP port 53 instead, but for A+ the key idea is that DNS is associated with port 53 over both TCP and UDP.

From a troubleshooting angle, a classic symptom of DNS trouble is a user saying, "I can't get to any websites, but I can ping 8.8.8.8." Being able to reach an IP address directly but not by name strongly suggests that traffic to UDP 53 is failing, or the configured DNS server is unreachable or misconfigured. You do not fix that by changing default gateways or cabling; you look at the DNS server settings, firewall rules affecting port 53, or the availability of the DNS service itself.

DHCP (Dynamic Host Configuration Protocol) takes care of automatically assigning IP addresses, subnet masks, default gateways, and often DNS server addresses to clients. DHCP uses **UDP port 67** on the server side and **UDP port 68** on the client side. When a client first joins a network and has no IP address, it broadcasts a DHCP Discover packet, and the server responds with an Offer. That DORA (Discover, Offer, Request, Acknowledge) sequence relies on those UDP ports being allowed through any host-based or network firewalls on the local segment.

You will see DHCP issues in practice when a workstation shows an APIPA address in the 169.254.x.x range instead of a valid network IP. That self-assigned address is Windows' way of saying, "I tried DHCP and did not get any response." The cause might be that the DHCP server is offline, the client is on the wrong VLAN, or something is blocking DHCP broadcast traffic on ports 67 and 68. Knowing the ports helps you rule out, for example, simple DNS trouble versus a more fundamental inability to get any configuration from DHCP.

Email Protocols: Sending and Receiving

Email problems are another daily reality for support technicians, and they map directly to a small cluster of well-known ports. When we talk about **sending** email, we are usually talking about **SMTP (Simple Mail Transfer Protocol)**. Traditionally, SMTP servers exchanged mail with each other over **TCP port 25**, and that port is still used for server-to-server communication. However, for client submission—the part where Outlook or a phone sends outgoing messages to the organization's mail server—modern environments often use **TCP port 587** (SMTP with STARTTLS) or sometimes **TCP port 465** (SMTP over SSL). Many ISPs block outgoing port 25 from residential networks to cut down on spam from infected machines, which can surprise users who try to point a local client directly at an external mail host over 25.

For **receiving** mail, clients typically use either **POP3 (Post Office Protocol version 3)** or **IMAP4 (Internet Message Access Protocol version 4)**. POP3 is the older approach and listens on **TCP port 110** in its plain form, and on **TCP port 995** when wrapped in SSL/TLS. POP3 clients tend to download messages and may remove them from the server, which works fine when you only check mail from one device. IMAP is more flexible and keeps messages on the server, synchronizing state (read/unread, folders, flags) across multiple devices. Plain IMAP uses **TCP port 143**, while secure IMAP uses **TCP port 993**.

This cluster of ports often shows up when a user says something like, "I can log into webmail, and I can browse the internet, but Outlook on my laptop says it can't connect to the mail server." Because webmail uses HTTPS over 443 and that is working, you know general connectivity is fine. What is failing is the separate client-to-server connections for sending and receiving. You open the account properties in Outlook and see that the incoming server is set to POP3 on port 110, but the organization's documentation specifies IMAP over 993. Simply correcting the protocol and port to match the server resolves the problem. The web works, the browser-based email works, but the dedicated client was misconfigured at the protocol/port layer.

Network Management and Monitoring: SNMP

Although you may not build large network monitoring systems in an entry-level role, you will certainly encounter references to SNMP in device configuration screens and exam questions. **SNMP (Simple Network Management Protocol)** is used to monitor and sometimes manage network devices such as switches, routers, access points, and printers. SNMP agents on those devices listen by default on **UDP port 161**, responding to queries from an SNMP management station. When a device wants to send an unsolicited alert—for example, to report that an interface has gone down—it usually sends an SNMP trap to **UDP port 162** on the monitoring system.

From a support perspective, you might not be the one tuning SNMP polling intervals, but you could be asked to ensure that a printer has SNMP enabled so that the central monitoring tool can read its status, or to avoid blocking SNMP traffic between a new switch and the network management server. Recognizing ports 161 and 162 as belonging to SNMP keeps you from accidentally cutting off the visibility that administrators rely on.

Once you start recognizing these services and their ports, firewall and router configuration pages become much easier to interpret. A rule that allows "TCP 80 and 443 from any" immediately translates in your mind to "users can browse web pages, both plain and secure." A port-forwarding entry sending "TCP 3389 to 192.168.1.10" tells you that someone has exposed RDP on that internal host to the outside world, which may be a security concern. When a security policy says "Block Telnet, allow SSH," you understand that as "deny TCP 23, permit TCP 22." Over time, this port knowledge stops being a list to memorize and becomes a diagnostic map you instinctively consult every time a user says, "I can't connect to..."

2.2 Wireless Networking Technologies

When you plug a PC into a switch with an Ethernet cable, the path between the device and the network is usually very predictable. Wireless changes that. The same IP traffic still flows, the same applications still run, but instead of copper you are relying on radio waves that share space with microwaves, cordless phones, neighbors' routers, and even your Bluetooth earbuds. As an entry-level technician, your job is not to become a radio engineer, but you do need to understand the main wireless technologies well enough to choose the right options, explain them to users, and troubleshoot when the signal in the conference room mysteriously collapses five minutes into a video call.

At the center of this story is Wi-Fi, the family of standards formally known as IEEE 802.11. Around it are shorter-range technologies like Bluetooth and NFC that solve different problems: connecting headphones, scanning barcodes, or handling tap-to-pay at a checkout counter. All of these live in the same general RF world but behave quite differently. The A+ exam, and real users, will not always name the technology for you; they will just say, "My wireless stuff doesn't work." You need to be able to recognize which technology is in play, which frequency band it's using, and how that interacts with distance, walls, and interference.

Radio Bands, Channels, and Trade-Offs

The most practical starting point is the idea of **frequency bands**. Most Wi-Fi you'll deal with operates in three ranges: **2.4 GHz**, **5 GHz**, and, on newer equipment, **6 GHz**. Think of these as three different "highways" in the air. A wireless access point (AP) can broadcast on one or more of these highways, and client devices like laptops or phones can listen on the ones their radios support.

The 2.4 GHz band is the original workhorse for consumer Wi-Fi. Because of its lower frequency, 2.4 GHz tends to travel farther and penetrate walls and floors better. That's why, in a large house or in the far corner of a warehouse, a 2.4 GHz signal may still be usable when 5 GHz has already faded. The trade-off is that 2.4 GHz is crowded. It is used by older Wi-Fi standards, many Internet of Things devices, Bluetooth, some cordless phones, baby monitors, and, notoriously, microwave ovens. On top of that, in many regions you effectively get only three **non-overlapping channels**—commonly channels 1, 6, and 11—so multiple neighboring networks have to share those same slices of spectrum. When too many devices yell at once on the same channel, everyone's performance suffers.

The 5 GHz band offers more usable channels and is generally less congested. Higher frequencies allow for wider channels and higher potential throughput. That is why standards like 802.11ac, which we will examine shortly, can deliver hundreds of megabits per second or more when conditions are good. The downside is physics: higher frequency signals do not bend around obstacles or penetrate materials as easily. A 5 GHz network can feel blazing fast when you are in the same room as the AP, yet drop off sharply a couple of walls away. Exam scenarios will often hint at this by describing a user whose Wi-Fi is excellent near the router but unreliable in distant rooms.

The newest player is 6 GHz, used by so-called Wi-Fi 6E equipment. This band was opened specifically for modern Wi-Fi and offers even more channel space with relatively little legacy interference for now. It is ideal for very high throughput in clean environments, but it suffers even more from range and obstacle limitations than 5 GHz. Also, both the router and client must support it; otherwise, it might as well not exist from the device's perspective. When you read about a cutting-edge office trying to support many high-bandwidth users in a dense space, 5 GHz and 6 GHz with modern standards are what make that workable.

Within each band, the radio spectrum is divided into **channels**. Two networks operating on the same or overlapping channels in the same physical area interfere with each other, even if they have different SSIDs and passwords. That is why APs are configured to use specific channel numbers, and why technicians sometimes resolve performance complaints simply by changing the channel to one that is less crowded. In a typical apartment building, for instance, you might open a Wi-Fi analyzer and discover that every neighbor's router is on channel 6 at 2.4 GHz. Moving yours to channel 1 or 11 can dramatically improve reliability without changing anything else.

Client-Side Wi-Fi Configuration

From the user's point of view, Wi-Fi configuration often reduces to two questions: "Which network name do I choose?" and "What is the password?" Behind those simple prompts are concepts you need to manage accurately.

The **SSID** (Service Set Identifier) is the human-readable network name broadcast by the AP. A router might advertise "OfficeWiFi-2G" and "OfficeWiFi-5G" as two separate SSIDs mapped to different bands, or it might present a single SSID and automatically steer clients between 2.4 and 5 GHz. Users frequently confuse SSID and password, so when someone says "My Wi-Fi is 'CoffeeShop123'," you need to clarify whether that is actually the network name, the passphrase, or both in a default setup.

Every SSID must also have a **security mode**. At the level you need now, focus on the difference between open networks (no password, anyone can connect) and secured networks using **WPA2-Personal** or **WPA3-Personal**. Both WPA2 and WPA3 in Personal mode use a **pre-shared key (PSK)**, which is the passphrase users type when they join for the first time. The best-practice answer on the exam, and in real environments, is to avoid ancient options like WEP or WPA and to prefer WPA3 when all hardware supports it, then WPA2 as a fallback. From a support standpoint, whenever the Wi-Fi password is changed on the router, every client must update its stored credentials. It is common to see half a department knock offline because one person updated the passphrase on the router but did not communicate that everyone's devices need to "forget" and reconnect with the new key.

Band issues frequently show up as "invisible network" complaints. Consider an older wireless printer that only supports 2.4 GHz 802.11g/n. The office upgrades to a sleek new router and, in the name of speed, the admin enables a 5 GHz-only SSID called "OfficeFast." Phones and newer laptops connect without issue, but the printer never sees the network at all. To the user, it looks like a printer problem. To you, it should immediately suggest a band compatibility issue: the printer's radio simply cannot tune into 5 GHz. The fix might be as simple as enabling a 2.4 GHz SSID or configuring the printer to use an existing mixed-band SSID.

Bluetooth: Short-Range Peripheral Connectivity

Where Wi-Fi focuses on network access for many devices over a room, house, or building, **Bluetooth** is usually about connecting two devices over a short distance. It is what links wireless keyboards and mice to PCs, earbuds to phones, fitness trackers to tablets, and many barcode scanners to point-of-sale systems. These connections typically operate reliably over a range of roughly 10 meters for common consumer equipment, sometimes more in line-of-sight conditions and with higher-power classes, but you should think of Bluetooth as "same room" rather than "whole building."

Bluetooth technology has evolved through multiple **versions** (2.x, 3.x, 4.x, 5.x and beyond), each improving speed, power consumption, and range. For the A+ exam, you do not need to memorize exact throughput numbers, but you should recognize that newer versions tend to be more capable and that very old devices may not support modern low-energy features. In real support scenarios, this comes up when users buy new accessories that require a newer Bluetooth version than their old PC or phone supports.

Connecting a Bluetooth device usually involves **pairing**. A common pattern is that the peripheral is put into a discovery or pairing mode—perhaps by holding a button until an LED blinks—and the host device (phone, laptop, tablet) scans for nearby Bluetooth devices and displays a list. The user selects the device, then enters a PIN or confirms a code if prompted. Under the hood, Bluetooth uses **profiles** that define what type of data the connection will carry, such as audio for headsets (A2DP, HFP), or keyboard and mouse input (HID). If a device pairs successfully but does not behave as expected—such as a headset that connects but passes no audio—it often turns out that the wrong profile is in use, or the device is paired only as a "hands-free phone" rather than as a full stereo headset.

Many everyday Bluetooth problems follow the same basic troubleshooting logic. If a wireless mouse keeps dropping, you first confirm that it has power, then check that it is within range and not buried behind a metal object, then verify that it is not currently paired to some other computer in the office. The user's complaint may be vague—"My Bluetooth is broken"—but your understanding of its short-range, device-to-device nature lets you systematically rule out distance, interference, and pairing conflicts.

NFC and Very Short-Range Communication

At the opposite extreme from Wi-Fi's room-scale coverage is **NFC (Near Field Communication)**. NFC operates over just a few centimeters—often less than 10 cm—and is designed for quick, low-bandwidth exchanges between devices that are almost touching. You encounter it most obviously in tap-to-pay systems, where a customer's phone or contactless card is held near a payment terminal to transmit payment credentials.

NFC can transfer only tiny amounts of data compared to Wi-Fi or even Bluetooth, so it is not used for general networking or media streaming. Instead, it either sends small data payloads, like identification tokens for access badges and transit passes, or it serves as a trigger mechanism. For instance, you might tap a phone against a Bluetooth speaker, and the NFC interaction automatically initiates the Bluetooth pairing process without the user having to open menus and search for devices. From a support perspective, this distinction matters: if a user complains that their tap-to-pay is not working, you think NFC and payment app configuration; if they say their headphones will not stay connected after pairing, you think Bluetooth.

Because NFC's range is so short, it benefits from a kind of built-in physical security: an attacker has to be very close to intercept or manipulate the communication. When troubleshooting, you often start by making sure NFC is enabled in the phone settings, that the correct area of the device is being held near the reader (the NFC antenna is not always obvious), and that any required payment or access application is set up properly. In retail environments, payment terminals may rely on Wi-Fi or Ethernet in the background to reach payment processors, so a tap-to-pay failure can blend issues from multiple wireless layers: NFC between phone and terminal, then Wi-Fi or wired networking between terminal and the internet.

Interpreting Wireless Symptoms

When users report wireless problems, the clues they give you indirectly reference all of these concepts: standards, bands, distance, and interference. A complaint such as "Wi-Fi is fine at my desk, but my calls fall apart in the conference room" suggests that signal strength or band choice is marginal in that room, possibly combined with an older client that can only connect via 2.4 GHz 802.11g while newer coworkers enjoy 5 GHz 802.11ac. Another user might tell you, "My laptop says it's connected, but everything is slow right after lunch." A quick look at your environment may reveal that a nearby microwave oven is used heavily during that period, injecting noise into the 2.4 GHz band and causing retransmissions. Simply moving the AP slightly farther from the microwave or shifting clients to 5 GHz can dramatically improve reliability.

You will also see issues that mix technologies. At a small retail counter, a clerk might say, "Customers can't tap to pay anymore, and my wireless barcode scanner keeps disconnecting." With a clear mental model, you separate these: NFC between phone and terminal for tap-to-pay, Bluetooth between scanner and point-of-sale tablet, and possibly Wi-Fi or Ethernet carrying transactions from the terminal to the payment gateway. Each link has different range, interference, and configuration considerations. Building the habit of first naming the technology involved, then identifying the band and expected range, and finally asking what else might be sharing that spectrum in that location, will serve you well both on the exam and in every real troubleshooting session.

Wireless networking gives users tremendous freedom, but it also introduces more variables than a simple Ethernet cable on a clean switch port. Your value as a technician comes from being able to see past the generic label "wireless" and into the specific standards, bands, and technologies at work, then explaining your choices in practical language: "We're going to move your laptop to the 5 GHz network so your video will be smoother," or "This printer can only use 2.4 GHz, so we need to enable that band on the router." As you progress into later chapters on SOHO router configuration and connectivity troubleshooting, this foundational understanding of wireless behavior will be what turns vague complaints into clear, targeted fixes.

2.3 Networked Host Services

Imagine a user walking into the office with a brand-new laptop. They connect to the corporate Wi-Fi, sign in with their usual username and password, open File Explorer to access the shared department drive, print a spreadsheet to the accounting printer down the hall, bring up the company intranet homepage, and then check email in Outlook. From the user's perspective, all of this is just "using the network." From your perspective as a technician, that simple five-minute sequence involves half a dozen different networked services running quietly on various hosts all over the environment.

This is the world of **networked host services**. These are software components that run on servers, routers, NAS boxes, and sometimes even workstations, providing capabilities that other devices consume. In earlier chapters, you met the idea of a **host** as any device with an IP address on the network: a PC, a server, a router, a printer, even a smart TV. When a host runs a background program that listens for requests on the network and responds, that program is a **service**. When we configure a host to provide a particular set of services to others, we often describe that configuration as a **server role**—for example, a DHCP server role, a file server role, or a web server role.

In a tiny home network, your all-in-one SOHO router might wear several hats at once: it could hand out IP addresses (DHCP), perform basic name lookups (a lightweight DNS proxy), share out a USB drive as a small file server, and of course route traffic to the internet. In even a modest business environment, those roles are usually spread across several dedicated machines: one host provides DHCP and DNS, another hosts file shares, another runs email, and so on. For the CompTIA A+ exams, you are not expected to build or deeply configure these servers, but you are absolutely expected to recognize what each service does, how client devices use it, and what it looks like when that service is failing.

Getting on the Network: DHCP and IP Configuration

The very first thing a new device does when it joins a typical network is look for **Dynamic Host Configuration Protocol (DHCP)**. When a Windows laptop is set to "Obtain an IP address automatically" (which is the default), it does not come with a preprogrammed address. Instead, as soon as it connects to wired Ethernet or Wi-Fi, it broadcasts a request that essentially says, "Is there a DHCP server out there? I need an IP address and configuration."

A DHCP server—often a router in a home or a firewall or Windows/Linux server in an office—listens for these broadcasts. When it hears one, it replies with an available IP address from a predefined pool and with other essential details the client needs: the **subnet mask**, the **default gateway**, one or more **DNS server** addresses, and the **lease time** that defines how long the client can use that address before checking back in. You might see the operation summarized with the DORA sequence (Discover, Offer, Request, Acknowledge), but at A+ level you mainly need to remember the purpose: DHCP automates the distribution and management of IP settings so you don't have to configure each device manually.

When DHCP is working, a client joins the network cleanly and can immediately communicate with other hosts and the internet. When DHCP is not working, the symptoms are very distinctive. In Windows, if the system does not receive a response from any DHCP server, it falls back to an **APIPA** (Automatic Private IP Addressing) address in the 169.254.x.x range. This allows limited, same-segment communication with other APIPA devices but not with routers, servers, or the internet. As a technician, if you see 169.254.x.x on multiple machines and hear that "the whole office has no internet," your mind should jump straight to the DHCP service or the device that provides it. Notice that this is very different from a DNS failure; DHCP is about obtaining valid IP configuration in the first place, while DNS is about using that configuration to locate hosts by name.

Finding Things by Name: DNS

Once a device has an address and a gateway, the next critical service is usually Domain Name System (DNS). Humans prefer names like www.example.com or fileserver.company.local. Computers, however, actually send packets to IP addresses. DNS is the system that translates between those two worlds. When a user opens a browser and types a URL, the client first asks its configured DNS server, "What is the IP address for this name?" Only after receiving that answer does it open a TCP connection to the web server.

Most clients learn which DNS server to use from DHCP, though you can also configure DNS servers statically. This relationship is important: DHCP doesn't just hand out IP addresses; it also typically tells clients, "Use this DNS server when you need to resolve names." If that DNS server becomes unreachable, the client keeps its IP address and can still communicate by IP, but it will fail whenever it tries to reach destinations by name.

You can use this distinction diagnostically. Suppose a user complains, "The internet is down," but you ask them to open a command prompt and ping a well-known public IP address (such as 8.8.8.8) and the ping works. Then you ask them to ping www.google.com by name and it fails. This pattern—IP connectivity to the outside world works, but name lookups fail—points strongly to a DNS problem, not a general network outage. Conversely, if they cannot even ping by IP, the issue is more fundamental, possibly with their local IP configuration, default gateway, or the WAN connection itself.

DNS is involved with far more than public websites. Internal hosts such as fileserver01, print01, or intranet.company.local often have DNS records in the organization's internal DNS servers. If those servers fail, users may not be able to map network drives or reach intranet applications by name, even if the servers themselves are technically up and reachable by IP. For A+ purposes, keep the conceptual view clear: DHCP answers, "What is my IP configuration?" DNS answers, "Given this name, what IP should I talk to?"

Sharing Storage and Printers: File and Print Services

Once a user is on the network and can find hosts by name, they usually start using more obvious, user-facing services—most commonly file and print sharing. A **file server** is simply a host whose primary role is to store and share folders for others. On Windows networks, this almost always uses the Server **Message Block (SMB)** protocol, sometimes referred to historically as CIFS. Users see this as mapped drives like H: or S:, or as UNC paths such as \\fileserver\department. The same SMB shares can be accessed from macOS and Linux as well, and in many small offices, a dedicated NAS device provides this role.

Centralizing files on a server rather than on individual PCs has obvious benefits. It makes backups more manageable, supports collaboration, and allows the organization to control who can see or edit which folders. From a client's point of view, saving a document to a mapped network drive feels almost identical to saving to the local Documents folder. Behind the scenes, though, their workstation is sending network file operations to a host dedicated to this file service role. If that host or its file service goes down, users across the office will report that "the shared drive disappeared" or "I get 'network path not found' when I open S:," even though their internet access is fine.

Closely related is the **print server** role. Although many standalone network printers can accept print jobs directly, organizations often centralize printer management on a server that hosts print queues. Users install the printer once via that server and then simply choose it in the print dialog. The server takes care of holding jobs in a queue, sending them to the printer, and handling drivers and permissions. In a small office, the printer itself may act as its own print server, exposing a shared printer name on the network. Either way, when users say "I cannot print to the accounting printer," but they can still open shared folders and browse the web, you are likely dealing with a print service or device issue, not a general connectivity problem.

Knowing Who You Are: Directory and Authentication Services

So far, we have looked at services that answer technical questions: "What IP should I use?" "What IP does this name correspond to?" "Where is this file or printer hosted?" In business networks, there is another fundamental question: "Who is this user, and what are they allowed to do?" That question is handled by **directory and authentication services**.

In Windows environments, the dominant example is **Active Directory**, which runs on servers known as domain controllers. A directory service maintains a structured database of user accounts, groups, computers, and policies. When a user logs onto a domain-joined workstation with DOMAIN\username or username@company.com, the workstation contacts a domain controller to authenticate that user. If the credentials check out, the directory service then controls what that user is allowed to access—file shares, printers, applications—often without asking them to type a password again. This is the single sign-on experience you see in most corporate offices.

Smaller SOHO networks often skip a full directory and rely on local accounts on the file server, NAS, or router. But any time you see domain logons, group policies, or centralized control over accounts, you are dealing with a directory/authentication role. Understanding the difference between a local account and a domain account becomes important in troubleshooting. If one user cannot log in but others can, the issue may be as simple as an expired password or locked account. If suddenly no one on a particular floor can log into the domain, yet local logons still work, that suggests an outage affecting a domain controller or the network path to it.

Authentication services dovetail with everything else we have discussed. The same directory might control who is allowed to map a particular network drive, who can add which printers, or who can access the internal web portal. As you study Windows administration and security in the Core 2 exam, this idea of a central authority that "knows who you are" will appear again and again.

Web, Email, and Application Services

Beyond generic file and print, organizations rely heavily on services that deliver web content and email. A **web server** hosts websites or web applications, presenting them over HTTP or HTTPS. Internally, that might be an intranet site at http://intranet.company.local where employees access HR documents or submit help desk tickets. Externally, it could be the public corporate site at https://www.company.com. Users think of this simply as "going to a website," but from the network's perspective, their browser is talking to a specific host whose role is to handle HTTP(S) requests.

When that host fails or its web service stops, users can often still reach other sites just fine. You will hear complaints like, "The internet is working, but the intranet page times out," or "Our public site is down, but I can go to other websites." That phrasing is a hint: if other external sites load, your WAN and ISP link are probably fine, and the issue is focused on a particular web server or its DNS records.

Email relies on multiple cooperating services. When a user sends a message, their email client talks to a server using **SMTP** to hand off the message for delivery. When they read mail, their client connects to a mail server that holds their mailbox, using **POP3** or more commonly **IMAP**. The same host may provide both roles, or they may be split across several servers. From the client's perspective, these show up as "outgoing mail server" and "incoming mail server" settings, often with hostnames like mail.company.com. For you, it is important to recognize the patterns when something goes wrong. If a user's browser can reach websites but Outlook cannot connect to imap.company.com, the problem may be with that specific mail service, the client's configuration, or possibly a firewall rule, rather than with general internet access. If they can receive mail but cannot send, that points specifically toward the SMTP side.

Business environments also depend heavily on specialized **application servers** that run line-of-business software: accounting systems, inventory tracking, CRM, and so on. Often, these applications are accessed through a browser that talks to a particular internal host, or through a dedicated client installed on the user's PC that connects to the application server. Here again, the troubleshooting clue is scope: if only that one application fails while other web pages, email, and file shares work, you usually focus on the application service or its host, not on DHCP or DNS.

Remote Access, Remote Management, and Time

Modern organizations rarely confine themselves to one building. Users work from home, travel, or connect from branch offices, and technicians manage equipment that might be in another city or data center. This is where **remote access** and **remote management** services come in.

A **Virtual Private Network (VPN)** server allows remote clients to create an encrypted tunnel into the corporate network over the public internet. Once the tunnel is established, the client appears—logically—as if it were on the internal LAN. It can then access file shares, printers, and intranet sites that would otherwise be inaccessible from the outside. The user experience is typically to launch a VPN client, enter credentials, and then work normally. If a user can browse public websites from home but cannot see the company shared drive until they connect the VPN, that is usually expected behavior. If the VPN client fails to connect, or connects but the user still cannot reach internal hosts, then you start thinking about the VPN service or routing on the internal network, not about their home ISP.

For technicians, **remote desktop** services are equally important. Protocols such as Remote Desktop Protocol (RDP) allow you to view and control a remote host's desktop as if you were sitting at its keyboard. IT staff use this to manage servers, assist users, or access their own office workstations from elsewhere. It is useful to keep the distinction clear: VPN connects you securely into the network as a whole, while remote desktop connects you to a specific machine.

Quietly supporting many of these services is **Network Time Protocol (NTP)**. Accurate timekeeping might sound trivial, but in a domain environment, authentication mechanisms and security protocols often depend on consistent clocks. Domain members typically sync their clocks from domain controllers, and those controllers may in turn sync from external time sources. If time drifts too far apart between a client and a server, logons and secure communications can start failing in bizarre ways. While you won't be configuring NTP in depth for A+, you should be aware that "time sync" is yet another service role often running in the background.

All of these examples illustrate a common theme: different tasks users perform—getting online, opening a shared folder, printing a document, visiting a web page, checking email, logging into the domain, connecting from home—map to different underlying services on specific hosts. When a user complains, "The internet is down," your job is to peel back that vague statement and figure out which service is actually involved. If they have an APIPA address, you look at DHCP. If they can ping by IP but not by name, you consider DNS. If they can browse the web but not open \\fileserver\share, you think about the file server or its connectivity. That habit of mapping symptoms to services is one of the professional skills that distinguishes an entry-level IT technician from a frustrated power user.

2.4 Network Configuration Concepts

By this point you've seen what networks are and what kinds of services run over them. The next big question is much more practical: what actually has to be correct on a PC, laptop, printer, or phone for it to work on that network? In real support work, most "I can't get online" tickets aren't about damaged cables or failing switches; they're about a handful of configuration values that live in one small dialog box. Learning to read and interpret those values is one of the most important skills for both the A+ exam and day-to-day troubleshooting.

A useful way to think about network configuration is to imagine that every device needs four basic pieces of information. It needs an **IP address**, which is its unique street address. It needs a **subnet mask**, which defines the edges of its neighborhood. It needs a **default gateway**, which is the route out of that neighborhood to the rest of the world. And it needs a **DNS server**, which acts like a phone book that translates human-friendly names into numeric addresses. On most networks, a service called **DHCP** quietly hands out all of this information automatically. When everything is correct, users get their email, web pages load, printers appear, and no one calls the help desk. When any of those values is wrong or missing, you get the classic "internet is down" complaint—even though the problem may be very specific.

Before we dive into each setting, it helps to separate physical connectivity from logical configuration. An Ethernet link light on a NIC or a strong Wi-Fi icon simply tells you the device can talk at the electrical or radio level to something else, usually a switch or access point. It says nothing about whether the device has a valid IP configuration. In other words, the cable might be perfect, the wireless password might be correct, and the access point might be right next to the user, but if the IP settings are wrong, the device still can't participate on the network in any useful way. New technicians often stop at "the Wi-Fi icon looks fine, so the network must be up." An experienced technician treats that as only step one and immediately moves on to IP configuration.

When you open the network adapter properties on a typical Windows system and look at the IPv4 settings, the first field that usually catches your eye is the **IP address**. In the IPv4 world, this looks like four decimal numbers separated by dots, such as 192.168.1.50. Each device on a given subnet must have a unique IP address; two devices with the same address will fight each other, and both will have intermittent or no connectivity. Within a given local network, devices also need to agree on which part of the address describes the network and which part describes the individual host. That division is handled by the next field: the subnet mask.

The **subnet mask** looks like an IP address, but its job is different. A common mask in small networks is 255.255.255.0. You can think of this as saying, "The first three numbers of the IP define the network, and the last number defines the specific device on that network." So if a user's PC is 192.168.1.50 with a mask of 255.255.255.0, then anything else that starts with 192.168.1 is considered local. A printer at 192.168.1.60 is in the same neighborhood; a server at 192.168.2.10 is not. You don't need to do binary math for the A+ exam, but you do need to recognize that a wrong mask can cause very strange behavior. If a device has an IP that "looks right" but a mask that tells it the rest of the network is somewhere else, it may try to send traffic to the router that should be local, or it may never send traffic to the router at all when it should.

That brings us to the **default gateway**. If the IP address is the house and the subnet mask is the neighborhood, the default gateway is the road out of the neighborhood. Technically, it is the IP address of the local router interface that knows how to reach other networks, including the internet. In a typical home network, this gateway might be 192.168.0.1 or 192.168.1.1, the LAN side of the ISP-provided router. In a small office, it might be a dedicated firewall or router performing the same job. When the device needs to talk to an IP address that is outside its local subnet, it forwards that traffic to the default gateway. If the gateway entry is missing, wrong, or unreachable, you usually see a very specific pattern: the user can access local resources—shares, printers, maybe an internal server—but cannot reach websites or remote offices. Being able to recognize "local OK, remote no" as a classic gateway problem will save you a lot of time.

Even if the device knows how to get out of its network, it still has one more key question: how do I turn www.example.com into something I can actually send packets to? That is the job of the **DNS server,** the component that many new technicians overlook. DNS, or Domain Name System, is the distributed "phone book" of the internet and of private networks. A client sends a query like "What is the IP for www.google.com?" to its configured DNS server, and if everything is working, it gets an answer back. When DNS is misconfigured, you get a different pattern of failure: the user may be able to ping an external IP like 8.8.8.8 successfully, but any attempt to browse to a name fails with "server not found" or a similar message. As soon as you see "IP works, name doesn't," you should think DNS.

Most of the time, end users (and even technicians) don't type in these values manually. They rely on **DHCP**, the Dynamic Host Configuration Protocol. A DHCP server—often built into the SOHO router—hands out an IP address, subnet mask, default gateway, DNS server, and a few other details when the device joins the network. The device's network adapter is set to "obtain an IP address automatically" and "obtain DNS server address automatically," and the whole process is invisible. This is ideal for laptops, phones, and most desktop systems because it avoids typos, duplicate addresses, and tedious reconfiguration when moving between networks. If DHCP is unavailable or blocked, the client must either be manually configured with static values or it will usually fall back to a special kind of address that signals trouble.

You will see those special addresses in two main flavors, depending on whether the device is using IPv4 or IPv6. In IPv4, when a Windows machine is configured for DHCP but does not hear back from a DHCP server, it assigns itself an **APIPA** address in the 169.254.0.0/16 range. You'll see something like 169.254.22.19 with a mask of 255.255.0.0, and no default gateway or DNS. This is Windows saying, "I couldn't get an address from anyone, so I gave myself something just so I can maybe talk to neighbors in the same situation." An APIPA address can sometimes communicate with other APIPA devices on the same switch, but it has no route to the internet or any routed networks. On the exam and in real life, recognizing 169.254.x.x as "no valid DHCP lease" is crucial, because it directs you to check the DHCP server, router, or Wi-Fi configuration rather than chasing DNS or firewall ghosts.

In IPv6, which you will increasingly see alongside IPv4, the picture looks different but follows similar ideas. IPv6 addresses are longer, written in hexadecimal, and separated by colons rather than dots, for example fe80::1c2d:3eff:fe4a:5b6c. Most modern operating systems assign themselves an **IPv6 link-local** address in the fe80::/10 range automatically, even without a DHCPv6 server. This allows for basic local communication and certain automatic functions, but, just like APIPA, it doesn't guarantee internet connectivity. For A+ purposes you don't need to design IPv6 networks; you just need to recognize that IPv6 addresses look very different from IPv4, that IPv4 and IPv6 can coexist on the same adapter, and that IPv4-style thinking about APIPA and DHCP still applies on the IPv4 side.

Another dimension of address interpretation you will encounter is the distinction between **public** and **private** IP addresses. Devices in homes and offices almost always sit on private address ranges such as 192.168.x.x or 10.x.x.x. These ranges are defined specifically not to be routable across the public internet. Instead, the router or firewall at the edge of the network has one **public IP** on its WAN side, provided by the ISP, and uses **Network Address Translation (NAT)** to let multiple private devices share that single public address. This is why it's perfectly normal for every PC in a small office to have a 192.168.1.something address, yet they can all browse the web simultaneously. For A+ purposes, you should be comfortable seeing 192.168.1.50 on a client and understanding that this is not a "direct internet" address, and you should know that if a device suddenly gets a public address directly, you may be looking at a mis-cabled connection that bypasses the internal router.

Up to this point, we've mostly been talking about devices that receive their configuration dynamically. There are plenty of situations, however, where you deliberately choose **static addressing**. You will often configure servers, network printers, routers, and other infrastructure devices with static IPs, masks, gateways, and DNS. The reason is predictability: you want the printer to be at the same address every day so that printer mappings and applications don't break whenever its lease expires. The price you pay is that a human has to get every field right. A wrong default gateway on a statically configured server produces a very consistent "can talk to local systems, cannot talk to remote networks" pattern. A typo in the IP that puts it on the wrong subnet can make it invisible to everyone. A duplicate static IP will create intermittent problems for both devices that share it. When you are deciding between DHCP and static, ask whether the device needs to be consistently reachable at a known address; if so, static (or at least a DHCP reservation, which you will see later in the SOHO section) is usually the way to go.

DNS deserves a bit more attention because name resolution failures are so common. In many small environments, the DNS server configured on clients is just the router's LAN IP. The router then forwards queries to the ISP's DNS servers or to public resolvers such as 8.8.8.8. In larger environments, clients might point to internal DNS servers that are part of Active Directory, responsible both for resolving internal names like fileserver01.corp.local and for forwarding external queries. When you troubleshoot "we can access our file server by name but no websites load," you are often seeing a situation where internal DNS records work but the internal DNS servers cannot reach or use external forwarders. On a single client, you may also run into stale or incorrect DNS entries left over from a previous network or VPN session. For example, a laptop that once lived in a corporate domain might still be configured to use 192.168.1.250 as DNS even though the small office it's now in has only a router at 192.168.1.1. The laptop will happily send DNS queries to 192.168.1.250, get no response, and then report that every website is down. If you happen to test by IP instead of name, you immediately see that routing is fine and only DNS is the culprit.

Beyond simple IP addressing, modern networks also use logical separation and secure tunneling that show up in endpoint configuration. One common mechanism is the **VLAN**, or Virtual LAN. A VLAN uses features of a managed switch to create multiple logical networks over the same physical hardware. For instance, you might have VLAN 10 for internal staff PCs, VLAN 20 for voice phones, and VLAN 30 for guest Wi-Fi. From an endpoint's perspective, being on a particular VLAN simply means it receives an IP address from the DHCP scope associated with that VLAN and can or cannot reach certain resources based on routing and firewall policies. You might connect a laptop to two adjacent Ethernet jacks that both go back to the same switch, but if one switch port is assigned to the wrong VLAN, the laptop suddenly gets an address from the "wrong" subnet and cannot reach the expected servers. On wireless networks with multiple SSIDs, each SSID may be mapped to its own VLAN; choosing the "Guest" SSID vs the "Corporate" SSID changes which network you are on, even though the radio hardware is the same.

Equally important for remote users is the **VPN**, or Virtual Private Network. A VPN creates an encrypted tunnel between the user's device and a remote gateway so that, from a networking perspective, the device behaves as though it were plugged into the remote LAN. On the client side, this usually appears as a separate network adapter or logical interface with its own IP configuration. When a user clicks "connect" in a VPN client, the system may receive a new IP address, new DNS servers, and new routing rules that send traffic for internal domains through the tunnel. Some organizations configure "full-tunnel" VPNs, where all traffic, including general internet browsing, passes through the corporate network. Others use "split tunneling," where only traffic destined for internal resources uses the VPN, while everything else goes out the user's normal internet connection. Many connectivity issues that occur "only when the VPN is on" are really routing or DNS issues within that VPN-specific configuration.

Putting this all into practice, imagine you sit down at a user's desk to troubleshoot a connectivity problem. The link light is on and the Wi-Fi icon looks healthy, so you move straight to the adapter's IP configuration. The address is 192.168.1.23, the subnet mask is 255.255.255.0, the default gateway is 192.168.1.1, and the DNS server is 192.168.1.250. You ping the gateway successfully, then you ping 8.8.8.8 successfully, but pinging www.google.com fails with "could not find host." From this, you infer that the basic network path to the internet works, but name resolution does not. The suspicious detail is DNS pointing at 192.168.1.250, which doesn't exist on this small network. You change the DNS setting to automatic, the client now picks up 192.168.1.1 as DNS, and suddenly names resolve and websites load. By reading those four fields together, you turned a vague "internet is down" into a precise configuration fix.

On another day, a home user calls and says the PC shows that it's connected to Wi-Fi, but it cannot browse the web, while their phone on the same Wi-Fi works fine. You open the IP configuration and see 169.254.22.19, subnet mask 255.255.0.0, no default gateway, and no DNS. Immediately you recognize an APIPA situation, which means the PC did not get a DHCP lease, even though other devices did. That suggests the router and its DHCP service are functional, but something about this PC's relationship to the Wi-Fi is broken. You have the user forget and rejoin the network, verify that the adapter is set to obtain an IP address automatically, and perhaps reset the adapter. On reconnect, the PC receives 192.168.0.105, mask 255.255.255.0, gateway 192.168.0.1, DNS 192.168.0.1, and everything starts working. Again, the specific values told you a story that guided your troubleshooting steps.

As you practice, you will find that every IP configuration you look at can tell you where the device "lives," how it tries to leave its local network, where it turns for name resolution, and sometimes even whether it is on the correct logical segment or inside a VPN. Being able to look at those values on Windows, on a mobile device, or in a SOHO router's web interface and mentally connect them to user-visible symptoms is exactly the kind of reasoning the A+ exam is testing, and exactly the mindset that separates someone who guesses from someone who truly understands network configuration.

2.5 Networking Hardware Devices

When you look at a simple home or small office network, it is tempting to think of it all as "the Wi-Fi" or "the internet box in the corner." For the CompTIA A+ exam—and for real troubleshooting work—you need to see something more precise: a chain of specialized devices, each doing a very specific job. Once you can picture that chain, most network questions become much easier to reason through.

A useful mental walk-through starts right at the user's device. Imagine a laptop on a desk. Inside that laptop, a **network interface card (NIC)** takes the data from the operating system and turns it into signals that can move across a network. If the laptop is plugged in with an Ethernet cable, those signals leave through an RJ-45 port and travel along copper wiring to a **switch** or to the LAN port of a SOHO router. If the laptop is using Wi-Fi instead, the signals move over the air from a **wireless NIC** to a **wireless access point (AP)**, which is often embedded inside the same SOHO router. From there, the traffic crosses the local wired network, arrives at the **router**, and the router decides where to send it next. To reach the internet, the router forwards the traffic out its WAN or Internet port to a **modem**, which converts between Ethernet and the ISP's transmission medium, whether that's coaxial cable, a phone line, fiber, or a cellular radio link. The modem hands the traffic off to the ISP's network, and from there it flows through many other routers you never see.

Every device in that path has a predictable role. When something breaks, your first job as a technician is to figure out which link in the chain is at fault: the NIC, the switch/AP, the router, the modem, or the ISP itself. The rest of this section is about learning what each of those devices actually does, how to recognize it on a desk or in a diagram, and what it means when that particular device misbehaves.

Network Interface Cards: Where the Host Meets the Network

The best place to begin is at the edge: the NIC inside each client and server. A **network interface card** operates at the physical and data link layers of the OSI model. Its job is to provide a hardware interface between the device and the network, whether that network is wired Ethernet or wireless Wi-Fi. In a desktop, a wired NIC might be an RJ-45 port soldered onto the motherboard, or it might be an expansion card inserted into a PCIe slot. In laptops, tablets, and smartphones, NICs are usually integrated components, sometimes implemented as tiny M.2 or soldered modules that support both Wi-Fi and Bluetooth.

Wired NICs expose an Ethernet port and support specific speed and duplex capabilities. On modern systems, "10/100/1000" megabits per second is common, and you will also see 2.5, 5, or even 10 gigabit NICs in higher-performance environments. When you plug in an Ethernet cable to a known-good switch or router, the quickest health check is the link and activity LEDs near the jack. A dark link LED with a cable connected suggests either a cable problem or a failed NIC or switch port. A solid light usually means the physical link is up, and a blinking light indicates activity—actual frames moving back and forth.

Wireless NICs replace the physical RJ-45 connector with a radio transceiver that talks to an access point. In many laptops this is hidden behind a small plastic panel or under the keyboard, with antenna wires snaked up into the display bezel. From the operating system's perspective, both wired and wireless NICs are "network adapters," and they are identified by a **MAC address**, the unique hardware address burned into the NIC. That MAC address becomes important when you learn how switches forward traffic and when you configure MAC filtering or static DHCP leases, but for now it is enough to remember that the NIC is the component that owns that address.

When a single computer on a network cannot reach anything, but its neighbors are fine, you should immediately think about the NIC, its driver, or its direct cabling. If the Ethernet cable is firmly connected at both ends and the switch port's LEDs show no link, you are probably looking at a physical problem with the cable or NIC rather than an issue with the router or the ISP. If the adapter does not appear at all in the operating system's list of network interfaces, then driver corruption, disabled hardware, or outright NIC failure jumps to the top of your suspects list. This "start at the edge" habit saves you from blaming the router for what is really a local hardware problem.

Switches: Building the Local Wired Fabric

Once you leave the NIC, the next device you typically hit on a wired LAN is a **switch**. A switch acts like the central nervous system of the local wired network, interconnecting multiple Ethernet devices and forwarding traffic only where it needs to go. Technically, a switch operates at Layer 2, the data link layer, and it forwards **Ethernet frames** based on MAC addresses. When a frame arrives on one port, the switch consults its MAC address table, which maps each known MAC to a specific port. The switch then sends the frame out only on the port associated with the destination MAC address.

On the exam, you should be ready to distinguish this behavior from that of an older **hub**, even though hubs are mostly historical at this point. A hub simply repeats incoming signals to all ports, creating a single big collision domain and wasting bandwidth in the process. Switches, by contrast, give each port its own collision domain and are smart enough to avoid blasting every frame to every device. If you see a picture or description of a box with a bank of numbered RJ-45 ports and almost nothing else—no antennas, no WAN port—that is almost certainly a switch.

In a small home or office, you will often encounter **unmanaged switches**. These are plug-and-play devices: you connect one port back to a LAN port on the router, and you connect additional devices to the remaining ports to expand the number of wired connections. There is no configuration interface and no VLANs or security policies to worry about. In larger environments, you will find **managed switches** with a web or command-line interface that allows administrators to carve up the network into VLANs, apply quality of service rules, and monitor port statistics. For A+ purposes, you mainly need to understand that switches concentrate local connections and forward traffic within a single IP network.

When a group of wired devices loses connectivity all at once, but wireless clients are fine and other wired areas are unaffected, you should visualize the wiring: are those affected devices all plugged into the same small 8-port switch under a desk or in a closet? If the answer is yes, that switch becomes your prime suspect. No link LEDs on any of its ports and a dark power LED typically means it has lost power. A single dead port, with other ports working normally, suggests a localized hardware problem on that port, which you can confirm by moving the cable to a different port and observing whether the link comes up.

Wireless Access Points: Bringing Wi-Fi Clients onto the LAN

Not every device connects with a cable. Wireless-capable phones, tablets, and laptops rely on **wireless access points** to join the network. Conceptually, an AP is to Wi-Fi what a switch port is to Ethernet: a connection point that provides access to the LAN. On the wired side, most standalone APs have an Ethernet port that you connect back to a switch or a router's LAN port. On the wireless side, the AP contains one or more radios that transmit and receive Wi-Fi signals in bands such as 2.4 GHz and 5 GHz, and it advertises a **service set identifier (SSID)**, the network name users see when they scan for Wi-Fi.

In many business environments, APs are dedicated ceiling- or wall-mounted units, often powered by Power over Ethernet from a switch. They do not route traffic to the internet themselves; they simply bridge wireless frames into the wired Ethernet domain. In a typical home, the AP is integrated into the broadband router, so the same plastic box acts as router, switch, firewall, DHCP server, and wireless AP. The exam may still refer to the "AP" even when describing this integrated device, so it is important to keep the function clear in your mind: the AP portion is responsible only for the radio-based connectivity between wireless clients and the wired network.

Because wireless is so visible to end users, AP problems are often reported as "the internet is down," even when the real issue is local. If wired devices in the same home or office are working perfectly, but wireless devices see no SSIDs at all, ask yourself whether the AP or the Wi-Fi feature on the router has been disabled or lost power. If users can see the SSID and connect, but performance is terrible while wired systems run quickly, then AP placement, interference, or overload comes to mind long before ISP problems. And if users can connect to the SSID and even reach local devices like a network printer, but cannot browse the web, that suggests that the AP's basic wireless function is fine and the trouble is further upstream, possibly at the router's WAN side or the modem.

Routers: Joining Your LAN to Other Networks

The next major device in the chain is the **router**. While switches focus on MAC addresses and local forwarding, routers operate at Layer 3, the network layer, and make decisions based on **IP addresses**. In a SOHO environment, the router is the point where your internal LAN meets an external WAN, usually your ISP's network and the wider internet. It has at least two logical sides: a LAN interface facing your private network and a WAN interface facing the provider's network.

Consumer-grade routers bundle several roles into one box. On the back you will usually see a single port labeled WAN or Internet, meant to connect to a modem or gateway, and a small group of LAN ports, which are essentially an internal switch. On the top or sides you may see antennas, indicating a built-in AP. Internally, the router runs services such as **NAT (Network Address Translation)**, which allows many internal devices with private IP addresses to share a single public IP, and **DHCP**, which automatically leases IP configurations to your clients. It also typically enforces a basic **firewall**, blocking unsolicited inbound traffic from the internet while allowing outbound connections from the LAN.

On exam questions, you will often be asked to choose between adding or configuring a router, a switch, or a modem. The key is to tie the device back to its primary job. If the requirement is to connect two different IP networks, or to allow multiple internal clients to share one internet connection, that calls for a router, because only a router understands IP subnets and can apply NAT. If the user says "we need more Ethernet jacks for local devices," that is switch territory, not router territory. Remember as well that while some ISP-provided devices combine modem and router functions, the logical roles are still separate. One part is handling the conversion to the ISP's medium; the other is doing routing, DHCP, NAT, and firewalling.

From a troubleshooting perspective, if both wired and wireless devices can talk to each other but none of them can reach anything on the internet, your thinking should jump to the router's WAN interface or its upstream connection to the modem. You can test this by attempting to reach the router's management IP address—for example, 192.168.1.1—from a client. If you can log in to the router but cannot browse external sites, the router's LAN side and switch/AP components are working, and you have narrowed the break to the router's internet-facing side, the modem, or the ISP.

Modems: Translating to the ISP's Medium

The **modem** is the unsung translator in this story. Historically, a modem's job was to modulate and demodulate signals between digital data and some analog communication medium, like a telephone line. The same idea persists today, even though the technology is more advanced. A **cable modem** connects to the ISP via coaxial cable, understands the provider's DOCSIS signaling, and presents a standard Ethernet interface to your router. A **DSL modem** connects using an RJ-11 phone line and translates between DSL signaling and Ethernet. A fiber installation uses an **ONT (Optical Network Terminal)** to convert light pulses on fiber into Ethernet, and cellular hotspots combine a cellular radio modem with routing functions to share LTE or 5G connectivity.

In many homes, the device the ISP drops off is a combination unit that includes both modem and router functions—and often Wi-Fi as well. Conceptually, though, you need to be able to separate these roles. If an exam question says the "modem's online light is blinking" and customers across a neighborhood are affected, that is pointing you toward a line issue between the modem and the ISP, not an internal routing configuration. On the other hand, if one house can see the modem as online but none of the internal devices are getting IP addresses, that suggests a problem on the routing side, perhaps with the DHCP server in the gateway.

Modem LEDs are valuable indicators. Typical labels include power, downstream, upstream, online or DSL, and sometimes link or Ethernet. If the router appears normal and clients can access the router's admin page but the modem's online light is off or flashing, resetting or power-cycling the modem and checking cabling make sense as early steps. When that does not resolve the issue, your focus should shift from local hardware to the provider's network, and the right next move is usually to contact the ISP.

Extenders, Alternative Media, and Network Bridges

Not every network problem can be solved by running a new Ethernet cable from the router to the farthest room, and not every building is friendly to Wi-Fi. This is where various extender and adapter devices come in. A **wireless range extender** or repeater is a device that listens to an existing Wi-Fi network and rebroadcasts it to extend coverage. You plug it into a power outlet within good range of the main AP or router, configure it to join that SSID, and then clients can associate with the extender in areas where the original signal was weak. The trade-off is that repeaters typically use the same radio to talk both to the upstream AP and to their clients, effectively halving available throughput. If users near the extender complain of slow speeds while those near the main router do not, you should consider whether the extender is poorly placed or overloading a single shared radio channel.

Other times, the RF environment is simply hostile: thick walls, interference, or long distances make Wi-Fi unreliable. **Powerline networking adapters** solve this by repurposing the building's electrical wiring as a data pathway. These devices usually come as a pair. One unit plugs into an electrical outlet near the router and connects to a LAN port with Ethernet. The second plugs in near the remote device and offers its own Ethernet port. With simple pairing, they encapsulate Ethernet frames over the power lines. Performance depends heavily on the quality and topology of the electrical system; outlets on different phases or behind noisy equipment can produce inconsistent speeds or dropouts.

In homes with existing coaxial cabling to many rooms, **MoCA adapters** (Multimedia over Coax Alliance) play a similar role, but over coax instead of power lines. You connect one MoCA adapter to the router via Ethernet and to a coax run; additional adapters in other rooms pick up the signal from coax and provide Ethernet jacks for TVs, consoles, or desktops. MoCA often delivers more stable throughput than powerline in buildings with good coax infrastructure. In enterprise or campus environments, you may also see **media converters** that bridge copper Ethernet to fiber for longer runs, and **wireless bridges** that join two wired LAN segments over a point-to-point Wi-Fi link, such as between two buildings.

The exam may describe these devices indirectly, for example by saying that a technician must connect a distant office where running new Ethernet is impractical but electrical outlets are available, or that a home has coax jacks in every room and needs high-speed connections for streaming devices. In those situations, being able to name powerline or MoCA adapters as the appropriate solution is exactly what is being tested.

Following the Chain and Reading the Clues

At this point, you can mentally trace a typical SOHO path: a host's NIC sends data to a switch or AP, which feeds into the router, which forwards it through a modem to the ISP. That simple chain—NIC -> Switch/AP -> Router -> Modem -> ISP—is a powerful framework for troubleshooting. When you hear a problem description, ask yourself where along that path everything is still working, and where it stops. If all wireless devices are offline but wired systems continue to work, your break is probably between the wireless NICs and the AP, or within the AP itself. If an entire group of wired devices in one part of the office goes dark, follow their cables in your mind (and in real life) until you reach their common switch. If all users, wired and wireless, can reach the router's web interface but not external sites, then the router and LAN are functional and your suspicion naturally moves towards the modem or the ISP.

You will notice that many exam scenarios are built exactly like this. A few sentences about which users are having trouble and which are not, plus a short note about status LEDs on a router, switch, AP, or modem, give you enough information to choose the device at fault or the device to add. As you move into upcoming chapters on configuring SOHO networks and wireless technologies, you will start logging in to these devices, setting SSIDs, enabling DHCP, and tightening security. Underneath those configuration screens, the same physical roles you have learned here remain constant, and the same chain of devices will guide you when it is time to troubleshoot.

2.6 Configuring a Basic SOHO Network

If you walk into a typical home or very small office today, you'll usually find the entire network built around a single box sitting under a desk or next to the TV. That one device, often called a wireless router, is doing almost everything: it connects to the Internet, it hands out IP addresses, it provides wired Ethernet ports, it broadcasts Wi-Fi, and it blocks basic attacks from the outside world. For the CompTIA A+ exam and for real-world work, being able to set up and adjust that box with confidence is one of the most valuable practical skills you can develop.

When we talk about configuring a "basic SOHO network," we are not talking about enterprise features like VLANs or complex firewall rule sets. The goal is much simpler and much more common: take the Internet connection from the ISP, share it safely with everyone in the home or small office, and make sure wired and wireless devices can get online reliably. To do that well, you need to understand not just where to click in the router interface, but what each part does in the bigger picture of how traffic flows from a laptop to the Internet and back.

Seeing the SOHO Router as a Collection of Roles

The easiest way to think about a SOHO router is not as a mysterious black box, but as several familiar network devices living in one chassis. Inside that plastic shell, you almost always have a **WAN interface**, a **LAN switch**, a **wireless access point**, a **DHCP server**, a **NAT router**, and a basic **firewall**. Each of those pieces is playing a distinct role in the path a packet takes.

On the outside-facing side is the WAN port, usually labeled "Internet" or "WAN." This is the link to the ISP's world: a cable modem, DSL modem, fiber ONT, or perhaps even a cellular connection. The address on this interface is either a true public IP or something assigned by the ISP's equipment. On the inside-facing side are the LAN Ethernet ports and the Wi-Fi radios. Those together form a single local network, typically using a private IP subnet such as 192.168.0.0/24 or 192.168.1.0/24. Every client device—desktops, laptops, smartphones, smart TVs, printers—lives on that LAN side.

The glue that makes this work is the combination of DHCP and NAT. The router's built-in **DHCP server** automatically hands out IP addresses to devices on the LAN, along with the subnet mask, default gateway, and DNS server information they need. The **default gateway** it gives them is the router's own LAN IP address, such as 192.168.1.1. When a client sends traffic to some Internet destination, that traffic is sent to the gateway. The router then uses **Network Address Translation (NAT)** to translate the internal private address into the single public IP on the WAN side, tracks the connection, and ensures replies are translated back and forwarded to the correct internal client. At the same time, the router's firewall keeps random unsolicited traffic from the Internet from reaching internal hosts.

Most SOHO routers ship with reasonable defaults so that a nontechnical user can plug them in and get basic connectivity. As a technician, though, you are expected to do more than accept the defaults blindly. You need to be able to verify that the WAN connection is using the right method for that ISP, adjust the LAN addressing if needed, configure Wi-Fi properly, and harden the security settings so that the network works reliably and is not an easy target.

Physical Setup and Getting into the Router

Configuration always starts with a sensible physical setup. In a small home, you may not have many options, but you still want to think about wireless coverage and interference. Placing the router in a central location, as high as is practical and away from large metal surfaces, large appliances, and the microwave can dramatically improve Wi-Fi performance. In a small office with several wired desktops, you also have to think about where the ISP's modem is located and how far Ethernet runs will need to go. You may decide to place the router near the demarcation point where the cable or phone line enters, then run longer Ethernet cables—or use additional switches—to reach work areas.

The cabling order matters more than many beginners realize. The ISP's medium (coax, twisted pair for DSL, fiber) connects first to the modem or ONT. From there, a single Ethernet cable goes from the modem's LAN port to the router's WAN or Internet port. Client devices and any downstream unmanaged switches plug into the router's LAN ports, not the WAN. A very common mistake is to accidentally plug the modem into one of the LAN ports, which will leave the router's WAN interface disconnected and all clients without Internet access even though their local network appears fine. Another pitfall you will see in the field is someone daisy-chaining a second wireless router behind the first, using its WAN port; this creates a double NAT situation that can complicate applications and remote access.

Once the cables are correct and the devices powered on, you need to reach the router's management interface. The easiest way is usually a wired connection from your laptop to one of the router's LAN ports. By default, your laptop will use DHCP to get an address. In Windows, when you run ipconfig, you should see a private IP such as 192.168.1.100 and a default gateway like 192.168.1.1. That gateway address is almost always the router's LAN interface and the URL you use to reach the web management page. Typing that address into a browser should prompt for login credentials. These are usually printed on a label on the router itself or in the quick-start guide, something like "admin/admin" or "admin/password." From a security perspective, that default login is a problem, but you need it initially to get inside and begin configuration.

If you cannot reach the interface at the expected address, the router may be using a different default subnet, or your laptop may have a static IP misconfigured from a previous job. In that case, re-checking your adapter settings and confirming that you are indeed receiving DHCP from the router are your first troubleshooting steps. Once you can reliably get to the management page, you are ready to handle the Internet side.

Configuring and Verifying the WAN Connection

Inside the router interface you will always find a section labeled something like Internet Setup, WAN, or Broadband. This defines how the router talks to the ISP. In most cable and many fiber scenarios, the correct choice is **Dynamic IP** or **Automatic Configuration (DHCP)**. In that mode, the router simply requests an IP configuration from the modem or directly from the ISP, just like your PC requests an IP from the router. You should see the WAN status screen showing an IP address, subnet mask, default gateway, and one or more DNS servers. If you see 0.0.0.0 or no address at all, there is a problem between the router and the ISP equipment.

DSL connections frequently use **PPPoE (Point-to-Point Protocol over Ethernet)**. When PPPoE is required, the ISP will have given the customer a username and password. These must be entered exactly in the router's PPPoE configuration, along with any service name if specified. If those credentials are wrong, the router may show a link light but never obtain a usable IP, and no client will reach the Internet. In some small business cases, the ISP provides a **static public IP** instead. There, your job is to type in the static IP, subnet mask, gateway, and DNS entries exactly as provided. Any typo will break connectivity.

A key habit for you as a technician is to always check WAN status before blaming local devices. If a user says, "No one can get on the Internet," and you can reach the router but its WAN address is missing or clearly wrong, the problem is upstream with the ISP or with the connection type configuration. If the WAN address looks like a private IP in the 192.168 or 10.x range, the router may be plugged into another router or gateway device from the ISP rather than directly to the Internet, which is common when the ISP gives customers an all-in-one modem/router and the user plugs in their own router behind it.

Once the WAN status shows a valid configuration, you can test from your laptop by browsing to a known site. If your PC can talk to the router (you can reach its web interface) but cannot reach external sites despite the router having a good WAN IP, then you start to suspect DNS settings, ISP issues, or a firewall misconfiguration. That layered reasoning—client to router, router to ISP—will appear repeatedly on the exam and in real troubleshooting.

LAN Addressing and DHCP on the Inside

With the Internet side functional, attention turns to the local network. SOHO routers almost always use one of the three private IP ranges: 10.x.x.x, 172.16–172.31.x.x, or 192.168.x.x. Recognizing these as **private addresses** is essential. If you see your PC with an address like 192.168.1.50 and gateway 192.168.1.1, you know you are on a private LAN, not directly on the Internet. The router's LAN IP—often 192.168.0.1 or 192.168.1.1—defines the network's subnet. For example, 192.168.1.1 with a 255.255.255.0 subnet mask means all IPs from 192.168.1.1 through 192.168.1.254 are on the same local segment.

In the router's LAN setup page, you can usually change this base address. You might do this if you are connecting two networks together and both happen to use 192.168.1.0/24 by default, which will cause conflicts. For instance, you could change one router to use 192.168.2.1/24 instead. Whatever LAN IP you choose, that will be the default gateway for all clients.

The DHCP server section is where you define the **DHCP pool** or range the router will hand out dynamically. A common default might be 192.168.1.100 through 192.168.1.199. The idea is that a subset of the subnet is reserved for automatic assignment, leaving some low-numbered addresses available for static assignments. For example, you might give a network printer a static IP at 192.168.1.20 and a NAS at 192.168.1.21, safely outside the pool so the DHCP server will never assign them to other devices.

When you configure DHCP, you can also specify the lease time and, in some routers, alternative DNS servers instead of those from the ISP. Changing DNS is sometimes useful when troubleshooting slow name resolution or when implementing content filtering. From an exam standpoint, it is important to realize that if a client cannot reach the DHCP server, it will assign itself an **APIPA** address in the 169.254.x.x range. Seeing that address immediately tells you there is a DHCP problem: either the server is down, the client is on the wrong VLAN or segment, or there is a cabling/connection issue.

There are situations where you want a device to have a stable IP but still use DHCP centrally. That is where **DHCP reservations** come in. In that mode, the router always assigns the same IP address to a device with a specific MAC address. For example, a VoIP phone in a manager's office might always receive 192.168.1.30, even though it is technically using DHCP like everything else. This avoids conflicts and makes it easy to find that device later.

Wireless Configuration: Names, Bands, and Channels

With the wired side in order, you can configure the wireless network. The first visible setting is the **SSID**, or network name. Almost every router ships with a generic SSID based on the brand and model. Changing this to something unique helps users identify the correct network, especially in apartment buildings where many routers of the same brand are visible. At the same time, the name should not give away too much personal information; "SmithFamilyWiFi" is fine, "123-Main-St-Apt-4B" is not ideal. Some routers allow you to hide the SSID so it does not show up in scans. This is not meaningful security and often makes support harder, so it is rarely the right choice.

Modern routers usually support at least two frequency bands: 2.4 GHz and 5 GHz, and many newer ones add 6 GHz for Wi-Fi 6E. The 2.4 GHz band offers better range and wall penetration but is crowded and has only three non-overlapping **channels** in the typical 20 MHz width: 1, 6, and 11. The 5 GHz band supports more channels and higher throughput but has shorter range. Many routers broadcast two SSIDs, one per band, such as "OfficeNet" and "OfficeNet-5G," or they use a single SSID with band steering to move capable devices to the faster band automatically. In congested environments, especially in 2.4 GHz, manually choosing channels 1, 6, or 11 can reduce interference from neighbors; the exam often expects you to know that those three are the non-overlapping options.

You will also see wireless mode settings like 802.11n-only, 802.11ac, or "mixed." Leaving the router in a mixed mode that supports older and newer clients is usually the most practical in a SOHO, because you never quite know what devices users will bring in. The trade-off is that some modes that support older standards might limit the maximum performance of newer ones, but in a small environment that is rarely critical.

Securing the SOHO Network

Once basic connectivity works, your job is only half done. An unsecured or poorly secured router is worse than no router at all, because it provides attackers a known foothold into the network. One of your first configuration changes after confirming WAN and LAN functionality should be to change the router's **administrative credentials**. Leaving "admin/admin" in place means any user on the LAN—or anyone who manages to connect to Wi-Fi—can alter settings or open the network further. Choose a strong, unique password for the management interface, and where the router allows you to change the admin username, do that as well.

The next major security decision is wireless encryption and authentication. The minimum acceptable standard in modern networks is **WPA2-Personal** using AES (also labeled WPA2-PSK [AES]). Where all client devices support it, **WPA3-Personal** is even better, offering stronger security against offline password attacks. You should avoid WEP entirely; it is cryptographically broken and should only appear in exam questions as a wrong choice. Similarly, open networks without any encryption should be reserved for extremely limited guest scenarios where you truly expect the traffic to be public and untrusted. Exam questions often present several options such as WEP, WPA, WPA2-TKIP, WPA2-AES, and WPA3; your task is to pick the strongest realistically supported method, which is almost always WPA2-AES or WPA3.

The Wi-Fi passphrase, or pre-shared key, should be long enough and complex enough that it cannot be guessed easily, but still something users can type without constant errors. A 14–20 character phrase made of several unrelated words and some numbers tends to strike a good balance, much better than a short, clever word with a few substitutions. Remember that changing this password later will require updating every client device, so it is worth getting it right early.

Many consumer and small business routers also support a **guest network** feature. A guest SSID creates a separate wireless network, often with Internet access but no access to internal LAN resources like file shares and printers. For a small doctor's office, for instance, this allows waiting room visitors to use Wi-Fi without ever being on the same logical network as medical records systems. Guest networks may also include bandwidth limits or time schedules. From an A+ perspective, recognizing that guest networks are about isolating untrusted users from internal resources is important.

Finally, consider firewall and remote management settings. SOHO routers typically run a **stateful firewall** that allows outgoing connections but blocks unsolicited incoming traffic. You should leave this enabled, and you should be wary of options like "DMZ host," which expose one internal system almost directly to the Internet. When something does not work from outside, beginners are tempted to shove that device into the DMZ to "just make it work," but this is a significant security risk. Targeted **port forwarding** to open only the specific ports you need to a specific internal IP is almost always safer. As for remote management of the router itself from the Internet, that should generally remain disabled unless there is a clear need and additional protections in place.

Connecting Clients and Verifying End-to-End Operation

With WAN, LAN, wireless, and security configured, you can start connecting client devices and validating that the entire chain works. Wired clients will usually be the least troublesome: plug in the Ethernet cable, confirm that the link lights come on, and then check that the device has received a DHCP lease in the correct private range with the right gateway and DNS. If a desktop shows 169.254.x.x instead, you know immediately it is not reaching the DHCP server on the router and you should look at cabling, switch ports, or adapter settings.

Wireless clients add one more step: the user must select the correct SSID and enter the correct passphrase. A very common support issue in homes is a laptop trying to connect to an old SSID from a previous router or to a neighbor's network with a similar name. Verifying that the device is really connected to the intended SSID, has an IP in the expected subnet, and has the router as its default gateway eliminates a lot of guesswork. If a phone can connect to Wi-Fi but shows "No Internet," you then look back toward the router's WAN status and ISP.

Networked printers, NAS devices, and other special clients are configured much the same way, but you often want them to have predictably stable addresses. You might connect a printer via Ethernet, then assign it a static IP like 192.168.1.25, or create a DHCP reservation for its MAC address. Once you can ping that address from your workstation and reach its web interface, you know the network layer is working and can move on to installing drivers or sharing settings, which are covered in later chapters.

As you work through setups like this, you are building not just a checklist of clicks, but a mental model of how a small network is supposed to look when it is healthy. When something breaks, you will be able to ask structured questions: Can the client see the router? Can the router see the Internet? Are the IP addresses in the right ranges? Is DNS functioning? That structured thinking, more than any single setting, is what turns basic SOHO configuration into a solid foundation for both the exam and real entry-level IT work.

2.7 Knowledge Check

Question 1: A user can browse to http://intranet.company.local but gets an error when browsing to https://intranet.company.local. Which TCP port is the MOST likely issue?

- **A.** 443
- **B.** 80
- **C.** 23
- **D.** 445

Question 2: A technician needs to enable secure remote command-line access to a Linux server over the internet. Which protocol and port combination should be allowed through the firewall?

- **A.** Telnet over TCP 23
- **B.** SSH over TCP 22
- **C.** RDP over TCP 3389
- **D.** HTTP over TCP 80

Question 3: Users report they cannot access Windows file shares using paths like \fileserver\dept, but they can browse the web and use email normally. Which port is MOST likely being blocked?

- **A.** TCP 23
- **B.** TCP 80
- **C.** TCP 445
- **D.** TCP 110

Question 4: A Windows administrator cannot use Remote Desktop to connect to a server, even though the server responds to pings and its web interface on port 80 is reachable. Which default port should be checked for RDP connectivity?

- **A.** TCP 21
- **B.** TCP 25
- **C.** TCP 161
- **D.** TCP 3389

Question 5: A technician suspects DNS issues because users can ping 8.8.8.8 but cannot browse to www.google.com. Which ports should be checked on the firewall for DNS client queries?

A. TCP 25 and TCP 110
B. UDP 53 and TCP 53
C. TCP 143 and TCP 993
D. UDP 67 and UDP 68

Question 6: A network printer's web configuration page on http://printer01 is accessible, but users cannot send print jobs using IPP. Which port is MOST likely blocked?

A. TCP 25
B. TCP 110
C. TCP 161
D. TCP 631

Question 7: A user cannot get an IP address from the DHCP server and is receiving an APIPA address. Which UDP port does the DHCP server listen on for client Discover messages?

A. 20
B. 21
C. 67
D. 143

Question 8: An SNMP monitoring system is not receiving traps from a network switch, but queries from the monitoring console to the switch work. Which destination port on the monitoring server should accept SNMP traps?

A. UDP 161
B. TCP 161
C. TCP 162
D. UDP 162

Question 9: A legacy POP3 mail server is configured for unencrypted access. Which default port must be open on the server for clients to download email in this configuration?

A. TCP 143
B. TCP 110
C. TCP 993
D. TCP 995

Question 10: A technician wants to disable insecure Telnet access to network devices and require a secure equivalent instead. Which port should be left open to support this secure remote CLI access?

A. TCP 22
B. TCP 23
C. TCP 443
D. UDP 69

Question 11: An internal monitoring system uses SNMP to query printers and switches for status. Which port must remain open on those devices to respond to SNMP polling?

A. UDP 162
B. UDP 161
C. TCP 162
D. TCP 161

Question 12: A mail client is configured to use IMAP without encryption. Which TCP port will it typically use to access the mailbox?

A. 993
B. 25
C. 110
D. 143

Question 13: A technician wants to block unencrypted web traffic while still allowing secure web traffic. Which ports should be configured to BLOCK on the firewall for this policy?

A. TCP 443 only
B. TCP 993 and TCP 995
C. TCP 80 only
D. TCP 22 and TCP 23

Question 14: A user can access an FTP server's login prompt but cannot list or transfer files in active mode FTP. Which port on the client is dynamically used by the server to initiate the data connection in active mode?

A. TCP 20
B. TCP 21
C. A random high TCP port above 1023
D. UDP 69

Question 15: Which protocol typically uses UDP and TCP port 427 to allow macOS clients to automatically discover services such as printers and file shares?

A. SMB
B. AFP
C. SLP
D. SNMP

Question 16: A user in a hotel Wi-Fi network is redirected to a login page when visiting non-secure sites but receives errors when trying to open secure sites. Which statement BEST explains this behavior with respect to ports?

A. HTTP/80 traffic is allowed and intercepted, but HTTPS/443 is blocked until authentication
B. HTTPS/443 traffic is allowed, but HTTP/80 is blocked until authentication
C. Both HTTP/80 and HTTPS/443 are blocked until a VPN is used
D. Only DNS/53 is allowed; all web ports are blocked permanently

Question 17: Which wireless standard operates only in the 5 GHz band and is commonly marketed as "Wi-Fi 5"?

A. 802.11n
B. 802.11ax
C. 802.11g
D. 802.11ac

Question 18: A user reports that Wi-Fi works near the access point, but the signal quickly drops off in distant rooms. Which configuration change is MOST likely to improve range at the cost of maximum throughput?

A. Move clients to the 5 GHz band only
B. Enable or use the 2.4 GHz band
C. Disable 802.11n support
D. Switch the SSID to hidden mode

Question 19: An older wireless printer can only connect to 2.4 GHz 802.11g/n networks. After installing a new router broadcasting only a 5 GHz SSID, the printer cannot see the network at all. What should the technician do?

A. Enable a 2.4 GHz SSID or mixed 2.4/5 GHz network on the router
B. Replace the router with an 802.11a-only model that supports legacy devices
C. Move the printer closer to the router without changing any wireless settings
D. Configure the printer for a static 5 GHz IP address and gateway

Question 20: A user complains that Wi-Fi is slow at lunchtime near the office kitchen, but performs well at other times. Which is the MOST likely cause?

A. DHCP lease expiration at noon causing frequent address renewals
B. DNS server maintenance window scheduled during lunch hours
C. Microwave oven interference in the 2.4 GHz wireless band
D. Router switching to IPv6 only during periods of heavy usage

ANSWERS

1: Correct Answer: A
Rationale: HTTPS uses TCP port 443, while HTTP uses TCP port 80. Since HTTP works but HTTPS fails, an issue with port 443 or its service is most likely.

2: Correct Answer: B
Rationale: Secure remote CLI access to Linux is provided by SSH on TCP port 22. Telnet (23) and HTTP (80) are unencrypted, and RDP (3389) is for Windows GUIs.

3: Correct Answer: C
Rationale: Windows file shares use SMB over TCP 445. If web (80) and email (110) work but UNC paths like \server\share fail, TCP 445 is likely blocked.

4: Correct Answer: D
Rationale: Remote Desktop Protocol listens on TCP 3389 by default. If ping and HTTP work but RDP fails, check connectivity to TCP 3389.

5: Correct Answer: B
Rationale: DNS uses UDP 53 for most queries and TCP 53 for larger transfers. If users can reach IPs but not hostnames, blocking these ports breaks DNS.

6: Correct Answer: D
Rationale: IPP printing uses TCP 631. If the printer's web page on port 80 works but IPP jobs fail, port 631 is likely blocked.

7: Correct Answer: C
Rationale: DHCP servers listen on UDP 67 for client Discover broadcasts and reply to clients on UDP 68. If UDP 67 is blocked, clients get APIPA addresses.

8: Correct Answer: D
Rationale: SNMP traps are sent from devices to managers on UDP 162. SNMP polling uses UDP 161, so trap issues point to UDP 162 on the manager.

9: Correct Answer: B
Rationale: Unencrypted POP3 uses TCP 110. TCP 995 is POP3 over SSL/TLS, and 143/993 are IMAP ports.

10: Correct Answer: A
Rationale: SSH, the secure replacement for Telnet, uses TCP 22. Telnet uses TCP 23; TCP 443 is HTTPS, and UDP 69 is TFTP.

11: Correct Answer: B
Rationale: SNMP agents respond to polling on UDP 161. Traps go to UDP 162, so for queries from a manager, UDP 161 must be open.

Question 12: Correct Answer: D
Rationale: Unencrypted IMAP4 uses TCP 143. Secure IMAP uses TCP 993. Ports 25 and 110 are for SMTP and POP3.

Question 13: Correct Answer: C
Rationale: HTTP uses TCP 80 and HTTPS uses TCP 443. Blocking TCP 80 while leaving 443 open enforces secure-only browsing.

Question 14: Correct Answer: C
Rationale: In active FTP, the client opens a random high TCP port (>1023) and tells the server. The server's data port 20 connects back to that client port.

Question 15: Correct Answer: C
Rationale: Service Location Protocol (SLP) uses UDP/TCP 427 for service discovery, used by macOS to find printers and file shares. SMB, AFP, and SNMP use other ports.

Question 16: Correct Answer: A
Rationale: Captive portals usually allow and intercept HTTP on port 80 for redirection, while blocking or limiting HTTPS on 443 until login, causing secure sites to error.

Question 17: Correct Answer: D
Rationale: 802.11ac operates only in the 5 GHz band and is marketed as Wi-Fi 5. 802.11n and 802.11ax can use 2.4 and 5 GHz; 802.11g is 2.4 GHz only.

Question 18: Correct Answer: B
Rationale: The 2.4 GHz band has better range and wall penetration than 5 GHz, at the cost of lower throughput and more interference, improving coverage in distant rooms.

Question 19: Correct Answer: A
Rationale: The printer supports only 2.4 GHz 802.11g/n, so it cannot see a 5 GHz–only SSID. Enabling a 2.4 GHz or mixed SSID allows it to connect.

Question 20: Correct Answer: C
Rationale: Microwave ovens operate around 2.4 GHz and can interfere with 2.4 GHz Wi-Fi, often degrading performance near kitchens during use.

CHAPTER 3

Hardware

3.1 Display Types, Components & Characteristics

Imagine a user stops by your desk with a complaint you'll hear many times in this career: "My new monitor is bigger, but it looks worse than the old one. The text is fuzzy and it hurts my eyes." On paper, the new display might sound better—larger size, maybe higher advertised specs—but size alone doesn't equal quality. What they are really running into is a collision of display technology, panel characteristics, and configuration choices. To give useful answers instead of guesses, you need to understand what is actually going on inside that rectangle of glass and plastic, and how the specs you see on the box translate into what the user sees on the screen.

At the heart of almost every desktop monitor and laptop today is some variant of **LCD**, or liquid crystal display. "LCD" refers to the core panel technology, not the lighting system behind it. A modern "LED monitor" is still an LCD panel; the difference is that its backlight uses LEDs instead of older fluorescent lamps. That distinction matters, because it affects both how the display behaves and how you interpret symptoms. Conceptually, an LCD works in layers. A backlight shines white light through the panel. In the middle sit liquid crystal cells, tiny structures that can twist when an electric field is applied. In front of those are color filters for red, green, and blue. By controlling how much light each subpixel allows through, the panel builds the full-color image you see. Once you have that mental picture, problems like "image is visible but the screen is very dim" start to make sense: the LCD is still forming the image, but the backlight layer isn't doing its job.

Within the family of LCDs, panel type has a huge impact on what the display is good at. One common type is the **TN (twisted nematic)** panel. TN technology is cheap to manufacture and very fast at changing pixel states, which translates into low response times and less motion blur. That is why many budget gaming monitors use TN: the fast transitions help fast-paced games look smoother. The tradeoff is that TN panels have relatively poor color accuracy and noticeably narrow viewing angles. If you look at a TN laptop screen from above or from the side, colors can shift dramatically and blacks can turn gray. You will occasionally see TN in office environments simply because it is inexpensive, but it is rarely the right choice when accurate color or wide viewing angles matter.

A step up in quality, and the current favorite for general-purpose use, is the **IPS (in-plane switching)** panel. IPS arranges and drives the liquid crystals differently, which significantly improves both color reproduction and viewing angles. An IPS monitor looks much more consistent when you move off-center; colors stay true rather than washing out or inverting. That makes IPS excellent for office productivity, web browsing, and especially any kind of content creation such as graphics work, video, or photography. The tradeoffs are cost and, historically, slightly slower response times than TN, though many modern IPS panels have become fast enough that only competitive gamers will really notice. When you see a scenario where a user needs "accurate color and wide viewing angles," IPS should be top of mind.

Sitting between TN and IPS in some respects is **VA (vertical alignment)**. VA panels can deliver very high native contrast ratios, with deeper blacks than most TN or IPS screens. That makes them attractive for watching movies or working with darker content. However, their pixel transitions can be less consistent, sometimes leading to more visible motion blur in games or fast-scrolling content. You are less likely to be tested on VA specifics than on the clear contrasts between TN and IPS, but it is helpful to recognize that not all LCDs fit cleanly into "fast but ugly" versus "pretty but slower." In the real world, VA panels often appear in TVs and some mid-range monitors where contrast is a selling point.

Alongside LCDs, you will increasingly encounter **OLED** displays, especially in high-end smartphones, tablets, and newer laptops. OLED stands for organic light-emitting diode, and it represents a different approach entirely. Instead of shining a backlight through a liquid crystal shutter, each pixel in an OLED panel emits its own light directly. When a pixel is supposed to be black, it can simply be turned off, giving OLED displays exceptionally deep blacks and extremely high contrast. They can also be made very thin and even flexible, which has driven their adoption in mobile devices and premium televisions. The drawbacks are cost, potential burn-in (where static images like toolbars leave a faint permanent "shadow" over time), and power usage that varies with content—bright, white-heavy content can draw more power than equivalent LCDs. For the A+ level, you mainly need to remember that OLED does not use a separate backlight, and that its per-pixel lighting is responsible for both its strengths and some of its unique failure modes.

While most of your daily work will involve flat panels on desks or attached to laptops, projectors are still common in conference rooms, classrooms, and training spaces. A projector is simply another type of display device, often based on LCD or DLP (digital light processing) technology, that throws the image onto a screen instead of directly to your eyes. Here, **brightness**, measured in lumens, becomes critical. A projector that is fine in a dark room might look washed out and unusable in a brightly lit classroom. Resolution and aspect ratio matter just as much as on monitors: pair a low-resolution projector with a modern laptop and you will immediately see fuzzier text and less usable workspace. Throw distance—the range at which the projector can create a properly sized, focused image—is another practical concern, especially in small rooms.

You will also see televisions repurposed as monitors, particularly in home offices and small businesses trying to save money. Technically, a TV is just a display with an integrated tuner and media features, and many of them use the same LCD or OLED technologies as monitors. However, TVs are optimized for video, not crisp text. They may use **overscan**, where the edges of the image are cut off, or processing that adds **input lag**, the delay between the signal arriving and the image appearing. Those behaviors can make a TV feel sluggish or slightly blurry when used as a PC monitor. It is not that they never work, but when a user complains that a big TV "doesn't look as sharp as my old monitor," it is often because of these design choices, combined with resolution and viewing distance.

All of these display types share certain key characteristics that you must be able to interpret. The most fundamental is **resolution**: the number of pixels horizontally and vertically. Common examples include 1920×1080 (often called 1080p or Full HD), 2560×1440 (1440p), and 3840×2160 (4K UHD). An LCD or OLED panel has a fixed grid of physical pixels, known as its **native resolution**. When you run the display at that native resolution, each source pixel from the graphics card maps cleanly to one physical pixel on the panel, giving the sharpest image. If the operating system is configured to a non-native resolution—say, you set a 1920×1080 monitor to 1366×768—the display has to scale the image. That scaling almost always introduces softness or blur, especially around text. When someone complains of "fuzzy text" on a new monitor, one of your first moves should be to check whether the OS is using the monitor's native resolution.

Aspect ratio describes the shape of the image, expressed as the ratio of width to height. For modern displays, 16:9 is the dominant standard; this is what most 1080p and 4K monitors use. You may also encounter 16:10 for slightly taller workspaces, and 21:9 or wider for ultrawide monitors. Older equipment and some specialized devices still use 4:3 or 5:4. When the aspect ratio of the signal does not match the aspect ratio of the display, you see familiar artifacts: black bars on the sides or top and bottom, or a stretched, distorted image. If a user complains that "everyone on the screen looks short and wide," the computer is probably sending a 4:3 image to a 16:9 display, or vice versa, and either the display or OS is stretching it instead of preserving the original shape.

Once resolution and aspect ratio are correct, **refresh rate** becomes a major factor in how the display feels. Refresh rate, measured in hertz (Hz), indicates how many times per second the display updates the image. A typical office monitor runs at 60 Hz, which is adequate for most productivity tasks. Gaming and high-motion applications benefit from higher refresh rates—120 Hz, 144 Hz, or even higher—because they can show smoother motion and reduce perceived blur. However, achieving those rates depends not just on the monitor but also on the graphics hardware and the cable or connector type. Trying to drive 4K at 144 Hz over an old HDMI or DisplayPort standard is likely to fail or fall back to a lower refresh. Symptoms can include flicker, loss of signal, or the system simply not offering the higher refresh rate as an option. When a user says, "My new 144 Hz monitor is stuck at 60," you should think about connector limitations and GPU capabilities before assuming the monitor is defective.

Another piece of the visual puzzle is **color depth**, sometimes called bit depth. This refers to how many distinct colors the system can represent for each pixel. A common standard is 8 bits per color channel (red, green, blue), often summarized as "24-bit color" or "True Color," which yields about 16.7 million possible colors. Lower color depths, such as 16-bit "High Color," support fewer colors and can show visible banding in gradients, where you can see distinct steps between shades instead of a smooth transition. In everyday office work, you may not notice or care, but for tasks like photo editing or professional design, higher color depth and accurate calibration are essential. On the exam, you might see color depth show up indirectly, with descriptions of banding or reduced color quality when settings are changed.

Brightness and contrast complete the basic set of visual characteristics. **Brightness** is typically measured in nits (candelas per square meter) and describes how much light the screen can emit. In a dim office, a moderate brightness level is fine; on a laptop used outdoors or near a sunny window, a dim panel can become effectively unreadable. When a user reports that the screen "washes out in bright light," insufficient brightness is a prime suspect, along with glossy screen coatings that reflect ambient light. **Contrast ratio** expresses the difference between the darkest black and brightest white the display can produce. Higher real-world contrast makes images pop and text easier to read, but you should be skeptical of marketing claims with absurdly high "dynamic" contrast numbers. OLED panels achieve excellent contrast because they can turn black pixels fully off, but well-tuned LCDs can be very usable in office environments despite lower theoretical ratios.

Two more technical characteristics are worth knowing, especially because gamers care about them and marketing materials emphasize them. **Response time** is how quickly a pixel can change from one value to another, often measured in milliseconds. Slower response times can cause motion blur or ghosting, where moving objects leave faint trails behind them. **Input lag** is the delay between the graphics hardware sending a frame and that frame actually appearing on the screen. High input lag can make controls feel sluggish, which is particularly noticeable in fast games or interactive applications. TVs used as monitors sometimes have high input lag due to image processing features; enabling a "Game Mode" or similar setting often reduces that lag.

So far we have focused on what the display shows, but the physical design and components matter just as much, especially from a support perspective. A monitor is more than just a panel; it includes a stand or mounting system, controls, power circuitry, and input electronics. A decent stand allows for height adjustment, tilt, swivel, and sometimes pivot into portrait orientation. That pivot capability, combined with operating system support for changing orientation, makes it possible to set up vertical monitors for coding or document review. When a user asks, "Can we rotate one of my screens so I can see full pages at once?" you need to know that some stands and panels support this and that you must adjust both the physical orientation and the OS settings to match.

Inside a desktop monitor, the components are typically not serviced by entry-level technicians beyond simple disassembly; if a logic board or power supply fails, the monitor is usually replaced. Laptops are different. A typical laptop display assembly includes the LCD panel, the backlight (almost always LED now, integrated into the panel), the cabling that runs through the hinge to the motherboard, the webcam, microphone, and often the Wi-Fi antennas. Older laptops used CCFL (cold cathode fluorescent lamp) backlights, which required an **inverter** to convert the system's DC power into the high-voltage AC the lamps needed. On the exam, you may still encounter scenarios involving inverter failure. A classic symptom is a screen that is extremely dim, but where you can still faintly see the desktop if you shine a flashlight at an angle. That tells you the panel is working and receiving video, but the backlight system has failed. In modern LED-backlit laptops, there is no separate inverter, but backlight power circuitry can still fail and produce similar symptoms.

Cabling and connectors form the bridge between the graphics source and the display. In this section we are less concerned with pinouts and more with how the connection type influences what is possible. Older **VGA** connections carry an analog signal. At low resolutions, a good VGA link can still look acceptable, but as resolutions climb, analog limitations lead to softness and increased susceptibility to interference. That is why high-resolution monitors connected via VGA often look slightly "off," especially around text. Digital connections such as DVI, HDMI, DisplayPort, and USB-C in display mode transmit discrete pixel values, preserving sharpness as long as the cable and port support the desired resolution and refresh rate. When a user replaces an old VGA cable with HDMI on the same monitor and immediately reports that the image looks sharper, this is precisely what is happening: the panel is still the same, but the connection is no longer adding analog fuzz.

When evaluating user complaints, it helps to mentally separate configuration issues from fundamental capability limits and hardware failures. Blurry or "soft" text on an otherwise bright, stable image often points to non-native resolution or an analog connection rather than a bad panel. A large display that "shows everything too small" is about resolution and pixel density interacting with viewing distance and operating system scaling; you may need to enable or adjust scaling rather than forcing a lower resolution. A secondary monitor that refuses to go above 60 Hz is probably limited by the graphics card, the specific output port used, or the cable specification, even if the monitor itself can support higher rates. Washed-out colors on a laptop compared to an external IPS monitor can be due to both panel type differences and misadjusted brightness and contrast. The more comfortable you are with the underlying technologies and characteristics, the easier it becomes to translate "it looks wrong" into "here is the specific setting or component I should check next."

Displays do not exist in a vacuum. Choosing the right type and configuration affects GPU requirements, power usage, desk ergonomics, and user satisfaction. An accountant may be happiest with dual 24-inch IPS monitors at 1080p for lots of spreadsheet columns, while a video editor might need a calibrated, high-resolution IPS or OLED panel with wide color gamut support. A call center might prioritize inexpensive TN panels, knowing that viewing angles and perfect color are less critical. On the exam and on the job, you will be asked, explicitly or implicitly, to make these kinds of matches between user needs, display types, and key characteristics. Understanding what is behind the glass is what lets you do that with confidence.

3.2 Cables, Connectors & Their Purposes

If computer components are the organs of a system, cables are the blood vessels and nerves that let everything communicate and stay powered. When a user says, "Nothing shows up on my monitor," or "The Internet is slow in the warehouse," there is a very good chance the story starts or ends with a piece of copper or fiber and the connector on the end of it. For the A+ exam, you are not expected to be an electrical engineer, but you are expected to look at a port or a plug and know, in practical terms, what it can carry (data, video, audio, power, or a mix), how fast it can move that information, and how far it can go before physics starts to get in the way.

A useful habit as you read this chapter is to mentally tag every connector you encounter with those three attributes: function, performance, and form. Function is what travels over the wire: is this mainly for network data, for a video signal, for audio, for power, or for some combination such as a laptop docking cable that does all three? Performance is about speed and distance: can this cable support 10 Gbps networking, or just a few megabits; does it work reliably over a few centimeters inside a PC or a 100-meter run across an office ceiling? Form is the physical shape and keying: is the connector reversible, is it wide and trapezoidal, is there a locking tab or L-shaped notch? At the help desk, users will not say "DisplayPort" or "RJ-45"; they will say "the squarish one with the little clip" or "the one that keeps falling out of my monitor." You need to be able to translate those descriptions into actual connector types and capabilities.

USB, Thunderbolt, and Peripheral Connections

On modern PCs and mobile devices, **USB** is the dominant general-purpose connector family, which ironically makes it one of the most confusing to learn. That confusion comes from two parallel dimensions: USB versions, which define speed and capabilities (USB 2.0, 3.x, 4), and USB connector shapes, which define how the port physically looks (Type-A, Type-B, mini, micro, USB-C). These two dimensions are independent; you can have USB 3 speeds running over what looks like a traditional rectangular Type-A connector, or you might have a USB-C connector that is limited to older, slower USB behavior.

The familiar full-size **USB Type-A** port is the classic flat rectangle you have probably plugged a thousand flash drives into. On a PC, Type-A is typically the "host" side, found on laptops, desktops, and docking stations. On the other end of older peripherals, you may still encounter **USB Type-B**, the squarish connector often used on printers and some scanners, or its smaller cousins. **Mini-USB** and **Micro-USB** connectors, used on older phones, cameras, and portable drives, are easy to learn by feel: mini is slightly wider and thicker, while micro is the very thin, asymmetrical connector that only fits one way and always seems to get inserted upside-down on the first try. These legacy shapes are still in use, which means you will get calls from users whose brand-new laptop has only USB-C and whose older device has a cable permanently attached ending in Micro-USB; your job is to recognize that this is a connector mismatch, not a dead device.

Newer systems increasingly rely on **USB-C**, a smaller, oval, completely reversible connector that has become the Swiss army knife of ports. USB-C is not a speed; it is a shape. Over that shape, a port might support USB 2.0 speeds, or it might support **USB 3.2** or **USB4**, or even **Thunderbolt**. It might be able to send video signals (using a feature called DisplayPort Alternate Mode), or it might be data-only. It might deliver a trickle of power to charge a phone, or it might support high-wattage **USB Power Delivery** capable of powering a laptop and monitor from a single cable. On the exam and in real life, this is where you must separate physical connector from protocol. A USB-C flash drive will physically plug into any USB-C port, but you should not assume the port can do things like drive an external 4K display just because the connector looks right.

Thunderbolt adds another twist. **Thunderbolt 3** and **Thunderbolt 4** ports use the same USB-C connector shape but run a much more capable protocol on top of it, bundling PCI Express, DisplayPort, USB, and power over a single cable. That is how modern Thunderbolt docks manage to provide network connectivity, multiple displays, and power to a laptop using just one cable. Earlier **Thunderbolt 1** and **Thunderbolt 2** ports used the **Mini DisplayPort** connector, which looks similar to the smaller DisplayPort used on some older laptops and Macs. A common exam trap is the assumption that any USB-C port equals Thunderbolt. In reality, many USB-C ports are just that—USB-C. They accept USB traffic and maybe video via Alt Mode, but they do not support all Thunderbolt features. When you see a scenario mentioning a Thunderbolt external SSD or dock, pay close attention to whether the laptop explicitly has Thunderbolt support or just generic USB-C.

Mobile devices add a couple of proprietary twists. For many years, Apple used the **Lightning** connector on iPhones and some iPads, a slim, reversible connector that is not the same as USB-C even though the size is similar. Android and other phones traditionally relied on Micro-USB and now overwhelmingly ship with USB-C. As an IT technician, you will quickly learn that "my phone won't charge" can be anything from a damaged port to a user trying to plug a Lightning cable into a USB-C-only device, or using a low-power charger that technically fits but cannot provide enough current for fast charging. Knowing that connector fit is only half the story, and that power standards and cable quality matter as well, helps you avoid chasing the wrong problem.

Video and Audio Connectors

Because you have just studied display types, the video connectors in this section will feel like the practical side of that discussion. On most office desktops and laptops, **HDMI** is the dominant connector for connecting to monitors, TVs, and projectors. The HDMI connector is a relatively wide, slightly tapered plug with two rows of contacts inside. Functionally, HDMI carries **digital video and audio** over the same cable, which is why you can plug a laptop into a TV and get both picture and sound through that single connection. Different HDMI versions (1.4, 2.0, 2.1) support different maximum resolutions and refresh rates, but at the A+ level you mainly need to know that HDMI is an all-in-one digital A/V cable and a strong first choice for most modern displays.

For PC-centric setups, especially higher-end or multi-monitor workstations, **DisplayPort** is very common. The full-size DisplayPort connector is slightly asymmetrical and usually has a small locking tab that clicks when you insert the cable. That latch is helpful for secure connections but can confuse users who do not realize they need to press it to remove the cable; more than a few ports have been damaged by someone yanking without releasing the latch. DisplayPort supports high resolutions and refresh rates and can also carry audio. One distinguishing feature is its ability to daisy-chain multiple monitors from a single port using Multi-Stream Transport on compatible devices. You may also see **Mini DisplayPort**, a smaller version with a different shape, especially on older Apple and ultrabook-style systems and some older Thunderbolt implementations.

In contrast, **VGA** and **DVI** represent older display connection technologies that you must still recognize, mostly to support legacy equipment. VGA is the classic blue, 15-pin **analog** connector with three rows of pins and two side screws. It was designed for CRT monitors and does not transmit a digital signal, which means it tends to produce a softer, sometimes slightly blurry image on modern LCD panels, especially at higher resolutions. DVI comes in several variants, but on the exam you mainly need to be able to recognize a **DVI-D** style connector as a larger white connector with a block of pins and sometimes a separate flat blade. DVI was a bridge between VGA and pure digital connectors like HDMI and DisplayPort; many PC monitors for years offered both VGA and DVI inputs. If you encounter a user complaining that their LCD display looks fuzzy even though it "works," suspect that they may be connected via VGA rather than a digital connector. Switching them to HDMI or DisplayPort often solves the issue instantly.

Audio connectors are frequently used alongside video but deserve their own mental slot. The workhorse here is the **3.5 mm analog audio jack**, sometimes called a TRS or TRRS connector depending on how many contacts it has. On a PC or laptop, you will see these as color-coded jacks (green for speakers/headphones, pink for microphone on older desktops) or combined headset jacks on newer notebooks. Headsets for phones, game consoles, and laptops typically use a TRRS style plug that can carry stereo audio plus microphone on a single connector. Even though HDMI and DisplayPort can carry audio, many users still plug in a separate 3.5 mm cable to their speakers or headphones, and you will need to trace which path is actually in use when troubleshooting sound issues. There is also **TOSLINK**, an optical audio connector that uses a small plastic fiber to carry digital audio, common in home theater receivers and soundbars, but you will see it less often in general IT support than in consumer AV setups.

Internal PC and Storage Connectors

So far we have focused on external cables you can see dangling off the back of devices. Inside a desktop case, different cables and connectors quietly move data and power between the motherboard, drives, and other components. The primary internal storage interface you will encounter is **SATA**. A **SATA data** connector is a small, flat, L-shaped plug and socket, designed so you cannot insert it upside-down. It connects the motherboard to storage drives such as 3.5-inch hard drives and 2.5-inch SSDs. Next to it on the drive, you will find the **SATA power** connector, which is wider and also L-shaped, coming from the power supply unit. An important point for both the exam and real troubleshooting is that these are two separate connections: a SATA drive that has power but no data cable will spin up but never appear in the BIOS or OS, and a drive with data but no power obviously will not respond at all.

Older systems may still use the classic 4-pin **Molex** power connector for some drives or fans. Molex is a chunky white plastic connector with four large round pins, originally used for PATA/IDE hard drives and optical drives. Its presence in a scenario is a strong hint you are dealing with legacy hardware. Newer solid-state drives can bypass cabling entirely using **M.2** slots on the motherboard. An **M.2 NVMe** drive looks like a slim circuit board "stick" that slides into a keyed M.2 slot and is held down with a small screw. There is no separate cable for data or power; everything flows through the motherboard socket. Exam questions sometimes play on this distinction: if a scenario mentions a missing SATA data cable, it affects only SATA devices, not M.2 NVMe modules. Being clear in your own mind that SATA implies an actual cable while M.2 NVMe is a direct-connect form factor will make storage installation and troubleshooting questions much easier.

You will also see a variety of internal power connectors from the power supply, including the large 24-pin ATX connector that powers the motherboard itself and supplemental 4/8-pin CPU power connectors, but those are covered in depth in the power supply chapter. For this section, it is enough to link in your mind that "internal drive with a thin data cable" usually means SATA, and "slim card-like SSD with a screw and no cable" usually means M.2 NVMe.

Network Cabling: Copper and Fiber

When it comes to network connections in an office, **twisted-pair copper Ethernet** is still the king. You know it as the slightly stiff cable that "clicks" into place at your laptop or desktop. Technically the connector is called an **8P8C** modular plug, but almost everyone—including the A+ exam—refers to it as **RJ-45**. This connector has eight small metal contacts and is noticeably wider than the smaller **RJ-11** connector used for analog phone lines and some DSL connections. RJ-11 usually has only two or four conductors and fits into a narrower jack. Mixing these up on the exam is a classic pitfall, so attach them to mental stories: RJ-11 is "old-school telephone to wall jack," RJ-45 is "PC to network switch."

The cable category—Cat 5e, Cat 6, Cat 6a, and beyond—defines how that copper cable is constructed and what speeds and distances it can reliably support. **Cat 5e** is common in slightly older structured cabling and typically supports up to 1 Gbps over runs up to 100 meters. **Cat 6** improves performance and can support 10 Gbps over shorter distances (around 55 meters) and 1 Gbps over the full 100 meters. **Cat 6a** is designed specifically to handle 10 Gbps at the full 100-meter standard Ethernet segment length and is what you will see in newer high-performance installations. When you troubleshoot a complaint like "we upgraded the switch to 10 gigabit but the back room is still slow," part of your thinking must be, "What category are these cables, and how long are the runs?" Because the effective throughput of a network link is limited by its weakest component, an ancient unmarked cable stapled along a 90-meter route can turn that shiny 10G switch port back into a gigabit or worse in practice.

The "twisted-pair" part of Ethernet cable is not just marketing. Inside that sheath are four pairs of copper wires twisted at different rates to reduce interference. In electrically noisy environments—near industrial machinery, fluorescent lighting ballasts, or in dense server racks—cables with additional shielding, called **STP** (shielded twisted pair), can help protect the signal. In typical office environments, **UTP** (unshielded twisted pair) is perfectly adequate and easier to work with. Regardless of shielding, you should mentally lock in that standard copper Ethernet segments are designed for a maximum of 100 meters end-to-end. Longer runs can work sometimes and then mysteriously drop packets or fluctuate in speed, which is exactly the kind of intermittent issue that drives users crazy and points you back to basic cabling limits.

Beyond copper, **fiber-optic** cabling uses glass or plastic fibers and light pulses instead of electrical signals. Fiber is immune to electromagnetic interference and supports very high data rates over long distances, which is why you see it used between telecommunications closets, between buildings, and by ISPs. While the exam expects you to recognize fiber as a concept and distinguish it from copper, it spends less time on the fine differences between fiber connector types. You may encounter **LC**, **SC**, or **ST** connectors in practice, but the critical awareness for A+ is that fiber connectors are completely different from RJ-45 and that you cannot terminate a fiber run with a copper connector. Fiber comes in **multimode** and **single-mode** varieties; multimode is common for shorter distances within a building, while single-mode is used for much longer spans, sometimes kilometers. In a troubleshooting scenario, if you see references to a patch panel with thin orange cables and small square connectors in a data closet, think "fiber uplink," not "regular Ethernet."

Power and Charging Cables

The last major group of connectors you should be comfortable with in this section are the ones that simply keep devices alive: power cords and chargers. Desktop PCs use a standard **IEC** power connector on the back of the power supply, often called a "kettle lead" in casual conversation. One end of that cable has the familiar three-prong plug for your country's wall outlets; the other end has the IEC C13 connector that fits into the PC or monitor. There is nothing exotic about it, but power issues are so common that being able to quickly verify that the cable is the right type, properly seated, and not obviously damaged is one of the first checks in any "my PC won't turn on" call.

Laptops historically have used proprietary **barrel connectors**, round plugs of various diameters and pin configurations, specific to the manufacturer and sometimes even the model line. A Dell laptop charger generally will not fit an HP laptop, even if the voltage happens to match, and mixing them can produce everything from slow charging to no charging to hardware damage. Newer laptops increasingly adopt **USB-C power delivery**, which allows standardized charging over a USB-C port. That is great for flexibility—you can charge from a docking station, monitor, or dedicated USB-C charger—but it also introduces subtle compatibility questions. A phone charger that outputs 15 watts over USB-C might keep a power-efficient ultrabook alive, but it will struggle with a workstation-class laptop that expects 65 watts or more, even though the connector fits perfectly. From a support perspective, this means you should think beyond "does it plug in" to "is this charger rated appropriately for the device."

On mobile devices, the distinction between **Lightning**, **Micro-USB**, and **USB-C** is part connector recognition, part ecosystem awareness. When a user in a mixed environment says, "The charging cable we got from the supply closet doesn't work with my phone," it might simply be that they grabbed a Lightning cable for an Android device, or vice versa. It may also be a data-only cable that does not support higher current charging, or a cheap cable with damaged pins. The more easily you can identify connector types and think about what each is supposed to carry—data, power, or both—the faster you can cut through vague user descriptions and get to a concrete solution.

Taken together, all of these cables and connectors form the physical layer of the systems you will support. Whether you are connecting a conference room laptop to an aging VGA-only projector with the right adapter, upgrading a desktop's hard drive, or tracing why a back-office PC cannot reach the new 10G switch at expected speeds, your ability to recognize ports, understand what each cable can and cannot do, and respect the limits of speed and distance will be as important as any software skill you develop.

3.3 Memory (RAM) Technologies & Compatibility

When users say, "My computer is slow," they are often feeling the limits of one component more than any other: system memory. **RAM**, or random access memory, is where the CPU keeps the data and instructions it is actively working with right now. It is dramatically faster than any storage drive, even the best SSD, but it is also **volatile**—everything in RAM disappears when the system loses power or shuts down. That volatility is why we still need drives for long-term storage, but the speed of RAM is why adding more (and the right kind) can transform a sluggish, tab-choked browser into something that feels smooth and responsive.

In day-to-day use, RAM size and RAM speed both affect performance, but capacity is usually the first and biggest factor. When a system runs out of physical RAM, the operating system starts using part of the storage drive as "fake" memory in a process often called paging or swapping. Even with a fast SSD, this is orders of magnitude slower than real RAM. That's when you see symptoms like slow application switching, long pauses when opening new programs, or a noticeable delay when you alt-tab between a game and a web browser. Understanding how RAM is built, what the different types mean, and how to pick compatible modules is therefore critical for both the CompTIA A+ exam and for making good decisions at the help desk.

Form Factors: Desktop vs Laptop Memory

Before diving into generations and speeds, it helps to recognize that RAM does not come in one universal shape. Desktop PCs and laptops almost always use different **form factors**. The standard desktop module is called a **DIMM**, which stands for Dual Inline Memory Module. These are the long, relatively tall sticks you see lined up in a row near the CPU socket on a motherboard. They have a row of gold contacts on each side and a small notch along the bottom edge that must line up with a key in the slot. That notch position is deliberately different for different memory generations, which we will come back to shortly.

Laptops, compact desktops, and some small form factor systems typically use **SO-DIMMs**, or Small Outline DIMMs. A SO-DIMM is shorter in length and slightly different in shape compared to a desktop DIMM. They also have a notch, but it is in a different location, and they have a different pin count. In practical terms, you cannot install a SO-DIMM into a desktop DIMM slot, and you cannot fit a desktop DIMM into a laptop SO-DIMM slot. Every now and then you will encounter more exotic varieties, such as **micro-DIMMs** in very thin laptops or embedded systems, but for most A+ scenarios you can safely think "desktop = DIMM" and "laptop = SO-DIMM." As a technician, just matching the physical form factor prevents a whole class of mistakes. A classic exam-style trap is offering a laptop SO-DIMM as the "right answer" for a desktop upgrade. In real life, the user simply would not be able to install the module, but from the exam's perspective it is testing whether you are paying attention to context clues like "tower case," "ATX board," or "notebook computer."

DDR Generations: DDR3, DDR4, DDR5 and Beyond

Once you know whether you are dealing with DIMMs or SO-DIMMs, the next question is: which **DDR generation** does this system use? Modern PCs use **DDR SDRAM**, which stands for Double Data Rate Synchronous Dynamic RAM. The "double data rate" part means the memory transfers data on both the rising and falling edges of the clock signal, effectively doubling the throughput compared to older single data rate SDRAM at the same base clock.

Over time, DDR technology has advanced through several generations: DDR, DDR2, DDR3, DDR4, and now DDR5 in many new systems. For the A+ exam, the important pattern is that each generation has its own electrical characteristics, its own pin layout, and its own notch position. That means they are not physically compatible. You cannot install a DDR3 module in a DDR4 motherboard; the notch will not line up, and if you try to force it you risk damaging both the RAM and the board.

In desktop systems, **DDR3 DIMMs** typically have 240 pins and operate around 1.5 volts, though there are low-voltage variants. **DDR4 DIMMs** increased the pin count to 288 pins and reduced the operating voltage closer to 1.2 volts. **DDR5 DIMMs** retain 288 pins but change the internal architecture and again push voltage and power management in a more efficient direction, generally around 1.1 volts or less. Even though DDR4 and DDR5 have the same number of pins on a desktop DIMM, the notch is in a different place, so they still cannot be mixed up or interchanged.

The same generational story plays out on the laptop side, with DDR3 SO-DIMMs, DDR4 SO-DIMMs, and DDR5 SO-DIMMs all using different pin counts and notch positions. From a compatibility standpoint, what matters is that the **motherboard is designed for exactly one DDR generation**. You will occasionally see "combo" boards in niche markets, but for mainstream client PCs you can assume that a DDR4 board takes only DDR4, a DDR3 board takes only DDR3, and so on. The CPU's memory controller is built to talk to a particular type of RAM at particular speeds; if the RAM generation does not match, the system simply will not work.

Names and labels can be another source of confusion. You might see a module described as "DDR4-3200" and also as "PC4-25600." These refer to the same speed in different ways. The DDR4-3200 name is telling you the effective data rate is 3200 mega-transfers per second. The PC4-25600 label is describing the theoretical maximum bandwidth in megabytes per second—about 25,600 MB/s. For exam purposes, you do not need to perform the math; you just need to recognize that both are speed-related identifiers for the same DDR4 module, not unrelated specifications.

Speed, Ratings, and Timings

Within a given generation, RAM modules support different **speeds**. This is usually advertised in terms of MT/s (mega-transfers per second) like DDR4-2400, DDR4-2666, DDR4-3200, and so on. Higher numbers mean more data transfers per second and, all else being equal, more memory bandwidth for the CPU. However, the memory controller in the CPU and the motherboard chipset impose a maximum supported speed. If you install RAM that is rated faster than the board supports, the common behavior is that the motherboard simply clocks it down to a supported speed.

For instance, suppose a motherboard's documentation states it supports DDR4-2666, and you install DDR4-3200 modules. The modules will still work, but they will typically run at 2666 MT/s. The system does not magically overclock itself to 3200 unless you explicitly configure overclocking features in the firmware and the hardware supports it. On the exam, the correct interpretation for this kind of scenario is that the RAM will "run at the slower, supported speed," not that it will cause boot failure just because it is technically faster than the spec.

You will also encounter **timings** or **latency** numbers, often written in a format like "CL16" or a series of numbers such as 16-18-18-38. These describe how many clock cycles the RAM takes to respond to certain commands. Lower numbers mean lower latency and marginally better performance. For the A+ level, you do not need to memorize how each timing parameter works; it is enough to know that latency affects performance more subtly than raw speed numbers, and that compatibility with the motherboard and CPU is far more important than chasing the lowest timing values.

As a junior technician, your priority is choosing RAM of the correct generation and form factor, with a capacity that fits the board's limits, and a speed equal to or higher than what the board supports. The fine details of timings are typically a concern only for enthusiasts and performance tuners, not for basic support scenarios.

Capacity and Memory Channels

Alongside type and speed, you need to consider how much RAM a system can physically and logically support. Each module has a **capacity**, usually measured in gigabytes, such as 4 GB, 8 GB, 16 GB, or 32 GB. The motherboard manual will list a **maximum total memory** and often a **maximum per slot**. A board might, for example, support up to 64 GB total, with a maximum of 16 GB per DIMM slot across four slots. If you try to exceed these limits, the system might refuse to boot, or it may only recognize part of the installed memory.

Modern systems also organize RAM into **channels**. A simple system running a single module in one channel operates in **single-channel** mode. If you install two matching modules in the correct paired slots, many consumer systems can use **dual-channel** mode, effectively doubling the available memory bandwidth because the memory controller can access both modules in parallel. Higher-end desktops and workstations may support triple-channel or **quad-channel** configurations, but the principle is the same: more channels mean more parallel pathways to memory.

To take advantage of dual-channel mode, you typically install two identical modules—same capacity, same speed, and ideally the same model number—in the specific slots indicated by the motherboard manufacturer. Boards often color-code these slots or label them as DIMM_A1, DIMM_B1, and so on, with the manual indicating which pair forms a channel. A common mistake is to install two modules next to each other physically, when the correct pairing might be slots 1 and 3 or 2 and 4. The system will still work, but it may drop back to single-channel mode, leaving performance on the table.

When planning an upgrade, you will often be choosing between a single larger module and two smaller ones. For example, if you want 16 GB, two 8 GB sticks installed in the appropriate slots can give you dual-channel performance, while one 16 GB stick would operate in single channel until you add a second 16 GB module. Real-world gains vary by workload, but dual-channel can noticeably improve integrated graphics performance and certain memory-heavy applications.

Installing, Verifying, and Troubleshooting RAM

All of these specifications only help if the physical installation goes well. RAM is one of the easiest components to upgrade, but it is also easy to get wrong if you rush. Before handling modules, you should protect against electrostatic discharge by grounding yourself or using an ESD strap, and always hold the module by its edges, avoiding contact with the chips and gold contacts.

On a desktop, you locate the DIMM slots near the CPU. Each slot has plastic retaining clips at the ends. To install a module, open these clips, align the notch on the RAM with the key in the slot, and press down firmly and evenly until both clips snap into place. If one or both clips do not close automatically, the module may not be fully seated. Many "new RAM won't boot" calls are solved simply by pressing the module in until it truly clicks. In laptops that use SO-DIMMs, the module usually inserts at an angle into the slot and then pivots down until side clips hold it flat.

Channel configuration matters at this stage as well. If you are installing two modules and the board supports dual channel, consult the manual or look for markings on the board so you place them in the correct paired slots. This is a small step, but on both the exam and in real systems it is a common detail that separates a fully optimized upgrade from a merely functional one.

After installation, the first test is whether the system passes POST without error beeps or diagnostic LEDs. Enter the BIOS or UEFI setup and check the reported total memory and, if available, the channel mode. In Windows, you can also open System Properties or Task Manager's Performance tab to confirm the operating system sees the expected amount of RAM. Keep in mind that a 32-bit operating system is generally limited to around 4 GB of usable memory; installing 16 GB of RAM in a machine running a 32-bit edition of Windows will not give you 16 GB of usable space, even if the hardware itself supports it.

When things go wrong after a memory upgrade, the symptoms vary. A system that fails to POST and emits a repeating beep code, or flashes a particular LED pattern, is often signaling a memory problem. Other times the machine boots but crashes randomly, throws blue screens, or locks up when under heavy load. These intermittent issues can also point to bad or incompatible RAM. Your first steps should be simple: reseat the modules, try each module individually in different slots, and confirm that the type, generation, and capacity match what the motherboard documentation specifies. If the hardware passes those checks, running a memory diagnostic such as Windows Memory Diagnostic or third-party tools like MemTest86 can help isolate a flaky module.

By combining your understanding of form factors, DDR generations, speed ratings, capacity limits, channel layouts, and special features like ECC and registration, you can approach any RAM-related scenario—exam question or real customer complaint—with a clear, methodical mindset. This is exactly the kind of practical reasoning CompTIA wants to see: not memorizing every timing number, but being able to look at a system, ask "What RAM should I buy? Will it work here? And how do I prove the system sees it?" and then follow through.

3.4 Storage Technologies & RAID Basics

If you ask users what makes their computer feel "slow," most won't mention the CPU or RAM. They'll describe long boot times, apps that take forever to open, and that ominous clicking from inside the case just before everything freezes. All of those symptoms point to one component: storage. Storage is where the operating system lives, where applications are installed, and where users keep their documents, photos, and projects. Unlike RAM, which is fast but forgets everything when the power turns off, storage is **non-volatile**. It remembers. That also means when storage is slow or failing, the entire system feels unreliable.

As an entry-level tech, you'll be asked to "speed up this system," "add more space," or "protect our files" far more often than you'll be asked about CPU clock speeds. To make good recommendations, you need a clear picture of the main storage technologies in use today, how they connect to the system, and how they can be combined into RAID arrays for better performance or redundancy.

Hard Disk Drives: The Classic Spinning Storage

For decades, the standard PC storage device has been the **magnetic hard disk drive**, or HDD. Internally, a hard drive is surprisingly mechanical. Inside the sealed enclosure are one or more circular **platters** coated with magnetic material, spinning at thousands of revolutions per minute. A tiny **read/write head** at the end of an actuator arm floats micrometers above the surface, moving back and forth to access different tracks on the platters. When data is written, tiny regions of the surface are magnetized in patterns representing bits. When it's read, the head senses those patterns and converts them back into electrical signals.

From an A+ perspective, the important characteristics of HDDs arise directly from this moving machinery. They offer very high capacities for relatively low cost. It's common to see multi-terabyte desktop HDDs that are significantly cheaper than SSDs of the same size. That cost-per-gigabyte advantage is why large media libraries, backups, and archival data often live on HDDs. The trade-off is performance. Because the heads must physically move to the right place on the disk before data can be read or written, there is a **seek time** penalty that doesn't exist in solid-state storage. Even once the head is in position, the platter must rotate so the correct sector passes under it. All of that adds up to higher latency and lower throughput compared to SSDs.

You'll frequently see desktop HDDs in a **3.5-inch** form factor and laptop HDDs in **2.5-inch** form factors. These measurements refer to the approximate width of the drive and correspond to different bay sizes and mounting hardware inside the case. A thin laptop has room for a 2.5-inch drive; a full-size desktop case will have one or more 3.5-inch drive bays. Most HDDs today connect via **SATA**, which we'll explore more in a moment. Manufacturers often advertise rotational speed—commonly 5400 RPM or 7200 RPM. In broad terms, a 7200 RPM drive can access data more quickly than a 5400 RPM drive, which is why you'll often find slower 5400 RPM HDDs in budget or low-power systems and faster 7200 RPM models in performance-oriented desktops and servers.

This mechanical nature also makes HDDs more fragile. A running drive bumped hard enough can cause the heads to crash into the platters, potentially scratching the magnetic surface and permanently damaging sectors. Over years of operation, bearings can wear, heads can misalign, and you might hear characteristic clicking or grinding sounds that indicate impending failure. In portable systems especially, this vulnerability to shock, along with lower performance, has pushed many manufacturers toward solid-state drives.

Solid-State Drives: Flash-Based Speed

Solid-state drives (SSDs) take a completely different approach. There are no spinning platters, no actuator arms, and no heads flying over a magnetic surface. Instead, SSDs use **flash memory**, a type of non-volatile memory that stores data as electrical charges in cells on silicon chips. A controller on the drive manages where data is stored, handles wear-leveling, and presents the drive to the system using familiar interfaces so the operating system doesn't have to care what's inside.

The practical impact of this design is dramatic. Accessing any block of data on an SSD is basically a matter of addressing the right memory cells. There's no mechanical movement and almost no latency compared to spinning media. Users notice this as incredibly fast boot times, applications that launch in a second or two instead of half a minute, and very responsive overall system behavior. An older laptop with a modest CPU and 8 GB of RAM can feel "like new" simply by replacing a mechanical HDD with a SATA SSD.

SSDs also have no moving parts to rattle around, which makes them more **shock resistant** and **silent** in operation. They use less power than magnetic drives, which is valuable in laptops where every watt translates into battery life. The main compromises are cost and, at a given price point, capacity. SSDs still tend to be more expensive per gigabyte than HDDs, and while multi-terabyte SSDs are increasingly common, bulk storage remains more economical on spinning disks in many environments.

Another technical detail that often gets misunderstood is SSD endurance. Each flash cell can handle only a finite number of program/erase cycles before it wears out. Modern SSD controllers use **wear-leveling** algorithms to spread writes across the entire drive, so some cells are not overused while others sit idle. For normal desktop and laptop workloads, this means you are unlikely to wear out a consumer SSD before the system is replaced. For the A+ exam and for everyday support work, the key point is that while SSDs do have finite write endurance, they are generally very reliable. You should still insist on backups—because failures do happen and users do accidentally delete files—but "SSD wear-out" is not a day-to-day crisis you'll be fighting.

In terms of physical form factor, many SSDs mimic the 2.5-inch size of laptop HDDs, with the advantage that they can drop into the same bays and use the same SATA connectors. You'll also encounter SSDs in more compact, circuit-board style shapes, especially **M.2**, which we'll cover when we talk about interfaces.

Interfaces and Form Factors: SATA, M.2, and NVMe

Understanding what's inside the drive is only half the story. You also need to know how the drive connects to the rest of the system, because that heavily influences performance and compatibility.

For many years, the default interface for both HDDs and many SSDs has been **Serial ATA (SATA)**. A SATA drive connects with a thin data cable to a SATA port on the motherboard, and with a separate power connector from the power supply. SATA has evolved through multiple generations, but for the A+ exam it's enough to recognize that SATA has an upper limit on throughput. Even though an SSD's flash memory could theoretically transfer data much faster, a **SATA SSD** is effectively capped by the SATA interface. It is still dramatically faster than a spinning HDD, but nowhere near the speeds that flash can reach when given a more modern path to the CPU.

This is where **M.2** comes in, and this is an area where exam writers love to test whether you understand the distinction between physical form factor and communication protocol. M.2 is a **form factor** and connector type: a slim, rectangular circuit board that plugs directly into an M.2 slot on the motherboard, lying flat against the board instead of mounting in a drive bay with cables. What M.2 does not tell you is how the drive communicates. You can have M.2 drives that speak **SATA**, and you can have M.2 drives that speak **NVMe** over the PCI Express (PCIe) bus.

NVMe (Non-Volatile Memory Express) is a storage protocol designed from the ground up for flash-based storage, running over PCIe. Unlike SATA, which traces its lineage back to protocols meant for spinning disks, NVMe takes advantage of multiple parallel command queues and the high bandwidth of PCIe lanes. The result is that an NVMe M.2 SSD can be several times faster than a SATA SSD, both in terms of maximum throughput and, more importantly, in how quickly it responds to many small I/O requests.

The confusion arises because people often say "M.2 drive" when they really mean "M.2 NVMe SSD," and others assume that "M.2" automatically implies NVMe performance. On real motherboards, you'll find M.2 slots that only support SATA, M.2 slots that support both SATA and NVMe, and some that support only NVMe. The drive and the slot must match. If you install an M.2 SATA SSD into a slot wired only for NVMe, it won't work, and vice versa. On the exam, when a question contrasts "SATA SSD" with "M.2 NVMe SSD," you should immediately think "cable-based, slower interface" versus "direct PCIe, high-performance interface."

There is also the question of boot support. Some older systems can use NVMe drives as secondary storage but cannot boot an operating system from NVMe. In practice, this is more relevant when upgrading older hardware than when dealing with modern systems designed around NVMe from the start. Still, it's a reminder to always consider both physical compatibility and firmware support when recommending a drive upgrade.

In laptops, M.2 NVMe SSDs have become very common because they offer excellent performance in a compact, low-power package without requiring a bulky drive bay. In desktops, you might use a combination of one NVMe SSD for the operating system and applications, and one or more SATA HDDs for bulk storage.

RAID Fundamentals: Why Combine Drives?

Even the fastest single drive can fail. It can also reach the limits of its performance, especially in environments where many users or applications are accessing data at once. **RAID**, which stands for Redundant Array of Independent (or Inexpensive) Disks, is a way to combine multiple physical drives into one **logical volume** to improve performance, increase redundancy, or both.

Before we look at specific RAID levels, it helps to understand the three core building blocks: **striping**, **mirroring**, and **parity**. Striping means splitting data into chunks and spreading those chunks across multiple drives. If you write a large file to a striped set of two drives, part of that file goes to drive A and part to drive B. Because both drives can be read from or written to simultaneously, striping improves performance and uses the combined capacity of the drives. The downside is that striping alone offers no redundancy. If either drive fails, part of every file is gone.

Mirroring is essentially the opposite focus. In a **mirrored** set, the same data is written to two or more drives. A common mirrored configuration uses two drives: anything written to one is written to the other. If one drive fails, the other still has an up-to-date copy of the data, so the system can keep running. The cost is capacity efficiency: with two 2 TB drives in a mirror, your usable capacity is 2 TB, not 4 TB.

Parity introduces some math into the picture. In a parity-based RAID, extra information is stored across the drives that allows the system to reconstruct the contents of a failed drive. You don't need to calculate parity on the exam; you just need to understand that parity provides **fault tolerance** (you can lose one drive and still recover all data) while using capacity more efficiently than pure mirroring. The price you pay is extra complexity and slower write performance, because parity must be calculated and updated with each write.

With those pieces in mind, you can understand the common RAID levels CompTIA expects you to recognize.

RAID 0, 1, 5, and 10 in Plain Language

RAID 0 uses striping only. It requires at least two drives and combines them into one large volume. Because data is striped across both disks, read and write performance can be significantly better than a single drive, and you get to use 100% of the combined capacity. The glaring weakness is redundancy: there is none. If either drive fails, all data in the array is effectively lost, because every file was split between the drives. A helpful way to remember this for the exam is that RAID 0 has "zero" redundancy. You might see RAID 0 used in scenarios where maximum performance and capacity are more important than data safety, such as temporary scratch space for video editing, but it is not appropriate where data loss is unacceptable.

RAID 1 is simple mirroring. It requires at least two drives of the same size. Everything written to one drive is written to the other. Your usable capacity is equal to the size of a single drive—the smallest in the pair—but you can survive the failure of one drive without losing data. Read performance can actually improve, since the system can read from either disk, but write performance is generally similar to a single drive. RAID 1 is attractive for small servers or important workstations where losing the system drive would be painful, and the extra drive cost is acceptable.

RAID 5 introduces striping with distributed parity. It requires at least three drives. Data and parity information are spread across all drives in the array. If any one drive fails, the remaining drives and the parity data can be used to reconstruct the lost data. The usable capacity is equal to the total capacity of the drives minus the capacity of one drive. For example, four 4 TB drives in RAID 5 give you about 12 TB of usable space. Read performance is generally good because data is still striped, but writes are slower due to the overhead of calculating and writing parity. Rebuilding a RAID 5 array after a drive failure can take a long time, and the remaining drives are under considerable stress during that process. Nonetheless, RAID 5 is common in small business servers and NAS devices because it balances effective capacity and single-drive fault tolerance.

RAID 10, sometimes written as RAID 1+0, combines mirroring and striping. The usual way to visualize RAID 10 is as mirrored pairs of drives, with those pairs striped together. It requires at least four drives. For example, in a four-drive RAID 10, you essentially have two mirrors, and then those two mirrors are striped. The result is strong performance and redundancy. The array can survive multiple drive failures as long as no mirrored pair loses both of its drives. Usable capacity is half of the total raw capacity, because of mirroring. RAID 10 is popular where both performance and reliability matter and where you can afford to "spend" half your raw capacity for redundancy, such as in database servers or heavily used file servers.

The exam may briefly mention RAID 0+1 as a separate combined level, but for A+ purposes the key is that RAID 10, as commonly implemented, is "striped mirrors" and is known for offering both good performance and good fault tolerance, at the cost of capacity efficiency.

3.5 Motherboards, CPUs & Expansion Cards

If you imagine a PC as a small city, the motherboard is the road network and infrastructure, the CPU is city hall where all decisions are made, and the expansion cards are special-purpose buildings added when you need something extra. Almost every performance upgrade, compatibility question, or mysterious "it just stopped working" call you'll see in an entry-level IT role touches one of these three. Understanding how they relate is what lets you look at a user's request—"Can we make this machine faster?"—and translate that into concrete hardware decisions that actually work.

A useful mental model is a simple triangle that governs most of your choices: **form factor**, **socket**, and **chipset**. If any corner of this triangle is wrong for the components you're planning to use, the build either won't fit, won't power on, or won't deliver the features you promised.

Motherboards: The Compatibility Triangle

Start with form factor because it is the most obvious. The most common desktop boards you will encounter are **ATX**, **microATX (mATX)**, and **Mini-ITX**. An ATX board is the full-size option, typically offering the most expansion slots, more RAM slots, and plenty of room around connectors for easier cabling. These are common in workstations, gaming systems, and any environment where you expect to add multiple cards or drives. MicroATX boards trim off some width, usually reducing the number of PCIe slots but still retaining a fairly standard layout. They are extremely popular in business desktops where cost, size, and "good enough" expansion matter more than maximum capability. Mini-ITX shrinks things further; it's a compact square that often has just one PCIe x16 slot and two RAM slots. You see Mini-ITX in small-form-factor builds, home theater PCs, and other places where the user wants a tiny box and is willing to accept limited expansion.

Form factor immediately constrains case and power supply choices. A full ATX board won't fit into a slim, small case that was only drilled for microATX or Mini-ITX mounting points, no matter what the sales rep said. On the exam, you might be told there is a small office tower with only two expansion slot openings visible on the rear panel; that should nudge you toward assuming a microATX or Mini-ITX layout inside and recognizing that a huge multi-slot graphics card simply won't have room, even if the PCIe slot type is technically compatible.

Once you know the board will physically fit, the next question is the **CPU socket**. Every motherboard exposes one (and only one) CPU socket in client systems. Intel's desktop sockets in recent years are various **LGA** designs, where the pins are in the socket and the CPU has flat contact pads. AMD's mainstream desktop platforms, such as **AM4** and **AM5**, use a different pin arrangement. From a support perspective, the rule is brutally simple: the CPU must match the socket exactly. An AM5 CPU will not fit an AM4 board; an Intel LGA 1700 CPU will not fit into an older LGA 1151 socket. There is no "close enough," and forcing a CPU into the wrong socket is an expensive way to learn about physical compatibility.

Then there is the quieter, but equally important, player: the **chipset**. The chipset is a collection of logic on the motherboard that defines which CPUs, memory speeds, storage options, and PCIe features the board can actually use. You can think of it as the personality of the board. Two boards may share the same socket and form factor, yet support different generations of CPUs and different maximum RAM speeds because the chipsets differ. It's not uncommon to see a scenario where a physically compatible CPU simply won't boot in a motherboard without a BIOS update, or at all, because the chipset never received support for that generation. For the A+ exam, you don't need to memorize vendor-specific chipset names; instead, you should be comfortable reasoning that "same socket" is not a guarantee by itself. In real work, this is when a professional checks the motherboard manufacturer's CPU support list rather than assuming.

When you combine these three—form factor, socket, and chipset—you get the practical compatibility picture. Faced with a user who wants a CPU upgrade, your first action is usually not ordering a processor, but looking up the existing board to see what it can handle. Maybe you can drop in a faster model that uses the same socket and is supported by the chipset. Or maybe any worthwhile upgrade would require a new board, which may in turn require a new case or power supply. Seeing this triangle clearly helps you communicate realistically with users and avoid promising upgrades that are impossible without a full platform change.

Touring the Motherboard: Connectors and Slots

Once you have the right board in hand, you need to be able to read it like a map. If you place a typical ATX motherboard on a bench and start at the top-center area, you'll find the **CPU socket** surrounded by mounting holes or brackets for the cooler and usually a row of chokes and heatsinks that belong to the **VRM**, the voltage regulator module. This region is mechanically delicate and thermally important. Misaligning the CPU, bending pins in an LGA socket, or failing to properly secure the cooler are all common causes of systems that never reach POST or shut down under load because of overheating.

To one side of the socket you will see the **RAM slots**. Modern boards generally support dual-channel configurations, which means the controller can access two memory modules in parallel to increase bandwidth. The slots are often color-coded or labeled as A1, A2, B1, B2, and the board's manual will specify an order: if you have only two modules, you might be told to populate A2 and B2 first. From a support standpoint, following that guidance is the difference between a system that achieves its rated performance and one that works but is slower than it should be.

Further down, you encounter the **PCI Express (PCIe) slots**, which are the backbone for expansion cards. PCIe slots have different physical lengths: x16, x8, x4, x1. The x16-length slot is typically used for graphics cards, but here you meet another subtlety: the **physical length** of a slot does not always reflect its **electrical lane count**. A budget board might provide a second x16-length slot that is electrically only x4. For a low-bandwidth card such as a basic network adapter or USB expansion card, that difference is irrelevant. For a high-end GPU, it certainly is not. The exam may ask you to reason about which slot should be used for a performance-critical card; in almost all mainstream boards, the top x16 slot, wired directly to the CPU, is the full-speed choice.

As you continue your tour, you'll see connectors for storage. Traditional **SATA ports** are usually grouped near the board's edge and support 2.5-inch and 3.5-inch drives and optical drives. Newer boards also have one or more **M.2 slots**, flat connectors designed to hold gumstick-sized SSDs. Here it's important to separate physical form factor from protocol. M.2 is just the physical slot and card type. The drive can speak **SATA** or **NVMe** over PCIe; some M.2 slots support both, some support only NVMe, and a few legacy boards support only SATA M.2 drives. In addition, many chipsets share bandwidth: installing a drive in a certain M.2 slot may disable a particular SATA port. A very common exam scenario is a user who installs an M.2 NVMe SSD, then wonders why one of the old SATA drives no longer appears. The subtle answer is that bandwidth sharing documented in the motherboard manual, not a bad drive.

Power connectors are another critical group. Near the right edge you will find the big **24-pin ATX power connector** that brings in most of the board's power. Near the CPU socket there will be one or more **CPU power connectors**, usually 4-pin or 8-pin EPS connectors. Forgetting to plug in the CPU power is a classic cause of "fans spin, lights come on, but no POST and no video." From a professional standpoint, every time you build or reassemble a system, doing a quick visual sweep to confirm these connectors are firmly seated prevents a lot of embarrassing callbacks.

Near the bottom edge of the board live a cluster of **headers** for front-panel connections and internal I/O. The **front-panel header** provides pins for the case's power switch, reset switch, HDD activity LED, and power LED. The arrangement is not standardized between manufacturers, so you do not win any prizes for memorizing pinouts; the right practice is to open the manual and follow the diagram. Alongside that, you'll see headers for **USB 2.0**, **USB 3.x**, and usually a **front audio** connector. Miswiring these doesn't usually stop the system from booting, but it will give you symptoms like dead front USB ports or a power button that does nothing. A surprising number of mysterious "my front USB ports never worked" complaints in the field come down to someone simply never having plugged in the correct header.

CPUs: Choosing and Understanding the Brain

Once you know where the CPU sits on the board, you can focus on what makes one processor different from another in a way that matters for your role. The first and non-negotiable attribute, as already discussed, is socket compatibility. Before you even look at performance numbers, you verify that the processor was designed for that socket and that the board's chipset and BIOS version support that specific model.

After that, you can evaluate performance-related characteristics. A **core** is an independent processing unit within the CPU. More cores mean the chip can handle more work in parallel, which is particularly important for heavily multithreaded tasks such as video rendering or running several virtual machines at once. **Threads** represent logical execution paths; many modern CPUs support some form of simultaneous multithreading, like Intel's Hyper-Threading, allowing each physical core to handle two threads. This doesn't double performance, but it does improve throughput for suitable workloads. **Clock speed**, measured in GHz, tells you how many cycles per second the core can perform. For light, single-threaded office workloads, higher clock speed on fewer cores can be more noticeable than having many cores at lower clocks. Your job is often to match the CPU's strengths to what the user actually does.

Behind the scenes, CPUs rely on **cache memory**—small, fast memory areas called L1, L2, and L3. L1 cache is the smallest and fastest, sitting closest to the execution units. L3 is larger and slower but still much faster than system RAM. You won't usually choose between CPUs primarily on cache size in an entry-level support role, but knowing that larger caches can smooth out performance helps you interpret specifications: a workstation-oriented CPU might have more cache per core than a low-end desktop CPU, and that contributes to its responsiveness under load.

Heat and power are expressed through **Thermal Design Power (TDP)**. TDP gives you a rough figure for how much heat the CPU will produce under typical maximum load, which in turn informs what kind of cooling and power delivery you need. A 65-watt CPU with the manufacturer's stock cooler will often be fine in a modest office case. A 125-watt high-end CPU in the same cramped case with poor airflow may constantly throttle to avoid overheating. If you upgrade a user from a low-TDP CPU to a much hotter model without checking the cooler's rating or case airflow, don't be surprised if they start seeing sudden shutdowns during video calls or batch jobs. In laptops, TDP is tightly linked to battery life and chassis temperature; low-TDP mobile CPUs trade raw speed for cooler, quieter operation.

Two other features are worth flagging because they surface both in exam questions and real-world requests. Some CPUs include **integrated graphics**, a GPU built into the processor itself. Others, particularly some AMD models labeled "F" and many server-class processors, have no GPU. If you build or upgrade a system with a CPU that lacks integrated graphics and do not install a discrete graphics card, there will be nowhere to send video output. Users will report "no signal" on the monitor even though everything appears to be powered on. Always mentally ask where the system's video is supposed to come from. In addition, CPUs may support **virtualization extensions** such as Intel VT-x or AMD-V. These instructions improve performance and compatibility for virtual machines. Hypervisors like Hyper-V or VMware Workstation may refuse to run 64-bit guests or complain about missing virtualization support if either the CPU doesn't implement these features or they are disabled in BIOS/UEFI. Enabling virtualization might simply be a matter of toggling a setting, but if the CPU doesn't have these capabilities in the first place, no software fix will help.

Installing and Replacing CPUs

The physical act of installing a CPU is one of those tasks that seems intimidating until you understand what each step is trying to protect. Before you ever open the case, you verify that the new processor is intended for that socket and is listed as supported for that motherboard and BIOS version. If the board requires a firmware update to handle newer CPUs, you generally want to perform that update while the old CPU is still installed and the system is stable. You also confirm that you have an appropriate cooler, either the stock cooler designed for that CPU's TDP or an aftermarket model rated for equal or greater heat output, and that it will physically fit the case without colliding with RAM or the side panel.

With the system powered down, unplugged, and your ESD protections in place, you open the socket by lifting the retention lever or unlocking the latch, depending on the design. CPUs have alignment markers, typically a small **gold triangle** on one corner that must match a mark on the socket, and notches along the edges that prevent wrong orientation. The correct technique is to gently lower the CPU into the socket and let gravity do the work. If it does not settle flatly and easily, something is wrong; forcing pressure here is how pins end up bent. Once seated, you lower the retention mechanism to clamp the CPU in place.

Between the CPU and the cooler, you must apply **thermal paste** unless the cooler comes with pre-applied compound. The goal of the paste is to fill microscopic gaps between the metal surfaces, not to act as a thick layer. A small, pea-sized dot in the center of the CPU or a thin line is usually enough; when you press the cooler down and secure it, the paste spreads into a thin film. Too little paste leaves air gaps that insulate and cause hotspots. Too much can squeeze out the sides and, in rare cases with electrically conductive compounds, cause shorts. After the cooler is firmly attached using its designed mounting points, you plug the fan into the motherboard's **CPU_FAN** header, not a random case fan header, so that the firmware can monitor its speed and respond to failures.

When you power on after a CPU change, your first stop should be the BIOS/UEFI setup to verify that the processor is identified correctly, that its base clock and core count are as expected, and that idle temperatures are reasonable. A CPU idling at extremely high temperatures points back to issues with paste application, cooler mounting, or case airflow. Only after this quick health check do you boot into the operating system and hand the machine back to the user.

Expansion Cards and PCI Express

While the motherboard and CPU set the platform, **expansion cards** let you customize it. Modern systems rely on **PCI Express (PCIe)** as the dominant standard for these cards. PCIe is organized into versions—3.0, 4.0, 5.0—and into lanes, with x1, x4, x8, and x16 representing the number of lanes a card or slot uses. Each newer version roughly doubles the bandwidth per lane compared to the previous generation. The good news is that PCIe is generally backward and forward compatible: a PCIe 4.0 card can run in a PCIe 3.0 slot at PCIe 3.0 speeds, and vice versa. For low-bandwidth devices like simple NICs or USB expansion cards, this usually doesn't matter. For high-performance GPUs or ultra-fast NVMe storage, the combination of lane count and PCIe version can be the difference between fully exploiting the hardware and bottlenecking it.

The most visible type of expansion card is the **graphics card (GPU)**. In gaming rigs, CAD workstations, and systems doing video editing or GPU-accelerated computation, these cards are often physically large and power-hungry. They are designed for x16 slots and, on modern boards, expect to be installed in the primary x16 slot wired directly to the CPU. In addition to drawing power from the slot, mid-range and high-end GPUs require extra **PCIe power connectors** from the power supply—6-pin, 8-pin, or combinations thereof. If you forget to attach these, the card may refuse to start, show warning LEDs, or cause system instability. It's common to see a user report that a new graphics card results in no video output, only to discover the display cable is still plugged into the motherboard's HDMI port instead of into the GPU, or that the card's auxiliary power cables were never connected.

Beyond graphics, you will encounter **network interface cards (NICs)**—both wired Ethernet and wireless adapters—added to systems that need more ports, higher speeds like 10 GbE, or Wi-Fi capabilities that the motherboard lacks. **Storage controllers** and **RAID cards** appear in systems that outgrow onboard SATA ports or need hardware RAID features. **USB expansion cards** add more ports or newer standards such as USB 3.2 to older systems. Less common in business environments but still exam-relevant are **sound cards** for improved audio fidelity and **capture cards** used in streaming and media production. Each of these cards will use some number of PCIe lanes; placing them in an appropriate slot, with enough bandwidth and physical clearance, is a key part of your planning.

Installing an expansion card uses the same disciplined approach as CPU installation, but with fewer ways to cause catastrophic damage. You power the system down, unplug it, and discharge static. After identifying the correct PCIe slot—taking into account performance needs and physical space—you remove the corresponding expansion slot cover from the case. The card's gold edge connector must align with the slot. A firm, even pressure should seat it; it should sit level, with the bracket flush against the case and no visible gold contacts still showing. Securing the bracket with a screw or tool-less retention mechanism prevents the card from working itself loose over time, which can happen from cable strain or vibration. If the card has its own power connectors, those need to be attached from the PSU with the correct cable type.

On first boot after installing a card, you watch for normal POST behavior and then verify that the BIOS/UEFI and operating system see the new device. Many operating systems will install generic drivers automatically, but for full functionality and performance you often install the manufacturer's drivers. This is particularly important for GPUs, advanced NICs, and RAID controllers. After the driver installation, you may need to tweak OS-level settings—for example, choosing the new sound card as the default audio device or setting the monitor connected to the GPU as the primary display.

Throughout all this work, habits distinguish a careful technician from a careless one. Using basic **ESD control**, handling boards by their edges, working on non-conductive surfaces, and storing components in anti-static bags greatly reduces the risk of subtle, latent failures. Maintaining simple documentation—recording, for each system, the motherboard model, CPU, RAM configuration, and installed cards—pays off later when you need to troubleshoot or plan upgrades remotely. And perhaps most importantly, learning to explain in plain language why a "simple" CPU swap might require a different motherboard, which in turn might require a different case or power supply, helps set expectations with users and managers who do not live in the details of sockets and chipsets but still depend on you to make the right calls.

3.6 Power Supplies & Power Protection

If the motherboard is the nervous system of a PC, the power supply is its heart. Every other component depends on it, yet power supplies are often chosen as an afterthought or the cheapest line item on a parts list. As a technician, you cannot afford that mindset. Both on the exam and on the job, you'll see that a huge number of "mysterious" problems—random reboots, odd lockups, systems that only fail under load—trace back to power. To work effectively, you need a practical understanding of how a PC's power supply unit (PSU) turns wall power into stable DC, how to choose and replace PSUs safely, and how to protect systems from the unstable and sometimes hostile world of building power.

From Wall Outlet to DC Rails

A desktop PC plugs into the same wall outlet that powers a lamp or a coffee maker, but what comes out of that outlet is very different from what the PC's internal components can use. Building wiring carries **AC (alternating current)** at a relatively high voltage, typically around 120 volts in North America and 230 volts in much of the rest of the world, at a frequency of 50 or 60 hertz depending on the region. The voltage is constantly changing direction and amplitude, which is convenient for power transmission but not for electronics. Inside the PC, the motherboard, CPU, RAM, and drives all expect **DC (direct current)** at low, tightly regulated voltages.

The PSU's main job is to take that high-voltage AC input and convert it into several low-voltage DC **rails**: primarily +12 volts, +5 volts, and +3.3 volts. Different components draw from different rails. Modern CPUs and GPUs essentially live off the +12-volt rail, which is then further regulated on the motherboard or video card to the exact voltages those chips need. Many logic circuits, chipsets, and some older devices use +5 volts or +3.3 volts. You don't have to understand the internal circuitry that performs the conversion, but you do need to appreciate what "clean" power means: the PSU must provide the correct voltage, within a very small tolerance, while supplying enough current for everything that's connected. If those voltages sag, spike, or ripple excessively, you get instability, corrupted data, or permanent damage.

Before the PSU can even begin that conversion, though, it has to accept the input correctly. Most modern PC power supplies are **auto-switching**, meaning they can accept a wide input range—typically something like 100 to 240 volts AC, 50/60 Hz—without you having to do anything. The PSU detects the input and adjusts internally. However, there are still units in the wild, particularly older or cheaper models, with a small red **voltage selector switch** on the back, often labeled 115/230 or 110/220. This is not a cosmetic detail. If you set that switch incorrectly—say, leaving it on 115 V and then plugging into a 230 V outlet—the PSU will likely fail immediately, sometimes with a loud pop and a burnt smell, and it may take other components with it. In the other direction, setting 230 V and plugging into a 120 V outlet usually results in a system that won't power on at all, because the PSU can't generate enough DC output. When you encounter one of these manual switch units, verify that it matches the local mains voltage before powering the system.

Physical Form Factor and Compatibility

Power supplies are not one-size-fits-all, even if the connectors look similar. In the desktop world, the most common design is the **ATX power supply**, which is built to fit ATX and many microATX cases. "ATX" here refers both to the dimensions of the metal housing and the arrangement of the mounting holes and rear cutout, where the power cord plugs in and the exhaust fan pushes hot air out. When you drop into a case with an ATX mounting point, an ATX PSU will line up, bolt in securely, and route its cables in sensible directions.

Smaller or specialized systems use different form factors. **SFX** units, for instance, are shorter and more compact, intended for small form factor (SFF) cases where space is at a premium. There are also narrow and low-profile designs like TFX, and many big-name manufacturers of prebuilt systems have used proprietary PSUs that look vaguely ATX-like but have odd dimensions or mounting patterns. When replacing a PSU in a prebuilt desktop, you cannot assume that any random ATX unit will fit. You should visually compare the old and new units, verify the measurements, and check whether the case can accept a standard replacement or whether you're locked into an OEM part or an adapter bracket.

Physical compatibility is not just about the metal box. You also need to think about **cable reach and routing**. In compact cases or unusually tall towers, a PSU with short cables might technically bolt in, but the CPU power connector might not reach the top of the motherboard without stretching over the CPU cooler or blocking fans. That's bad both for airflow and for safety. In cramped SFF systems, you may have to plan your cable paths carefully and sometimes choose an SFX unit with longer cables specifically designed for tight spaces. Part of your professional mindset is looking beyond "it physically fits" to "it fits in a way that allows safe, neat cable management."

PSU Connectors and What They Power

Once the PSU is mounted, its personality is defined by its connectors. The most central cable is the **ATX main power connector**, which is almost always a 24-pin plug on modern systems. This connects to the motherboard and supplies a mix of voltages and control signals—enough to power chipsets, RAM slots, integrated devices, and to let the motherboard tell the PSU when to turn on and off. Without this connection, nothing meaningful happens, but having only this connection is not enough either.

Near the CPU socket you will find one or more separate **CPU power connectors**, often labeled CPU_PWR, ATX12V, or EPS. These are typically 4-pin, 8-pin, or a split 4+4-pin design. Their job is to deliver high current 12-volt power directly to the voltage regulators that feed the CPU. This is why, in practice, a system may appear to "almost" start with this connector missing—fans may spin briefly using power from the main 24-pin—but the CPU never truly initializes, and you get no POST, no video, and no beeps. Plugging in the CPU power connector is not optional, and confusing it with other similar-looking connections can be disastrous.

A common exam and real-world trap involves mixing up CPU and **PCIe power connectors**. Discrete graphics cards often require their own direct 12-volt feed through 6-pin, 8-pin, or 6+2-pin PCI Express power plugs. These are keyed and sometimes labeled, but to an untrained eye, an 8-pin EPS (CPU) connector and an 8-pin PCIe connector can look alike. Under no circumstances should you try to force one where the other belongs. The pinouts and current limits are different. Plugging a CPU power cable into a GPU, or a GPU cable into a motherboard CPU socket, can permanently damage the components. When you are working inside a case, slow down, read the small labels on the cables and the markings next to the sockets, and remember that if it does not slide in smoothly with gentle pressure, something is wrong.

For storage and accessories, the PSU provides **SATA power connectors**, with their characteristic flat, thin, L-shaped form that prevents incorrect orientation. These carry 3.3 V, 5 V, and 12 V in a compact plug suitable for hard drives, SSDs, and optical drives. Older devices and some case fans use the classic 4-pin **Molex** connector, which primarily supplies 5 V and 12 V. As systems age and get upgraded, you will often see both in use, sometimes through adapters. Be cautious with adapter chains; they can make cable management easier in the short term but increase resistance and heat if overloaded.

Another dimension of PSU design that affects your day-to-day work is whether the unit is non-modular, semi-modular, or fully modular. A **non-modular** PSU has all cables permanently attached, which means unused connectors must be bundled and tucked away somewhere inside the case. This can clutter airflow and make maintenance more awkward. **Semi-modular** units have some permanently attached cables (usually the 24-pin and CPU power) and provide modular connectors for extras like PCIe and SATA. **Fully modular** PSUs allow you to connect only the cables you need and remove everything else. This can greatly simplify builds and upgrades, but it also introduces a subtle hazard: you must use the cables that came with that specific PSU model. Different manufacturers, and even different models from the same manufacturer, may wire their modular ports differently. Mixing cables from different units can silently mis-wire voltages and destroy hardware. The safe habit is to keep PSU-specific cables labeled and never assume they are interchangeable.

When you're planning a build or diagnosing issues, think in terms of "does this PSU have all the connectors required, in the right quantity?" A high-end GPU that expects two 8-pin PCIe connectors is not an ideal match for a budget PSU that only has a single 6-pin output, no matter what adapters Amazon is happy to sell you. The exam will test this kind of reasoning directly.

Wattage, Rails, and Efficiency

From the outside, PSUs tend to advertise a single number: 400 W, 650 W, 850 W, and so on. It's tempting to treat that as the whole story: pick a wattage that "sounds big enough" and move on. As a technician, you need to read one level deeper, starting with the label on the side of the PSU. That label breaks the output into rails, most importantly the combined capacity of the **12-volt rail or rails**, since that's where CPUs and GPUs draw most of their power. Two different "600 W" PSUs can have very different 12 V capabilities; one might provide 540 W on 12 V with the rest on 3.3/5 V, while another cheap design might put much less on 12 V and disappoint in real-world performance.

You will see references to **single-rail** and **multi-rail** 12 V designs. In a single-rail PSU, all 12 V output is effectively one big pool of current, protected by a single overcurrent protection (OCP) threshold. In a multi-rail design, the 12 V output is divided into several separately protected rails, each with its own OCP limit, even though they ultimately originate from the same source. For A+ purposes, you do not need to perform calculations or design these systems; you just need to know that both approaches are acceptable and safe if properly designed. Multi-rail units can offer finer-grained protection against a single cable or connector drawing too much current, while single-rail units can be simpler to distribute power across multiple connectors without hitting per-rail limits. You are not expected to choose based on rail count alone, but you should recognize the terminology.

A more important practical spec is **efficiency**. Efficiency describes how much of the AC power drawn from the wall actually makes it to the DC outputs, versus how much is wasted as heat inside the PSU. A common certification system you will encounter is **80 PLUS**, with tiers such as Bronze, Silver, Gold, Platinum, and Titanium. An 80 PLUS Gold PSU, for example, is certified to reach specified efficiency levels at typical loads. This matters for several reasons. A more efficient PSU runs cooler, because less energy is wasted as heat. That usually means its fan can spin more slowly and quietly, and the internal components experience less thermal stress, which can improve reliability over time. It also draws less power from the wall for the same workload, which reduces electricity costs—more relevant in environments with many systems or 24/7 operation.

When sizing a PSU for a system, you don't want to hug the minimum. Component manufacturers and online calculators can give you a rough total wattage requirement for a configuration, often based on worst-case simultaneous loads. In practice, it is wise to choose a PSU with a comfortable margin—many technicians aim for something like 25–30 percent headroom above the calculated draw. This leaves room for transient spikes, future upgrades, and the natural aging of components, which can reduce maximum output slightly over years of use. At the same time, there's no benefit to buying a 1600 W monster supply for a small office desktop that will never exceed 150 W. Overspec'd PSUs tend to be more expensive and operate less efficiently at very low loads, so balance cost, headroom, and realistic usage.

Guarding Against Bad Power: Surge Protection, UPS, and Conditioning

Not every power problem starts inside the PC. Building power can be noisy, unstable, and occasionally violent. Voltage spikes from lightning, utility switching, or large motors starting up in the same building can exceed what your PSU's internal protection circuits can handle. That's where external **power protection devices** come in.

The most basic line of defense is a **surge protector**. Unlike a plain power strip, which is just an extension of the wall outlet, a surge protector includes components that divert short, high-voltage spikes away from your equipment, usually to ground. On the outside, they look similar, so you have to read the labeling. A proper surge protector will typically list a **joule rating**—a measure of how much surge energy it can absorb over its life—and may have an indicator light showing whether protection is still active. Once the internal components have taken enough hits, the strip may silently degrade into just a dumb power bar, still passing power but no longer offering protection. For sensitive electronics like PCs, monitors, and networking equipment, plugging directly into the wall or into a basic power strip with no surge protection is a risk, especially in areas prone to storms or known power issues.

While surge protectors help against spikes, they do nothing when the power simply goes away or sags for seconds at a time. In many environments, that sudden loss of power is the real hazard, leading to file system corruption, lost work, and even hardware stress as systems repeatedly crash and reboot. To handle that, you turn to a **UPS (uninterruptible power supply)**. A UPS combines surge protection with a battery and inverter, so that when mains power drops or fluctuates beyond limits, the UPS can supply stable power for some period. On the A+ exam, you should recognize the basic **UPS types**. Standby (or offline) UPS systems normally pass wall power straight through and only switch to battery when they detect an outage. Line-interactive UPS units can actively adjust voltage up or down slightly, helping ride through brownouts and minor overvoltage without fully switching to battery. Online, or double-conversion, UPS systems constantly feed the load from their inverter, with the battery and incoming AC keeping that inverter powered; this provides the cleanest and most consistent output and is common in data centers and for truly critical gear.

Every UPS is rated in both **VA (volt-amperes)** and watts. You don't need to become an electrical engineer to use those numbers. Practically, when choosing a UPS for a set of devices—say, a server and a network switch—you add up their wattage requirements, then select a UPS whose watt rating comfortably exceeds that sum, taking into account how long you want them to run on battery. Vendors often provide runtime charts that show how many minutes of battery you can expect at different loads. For typical office setups, the goal is not to keep users working through an all-day blackout; it is to bridge brief outages and provide enough time for a controlled shutdown during longer ones. Many UPS units can connect to a PC or server via USB or network and, with the right software, automatically initiate shutdown when the battery is running low.

A related but distinct category is the **line conditioner** or power conditioner. These devices are designed to smooth out voltage fluctuations and filter electrical noise without providing battery backup. They are useful in environments where power is dirty—frequent minor sags, interference from heavy equipment—but outright blackouts are rare, or where very consistent voltage is important for specialized equipment. Sometimes, line conditioning is built into higher-end UPS units, giving you both regulation and battery in one device.

Choosing among a simple surge protector, a UPS, and a line conditioner is a matter of risk assessment. A single home desktop used for casual browsing may be adequately protected by a decent surge strip. A small office file server that multiple users depend on should absolutely be on a UPS, so it can ride through short drops and shut down safely during extended cuts. Networking gear like routers and switches also benefit from UPS protection; it is often more disruptive for a whole office to lose connectivity than for one PC to reboot.

Safety and Professional Practice Around Power

Working with power is where your habits directly intersect with personal safety. The first rule is that a **PSU is not a user-serviceable device**. Inside, large capacitors store charge that can remain dangerous even after the unit is unplugged. Entry-level technicians should never open a PSU housing. If a unit fails, smells like burning, or shows visible damage, your options are to power it down, disconnect it, and replace it as a whole. Any notion of "maybe I can fix that scorch mark" is both unprofessional and unsafe.

Before you work inside any PC, you must remove power properly. That means shutting the system down through the operating system when possible, flipping the rear PSU switch off if it has one, and unplugging the AC cord from the wall or from the surge protector/UPS. A good habit is to press the front power button once after unplugging; you'll often see fans twitch or LEDs flicker briefly as residual charge drains from the motherboard. Only after this should you start disconnecting internal cables or removing the PSU from the case. Avoid working in wet or humid conditions, and never defeat the ground pin on a plug with an adapter just to make it fit an older outlet. That grounding is a key part of both your shock protection and the PSU's ability to safely handle faults.

You also need to distinguish between **ESD (electrostatic discharge) protection** and AC shock protection. Wearing an antistatic wrist strap clipped to a grounded point helps prevent you from zapping sensitive chips with static, but it is not a shield against mains voltage. When the system is plugged in, you treat the PSU and any exposed AC contacts with caution, regardless of your ESD setup. Ideally, you will ensure that the outlet itself is properly grounded and wired; in a professional environment, facilities or electricians may handle verification, but you should be alert for signs of bad wiring, like frequent breaker trips or tingling when touching metal chassis.

When replacing a PSU, approach it as a controlled procedure rather than a cable yank-and-swap. Before you pick up a screwdriver, confirm that the replacement unit matches the system's requirements: same or compatible form factor, adequate wattage with some headroom, and the necessary connectors in the right quantities. With the system powered down and unplugged, open the case, examine how the existing cables are routed, and consider taking a quick photo to document the original layout. Disconnect cables gently from the motherboard, drives, and GPU, using any latches or tabs rather than pulling on wires. Then remove the mounting screws at the back of the case and slide the old PSU out carefully, watching that cables don't snag on components.

Installing the new unit is the reverse in principle but an opportunity to improve. Mount it securely, then route cables in a way that avoids blocking fans or pressing tightly against sharp case edges. Connect the 24-pin main power, CPU power, PCIe power, and drive power deliberately, confirming each connector clicks or seats fully and matches the labeled socket. Resist the temptation to use random modular cables that were "lying around"; stick with those that shipped with the new PSU. Once everything is connected and any loose cables are tied back, close the case, reconnect the AC cord (ideally to an appropriate surge protector or UPS), and power on. Stay with the system for a few minutes, watching and listening for abnormalities—strange noises, flickering lights, or the unmistakable smell of overheating components. Power work is one area where "set it and forget it" is not your friend; your diligence in those first minutes can prevent an expensive failure.

By approaching PSUs and power protection with this combination of technical understanding and disciplined safety habits, you turn what many people treat as a mysterious black box into a predictable, manageable part of your toolkit. That, in turn, will make you far more effective when you later troubleshoot "dead" systems, intermittent crashes, and offices plagued by unstable power.

3.7 Printer Deployment & Configuration

If you ask most entry-level technicians what kind of tickets they see the most, printers will be near the top of the list. Not because printers are mysterious, but because they sit right where hardware, networking, and user expectations collide. From the A+ exam's point of view, "printer deployment and configuration" means everything that happens after someone opens the box but before the first user successfully prints a job without complaining. In this section, we will walk through that journey: deciding how to connect the printer, getting it on the network if needed, installing the right drivers, exposing it to users through the operating system, and tuning the settings so it behaves in a predictable, business-friendly way.

It helps to draw a clear line in your mind between configuration and hardware faults. In this chapter, you should assume the printer itself is healthy—no paper jams, no empty toner cartridges, no broken fusers. Your job is to make that healthy printer visible, reachable, and correctly configured. In a later chapter, you will look at what to do when something inside the printer goes wrong. For the exam, being able to tell "this looks like a misconfiguration" from "this is a mechanical or maintenance issue" is a big part of what CompTIA expects from an A+ candidate.

Choosing How the Printer Connects

The first decision in any deployment is how the printer will connect to the rest of the environment. That choice drives almost everything that follows. At one extreme, you might have a single user in a home office with a small inkjet printer sitting next to their PC. At the other, you might have a busy laser printer in a small office that needs to serve a dozen employees. The basic question is always the same: is this a **local** device for one system, or a **shared** device for many?

Most modern desktop deployments start with **USB**. A USB-connected printer is treated as a local hardware device. You physically plug the printer into the computer with a USB-A–to–USB-B cable (or USB-C on newer hardware), the operating system detects it, and you install drivers. This is straightforward and usually reliable, which is why it shows up so often in small setups and exam questions. On older or very specialized systems, you might still encounter **parallel** (LPT) or **serial** ports, especially with legacy laser printers or dot-matrix devices in industrial settings. These are slow and limited compared to USB, but on the exam you should be able to recognize them as direct, point-to-point connections that normally serve a single host.

If several people need to print to the same device, you move into **network printer** territory. A printer with an **Ethernet** port connects to the same switch or router as the computers in the office, gets an IP address, and behaves like a little computer of its own. That is usually the best choice for a small office: wired Ethernet is stable, fast, and easy to manage. Many business-class printers include a built-in web interface you can reach by typing the printer's IP address into a browser; from there you can adjust network settings, security, and features without touching any PC. In environments where running cable is difficult or the printer must sit far from the switch, you might turn to **Wi-Fi**. In that case the printer becomes a wireless client on the existing wireless network, joining an SSID and authenticating with the same passphrase as any laptop. You may see exam scenarios mention **WPS** (Wi-Fi Protected Setup), where you press a button on the router and on the printer to pair them, but you should also understand that wireless reliability depends heavily on placement and signal strength.

There are also peer-to-peer and short-range connection methods that appear more often with mobile devices. **Wi-Fi Direct** allows a printer and a device, such as a smartphone, to connect directly to each other without going through a traditional access point. This can be useful in situations where there is no usable network but users still need to print. **Bluetooth** printing plays a similar role for very short ranges, for example with portable printers used in field work. Finally, many vendors now offer **cloud printing** services, where the printer associates with a vendor account over the internet and users print through that cloud service instead of talking directly to the device on the LAN. For A+ purposes you do not need to master each vendor's implementation, but you should recognize that some printers can be managed and accessed through the cloud rather than purely through local network protocols.

The exam frequently hides a simple logic test inside these connection choices. If a scenario describes one user at a desk with a printer next to their tower, USB is often the most practical answer. If a scenario talks about ten users in different rooms who all need access, a network-attached printer via Ethernet or Wi-Fi is the better answer. That choice determines whether you will add the printer as a local device on one machine or a network resource that many devices can discover.

Giving the Printer an Address on the Network

Once a printer joins the network, it behaves like any other host. It needs an IP address, subnet mask, and typically a default gateway. Many printers default to **DHCP**, meaning they ask the DHCP server (commonly the SOHO router) for an address automatically. That is fine for a quick setup, but in a business environment a constantly changing printer IP tends to cause problems. If a user's computer thinks the printer is at one address but the DHCP server later gives the printer a different one, print jobs no longer reach the correct device. That is why stable addresses matter for shared printers.

You can provide stability in two main ways. One is to configure a **static IP address** directly on the printer, using either its front-panel menu or its web interface. There, you manually specify an address, subnet mask, and gateway and ensure you choose an address that fits the network's addressing plan and is not in the DHCP pool. The other approach is a **DHCP reservation** configured on the DHCP server. In that model, the printer still uses DHCP, but the server always hands out the same address based on the printer's MAC address. The A+ exam will likely refer to both; either method gives you a predictable printer IP that never surprises users.

Accessing the printer's configuration depends on its capabilities. Many devices have a small LCD panel and navigation buttons that allow you to browse to a "Network Settings" menu and view or set IP information. Others provide richer management through an embedded web server: you type the current IP address into a browser, log in with an administrative account, and configure everything from security to paper trays. From a troubleshooting perspective, if the printer works fine over USB but network users cannot print, that is your cue to verify that the network interface has a valid IP, that you can ping that IP from a workstation, and that any required ports and protocols are enabled.

On the protocol side, modern environments often rely on **IPP** (Internet Printing Protocol) or printer sharing over **SMB**, especially with Windows. Older or Unix-like systems may still refer to **LPR/LPD**. You are not expected to memorize every port number here (that is covered in networking sections), but you should recognize the names and understand that the printer or print server must speak a protocol that matches what clients expect. If users can browse to the printer's web page but print jobs never arrive, a misconfigured protocol or blocked port might be the missing link.

Installing Printer Drivers and Software

With the hardware connected and, if applicable, network settings in place, the next major step is installing **printer drivers** on each system that will send print jobs. A driver acts as a translator between the operating system and the device. Applications generate printing instructions using a generic model; the driver converts those instructions into a language the printer understands, such as **PCL**, **PostScript**, or a vendor-specific format. If the driver is wrong, incomplete, or too generic, you often see missing features in the interface, strange output, or even no output at all.

Modern operating systems try to make this easy with plug-and-play detection and built-in driver libraries. When you connect a USB printer to Windows, for example, you will often see it automatically identify the model, search Windows Update, and install a matching driver. macOS does something similar through its built-in database of printer definitions and its **AirPrint** support, which can talk to many devices without extra software. However, automatic detection does not always expose advanced features. For business-class devices, especially those with duplex units, extra trays, or finishing options, you often get the most complete support by downloading the latest driver package from the manufacturer's website.

Drivers must also match the operating system architecture. A 64-bit version of Windows needs a 64-bit printer driver; installing a 32-bit driver there will fail or result in a nonfunctional device. In shared environments, such as when a Windows print server shares a printer to multiple clients, you may need to install both 32-bit and 64-bit drivers on the server so that clients with different architectures can connect seamlessly. On the exam, if a scenario describes a printer that installs but fails to produce any output on a particular workstation, while working fine for others, an architecture mismatch or wrong driver version is a strong suspect.

The installation path looks slightly different on each platform, but the concepts are consistent. In Windows, you usually open the Printers or Printers & Scanners interface, choose to add a printer, and then decide whether it is a local printer (for USB or legacy ports) or a network, wireless, or Bluetooth printer. If Windows cannot automatically identify the device, you might need to select the manufacturer and model from a list or point the wizard to a driver file you downloaded earlier. On macOS, you visit the Printers & Scanners pane, click the plus sign, and either choose a discovered device or specify an IP printer, selecting the appropriate driver or AirPrint. Linux and other Unix-like systems commonly use **CUPS**, which offers a web-based interface where you can add printers, choose the connection type, and associate a driver, although command-line tools exist as well.

When users complain that certain options they expect—like duplex printing or selecting a particular tray—are missing in the print dialog, an incomplete or generic driver is very often the root cause. A common real-world pattern is a printer that supports duplexing, but Windows only shows single-sided options. Installing the full-feature driver from the vendor instead of a basic class driver usually restores all those missing controls.

Configuring the Printer in the Operating System

After the driver is installed, the operating system treats the printer as a defined object with a name, capabilities, and configuration. In a multi-printer environment, users and applications need to know which printer to use by default. Setting a **default printer** on a workstation tells the OS which device to choose if the user does not explicitly select one in the application. If a user keeps accidentally printing to the wrong device, one of the first things to check is which printer is currently marked as default on their machine.

In Windows, it is important to distinguish between **printing preferences** and **printer properties**, because the exam does. Printing preferences are user-oriented. They control how documents should be printed by default for that user: whether to print in color or grayscale, whether duplexing should be used, what paper size to assume, or whether to use draft quality to save toner. Printer properties, by contrast, are device-oriented. They describe and control the printer's capabilities, such as whether a duplex unit is installed, how many trays exist and what paper they hold, and which port the printer uses.

Port configuration is central for Windows-managed printers. On the Ports tab in the printer's properties, you see how the operating system sends jobs to the device. A USB-connected printer might use a USB or DOT4 port. A true network printer will usually be configured with a **Standard TCP/IP Port** that points to the printer's IP address, or sometimes a **WSD** (Web Services for Devices) port that uses discovery services to find the printer on the network. A shared printer hosted on another PC will appear with a path like \\HOSTPC\PrinterShare. When troubleshooting, if jobs appear to print but never reach the device, confirming that the printer is using the right kind of port, with the correct address or share name, is a fundamental check.

Windows also allows you to tune **spooling** behavior under Advanced properties. By default, the print spooler accepts the job from the application, stores it on disk, and begins sending it to the printer as soon as enough of the job is buffered. This allows the application to finish quickly, even for long documents. You can change this to "start printing after last page is spooled," which waits until the entire document is buffered before sending it, sometimes improving reliability on slow networks or older printers. There is also an option to "print directly to the printer," bypassing the spooler entirely. That setting is rarely used in production, but can help isolate spooler-related issues when diagnosing odd behavior.

Sharing Printers and Controlling Access

In a small office or home office, budgets often push people to share a single device among multiple computers. There are two main models for this. A network printer shares itself by being a network host; each client connects to the printer's IP or hostname. Alternatively, a locally attached printer—typically USB—can be shared from a host PC. In that case, the operating system on the host publishes the printer on the network, and other systems connect to it as though it were a network resource, even though the actual path is host PC → USB → printer.

Sharing a locally attached printer in Windows is as simple as opening its properties, going to the Sharing tab, enabling sharing, and assigning a share name. Other users can then browse the network to find it or connect directly via a UNC path such as \\OFFICE-PC\HP-Laser. When they connect, they may automatically download a driver from the host PC, or they may need to provide their own, depending on configuration. The obvious limitation of this arrangement is that the host system must be powered on and connected to the network for anyone else to use the printer. A surprisingly common real-world help desk call is "the network printer is down" when in fact the host workstation has been turned off for the day. Recognizing that dependency is something the exam tests.

Because printers are shared resources, there are basic **permissions** associated with them. Windows distinguishes between the ability to print, the ability to manage documents in the queue, and the ability to manage the printer itself. Typical practice is to grant ordinary users permission to print but reserve management tasks, such as pausing the printer or changing device-wide settings, for administrators or specific support roles. Network printers themselves also have administrative interfaces, usually web-based, that should be protected with non-default passwords. Disabling unused protocols on the printer—turning off features like FTP, Telnet, or older discovery services that are not needed—slightly reduces the attack surface and is a good habit to develop as you move into more security-conscious roles.

Tuning Printer Features and Job Settings

Once the printer is visible and shared as needed, the remaining work focuses on shaping how it behaves day to day. Paper handling is one of the most important aspects. Many printers have multiple trays, each loaded with different media: perhaps plain letter paper in tray 2, legal-size sheets in tray 3, and pre-printed letterhead in tray 1. In the driver's device settings, you specify which trays exist and what size and type of paper each contains. If that configuration does not match reality, the printer may constantly demand the "wrong" paper size, or users may unknowingly print confidential letters onto scrap paper in a bypass tray. Page orientation (portrait versus landscape) and paper size settings also live in preferences; a mismatch between the document's settings and the printer's settings can create clipped output or content shrunk to fit.

Print quality and color options directly affect both user satisfaction and consumable costs. Most drivers allow you to choose between draft, normal, and high-quality modes. Draft prints quickly and uses less ink or toner, which can be useful for internal drafts and large documents where perfect sharpness does not matter. High-quality settings slow down printing and increase consumption but are appropriate for final reports or presentations. Similarly, many organizations set the default to **grayscale** or mono printing, requiring users to consciously choose color when necessary, because color toner and ink are significantly more expensive. You configure these defaults in the printing preferences, and they apply to most applications on that workstation unless an app overrides them.

Duplex printing is another area where hardware capabilities must be matched by software configuration. A printer that physically supports duplexing needs the driver to know that a duplex unit is installed. In the device settings or properties you will typically see a check box or drop-down to indicate the presence of a duplexer. Once that is enabled, users will see a duplex option in their print dialogs and can choose long-edge or short-edge binding. If they report that "this printer should print on both sides, but the option is missing," you should first verify that the correct driver is installed and that duplexing is enabled in the driver, before assuming a hardware failure.

Higher-end devices introduce finishing options such as collation, stapling, and hole punching. Collation simply means printing multi-page documents in complete sets—pages 1 through 10 together, repeated—rather than all copies of page 1, then all copies of page 2, and so on. Stapling and punching require physical modules in the printer. As with duplexing, those modules must be declared in the driver's properties. If they are installed but not enabled in software, users will never see the corresponding options.

Managing Print Queues and Recognizing Configuration Clues

Behind every printer definition in the operating system is a **print queue**, where jobs wait their turn to be sent to the device. In Windows, double-clicking a printer icon shows you the current queue: each job has an owner, a size, a status, and a position. From here you can pause, resume, or cancel jobs. A single malformed or very large job can sometimes clog the queue, preventing subsequent documents from printing. Users might simply say, "nothing is printing," even though the underlying issue is a stuck job at the top of the queue. Clearing that job often restores normal operation immediately.

In larger environments, a dedicated **print server**—whether a Windows Server system, a NAS, or a specialized appliance—hosts the queues and drivers for multiple printers. Clients connect to the server, not directly to each printer. This centralizes driver management and simplifies deployment, but the basic concepts are the same: queues, drivers, permissions, and network connectivity.

Being familiar with these configuration layers allows you to quickly decide whether a symptom sounds like configuration trouble or hardware trouble. If the printer's own internal test page, printed from its control panel, looks fine, but Windows cannot print a test page to it, you are dealing with a driver, port, or network configuration issue, not a broken fuser. If the printer accepts jobs from one PC but not from another, the hardware and network path clearly work; your focus should shift to the failing workstation's drivers, ports, or permissions. If duplex options, tray choices, or finishing selections are missing from the print dialog even though the device supports them, the driver or device properties are misconfigured. Over time, you will develop the habit the exam is trying to reinforce: when someone says, "the printer doesn't work," you mentally walk through connection type, addressing, drivers, OS configuration, sharing, and queue status before you ever reach for a screwdriver.

3.8 Printer Maintenance Procedures

If you only ever touch printers when someone yells that one is broken, you will spend a lot of your IT life putting out fires. Experienced technicians approach printers the way good car owners approach vehicles: regular oil changes, tire rotation, and inspections prevent breakdowns on the highway. In the same way, **printer maintenance** is about keeping devices running predictably, avoiding emergency downtime, and extending the life of components that are not cheap to replace. For the A+ exam, you are expected not just to know the parts of a printer, but to recognize what "normal care and feeding" looks like for each printer technology and how to perform that care safely and correctly.

Before getting into the specifics of laser, inkjet, thermal, and impact printers, it helps to think in terms of general principles that apply to almost every device. Any maintenance task begins with the same preparation. You review the **manufacturer's maintenance guide**, not because you enjoy reading manuals, but because each vendor defines exactly what should be cleaned, replaced, and reset at particular intervals. You power down the printer, disconnect it from power if the procedure calls for opening covers or removing assemblies, and you allow hot components—especially the fuser in a laser printer—to cool down. You work in a clean, well-lit space, ideally on an ESD-safe surface, and you gather the right tools: lint-free cloths, manufacturer-approved cleaning solutions, and any **maintenance kits** or consumables you plan to replace. This is the baseline professional behavior CompTIA wants you to internalize.

The idea of a maintenance kit is important enough to call out clearly. Vendors package sets of high-wear parts into a single **maintenance kit** and associate that kit with a page count or usage threshold. In a typical business-class laser printer, that kit may include a fuser assembly, transfer roller or belt, and certain pickup and feed rollers. When the printer reaches a predetermined number of pages—say 100,000 or 200,000—it will prompt for maintenance or show a "Replace maintenance kit" message. The goal is to replace these components proactively before they fail in service, in much the same way you change timing belts or brake pads on a car before they catastrophically fail. On the exam, when you see a scenario involving a scheduled page-count threshold and a maintenance warning, you should be thinking in terms of swapping those vendor-specified parts and then resetting the maintenance counter, not reinstalling drivers or rebooting the printer.

Laser Printer Maintenance

Laser printers tend to be the workhorses of office environments, so CompTIA puts a lot of emphasis on their upkeep. If you remember the sequence "toner, drum, fuser, rollers," you have a good starting mental map for laser maintenance. Each of these components gradually wears out in a different way, and recognizing the symptoms will help you connect complaints to maintenance tasks.

The most frequent interaction you will have is with the **toner cartridge**. Modern cartridges are usually easy to replace: you open a front or top cover, carefully pull the old cartridge straight out, and slide the new one in until it clicks. The key is to treat toner as a fine plastic powder, not simple dirt. You avoid shaking cartridges violently, because that can cause leaks, and you keep the cartridge level to prevent spills. You do not touch the surface of an exposed **imaging drum**; oil from your fingers can permanently mark it, leading to repetitive print defects. If the cartridge and drum are separate, you follow the manufacturer's instructions about which piece to remove and how to protect the drum from light during handling. Many vendors recommend gently rocking a new cartridge end to end before installation to distribute toner, but always within their guidelines.

Cleaning inside a laser printer must be done with the right tools and a light touch. Paper dust and stray toner naturally accumulate along the **paper path**—the route pages take from the input tray through the imaging and fusing process to the output tray. Your instinct might be to blow this out with a can of compressed air, but that is exactly what most vendors tell you not to do. Compressed air can drive fine toner into places it should never go, such as optical assemblies, sensors, or vents, and can cause malfunctions that are much harder to fix than a bit of dust. Instead, you use a slightly damp, lint-free cloth to wipe up loose toner and dust, or a vacuum that is specifically rated for toner, with filters designed to trap fine particles without generating excess static. A household vacuum is not acceptable; it can both spread toner into the air and generate harmful static discharges.

The **fuser assembly** deserves special respect. Its job is to melt toner into the paper, which means it routinely reaches high temperatures. If you open a printer that has just finished a large print job, the fuser will be very hot. Any maintenance that involves the fuser starts with powering down, unplugging, and waiting for the fuser to cool according to the vendor's recommended time. When a printer approaches its maintenance interval, the fuser is often one of the parts scheduled for replacement because worn fuser rollers lead to smearing, ghosting, or toner flaking off pages. Exam scenarios describing toner that rubs off easily after printing, or pages with partly unfused areas, often point toward fuser problems and, by extension, replacement as part of a maintenance kit.

Another group of components that quietly cause a lot of trouble when neglected is the set of **pickup and feed rollers** and any **transfer roller or belt**. Over time, rubber rollers lose their grip and become smooth or glazed. Users describe this as recurring paper jams in the same location, multiple pages being pulled at once, or the printer simply failing to pull paper from the tray. During maintenance, visual inspection of these rollers is important: if they look shiny, cracked, or flattened, it is time to replace or, in some models, clean them with manufacturer-approved rubber rejuvenator. The transfer roller or belt, which helps move toner from the drum to the paper, can also accumulate toner and wear; streaking or banding across the page can be a symptom of a failing transfer component.

From a process standpoint, a thorough laser printer maintenance session follows a logical sequence. You often begin by printing a **configuration or status page** to capture current page counts and consumable life estimates. Many enterprise printers will tell you the percentage life remaining on the fuser, transfer belt, and even roller sets. You then power down, unplug, and open the printer to inspect the paper path, rollers, and visible assemblies, cleaning out paper scraps and dust. You replace components identified by the vendor's maintenance kit for that usage level, taking care with any hot or static-sensitive parts. When you are done, you reassemble the printer, power it on, reset the **maintenance counter** through the control panel or embedded web interface, and print test pages to confirm normal operation and acceptable print quality. Only at that point do you consider the maintenance task complete.

Inkjet Printer Maintenance

Inkjet printers have a very different "personality" from laser devices. Instead of dealing with powdered toner and hot fusers, you are dealing with liquid ink, microscopic nozzles, and delicate mechanics in the carriage assembly. The maintenance focus shifts from heat and dust to **ink flow**, clogs, and alignment.

The most visible maintenance task here is dealing with **ink cartridges** and the **print head**. In some designs, the print head is built into the cartridge itself; in others, the cartridges simply hold ink and feed a fixed print head mounted in the carriage. Either way, the primary enemy is dried ink. If a printer sits idle for weeks, the ink at the nozzles can dry and clog, leading to missing lines, faint colors, or banding across the page. A user might report that blue text is missing or that photos print with odd stripes. Before you assume a hardware failure, you typically run the printer's built-in **print head cleaning** utility through the driver software or control panel. This process forces extra ink through the nozzles to clear minor clogs. It often needs to be run more than once, followed by a **nozzle check** or test pattern print to see if the gaps have disappeared.

After cleaning, many inkjets also benefit from an **alignment** procedure. This prints a series of patterns and uses either user input or an optical sensor to fine-tune the timing and position of the nozzles. Misalignment shows up as jagged text or colors that do not quite line up at their edges. In the exam context, if you see a scenario involving blurry or misregistered text after cartridge replacement, the correct maintenance step is usually to run the alignment utility, not to replace cartridges again.

Physically replacing cartridges is simple, but there are details that matter. You always begin by using the printer's controls to move the carriage to its replacement position so you are not forcing it by hand. When installing a new cartridge, you remove any protective tape over the nozzles or vents, but you avoid touching the nozzles themselves or the electrical contacts. Finger oils and static can both cause poor contact or flow problems. The area around the carriage tends to accumulate dried ink and paper dust, which you can gently clean with a slightly damp lint-free cloth, being careful not to smear ink into sensors or onto belts.

Unlike lasers, inkjets like regular use. A surprising amount of preventive maintenance is simply ensuring that somebody prints a small test page every week or two so that ink continues to flow and does not solidify in the nozzles. In some organizations, IT schedules automatic test prints for rarely used devices just to keep them alive. On the exam, any discussion of faint or missing ink lines in an inkjet should make you think in terms of cartridge replacement, nozzle cleaning, and alignment—once you have ruled out trivial issues like empty cartridges.

Cross-Cutting Practices and Professional Behavior

Regardless of printer type, certain habits separate a professional technician from someone who just swaps cartridges. One of the most underrated is controlling the environment around the printer. Excess dust, high humidity, and direct sunlight all accelerate wear. A dusty warehouse floor is hard on rollers and fans; a humid room can cause paper to curl and feed poorly; constant exposure to sunlight can degrade plastics and even affect thermal paper. Part of being proactive is recommending better placement when you notice printers living next to open windows, heaters, or industrial machinery.

Documentation is another theme that shows up explicitly and implicitly on the exam. After you complete maintenance, you record what you did: which consumables were replaced, which maintenance kit was installed, what the page count was before and after, and any anomalies you observed. Many enterprise printers can print **configuration pages** that show total page counts and detailed consumable status. Learning to interpret these reports is a valuable skill. When a printer shows "Maintenance required" or "Replace maintenance kit soon," the proper response is to confirm the exact kit in the service manual, schedule downtime with the affected users or department, gather parts, perform the maintenance, reset the maintenance counter, and print a test page to prove everything is back to normal. Simply clearing the message without replacing parts is unprofessional and often leads to failures at inconvenient times.

Finally, maintenance procedures and troubleshooting are deeply linked in practice. A user complaining of repetitive marks at fixed intervals down the page in a laser printer should make you think about surfaces that contact the paper in a repeating pattern—typically the drum or fuser. If the device is also at or beyond its maintenance interval, that strengthens the case for replacing the drum or fuser as part of a maintenance kit. Similarly, when you see repeated paper jams at the same point in the printer, worn rollers are a more likely culprit than user error loading paper. Exam questions often give you just enough detail to choose between cleaning, replacing, or calibrating. The key is to identify the printer type first, think about its main wear points, and then match the symptom to the appropriate maintenance action rather than reaching for generic fixes like "update the driver."

As you build experience, printer maintenance stops feeling like a set of isolated tasks—change toner here, clean a head there—and starts to feel like part of a broader operational discipline. You follow manufacturer guidelines, respect safety and ESD precautions, manage consumable inventory so you are never caught without a needed kit, communicate with users about short planned outages, and never walk away without printing a test page and checking for warning indicators. That mindset, as much as the specific procedures, is what CompTIA wants you to carry into both the exam and your first real support job.

3.9 Knowledge Check

Question 1: A user replaced a 22-inch 1680×1050 monitor with a new 27-inch display. They complain that text now looks fuzzy and hurts their eyes. What is the FIRST setting you should verify in the OS display configuration?

A. That the monitor is set to its native resolution for the new 27-inch panel
B. That HDR is enabled for the new display in the graphics settings
C. That the refresh rate is set to at least 144 Hz in the display options
D. That the display color depth is set to 16-bit instead of 32-bit

Question 2: A customer wants a monitor for photo editing and accurate color reproduction with wide viewing angles. Which LCD panel type is MOST appropriate?

A. IPS, which is designed for accurate color and wide viewing angles
B. TN, which is optimized mainly for low cost and fast response times
C. VA, which focuses on high contrast but has narrower viewing angles
D. OLED, which is not an LCD panel type and uses self-emitting pixels

Question 3: A technician shines a flashlight at an older laptop's screen and can faintly see the desktop, but the image is extremely dim. The laptop uses a CCFL backlight. Which component has MOST likely failed?

A. Inverter, which supplies high voltage power to the CCFL backlight
B. LCD panel, which would show no image at all if it had failed
C. GPU, which would typically cause artifacts or no video output
D. Wi-Fi antenna, which is unrelated to the laptop's display backlight

Question 4: A gamer connects a new 144 Hz 1080p monitor but can only select 60 Hz in Windows. The monitor is on HDMI, and the PC has both HDMI and DisplayPort outputs. Which is the MOST likely cause?

A. The monitor is not IPS, which does not affect maximum refresh rate
B. The monitor's response time is too slow to allow 144 Hz operation
C. The HDMI port/cable standard on the PC cannot support 1080p at 144 Hz
D. The monitor's brightness is too low to display higher refresh rates

Question 5: A smartphone's OLED screen shows a faint ghost of a navigation bar that never completely disappears, even on different apps. What display characteristic BEST explains this symptom?

A. Burn-in due to per-pixel self-emission on the OLED display
B. Poor native contrast ratio causing washed-out dark areas
C. Incorrect aspect ratio stretching the image on the screen
D. Too low color depth reducing the number of visible colors

Question 6: A projector looks washed out and hard to see in a bright conference room, even though it is sharp when the lights are off. Which specification should you prioritize when replacing it?

A. Native contrast ratio to improve dark and light area separation
B. Aspect ratio to better match the connected source devices
C. Response time to reduce motion blur in fast-moving images
D. Brightness (lumens) to overcome the ambient room lighting

Question 7: A user complains that people in a video appear short and wide on their 16:9 monitor. What is the MOST likely cause?

A. The color depth is set too high, distorting the video image
B. A 4:3 signal is being stretched to fill a 16:9 widescreen display
C. The refresh rate is too high for the video content being played
D. The monitor is not using the correct HDMI port for the source

Question 8: A user has connected a large TV as a PC display and complains that it feels sluggish when moving the mouse and that some of the desktop edges are cut off. Which tv characteristic are MOST responsible?

A. Low brightness, making the image appear dim in the room
B. Low contrast ratio, reducing the difference between dark and light
C. Low color depth, limiting the number of colors that can be shown
D. Input lag and overscan, causing delay and cropping of the desktop

Question 9: A user describes a port on the back of their PC as "the wide, slightly trapezoid-shaped one that I plug my monitor into and it carries sound too." Which connector are they MOST likely referring to?

A. HDMI, a wide, slightly trapezoidal port that carries audio and video
B. DisplayPort, which has a different shape with one beveled corner
C. VGA, a blue 15-pin D-sub connector that carries only analog video
D. DVI-D, a larger rectangular connector that does not carry audio

Question 10: A user's ISP has installed fiber service. In the network closet you see thin orange cables with small square plastic connectors going into a patch panel. What type of medium is this MOST likely using?

A. Coaxial copper, which is thick round cable with metal connectors
B. Shielded twisted pair copper, which uses RJ-45 style connectors
C. Unshielded twisted pair copper, commonly used for Ethernet cabling
D. Multimode fiber-optic, often orange with small square LC connectors

Question 11: A user wants to connect an external high-speed NVMe SSD and a dual-monitor dock to a laptop over a single reversible connector that can also deliver power. Which interface MOST closely matches these requirements?

A. USB 2.0 Type-A, which is not reversible and has limited bandwidth
B. Micro-USB, which is reversible only on some variants and slower
C. Thunderbolt 3/4 over USB-C, supporting PCIe, video, and power
D. Mini DisplayPort, which carries video but not full USB-C features

Question 12: A technician is upgrading RAM in a laptop. The new module physically will not fit into the existing slot, even with firm pressure. The old module is DDR3 SO-DIMM and the new one is DDR4 SO-DIMM. What is the BEST explanation?

A. The capacity of the new module is too large for the laptop to use
B. The new RAM must be overclocked first before it can be installed
C. The OS does not support additional RAM until it is upgraded
D. DDR3 and DDR4 SO-DIMMs have different notches and are incompatible

Question 13: A desktop motherboard has four DIMM slots labeled A1, A2, B1, and B2 and supports dual-channel memory. The user has two identical 8 GB sticks. To enable dual-channel mode, how should the RAM be installed?

A. Both sticks in A1 and A2, using only the first memory channel slots
B. Both sticks in B1 and B2, populating only the second memory channel
C. One stick in A1 and one in A2, leaving both B-channel slots empty
D. One stick in A2 and one in B2, following typical dual-channel pairing

Question 14: A small business server requires error detection and correction in memory to protect critical data. Which RAM type should you recommend?

A. Non-ECC unbuffered, which does not provide error correction features
B. ECC, which can detect and correct certain memory bit errors
C. Registered non-ECC, which buffers signals but lacks ECC capability
D. DDR2, which is an older standard without guaranteed ECC support

Question 15: A user complains that their PC is extremely slow when multiple applications are open, and the hard drive activity light stays on constantly. Which upgrade is MOST likely to improve performance in this scenario?

A. Replace the CPU with a higher core-count model for more threads
B. Replace the PSU with a higher wattage unit for better stability
C. Increase the amount of system RAM to reduce paging to disk
D. Replace the GPU with a more powerful model for better graphics

Question 16: A technician is installing a 3.5-inch SATA hard drive in a desktop. After booting, the drive spins up but does not appear in BIOS. What is the MOST likely cause?

A. The drive is formatted with the wrong file system for the OS
B. The SATA power connector is unplugged, preventing the drive from spinning
C. The drive is using M.2 NVMe and needs a different motherboard slot
D. The SATA data cable is not connected or is on a disabled controller port

Question 17: A small office wants to protect against a single drive failure in their file server while also gaining better read performance. They have three identical 4 TB drives. Which RAID level is MOST appropriate?

A. RAID 0, which stripes data but offers no fault tolerance at all
B. RAID 1, which mirrors data but uses only two drives effectively
C. RAID 5, which stripes data with parity across three or more drives
D. RAID 0+1, which requires more drives and is less space-efficient

Question 18: A database server requires both high performance and fault tolerance and has four identical drives available. Which RAID configuration is MOST suitable?

A. RAID 0, which provides performance but no redundancy at all
B. RAID 10, which mirrors and stripes for speed and fault tolerance
C. RAID 1, which mirrors only and does not improve write performance
D. RAID 5, which adds parity but has slower write performance than RAID 10

Question 19: A user wants to upgrade the CPU in their desktop. The existing motherboard has an LGA 1200 socket and a chipset that only supports 10th-generation Intel Core CPUs. They purchase a newer 13th-generation Intel CPU for LGA 1700. Why will this upgrade fail?

A. The PSU wattage is too low to power the newer 13th-generation CPU
B. The CPU does not match the motherboard socket and supported chipset
C. The RAM speed is too slow to meet the requirements of the new CPU
D. The case does not have enough cooling fans for the upgraded processor

Question 20: A technician installs a new discrete graphics card in a PCIe x16 slot, but the system still outputs video only from the motherboard's HDMI port and not from the card. Which is the MOST likely cause?

A. The card is installed in a legacy PCI slot instead of a PCIe x16 slot
B. The monitor cable is DVI instead of HDMI and cannot carry the signal
C. The motherboard's chipset does not support PCIe expansion slots
D. The monitor is still connected to the motherboard output instead of the GPU

ANSWERS

1: Correct Answer: A
Rationale: LCDs look sharpest at their native resolution. If the OS uses a non-native resolution, the image is scaled, making text appear fuzzy and causing eye strain. HDR, refresh rate, and color depth do not typically cause this specific softness.

2: Correct Answer: A
Rationale: IPS panels are known for accurate color and wide viewing angles, ideal for photo work. TN favors speed and low cost, VA emphasizes contrast with more limited viewing angles, and OLED is a different, non-LCD technology.

3: Correct Answer: A
Rationale: With CCFL backlighting, a very dim but visible image usually means the inverter that powers the backlight has failed. The LCD and GPU are still producing an image. The Wi-Fi antenna is unrelated.

4: Correct Answer: C
Rationale: Older HDMI ports/cables may only support 1080p at 60 Hz. To use 144 Hz, you need DisplayPort or a newer HDMI standard that supports higher refresh rates. Panel type, response time, and brightness do not cap the selectable refresh rate this way.

5: Correct Answer: A
Rationale: OLED pixels emit their own light and can suffer burn-in when static elements remain for long periods, leaving a persistent ghost image. Contrast, aspect ratio, and color depth do not cause permanent ghosting.

6: Correct Answer: D
Rationale: In bright rooms, projector brightness (lumens) is critical to overcome ambient light. If lumens are too low, the image looks washed out even if it is sharp in the dark. Contrast, aspect ratio, and response time are secondary here.

7: Correct Answer: B
Rationale: Stretching a 4:3 source to fill a 16:9 screen makes images look short and wide. Color depth and refresh rate do not cause this distortion, and the HDMI port choice does not change aspect ratio handling.

8: Correct Answer: D
Rationale: Many TVs add processing that causes input lag, making the mouse feel sluggish, and overscan, which crops the desktop edges. Brightness, contrast, and color depth affect image quality, not lag or cropping.

9: Correct Answer: A
Rationale: A wide, slightly trapezoidal connector that carries both video and audio matches HDMI. DisplayPort has one beveled corner, VGA is a 15-pin D-sub analog connector, and DVI-D is larger and typically does not carry audio.

10: Correct Answer: D
Rationale: Thin orange fiber with small square connectors (often LC) is characteristic of multimode fiber-optic cabling. Coaxial and twisted pair copper use different shapes and connectors such as F-type or RJ-45.

11: Correct Answer: C
Rationale: Thunderbolt 3/4 over USB-C supports PCIe (for NVMe SSDs), DisplayPort (for multiple monitors), USB data, and power delivery over one reversible connector. USB 2.0 Type-A and Micro-USB lack bandwidth and features, and Mini DisplayPort does not provide full USB-C/Thunderbolt or power delivery.

12: Correct Answer: D
Rationale: DDR3 and DDR4 SO-DIMMs have different notch positions and electrical specs, so they are not physically or electrically compatible. Capacity, overclocking, or OS limits do not prevent the module from fitting.

13: Correct Answer: D
Rationale: Dual-channel mode requires installing modules in the correct paired slots, commonly A2 and B2 as indicated by the motherboard manual. Filling only one channel (A1/A2 or B1/B2) prevents dual-channel operation.

14: Correct Answer: B
Rationale: ECC RAM can detect and correct certain memory bit errors, which is important for servers and critical systems. Non-ECC and registered non-ECC lack error correction, and DDR2 is just an older standard that may or may not support ECC.

15: Correct Answer: C
Rationale: Slow performance with many apps open and constant disk activity usually indicates heavy paging due to insufficient RAM. Adding RAM reduces paging and improves responsiveness. CPU, PSU, and GPU upgrades do not resolve this memory bottleneck.

16: Correct Answer: D
Rationale: If the drive spins, it has power. If it does not appear in BIOS, the SATA data cable is likely disconnected or connected to a disabled controller port. File system format affects OS-level access, and an M.2 NVMe drive would not be a 3.5-inch SATA device.

17: Correct Answer: C
Rationale: RAID 5 stripes data with distributed parity across three or more disks, providing single-drive fault tolerance and improved read performance. RAID 0 has no redundancy, RAID 1 uses only two drives effectively, and RAID 0+1 is less space-efficient and needs more drives.

18: Correct Answer: B
Rationale: RAID 10 (striped mirrors) combines mirroring and striping for both high performance and strong fault tolerance, ideal for databases. RAID 0 has no redundancy, RAID 1 does not boost write performance, and RAID 5 has slower writes due to parity overhead.

19: Correct Answer: B
Rationale: The new CPU is for an LGA 1700 socket and compatible chipset, while the board uses LGA 1200 and supports only 10th-gen CPUs. Socket and chipset mismatch means the CPU cannot be installed or recognized, regardless of PSU, RAM, or cooling.

20: Correct Answer: D
Rationale: If the monitor remains plugged into the motherboard's HDMI port, the system will keep using integrated graphics. The monitor must be connected directly to the discrete GPU. The other options do not explain video still coming from the motherboard.

CHAPTER 4

Virtualization & Cloud Computing

4.1 Understanding Virtualization, Hypervisors & the Cloud

Imagine a neighborhood where every family has its own standalone house on its own lot. Each house has its own walls, its own roof, its own furnace, and its own driveway. That is how traditional computing works: one operating system installed directly on one physical computer, using all of that computer's hardware for itself. Now imagine an apartment building instead. Dozens of families live in the same structure, sharing the same foundation, walls, plumbing, and electrical service, but each family has its own apartment that feels like a separate home. That apartment building is a good mental model for **virtualization**. The physical building is the real hardware, and the individual apartments are **virtual machines**—self-contained environments that seem like separate computers, even though they share the same underlying physical resources.

At its core, virtualization is the process of using software to simulate hardware so that multiple virtual computers can run on a single physical system. The physical computer underneath is called the **host**. The host provides real CPU cycles, real RAM, real storage devices, and real network ports. Sitting on top of that host is a specialized layer of software called a **hypervisor**. The hypervisor's job is to carve up the host's resources and present each slice as if it were an independent computer. Each **virtual machine**, often shortened to VM, is one of those slices. Inside a VM, you install an operating system just as you would on a physical PC. That operating system is called the **guest OS**, and from its point of view, it is running on a real processor, a real motherboard, and real network hardware. It "sees" a CPU, memory, a disk, and a network adapter, but those are all virtual devices provided and managed by the hypervisor.

This illusion is powerful and easy to forget when you are working inside a guest OS. You open Task Manager or top or Activity Monitor in the guest and you see CPU and memory usage, just like you would on a physical computer. You can install drivers, applications, and updates. You can misconfigure it and crash it. But behind the scenes, everything that VM does is really just a set of requests to the hypervisor, which then schedules access to the host's actual hardware. For an A+ technician, keeping that relationship in your head—guest OS and VM on top, hypervisor in the middle, host hardware at the bottom—is critical. Many exam scenarios, and many real tickets, come down to figuring out whether a problem lives inside the guest, inside the hypervisor configuration, or down on the host hardware.

Host, Hypervisor, and Hypervisor Types

The hypervisor is the traffic cop and building manager of the virtual environment. It decides when each VM gets CPU time, how much physical RAM is reserved for each VM, where VM disk files live, and how virtual network adapters connect to the outside world. There are two broad categories of hypervisors that you need to recognize for the A+ exam: **Type 1** and **Type 2**. The difference is all about where the hypervisor sits in the stack.

A **Type 1 hypervisor**, sometimes called a **bare-metal hypervisor**, runs directly on the host hardware. When you power on a server that uses a Type 1 hypervisor, it does not boot into Windows, macOS, or Linux in the traditional sense. Instead, it boots directly into the hypervisor itself. That hypervisor then loads and runs multiple VMs, each with its own guest OS. If you imagine a stack of layers from bottom to top, you would see hardware at the bottom, then the Type 1 hypervisor, and then the VMs on top. This design is very common in server environments because it minimizes extra overhead and gives the hypervisor more direct control over hardware resources. Examples you are likely to hear in entry-level roles include Microsoft Hyper-V when installed as a dedicated server platform, VMware ESXi, and KVM as used in many Linux-based virtualization platforms.

A **Type 2 hypervisor**, also called a **hosted hypervisor**, runs as an application inside a normal operating system. In this model, you first boot the host into Windows, macOS, or Linux, and then you launch the hypervisor software from within that OS just like any other program. When you start a VM, the hypervisor asks the host OS for CPU time, RAM, disk access, and network access, and then it hands slices of those resources to the VM. The layer stack looks different here: hardware at the bottom, then the host operating system, then the Type 2 hypervisor as an application, and then the VMs on top of that. This is the style you encounter most often on desktops and laptops. Oracle VirtualBox, VMware Workstation and VMware Player, Parallels Desktop on macOS, and VMware Fusion for macOS are all Type 2 hypervisors.

Where students often get tripped up is with products like Hyper-V that can appear in both worlds. Hyper-V can be a true Type 1 hypervisor when a server boots directly into it, but you can also install Hyper-V as a role on top of Windows Server or as a feature of Windows 10 or Windows 11 Pro. Even in those cases, the underlying technology is still Type 1—the hypervisor is running closest to the hardware and Windows is partly acting as a management layer. For A+ purposes, rather than obsessing over marketing labels, pay attention to the functional question: does the hypervisor run directly on the metal, managing hardware access itself (Type 1), or does it run on top of a conventional OS that is managing the hardware (Type 2)? On the exam, if you see VirtualBox installed on a Windows 11 laptop, you are dealing with a Type 2, hosted hypervisor scenario.

In everyday IT work, you will see both types. A small office might invest in one or two physical servers running ESXi or Hyper-V to host the file server, a domain controller, and a couple of application servers as VMs. At the same time, developers and IT staff will often have VirtualBox or VMware Workstation on their laptops so they can run Linux test systems, older versions of Windows, or isolated lab environments without needing extra hardware.

Virtual Hardware and Resource Allocation

Once you are comfortable with hosts and hypervisors, it helps to think about what "hardware" a VM actually has. Every VM is configured with a set of **virtual hardware components** that mirror the real components you have learned about earlier in this book. The VM has one or more **virtual CPUs** (often called vCPUs), which are essentially scheduled slices of the host's physical processor cores. It has a specific amount of **virtual memory**, which is a reserved portion of the host's physical RAM. It uses one or more **virtual disks**, which are really just files sitting on the host's storage system, formatted and managed by the hypervisor. And it has at least one **virtual network adapter**, or vNIC, that connects through virtual switches and, eventually, out to the physical network.

The key mental model here is that the host is a pool of resources, and each VM is dipping a bucket into that pool. If your host has a quad-core CPU and 16 GB of RAM, then all running VMs together must share those four cores and that 16 GB. If you create four VMs and assign each of them 8 GB of RAM, on paper you have "allocated" 32 GB—double what actually exists. Some hypervisors will not even let you power on that last VM because there is not enough physical memory available. Others will allow overcommitment, but you then start seeing serious performance issues as the hypervisor tries to juggle memory, swapping to disk and slowing everything down. The same is true with CPUs. Giving every VM the maximum number of vCPUs might sound like you are making them faster, but if the host only has a few physical cores, all you are really doing is creating more scheduling work and contention for the hypervisor.

Under-allocation causes a different kind of pain. Suppose you create a Windows 11 VM with only 2 GB of RAM and a single vCPU, and then you try to run a modern development environment or a database on it. The guest OS will start, but once applications launch, you might see constant disk activity and high CPU usage inside that VM's Task Manager, with everything feeling sluggish. From the inside, it looks like "this computer is slow," but the host might be almost idle. In that case, the fix is to adjust the VM's configuration and give it more memory or another vCPU, assuming the host has enough to spare.

The art at the A+ level is learning to look at both the VM and the host when someone says, "The VM is slow." You should get in the habit of asking yourself where the bottleneck might be. If you check the host and see CPU pinned at 100 percent and memory nearly exhausted, and you notice that someone has created a big "test" VM with 8 GB and 4 vCPUs on a modest host, the problem is not inside the guest operating system at all. The problem is that the test VM is hogging resources and starving the others. A common pattern in small environments is exactly that: a new VM is created with generous settings "just to try something," and suddenly another VM that everyone depends on becomes unusably slow. In that situation, shutting down or resizing the test VM restores performance without any changes to the inventory VM's guest OS.

Storage is another critical part of the resource picture. Each VM's virtual disk is usually stored as a single large file (or set of files) on the host's physical drive. Common formats include VHD or VHDX for Microsoft platforms and VMDK for VMware, but for A+ purposes, the key idea is that from the host's point of view, these are just big files. If the host's physical drive is nearly full, there may not be room to expand a dynamically growing virtual disk, which can cause VMs to fail to start or to crash when they run out of space. Even before you hit that wall, too many VMs doing disk-intensive work on a single, slow spinning hard drive can lead to "laggy" behavior in all guests. When troubleshooting, do not overlook the simple step of checking disk free space and disk performance on the host.

Basic Virtual Networking

Networking inside VMs can be a source of confusion because there are multiple layers involved. Each VM has a vNIC that can be connected to different kinds of virtual networks. In Type 1 environments, these virtual networks are often tied to virtual switches that bridge to physical NICs. In Type 2 environments like VirtualBox or VMware Workstation, you typically choose from a few basic modes that control how the VM sees the outside world. Although this book goes deeper into networking elsewhere, there are three modes that are particularly important for virtualization questions: bridged, NAT, and host-only.

When a VM's vNIC is set to **bridged** mode on a desktop hypervisor, the VM behaves like just another device plugged into the same LAN as the host. It gets its own IP address on that network, usually from the same DHCP server that gives addresses to physical PCs. From the point of view of the office network, it is a separate machine. This is ideal when the VM needs to access and be accessed by other LAN resources, such as file servers or application servers, using standard IP addresses on the same subnet.

With **NAT** mode, short for Network Address Translation, the VM usually still gets internet access, but it is hidden behind the host. The VM sits on a private virtual network, and the hypervisor translates its outbound connections to appear as if they are coming from the host's IP address. To external servers on the internet, it looks like only the host is talking. This is often the default mode for desktop hypervisors because it is easy and reasonably safe: the VM can browse the web and download updates, but other devices on the LAN cannot directly initiate connections to the VM unless special port forwarding is configured.

In **host-only** mode, the VM can talk to the host and to other VMs on the same host-only network, but it cannot directly reach the wider LAN or the internet. This mode is useful for isolated lab environments where you want to test software without risking unintended connections to production networks, or when you want a completely contained playground for malware analysis or configuration experiments.

Misunderstanding these modes is a very common cause of "my VM can't reach X" tickets. Consider the scenario where a developer runs an Ubuntu VM in VirtualBox on a Windows 11 laptop. The developer can browse the web from inside the Ubuntu VM but cannot access the company's file server by name or IP, even though the Windows host can. The likely explanation, once you recognize the pattern, is that the VM is using NAT mode. The VM's traffic to the internet is being translated and allowed out, but the VM is not directly on the corporate LAN, so it cannot see internal-only resources. Switching the VM's vNIC to bridged mode so it pulls an address on the corporate subnet immediately fixes the issue, because now the VM appears to the network just like any other workstation.

Snapshots, Clones, and Operational Considerations

Beyond just running VMs, hypervisors also offer features that make managing them easier. One of the most important to understand conceptually is the **snapshot**. A snapshot is like a point-in-time picture of a VM's state—usually including its disk contents and sometimes its memory. Before you make a risky change, such as installing a complex piece of software or applying a major patch, you can take a snapshot. If the change goes badly, you can roll back to that snapshot and the VM will return to exactly how it was at that moment.

Snapshots feel almost magical when you first use them, and that leads many people to treat them as if they were **backups**. They are not. A snapshot depends on the original virtual disk file and a chain of changes layered on top of it. The longer a snapshot exists and the more changes occur, the larger and more complex that chain becomes. Over time, that can slow down performance and consume large amounts of disk space. If something happens to the underlying virtual disk, your snapshots are useless. Proper backups, by contrast, are designed as independent copies stored on different media or in different locations, intended for long-term recovery. As an entry-level technician, you should think of snapshots as short-term safety nets for testing and upgrades, and of backups as the real disaster recovery plan.

Hypervisors also support creating **templates** and **clones**. A template is a master VM image configured with a base operating system, patches, and standard applications. From that template, you can quickly deploy multiple new VMs with identical starting configurations, saving time and reducing the chance of inconsistent builds. A clone is a copy of an existing VM, which can be useful when you want to create a test environment that looks exactly like production but with a different hostname or IP address. These concepts show up more often in server environments than on individual desktops, but you may encounter them if your help desk role includes supporting a small virtualization host.

Finally, there are operational behaviors that matter both for the exam and for real professionalism. Remember that all VMs on a given host depend on that host's hardware and on the hypervisor. If you reboot or power off a Type 1 host, every VM running on it goes down. Before doing maintenance on a host, you need to know which VMs are running, who uses them, and when it is safe to shut them down or migrate them elsewhere. Even on a single-user laptop with a Type 2 hypervisor, abruptly killing the hypervisor process or forcing the laptop to power off can corrupt VM disks just as pulling the plug on a physical computer can corrupt its drive. When you adjust a VM's CPU or RAM allocation, recognize that you are taking those resources out of the shared pool and that other VMs may feel the effect. In small offices, that often means coordinating with colleagues before spinning up a large test VM or increasing allocations on a production VM.

As you move deeper into cloud concepts and more advanced troubleshooting, you will see these same patterns repeated at larger scales. Underneath many "cloud servers" are just VMs managed by a hypervisor in someone else's data center. Whether those systems are sitting in a rack you can touch or running in a public cloud, the ideas you have just seen—hosts, hypervisors, guest OSs, shared pools of CPU, RAM, storage, and basic virtual networking—give you the mental tools to reason about what is really happening when someone says, "The virtual machine is down," or "The VM can't reach the network."

Cloud Concepts & Service Models

When most users say "it's in the cloud," what they really mean is "I don't know where it is, but it works when I open my browser or app." As an entry-level technician—and as an A+ candidate—you don't get to stop there. For you, "the cloud" has to become something concrete: whose computers are we using, who manages which parts, and what does that mean when something breaks? Once you strip away the marketing, the cloud is simply someone else's infrastructure and software, delivered over the internet, under a service agreement. The magic feeling users get is really just good engineering, automation, and clear divisions of responsibility behind the scenes.

Whenever you work with a cloud service, it helps to mentally separate three pieces. First, there is the local device: the user's laptop, smartphone, tablet, or thin client. Second, there is the network path: the local Wi-Fi, the organization's LAN, and the internet connection in between. Finally, there is the cloud service itself: remote servers, storage, and applications running in a provider's data center. Support work involves deciding which of those three layers is actually responsible for the symptom you are seeing. For example, if a user can't open any websites, that feels different than "I can browse the web but our cloud-based ticketing system just spins." The first points toward network or local issues; the second is more likely a problem with that specific cloud service or how the user's account is configured.

You will also need to learn to classify what kind of cloud service you are dealing with. Are users simply accessing a complete application over the web, like Microsoft 365? That is a classic **Software as a Service (SaaS)** situation. Are developers in your company pushing code to a web-based application platform that they do not patch or maintain at the operating system level? That is **Platform as a Service (PaaS)**. Is your organization renting virtual machines and virtual storage that your admins fully control and configure? That is **Infrastructure as a Service (IaaS)**. The more precisely you can identify the model, the more accurately you can say what you are responsible for and what belongs to the cloud provider.

Essential Cloud Characteristics

Before diving into the service models, it is worth looking at the common characteristics that make something truly "cloud" in the exam sense. Cloud services are not just "on the internet." They follow some standard traits that shape how they behave and how you support them.

Cloud resources are typically **on-demand and self-service**. That means an administrator at the customer side can create resources—such as a new virtual machine, a user account, or additional storage—through a web portal or API without opening a ticket with the provider each time. In practical terms, instead of calling a vendor to ask them to install a server next month, someone in IT can log into the provider console and spin up a server in minutes. When you are supporting users, that also means many tasks you perform—creating a mailbox, granting access to a shared folder, provisioning a virtual desktop—happen in a web interface for that cloud service, not by running installers on local machines.

Cloud services also offer **broad network access**. They are designed to be reachable over standard networks and protocols from a variety of client types: PCs, smartphones, tablets, and thin clients. This is why your users can open the same email system on their desktop Outlook client, in a browser, and on a mobile app. From a troubleshooting point of view, this flexibility is revealing. If a user cannot access the CRM system from their laptop but easily reaches it from their phone on cellular data, the evidence points strongly toward an issue with the laptop or its current network, not with the CRM service itself.

Under the hood, cloud providers make all of this work economically by **pooling resources**. Your organization's virtual machines, storage, and applications are running on shared physical hardware alongside many other customers' workloads. You do not know—and cannot choose—the exact physical server or disk your data is on. That is the provider's problem, not yours. For you as a technician, this means you rarely, if ever, troubleshoot physical server failures in a public cloud. If a host fails, the provider's automation migrates your workloads elsewhere. You deal instead with virtual machines, service dashboards, and status pages.

Another key characteristic is **rapid elasticity**. Cloud resources can scale up or down quickly based on demand. A web application might automatically add more virtual servers behind a load balancer during busy hours and shut them down overnight. Storage allocation can be increased on short notice when a department fills its shared drive. This elasticity can directly affect end users. If autoscaling is misconfigured, a site may feel slow or unresponsive during peak times. As a front-line tech, you will not redesign autoscaling policies, but you should recognize that "the app is slow every day at 10 a.m." might be a capacity or scaling issue in the cloud, not a problem with an individual user's PC.

Finally, cloud services are usually a **measured service**. Usage is metered—by gigabytes of storage, number of user accounts, CPU hours, database transactions, or outbound bandwidth—and billed accordingly. This is why a small business can start with a handful of licenses and then notice their bill increasing as more staff are added or as users store more data in cloud drives. You may be drawn into investigating why the organization hit a storage quota or why a project suddenly doubled its cloud spending. Often the answer is straightforward: someone uploaded a large archive, turned on a high-retention backup option, or left a test virtual machine running for weeks. Understanding that usage is tracked and charged helps you explain to managers why limiting unneeded resources matters.

Service Models: IaaS, PaaS, and SaaS

With those characteristics in mind, it becomes easier to understand the three main service models. One way to picture them is as a vertical stack of layers, from physical hardware at the bottom up to the end-user application at the top. The question for each model is: which layers does the provider manage, and which layers does the customer manage?

Infrastructure as a Service (IaaS) is the lowest level in that stack that still counts as cloud from the A+ perspective. In IaaS, the provider gives you virtualized hardware: virtual machines, virtual networks, load balancers, and storage volumes. You, as the customer, are responsible for installing and configuring the operating system on those machines, hardening them, installing applications, and managing the data. Think of Amazon EC2 instances, Microsoft Azure Virtual Machines, or Google Compute Engine. When a small business "moves its servers to the cloud," they often start with IaaS: the same Windows Server they used in their own rack, now running as a virtual machine in a provider's data center.

From the support technician's point of view, IaaS feels a lot like working with traditional servers, except that you access them remotely and never see the underlying hardware. You might be asked to connect to a cloud virtual machine using RDP or SSH and troubleshoot why a service is not starting, why a Windows update failed, or why a database process is consuming too much memory. If the organization's application cannot reach its database, you might check the firewall on the database VM, verify that the database service is running, or ensure DNS is resolving the correct internal hostname. On the exam, phrases like "the technician must install the operating system on a rented virtual server" or "you are responsible for configuring and patching the server OS in the provider's data center" are strong signals that you are dealing with IaaS rather than a higher-level service.

Platform as a Service (PaaS) sits above that. In a PaaS model, the provider manages the physical infrastructure, the virtualization, and the operating system environment, and often much of the runtime stack. Your organization provides application code or configuration, but does not patch or administer the underlying OS. Developers might deploy a web application to Azure App Service, Google App Engine, or Heroku, or they might use a managed database service such as Azure SQL Database. They write the code, upload it, configure environment variables or connection strings, and the platform handles details such as scaling, OS updates, and runtime versions.

An entry-level tech is not usually writing the code that runs on PaaS, but you may support its integration with the rest of the environment. You might be asked to verify that a DNS record points the company's custom domain to the PaaS web app, or to help a user who cannot reach a PaaS-hosted internal application because of a firewall or VPN configuration. You might log into the provider portal to collect logs or error messages for escalation. Exam questions that mention "developers deploy their code to a managed web environment and do not manage the operating system or hardware" are describing PaaS, even if they do not use the term directly.

At the top of the stack is **Software as a Service (SaaS)**, the model users encounter most often. In SaaS, the provider delivers a complete application over the network. The provider manages the servers, the operating systems, the databases, the application updates—everything under the hood. The customer primarily manages user accounts, permissions, and how the service is used within the organization. Familiar examples include Microsoft 365 or Office 365, Google Workspace, Salesforce, Dropbox, Slack, and most web-based email and productivity platforms.

SaaS is where you will probably spend much of your time supporting users. Typical tickets involve password resets, account lockouts, "I was removed from this shared folder," or "my files are not syncing between my laptop and the web." You may troubleshoot browser issues ("it works in Chrome but not in this outdated browser"), local cache or profile problems, or network restrictions such as a corporate firewall blocking access to a particular SaaS domain. You do not, however, log into a SaaS provider's server to restart a service. If the provider's status page shows an outage, your role is to confirm the impact, communicate with users, and monitor for resolution. On exam questions, wording like "users access the application entirely via a web browser, with no local installation required, and the provider handles all updates" is a direct pointer to SaaS.

The key mental model is that the closer you are to the hardware, the more control and responsibility you have (as in IaaS). The closer you are to the end-user application, the less you manage yourself and the more the provider handles for you (as in SaaS). PaaS sits in the middle, taking infrastructure and OS management off your plate while still requiring your organization to manage the applications themselves.

Deployment Models: Public, Private, Hybrid, and Community

Service models describe what you are renting; deployment models describe where the cloud runs and who shares it. In a **public cloud** deployment, the infrastructure is owned and operated by a third-party provider and shared among many customers. Amazon Web Services, Microsoft Azure, and Google Cloud Platform in their standard forms are public clouds. Your organization's virtual machines, storage, and applications coexist with countless others on the provider's hardware, isolated logically but not physically. Public clouds are attractive because you avoid buying and maintaining servers, you can scale quickly, and you pay only for what you use. From a support standpoint, you interact mainly with provider web portals, command-line tools, and status dashboards, and you follow their maintenance and outage notifications.

A **private cloud** resembles public cloud in technology and user experience but is dedicated to a single organization. It might be hosted on-premises in the company's own data center using platforms such as VMware or OpenStack, or managed by a third party in a hosted facility but not shared with other customers. The appeal is greater control over security, compliance, and customization, at the cost of more responsibility and usually higher expense. For a technician, private cloud often looks like "internal virtual infrastructure with a management portal." You might deploy internal virtual machines for departments, manage access to internal web applications, or troubleshoot connectivity between users and services that never leave the corporate network.

A **hybrid cloud** combines public and private environments so that data and workloads can move or integrate between them. An organization might keep sensitive data and critical databases in its private cloud while using public cloud resources for burst capacity or public-facing web servers. It might synchronize user identities from on-premises Active Directory to a cloud identity provider so that users sign in once and gain access to both internal and SaaS applications. Hybrid designs introduce new support scenarios. When a user cannot reach a cloud application that depends on a VPN or dedicated link back to the private data center, you may need to consider both sides of the connection. On the exam, be careful to reserve "hybrid cloud" for situations where there is an actual mix of public cloud and private/on-premises environments working together, not just "we have two office locations."

Finally, a **community cloud** is infrastructure shared by several organizations with common needs, such as regulatory requirements, mission alignment, or industry membership. Multiple hospitals in the same region might use a shared cloud platform tailored to healthcare compliance, or several universities might share infrastructure for research projects. As an A+ technician you are less likely to directly encounter or design community clouds, but you should recognize the term. From your perspective, it behaves like a cloud environment where the "customer" is a defined group rather than a single company.

Everyday Cloud Use and Support Scenarios

Most of your daily interaction with cloud services will revolve around very practical use cases. One of the most visible is cloud storage and file synchronization. Services like OneDrive, Google Drive, Dropbox, and similar tools are SaaS applications that present as web interfaces plus sync clients installed on desktops and mobile devices. Users expect their Documents folder to be available everywhere, often without fully understanding what is local and what exists only online. You may find yourself explaining why a file marked as "online-only" disappeared when the user went offline, or why two versions of the same document exist after a sync conflict. Troubleshooting often involves confirming that the user is signed into the correct account, that the sync client is running and not blocked by a firewall, and that they have not exceeded their storage quota.

Cloud-hosted applications and virtual desktops are another common area. Some organizations move line-of-business applications entirely into the cloud, accessed through a browser or thin client. Others adopt desktop-as-a-service solutions, where users connect to full Windows desktops running as virtual machines in a cloud provider. Your job may include confirming that users have the right client software, checking that their local firewall allows outbound connections on the required ports, and determining whether a given problem lies with the endpoint, the network, or the remote environment. If a user reports that their virtual desktop is slow while another user in a different office sees normal performance, your investigation will follow a different path than if everyone connected to that desktop pool is complaining at once.

Cloud-based backup and redundancy also impact support work. Endpoint backup agents may upload user data to a cloud backup provider on a schedule, while servers might use cloud storage for snapshot backups or long-term archiving. When a user accidentally deletes an important folder, you may check the backup console in a web browser to confirm whether recent backups exist and initiate a restore to the original or an alternate location. Part of your role is also verifying that backups are actually running; a red "last backup failed" indicator may lead you to inspect credentials, available storage, or network connectivity between the client and the backup service.

4.2 Knowledge Check

Question 1: A user launches Oracle VirtualBox as an application on their Windows 11 laptop and starts an Ubuntu virtual machine. What type of hypervisor is VirtualBox in this scenario?

A. Type 2 hosted hypervisor
B. Type 1 bare-metal hypervisor
C. Cloud hypervisor
D. Embedded firmware hypervisor

Question 2: A help desk technician is troubleshooting a slow VM. Inside the guest OS, Task Manager shows high CPU and memory usage, but the host appears mostly idle. What is the BEST first step?

A. Replace the host's physical CPU
B. Increase the VM's vCPU or RAM allocation, if available on the host
C. Power off all other VMs on the host
D. Reinstall the hypervisor software

Question 3: A developer reports that their Ubuntu VM in VirtualBox can browse the internet but cannot access the company file server on the internal LAN. The Windows host can access the file server. Which virtual NIC mode is MOST likely causing this behavior?

A. NAT
B. Bridged
C. Host-only
D. Loopback

Question 4: Before installing a complex software package on a production VM, the administrator wants the ability to quickly revert if something goes wrong. Which feature should be used?

A. Full backup to external tape
B. Adding an extra vCPU
C. New VM from template
D. Snapshot of the VM

Question 5: A technician must perform maintenance on a Type 1 hypervisor host. Several production VMs are running on this host. What is the MOST important consideration before rebooting the host?

A. Ensuring the host OS has the latest antivirus signatures
B. Verifying the host's BIOS supports hardware virtualization
C. Identifying which VMs are running and coordinating downtime or migration with their users
D. Creating a new local user account on each guest OS

Question 6: A small business rents virtual servers from a provider and installs its own operating systems and applications on them. The admin is responsible for patching the OS and configuring services. Which cloud service model is this?

A. SaaS
B. PaaS
C. DaaS
D. IaaS

Question 7: Which characteristic of cloud computing refers to the ability of resources to automatically scale up or down quickly based on demand?

A. Rapid elasticity
B. Measured service
C. Broad network access
D. Resource pooling

Question 8: In public cloud environments, physical servers and storage are shared among many customers, with logical separation between them. Which cloud characteristic does this describe?

A. Rapid elasticity
B. Measured service
C. Resource pooling
D. Broad network access

Question 9: A company keeps sensitive databases on servers running in its own data center but uses a major public cloud provider to host its public-facing web application. The two environments are connected so the web app can query the internal database securely. Which deployment model is in use?

A. Public cloud only
B. Hybrid cloud
C. Private cloud only
D. Community cloud

Question 10: A backup solution uploads user data from endpoints to a cloud-based backup provider. A user accidentally deletes a folder and requests it be restored. Where will the technician MOST likely initiate the restore process?

A. From the hypervisor console on the backup provider's host
B. From the provider's web-based backup management portal or client application
C. From the endpoint BIOS configuration screen
D. From a snapshot taken on the user's local disk

ANSWERS

1: Correct Answer: A
Rationale: VirtualBox runs as an application on top of Windows, so it is a Type 2 (hosted) hypervisor.

2: Correct Answer: B
Rationale: Since the host is mostly idle but the VM is resource-constrained, the best first step is to increase the VM's vCPU and/or RAM allocation if the host has capacity.

3: Correct Answer: A
Rationale: In NAT mode, the VM uses the host's IP to reach the internet but is not directly on the internal LAN, so it often cannot access internal-only servers like a file server.

4: Correct Answer: D
Rationale: A snapshot captures the VM's state at a point in time so the admin can quickly revert if the software installation causes problems.

5: Correct Answer: C
Rationale: Rebooting a Type 1 host will shut down or pause all VMs on that host, so it is critical to identify affected VMs and coordinate downtime or migration with their users.

6: Correct Answer: D
Rationale: Renting virtual servers while managing the operating systems and applications yourself is Infrastructure as a Service (IaaS).

7: Correct Answer: A
Rationale: Rapid elasticity is the cloud characteristic that allows resources to be quickly scaled up or down based on demand.

8: Correct Answer: C
Rationale: Resource pooling describes how providers share physical resources among multiple customers while keeping their environments logically separated.

9: Correct Answer: B
Rationale: Using both on-premises resources and public cloud services together, with connectivity between them, is a hybrid cloud deployment.

10: Correct Answer: B
Rationale: Cloud backup restores are typically initiated from the provider's web-based management portal or client application, not from local system tools or hypervisor consoles.

CHAPTER 5

Hardware & Network Troubleshooting

5.1 Troubleshooting Core PC Hardware (Board/RAM/CPU/Power)

When someone says, "My computer is dead," they rarely mean that literally. What they are really telling you is that somewhere in the chain of core hardware—power, motherboard, CPU, or RAM—something has failed, misbehaved, or simply come loose. Your job, both on the exam and in the field, is not to guess what that "something" is, but to work your way toward it methodically. The general troubleshooting process you saw earlier still applies here: you identify the problem, form a theory, test it, adjust your theory if needed, implement a fix, verify that the system really is healthy again, and then document what you did. In this chapter, you are simply narrowing that process to the engine room of the PC.

Two habits make core hardware troubleshooting dramatically easier. The first is to always start with power. If power isn't right, nothing else can be. The second is to always start with the least invasive step. On the A+ exam, that translates to choosing answer options like "verify the power strip is on" or "reseat the RAM" before options like "replace the motherboard." In a real environment, those habits save time, parts, and a lot of frustration. The exam loves to hide very simple causes inside wordy scenarios; if you discipline yourself to think from the outside in, and from simple to complex, you'll see those tricks coming.

Before you dig into individual failure types, it helps to have a mental framework for what a "sick" PC looks like at startup. Most startup problems fall into four broad states. There is the completely dead system: no lights, no fans, no sounds. There is the system that seems to have some power—fans spin, maybe some LEDs—but you get no POST beeps and no video output. There is the system that does perform **POST** (the **Power-On Self Test**) but stops with beep codes or error messages. Finally, there is the system that boots an operating system but then shuts down unexpectedly, reboots, or behaves erratically. If you can quickly place a problem into one of these four categories, you immediately narrow the suspects and pick a reasonable next step.

Power and Startup Fundamentals

Think of power flow as a simple path: AC leaves the wall outlet, passes through any surge protector or UPS, enters the power supply unit, and is converted into DC voltages that feed the motherboard through the main 24-pin ATX connector and separate CPU power connector. From there, the board distributes power to RAM, CPU, chipset, and other devices. A failure at any point can give the appearance of a dead or unstable PC, which is why the chapter starts with this chain.

Power problems can be subtle, but very often they are not. A wall outlet controlled by a light switch, a surge protector that someone turned off while vacuuming, or a UPS with a dead internal battery can all leave a computer unresponsive even though "everything is plugged in." Internally, a half-seated power connector, a missing 4- or 8-pin CPU power line, or a failing rail inside the PSU can also create confusing symptoms: fans that twitch and stop, LEDs that flicker, or a system that works one moment and fails the next. Remember that a defective PSU can damage other components, so you never want to ignore clear power irregularities.

When a system appears dead, you begin at the wall. Testing the outlet with a phone charger or a lamp is often faster than pulling out meters. On the exam, if you see a scenario where the monitor's LED is off and nothing in the room seems to have power, checking the outlet or breaker is the answer CompTIA is fishing for, not "replace the motherboard." Once you know the outlet is good, check intermediate devices: is the surge protector on, are its status lights normal, is the UPS online rather than in bypass or fault mode? Only after the external pieces are ruled out do you move to the PC's own PSU.

A **PSU tester** or multimeter lets you confirm that the PSU's main voltage rails are present. A standard ATX supply should deliver approximate +12 V, +5 V, and +3.3 V outputs within reasonable tolerance. From a troubleshooting perspective, you do not need to memorize exact tolerances for the exam; what matters is recognizing that a missing or significantly low rail points to a bad PSU. If you connect a tester and some rails do not come up at all, or if the PSU will not even power on under test, you have strong justification to replace or swap with a known-good unit. Technicians often keep a spare, lower-wattage but known-good PSU just for this kind of diagnostic work.

If a system shows absolutely no signs of life, even when connected to confirmed good AC power, there are a few plausible culprits. The PSU might have failed entirely, the motherboard might be shorted or otherwise dead, or the front-panel power button circuit may not be sending the "power on" signal to the board. Because power supplies fail more often than motherboards, and because they are easier to replace, you test or swap the PSU first. Only after a known-good PSU produces no response do you seriously consider the motherboard or power button wiring as prime suspects.

Scenario 1 illustrates this mindset nicely. A user claims their desktop "just died." When the technician arrives, both monitor and PC are lifeless. Instead of immediately disassembling the system, the tech plugs a phone charger into the wall outlet and sees that it does not power on. They notice a wall switch that controls the outlet is off, flip it, and the monitor comes back to life—but the PC still doesn't start. Now attention shifts to the PC's rear panel, where the technician notices the PSU's rocker switch set to off. One small flip later, the fans spin and the system boots normally. On the exam, if you are offered choices such as "verify the PSU switch is on" and "replace the motherboard," you now know which path CompTIA expects you to take.

When the System Powers On but Does Not POST

Once you move beyond the completely dead system, the second major category is the machine that appears to have some power—fans spinning, maybe case LEDs lit—but does not actually perform POST. You might see no video signal, no beep codes, and no keyboard LEDs toggling. In this state, the motherboard is at least getting some power from the PSU, but something is preventing it from starting or completing the self-test.

Because POST is where the firmware checks for a working CPU, usable RAM, and basic chipset health, missing or failed core components are common causes of a no-POST condition. Before assuming parts are bad, however, you verify simple things. The front-panel header is one: if the power button leads are incorrectly connected or loose, you can get bizarre behavior where fans spin from residual power or test switches but the system never truly attempts a full startup. Double-checking that the power switch pins are wired correctly is quick and non-destructive.

Next, you confirm that all required power connectors are firmly attached. The 24-pin ATX connector can look seated when it is not fully latched; giving it a firm push until the clip clicks into place can suddenly "fix" a stubborn system. The separate 4- or 8-pin CPU power connector is even more critical. It is a classic exam scenario: the system builder connects the big 24-pin plug but forgets the smaller CPU power plug near the processor socket. The symptom is "fans spin, no POST." The best next step is not to install a new graphics card or reload the operating system—it is to verify that the CPU power cable is connected.

When these simple checks do not produce a working POST, it is time to simplify. Technicians call this going to a **minimal boot configuration** or "breadboarding." You remove everything not strictly required to POST, leaving only the motherboard, CPU with its cooler properly attached, a single known-good RAM module, and the PSU. If the board does not include onboard video, you add a basic, known-good GPU. Storage drives, extra expansion cards, and all but the essential front-panel connections come out of the equation. The idea is simple: if the system POSTs in this stripped-down state, one of the removed components or connections was causing the problem; you can add them back one at a time to identify the culprit. If it still refuses to POST, you know the problem lies in the remaining core components.

Recognizing and Confirming RAM Problems

RAM issues are especially interesting because they can appear at multiple phases of startup. Sometimes they stop POST completely. In those cases, the motherboard may emit a repeating beep pattern, flash a diagnostic LED, or display an on-screen message like "Memory error" or "No usable RAM detected." Modern boards often include a "DRAM" status light or POST code display that will stick on a memory-related code when something is wrong. On the exam, when you see a description of continuous beeping or manufacturer-documented RAM beep codes, the next logical action is to reseat or replace memory modules, not to reinstall Windows.

Other times, RAM may be just functional enough to pass an initial POST but unstable under load. That is when you encounter random blue screens, freezes, reboots, or application crashes. These symptoms are easy to blame on drivers or the operating system, and sometimes that is the cause, but bad or marginal DIMMs are common enough that you should always keep them on your radar. A pattern of varied stop codes—different blue screen messages each time—after a recent memory upgrade is a strong hint that the new RAM is not entirely healthy or compatible.

Your first step with suspected RAM is always to power the system down completely, unplug it, and discharge any residual power by pressing the power button briefly. Using appropriate ESD precautions, you then check that each memory module is fully seated, with its edge gold contacts completely inside the slot and both latches on the sides snapped firmly into place. Half-seated RAM is a textbook cause of no-POST conditions and intermittent crashes. You also confirm that the modules occupy the correct slots for dual-channel configurations according to the motherboard manual; mixing slots or mixing incompatible speeds and voltages can destabilize an otherwise working system.

To move from suspicion to confirmation, you can run diagnostic tools. Windows includes **Windows Memory Diagnostic**, which you can trigger from within the OS; it reboots the machine into a simple test environment and walks through patterns designed to stress the memory. Many motherboard vendors or RAM manufacturers also offer their own tools or recommend third-party utilities for deeper testing. If a diagnostic reports errors, you do not stop there; you pull all but one module and test each stick individually, ideally in a known-good slot. When you identify a specific module that fails consistently while others pass, you have a clear answer and can recommend replacement. Scenario 2 demonstrates this: the technician sees random restarts, checks CPU temperatures to rule out overheating, then runs a memory test. By isolating each module, they track the problem to one bad stick rather than replacing the entire set or the PSU.

RAM's relatively low cost and ease of replacement also influence your decision-making. If you have a system with ambiguous symptoms but strong hints of memory trouble, swapping in a known-good DIMM is often a faster and safer test than tearing down the CPU or replacing the motherboard. On the exam, answers that involve reseating or swapping RAM when you have memory-related beep codes or POST messages are almost always favored over more drastic steps.

Motherboard and CPU: The Last Suspects

The **CPU** and **motherboard** sit at the heart of the system, and replacing either is a major surgery compared to swapping a PSU or RAM stick. Both in practice and on the exam, you should treat them as last suspects, to be blamed only after you have verified power, memory, and obvious connections. That does not mean they never fail; it just means they fail less frequently, and misdiagnosing them is expensive.

Typical CPU-related problems fall into two broad categories: total failure to POST (even with known-good PSU and RAM) and rapid shutdown or reboot, often tied to overheating. CPUs are designed with thermal protection. If the cooler is not properly attached, if there is insufficient or missing thermal paste, or if the CPU fan is not connected to the appropriate header, the chip can overheat almost immediately. The motherboard firmware detects this and cuts power within seconds to protect the processor. The result is a system that powers on briefly—fans spin, LEDs flash—and then shuts off. Exam questions that mention a recently installed CPU, a misplaced or non-spinning CPU fan, or prompts about "CPU over temperature" are steering you toward checking cooling and thermal contact, not swapping the power supply.

Motherboard issues are more varied. Modern boards often provide diagnostic LED clusters or small numeric POST code displays that indicate which subsystem is failing: CPU, RAM, boot device, and so on. When the system powers on but hangs at a certain code, your next step is to consult the motherboard manual or manufacturer's support site to interpret that code. Built-in speakers or piezo buzzers can also emit **beep codes**; different beep patterns correspond to different failures. CompTIA does not expect you to memorize vendor-specific beep codes, but it does expect you to know that referencing the documentation is the correct move.

Physical inspection is also valuable. With the system unplugged and discharged, you can examine the motherboard for **bulging or leaking capacitors**, scorch marks, or other visible damage. In socketed CPU designs, especially LGA (land grid array) sockets where the pins are in the motherboard, bent pins are a common cause of strange behavior. A pin bent out of place can prevent the CPU from making solid contact on certain power or data lines, leading to no-POST or intermittent crashes that are very difficult to explain otherwise. If you find extensive pin damage or multiple bulging capacitors, the board is generally considered not worth repairing in a typical desktop support context.

One subtle but important distinction is that truly bad CPUs are comparatively rare. If you encounter a system where multiple components are behaving oddly—USB ports failing, RAM slots only working intermittently, onboard video glitching—your first suspicion should be the motherboard or its power delivery, not the CPU itself. Likewise, if you connect a known-good PSU and RAM to a board and still get no POST, with no diagnostic codes or LEDs indicating life, the board becomes the primary suspect.

Throughout all of this, safe handling is non-negotiable. Working inside a system always starts with power down and unplug. Pressing the power button briefly after unplugging helps discharge residual power in the PSU and motherboard capacitors. Using **ESD precautions**, such as an antistatic wrist strap clipped to the case or regular contact with a grounded metal part of the chassis, protects sensitive components from static damage. On the exam, if two answers both seem to fix the problem but only one mentions taking ESD precautions or disconnecting power first, the safer, more professional step is usually the correct one.

5.2 Storage & RAID Troubleshooting

Storage troubleshooting is one of those areas where technical skill and professional judgment have to work together. With a bad video card, you might lose a display; with a bad drive or misconfigured RAID, you can lose someone's thesis, a year of accounting data, or the only copy of critical photos. For the A+ exams, and even more in real work, the way you think about storage problems matters as much as the tools you use. You'll constantly balance "How do I fix this?" against "How do I avoid making it worse?" The safest approach is to move in stages, from least invasive to more invasive, keeping data protection in the front of your mind.

It helps to remember that storage problems rarely live at just one layer. You have the **physical** device itself (HDD, SATA SSD, NVMe SSD, or external drive). On top of that sit **logical structures** like partitions and file systems. Wrapped around all of it are **configuration** choices in BIOS/UEFI, RAID controllers, and the operating system. When a user complains that a system won't boot, or that files keep disappearing, any one of these layers—or a combination—might be responsible. A systematic mindset keeps you from jumping straight to "the drive is dead" when the real issue is something as simple as boot order or a loose cable.

A very common storage-related incident is a boot failure. You'll see messages like "No boot device found," "Operating System not found," or the system may simply sit at the logo screen and never progress. Sometimes the machine enters an endless reboot loop. You can think of these broad symptoms as falling into three main categories: misconfiguration, logical corruption, and physical failure. Misconfiguration covers things like a boot order that points to the wrong disk, a disabled SATA or NVMe controller, or a RAID mode change that Windows doesn't understand. Logical issues mean the hardware is working, but the boot loader or file system is damaged. Physical problems involve the drive or its connection actually failing.

Your first checkpoint for almost any boot failure is BIOS/UEFI. If you enter setup and the primary drive is missing from the list of detected devices, that strongly suggests a physical or connection problem, not an operating system issue. The scenario where a PC is moved and then displays "No boot device found" is a classic example. If you know the system worked earlier and now the drive doesn't appear in BIOS, you should be thinking about a disturbed SATA cable, a power connector that worked loose, or in rarer cases, ESD or impact damage to the drive or port. Reseating data and power cables and verifying that the drive shows up again in BIOS is a non-destructive, high-value step before you ever consider reinstalling an OS or replacing hardware.

If the drive does appear in BIOS/UEFI and is set as a boot device but the system still won't load Windows, your focus shifts away from raw connectivity. Now you're likely dealing with logical structures: the system partition, the boot manager, or the file system on the boot volume. In such cases, other tools such as Windows recovery options, bootrec utilities, or CHKDSK come into play, but you should already be thinking about data. Is there recent backup? Can you still access the drive's files from a recovery environment or a different system? The professional approach is to salvage accessible data before performing operations that rewrite boot sectors or repair file system structures, because those changes can make recovery harder if something goes wrong.

Not all storage problems present as clean "no boot" errors. Many start as **read/write** or performance complaints. A user might tell you that the system freezes whenever they open large files, or that saving documents "takes forever." Others report intermittent "file not found" errors for files they are sure they saved. On traditional HDDs, these symptoms can be early signs of **bad sectors**, mechanical wear, or heat problems. You might hear clicking or grinding from the drive, which is an ominous clue that the read/write heads or platters are in trouble. Loose SATA cables can also cause intermittent read/write errors, so, again, you start with easy physical checks before assuming the disk itself is dying.

Solid-state drives behave differently. They have no moving parts, so they won't click or grind, but they can develop controller issues or firmware bugs that cause stalls, freezes, or sudden read-only behavior. Most typical desktop users never hit the write endurance limits of modern SSDs, but the A+ exam expects you to know that this is at least a theoretical concern. For both HDDs and SSDs, more mundane factors can also cause storage slowness: very low free space, especially on the system drive; many background tasks hammering the disk, such as antivirus scans or indexing; or a heavily fragmented HDD. Fragmentation is far less of a concern on SSDs, but on spinning disks a badly fragmented volume can slow access significantly.

This is where **SMART**—Self-Monitoring, Analysis and Reporting Technology—starts to matter. Most modern drives track internal health metrics and can raise warnings before catastrophic failure. Many BIOS/UEFI implementations have a SMART status field, and you can get more detailed reports through vendor utilities or third-party tools. SMART is not magic; drives can still fail suddenly with no prior warning. However, if you see a SMART message like "Predicted failure" or "Hard disk failure imminent," the correct mindset is not "How do I fix this drive?" but "How do I get this data off and replace the drive right away?" Exam scenarios that mention SMART warnings are usually pointing you toward immediate backup and replacement, not extended attempts to repair the existing disk.

So far we've talked about whether the system can see the drive and how well the drive can read and write data. The next layer is the logical organization of that data: partitions and file systems. In Windows environments, this is where **Disk Management** becomes one of your main tools. Suppose a user reports that a secondary data drive has vanished from File Explorer. You open Disk Management and see the physical disk listed, but the volume shows as "Offline" or its file system is listed as "RAW" instead of NTFS or exFAT. That tells you that the hardware is present and talking to the system, but the logical structures are damaged or missing.

Different Disk Management states point to different corrective actions. If you see a disk with a large "Unallocated" region and no partitions, the drive may never have been partitioned, or a partition table was wiped. In an exam question where a newly installed drive shows as unallocated, you would expect to create a new partition and format it. When a volume appears as RAW, that usually indicates a corrupted file system. Windows will often pop up a message such as "You need to format the disk before you can use it." In a home setting with no important data, formatting might be acceptable. In a business setting with critical, unbacked-up data, the right answer is to stop, avoid formatting, and either attempt to back up whatever can still be read or escalate to specialized data recovery.

Logical file system issues are where tools like **CHKDSK** come in. CHKDSK can scan and fix file system errors, locate bad sectors, and attempt to recover readable information. It is powerful—and potentially destructive. On the exam, and in practice, you should treat file system repair operations as a second phase, not the first. If the volume still mounts and data is accessible, you prioritize copying that data somewhere safe. Only then do you run CHKDSK with repair options, because it may mark damaged files as lost, move them to FOUND folders, or update indexes in ways that make professional recovery more difficult later. The pattern you want to internalize is assessment, backup where possible, then repair.

Once you're comfortable distinguishing physical, logical, and configuration problems on single drives, you're ready to layer RAID on top, which is where things become more interesting. The key to RAID troubleshooting is remembering what each level actually provides. **RAID 0** is striping for performance only; there is no redundancy. If any drive in a RAID 0 array fails, the entire array goes down and you typically lose all data. There is no rebuild, only recreation and restore from backup. **RAID 1** is mirroring. Two drives hold identical copies of data. If one fails, the system can continue running off the surviving disk while you replace the bad one and rebuild the mirror. **RAID 5** combines striping with parity. It can survive the loss of a single drive, but if a second disk fails before the rebuild completes, the array usually fails completely.

RAID arrays are usually managed and monitored through a RAID BIOS/UEFI screen that appears during POST, through dedicated RAID controller utilities in the operating system, or, in the case of software RAID, through tools like Windows' Storage Spaces or Disk Management. These utilities describe array health with status terms such as **Optimal** or **Healthy**, **Degraded**, **Rebuilding**, and **Failed**. Degraded means you've lost redundancy but still have access to data. In a two-drive RAID 1, that corresponds to one failed disk. In a RAID 5, it means one drive has failed and the array is using parity data to keep going. Rebuilding indicates that the controller is reconstructing data onto a replacement disk. Failed generally means the array is offline or its data is inaccessible by normal means.

The nuance here is in how you respond to those statuses. A degraded array is not yet a disaster, but it is urgent. For example, imagine a small office file server with a two-disk RAID 1 showing a front-panel warning light. When you open the RAID management utility, it reports the array as degraded and flags one disk as failed. Because you understand RAID 1, you know the system is currently running entirely on the remaining drive and any further issue could take it down. Before you touch any disks, you verify which physical bay corresponds to the failed logical drive. You also confirm that last night's backup completed successfully, because while RAID protects against a single drive failure, it isn't a backup. Only then do you replace the identified disk with a compatible one, allow the controller to start the rebuild, and inform users that performance may be slower until the status returns to optimal.

In RAID 5, that rebuild window is even more sensitive. The array can survive one failed disk, but during the rebuild it is under heavy load as parity data is used to reconstruct the missing information. If another disk fails during this time, or if you accidentally remove the wrong disk, you can end up with a completely failed array. That's why good practice, and good exam reasoning, involves verifying backups and minimizing stress on the system while the rebuild completes. You don't schedule large file migrations or heavy maintenance tasks during that period if you can avoid it. The question on the exam that describes a RAID 5 array in degraded status with one failed drive is basically asking whether you know to replace that single failed disk and let the rebuild run—while understanding the associated risk.

RAID 0 stands out because its troubleshooting path is fundamentally different. There is no degraded state with redundancy; a single failed disk renders the striped volume unusable. If the scenario describes a RAID 0 gaming system where one disk dies, the appropriate response is to replace the failed drive, recreate the array, and restore from backups. Any answer that suggests you can rebuild a RAID 0 array or that RAID 0 somehow "protects" data is incorrect. The exam writers like to test that misunderstanding.

RAID also introduces a class of configuration problems that can look like drive failure but aren't. Changing SATA mode in BIOS from RAID to AHCI or the other way around can make Windows unbootable, because the OS was installed with one type of controller driver and is now seeing a different one. Moving disks between ports or controllers can confuse certain onboard RAID implementations that expect drives to appear in a particular order. In practice, if a machine suddenly stops booting right after someone "tweaked" BIOS storage settings, your first instinct should be to revert those changes and see if the array or drive becomes available again. Just as with single-drive systems, always think about configuration before declaring that hardware is dead.

Throughout all of this, it's worth reinforcing the distinction between **RAID and backup**. RAID 1 and RAID 5 keep systems running when a drive fails, which helps with uptime. They do nothing for the user who accidentally deletes a critical folder or for a company that gets hit by ransomware encrypting all disks in an array. Fire, theft, power surges, or controller failures can also affect all members of a RAID set at once. Exam questions sometimes deliberately include both RAID and backup as options; the safest answer for long-term data protection is always backup. RAID complements backups; it never replaces them.

When you put everything together, a consistent troubleshooting rhythm emerges for storage issues. You start with the story: when did the problem begin, what changed, has anyone moved the system or modified BIOS? You check physical signs like noises, drive LEDs, cabling, and power. You confirm in BIOS/UEFI that the system sees the drive or RAID controller, and that boot order makes sense. You move up to operating system tools—Device Manager, Disk Management, SMART utilities, RAID consoles—to determine whether the issue is physical, logical, or purely configuration. At every step where data might be at risk, you pause to consider backup and, if possible, copy off important files before doing anything that writes to the disk or array. Only after those bases are covered do you dive into repairs: running CHKDSK, replacing failing hardware, rebuilding RAID arrays, and finally verifying that the system is stable again and documenting what you did for whoever has to troubleshoot it next.

5.3 Video, Projector & Display Troubleshooting

Among all the problems you will see in an entry-level support role, display issues are some of the most visible and the most urgent. When a user cannot see anything on the screen, their work stops immediately, and the stress level in the room goes up fast. The good news is that many video and display issues turn out to be very simple: the monitor is on the wrong input, the cable is loose, the brightness is turned all the way down, or Windows is sending the image to a non-existent second screen. The challenge, and what the A+ exam is really testing, is whether you can interpret the symptoms, keep your cool, and follow a structured process instead of jumping straight to "the monitor is dead" or "the video card is fried."

If you think back to the general troubleshooting methodology you saw earlier in this part of the book, video troubleshooting is a perfect place to apply it. You start by identifying the problem through observation and a few smart questions. What exactly does the user see? Has this ever worked on this system? Did it stop working after a change, such as moving desks, installing a driver, or connecting a projector? From there you form a theory: is this likely to be a power issue, a cabling problem, a misconfiguration in the operating system, or an actual hardware failure? Each next step should be low risk and easy to reverse, and you verify your results as you go. Over time, this becomes second nature, and you can walk into a room, glance at the display, and already have a short list of likely causes in your mind.

A useful starting point with any display complaint is to decide very quickly whether you are dealing with **no display** or a **bad display**. No display means the user cannot see an image at all. The screen may be completely black with no power light, it may show a "No signal" message, or you may see a lit but blank panel where the backlight is on but nothing is being drawn. Bad display, on the other hand, means some sort of image is present, but it is distorted, fuzzy, the wrong size, flickering, oddly colored, or otherwise wrong. That distinction matters because it tells you where to focus your effort.

When you have absolutely no image, even during boot, the first thing you must sort out is whether the monitor or projector itself is alive. Look for a power LED and any on-screen messages, such as "No Signal" or a menu overlay. If the front panel is dark, you are not yet troubleshooting video; you are troubleshooting power. That might mean asking whether the monitor is plugged in to a working outlet or power strip, whether the power switch on the back is accidentally off, or whether the brightness has been turned so low that the screen appears black even though the panel is technically on. With projectors, lamp indicators and fan noise are important clues; a running fan and a "No Signal" message tell you the projector is functioning and simply not receiving a usable video signal.

Once you are confident the display device has power, your attention shifts to the **signal path**. This is where a huge number of "dead monitor" calls are resolved. You check that the video cable—HDMI, DisplayPort, VGA, DVI, USB-C, whatever is in use—is fully seated on both ends and is connected to the correct ports. On a desktop with a discrete graphics card, it is surprisingly common for the user to plug the cable into the motherboard's video port instead of the card's ports, which leaves the monitor waiting on a connector that may be disabled in BIOS. On the display side, modern monitors and TVs usually have multiple inputs, and the device does not always automatically switch to the one you just plugged in. A TV stuck on HDMI1 will happily show "No Signal" while the laptop is sending a perfect image into HDMI2. Simply pressing the Input or Source button on the remote and selecting the matching port can instantly "fix" what the user thought was a hardware failure.

If the monitor reports "No signal" but the PC seems to power on—fans spinning, lights on, maybe a single POST beep—your next step is to decide whether the computer is actually booting far enough to talk to a display. A quick trick is to see whether the system shows a BIOS or manufacturer logo during startup. If you can see BIOS but lose the image once the operating system loads, the basic hardware path is working and you should suspect software or configuration issues, such as a bad video driver or an inappropriate resolution. If you never see BIOS, or if the system does not beep, light keyboard LEDs, or show any other signs of a successful POST, the problem may be deeper than video: motherboard, RAM, CPU, or power supply issues can all present as a blank screen to the user.

Sometimes there actually is an image present, but it is nearly invisible because the backlight has failed. In older LCD panels, the cold cathode fluorescent backlight and its inverter board were common failure points. The panel would still draw the image, but with no light behind it, you would only see a very faint ghost of the desktop if you shined a flashlight at an angle across the screen. In that case, the computer and graphics subsystem are fine, but the cost and complexity of replacing backlights or inverters usually push these repairs into the "replace the display" category for entry-level technicians.

Most of the calls you receive will not be total black screens but some kind of **degraded display**, where an image is present but clearly not right. One very common scenario is a desktop that looks stretched, squished, or strangely blurry. Users might say the text looks fuzzy or that the picture does not fill the screen properly. This almost always points to a **resolution or aspect ratio mismatch**. LCD and LED panels have a single **native resolution**—for example, 1920×1080 for a typical 1080p monitor—and if the operating system is set to a lower or non-native resolution, the monitor has to scale the image, which introduces softness and distortion. The fix is to go into Windows Settings, open the System and Display section, and select the recommended resolution, which will usually be the panel's native mode. Once you apply that change, fonts snap back into focus and circles look like circles again.

On projectors, similar complaints show up as images that are either letterboxed with black bars or stretched out so that people look unnaturally wide. Here you have to coordinate two things: the computer's resolution and the projector's **aspect ratio mode**. Many projectors can operate in 4:3, 16:9, 16:10, or an auto mode. If the projector is locked to 4:3 and you send it a widescreen 16:9 signal, it will probably add black bars or distort the image. Matching the projector to the laptop's aspect ratio—or setting both sides to auto detection—usually brings the picture back to a proper shape.

Another category of degraded video involves **artifacts and corruption**. Users might describe "weird colored lines," "blocks," or "garbage" on the screen, especially when doing something graphics-intensive like gaming or video editing. You may see horizontal tearing during motion or patterns that worsen as the system warms up. When these artifacts appear even before the operating system loads, during POST or BIOS screens, they strongly suggest a hardware problem with the graphics card or integrated GPU. Overheating is a classic culprit: dust-clogged heatsinks, failed GPU fans, or poor case airflow can allow the GPU to reach temperatures where it starts to misbehave. Opening the case (after powering down and unplugging, of course), checking that the card is fully seated, cleaning out dust, and verifying that the fans spin freely are all reasonable steps. If the artifacts only appear after a particular driver loads, or in a specific OS user session, it is worth booting into Safe Mode or using a basic display driver to see whether the issue disappears, which would point to driver corruption rather than failing hardware.

Color and brightness issues form another cluster. A user might say the display has a red tint, or that everything looks washed out and flat. With older analog VGA connections, a bent or broken pin can drop a single color channel, leaving the entire image skewed toward blue or green. Swapping the cable or switching to a digital connector like HDMI is an easy way to test that theory. Before declaring the monitor bad, you should also check the on-screen display controls for brightness, contrast, and color temperature, as well as the OS-level brightness and night-mode settings. It is very easy to mistake a misconfigured color profile for a dying panel. When the complaint is "the screen is very dim even with brightness turned up," and you can barely make out the image, that takes you back to the backlight and power circuitry scenario mentioned earlier.

Flickering, ghosting, and motion problems can be subtle but are still driven by the same basic principles. If a user complains of a flicker or rolling bar effect, especially on older displays, the **refresh rate** may be set too low or to a value the monitor does not handle well. Adjusting the refresh rate in the OS display settings to a supported, higher value usually clears that up. On digital interfaces, flickering more often indicates a marginal or damaged cable, a loose connection, or electrical interference. Ghosting—where moving objects leave trails behind them—is usually more about the panel's response time than a configuration error, although very low-quality cables or certain scaling modes can exaggerate it.

When you move from desktop monitors to **projectors and TVs**, the troubleshooting ideas stay the same, but a few additional variables come into play. First is input selection, which we have already touched on. TVs are notorious for defaulting to the last input used, so if someone unplugged a Blu-ray player from HDMI1 yesterday and you plug a laptop into HDMI2 today, the TV will calmly sit there silently waiting for HDMI1. In a conference room, it is common to find multiple inputs connected to a projector—VGA, HDMI, maybe a wireless adapter—and users do not realize they have to choose the input that corresponds to the physical port they are using.

Second is the way the operating system decides where to send the image. On Windows, pressing Windows key + P brings up the display mode options: PC screen only, Duplicate, Extend, and Second screen only. These modes are at the heart of many exam questions and many real-world tickets. If the laptop is set to PC screen only, the internal display will work and the projector will remain dark, no matter how many times the user reseats the HDMI cable. If it is set to Second screen only, the internal display will go black and the user may think the laptop has crashed, when in fact it is rendering the desktop exclusively on an external monitor that is not currently attached. With Extend, the projector becomes a second desktop, which confuses users who expect to see the same thing on both screens and cannot find their mouse pointer "on the projector." For presentations, Duplicate is usually what the user wants, and simply switching to that mode often resolves the complaint in seconds.

Projectors add a couple of optics-related adjustments that are easy to confuse with computer problems. **Keystone correction** compensates for placing the projector at an angle to the screen, turning a trapezoidal image back into a rectangle. If keystone is misadjusted, the image will look distorted regardless of what the computer is sending. Focus is another; if you see a uniformly blurry picture but the resolution settings look correct, reach for the focus ring on the projector lens before diving into drivers. Screen size complaints with projectors—"the image is too big and spills off the screen", or "it is too tiny in the middle"—are usually resolved by moving the projector closer to or farther from the screen, or by adjusting its zoom, not by changing desktop resolution. And then there is the room itself: in a brightly lit conference room, a perfectly functioning projector may still look washed out and low contrast; that is not a PC problem at all, but an ambient light issue that you can only solve with blinds, dimmer switches, or a brighter projector.

Multi-monitor configurations on desktops and laptops combine many of these concepts. When a second monitor does not seem to work, start by confirming that the hardware path is good: the cable is connected to an active output, and the monitor is powered on and set to the right input. Then, in the OS display settings, check whether the computer even sees the second display. Windows offers a Detect button for this purpose; if pressing Detect suddenly makes a "new" monitor appear, you know the system simply had not enumerated it yet. Orientation and arrangement are another frequent source of complaints. Users will say "my mouse goes the wrong way" because Windows thinks the second monitor is to the left of the first when it is physically on the right. Dragging the monitors into the correct positions in the layout diagram so that cursor movement matches the physical arrangement quickly fixes that disorientation.

Laptops add their own twists. Many models have a function key combination, such as Fn + F8, to cycle between internal display, external display, and both. If a user has accidentally pressed that combination, the laptop might be driving only the external port, leaving the built-in panel black until you toggle it back. Power management settings can also affect behavior: some laptops are configured to turn off the internal screen or even go to sleep when the lid is closed, which might surprise someone trying to present with the lid down. Docking stations bring additional connectors, firmware, and drivers into the picture, so reseating the laptop in the dock, verifying the dock has power, and checking for dock-specific driver updates are all part of the troubleshooting routine when docked displays misbehave.

While all of this is happening, you still have to think about safety and professionalism. Never open an LCD or LED monitor chassis unless you are explicitly trained and authorized; even when unplugged, internal power supplies and capacitors can hold potentially dangerous voltages. Always power devices down before disconnecting or reconnecting video cables to avoid arcing at the connectors or electrostatic damage to ports. Be mindful of the physical size and weight of large TVs and projectors; moving them carelessly is a recipe for injuries and expensive accidents. And when you explain what you found to the user, keep the language accessible. Saying, "Your laptop was set to send the picture only to a second screen that wasn't plugged in—that's why you saw black; I switched it to show on both," is far more useful than a deep dive into GPU pipelines.

The final skill to develop is knowing when you have to stop adjusting settings and start talking about replacement. A cracked panel, a backlight that no longer turns on, a GPU that continues to artifact even after cleaning, reseating, and driver updates—these are not things you can "tune" back into working condition. For an A+-level technician, the correct decision is often to document the steps you took, back them up with clear observations, and recommend replacing the faulty component, whether that is a standalone monitor, a laptop display assembly, or a failing graphics card.

5.4 Mobile Device Troubleshooting

If you think about how people react when their desktop freezes versus when their phone "dies," you quickly see why mobile troubleshooting deserves special attention. A desktop crash is annoying; a smartphone failure often feels like a crisis. The device holds their two-factor codes, work email, family photos, ride-sharing apps, payment apps, and social life. That emotional energy is part of what you're really troubleshooting. On the CompTIA A+ exam and in the real world, success with mobile devices depends less on memorizing every menu and more on approaching vague complaints with a calm, structured mindset and using the tools that Android and iOS already provide.

You have already seen the general A+ troubleshooting method: identify the problem, establish a theory, test it, plan and implement a fix, verify full functionality, and document. Mobile devices still follow that pattern, but the constraints are different from desktops and laptops. You usually cannot open the case to reseat RAM or swap a power supply. Batteries are sealed, ports are tiny, radios are always in play, and much of the "hardware" behavior is actually software-controlled. A cracked screen, a flooded charging port, a misbehaving app, and a dropped Wi-Fi connection can all present as "my phone won't work." To stay organized, it helps to mentally bucket symptoms into four areas: **power**, **output/input**, **data/OS**, and **signal**. You will subconsciously run through this "PODS" check every time you hear a new complaint: is it really a power issue, a display or touch problem, an app/OS problem, or a connectivity problem?

Power and Charging Problems

Power complaints are among the most urgent, and also among the most commonly exaggerated by users. When someone says, "My phone is dead," your first job is to carefully define what "dead" means. If the device shows no sign of life—no screen, no vibration, no charging indicator—you start by confirming that it really is powered off and not simply locked or in a very low brightness state. Try a normal power-on first. If that fails, use the platform's **forced restart** combination, which is usually some variation of holding the power and volume buttons for several seconds. You do not need to memorize specific combinations for the exam, but you should recognize that mobile OSes provide a non-destructive forced reboot as an early troubleshooting step.

If there is still no response, think about the most likely and easiest-to-test variables before jumping to conclusions about the battery or motherboard. Mobile devices are often run down to empty, so assume a fully discharged battery is possible. Connect the phone or tablet to a known-good charger and cable, ideally one you have verified on another device. Watch closely for any sign of charging: an LED, a battery icon on the screen, a vibration, or even a subtle backlight glow. If the device stays dark and the charger is known good, you are looking at either a failed battery, a damaged charging port, or deeper hardware trouble. On the other hand, if the device wakes up and starts charging, you have already isolated your theory: the original charger, cable, or outlet is probably at fault. This is exactly the reasoning CompTIA expects: start with the simplest, least invasive tests such as swapping in a known-good accessory before you assume a board-level failure.

Sometimes the device powers on, but the user complains that the **battery drains very quickly** or that the phone gets uncomfortably hot. Both Android and iOS offer battery usage screens that show which apps or services are consuming the most power. When you open these, you might see that a social media app has 30–40% of the usage, that the screen itself is consuming a large portion, or that constant GPS navigation is active. This is where you translate technical information into practical advice: reduce screen brightness, disable unnecessary background app refresh, turn off GPS when not needed, and uninstall or restrict apps that are behaving badly. A runaway app can also drive the CPU hard, producing heat. If the device is hot to the touch and the battery is dropping rapidly even when idle, power it down, let it cool, and investigate recently installed apps or updates once it is safe to work with again.

You also have to be aware of hazards. A **swollen battery** may cause the screen to lift slightly from the frame or the back cover to bulge. That is not a cosmetic issue; it is a safety problem. As an entry-level technician you should recognize this symptom, power the device off, and remove it from use. Do not puncture, squeeze, or attempt to disassemble the device yourself unless you are trained and authorized. Escalation to a specialized repair technician or manufacturer service is the correct step. The exam will not ask you to repair a swollen battery, but it may expect you to choose the safe response rather than continuing to troubleshoot as if it were a software problem.

Power complaints also include **"won't charge"** or "charges very slowly." Here, your job is to isolate variables systematically. The user may be charging from a USB port on a PC that supplies only 500 mA, while the device is designed for a 2-amp wall charger. If they are scrolling through video while plugged in, the battery might still drop or creep up very slowly. Testing with a proper wall adapter immediately clarifies whether the problem is the power source. If multiple chargers behave the same way, inspect the charging port with a light. Pocket lint and dust often accumulate, preventing a solid connection; a gentle cleaning with a non-metallic tool can solve many "intermittent charging" issues. If there is visible corrosion or mechanical damage, it is again time to escalate to hardware repair instead of forcing connectors or improvising tools that could short the contacts.

Display and Input Issues

Mobile devices blur the line between power and output problems because the display is the primary interface. A **black or dim screen** does not always mean a dead phone. One useful question for the user is whether they still hear notification sounds, vibrations, or ringtones. If they can hear incoming calls or message alerts, the phone is likely running but the display subsystem is not cooperating. Before assuming a hardware failure, try simple adjustments: increase brightness via the physical or on-screen controls if you can access them, disable auto-brightness in favor of a fixed level, and verify that no power-saving mode is aggressively dimming the display. Some power-saving profiles darken the screen significantly, which can be misinterpreted as a fault.

However, if the device clearly plays sounds, responds to button presses, but the screen never shows an image, that pattern suggests a backlight, display, or display connector issue rather than a battery or OS failure. For the exam, it is important to distinguish "no video, but device seems on" from "no power at all." In the first case, screen replacement or hardware service is likely. In the second, you return to your power troubleshooting path.

Modern phones and tablets rely heavily on **capacitive touchscreens**, so touch issues can make a functional device essentially unusable. When someone complains that "the screen doesn't respond" or that it is "pressing things by itself," start with the easy, non-destructive steps. Remove the case and any screen protector to eliminate mechanical pressure or poor alignment. Clean the surface to get rid of oils or moisture that can confuse touch detection. Ask whether the device is being used with gloves or in the rain, both of which affect capacitive sensing. Then, reboot the device. A frozen touch controller or OS glitch often clears with a restart.

If the display looks fine but touch input is still unreliable, you can use platform features to narrow down the cause. On Android, **safe mode** boots the device with only core system apps, disabling third-party apps temporarily. If touch input is normal in safe mode but misbehaves in normal mode, an installed app is probably responsible. On iOS, you do not have safe mode in the same way, but a restart followed by testing before opening any third-party apps serves a similar purpose. Persistent touch failure in all contexts, especially with visible cracks or after a liquid spill, points toward hardware damage and screen replacement.

Physical **buttons and sensors** are another category you will see just enough to matter. Stuck power or volume buttons can cause unexpected reboots or prevent a device from waking properly. A user might think the phone is boot looping, when in reality a jammed power button is holding the device in a reset state. Carefully testing the tactile feel of the button and removing the case to check for mechanical interference can reveal this quickly. Similarly, when the display fails to rotate from portrait to landscape, you should first check the orientation lock setting in the quick controls, then consider whether the case is obstructing the accelerometer area. Only after those checks should you suspect an internal sensor failure.

Performance, OS, and App Behavior

A huge portion of daily support tickets can be summarized as "my phone is slow" or "this app keeps crashing." These are **data and OS** category problems, and the trick is to separate heavy usage from genuine malfunction. Mobile operating systems manage resources aggressively, but they are still limited. The first line of defense is simple: reboot the device. Many performance issues, especially after long uptimes, vanish after a restart as temporary files are cleared and processes are reset.

Next, look at storage. A nearly full device can slow dramatically because there is no room for caches, logging, and updates. Both Android and iOS provide storage breakdowns showing how much space is used by apps, photos, videos, and system data. If usage is above 90–95%, you will almost certainly see lag, failed app updates, and crashes. Helping the user remove unused apps, offload photos and videos to cloud storage or a computer (consistent with your organization's policies), and clear large caches can restore normal performance. Many platforms also show per-app memory or CPU usage; when one app consistently sits at the top, that is a hint that it may be poorly written or misconfigured.

When **specific apps crash, fail to open, or behave erratically**, the pattern matters. If only one app misbehaves while others are fine, the most sensible approach is to update that app first. Outdated versions may not be compatible with the current OS, or the developer may have fixed stability issues. On Android, clearing an app's cache and data can resolve corruption in local files, but be aware this may sign the user out or reset preferences. On both platforms, uninstalling and reinstalling the app is an effective test—provided you have the user's consent and credentials for re-authentication. The exam is fond of this hierarchy: first, check for updates; then, clear cache or settings; then, reinstall if necessary.

If multiple apps crash or the whole system seems unstable, you step back and consider OS-level issues. Is the OS several versions behind and unable to run newer apps? Is there a pattern that suggests malware, such as random pop-ups, unfamiliar apps, and excessive data usage? You might run a trusted mobile security scan if your organization uses such tools, and you should certainly recommend uninstalling untrusted sideloaded apps. In corporate environments, mobile device management (MDM) policies can also remove apps or enforce restrictions that users interpret as "broken." Always check whether a problem started right after a policy update or enrollment change.

A more dramatic OS problem is an **update failure** or **boot loop**, where the device repeatedly restarts or gets stuck on the manufacturer's logo. The correct order of operations here is very important for the exam. First, try a forced restart; transient issues may resolve themselves. If the device boots, ensure it has adequate battery charge and a stable Wi-Fi connection before attempting the update again. If it continues to loop, Android devices often offer a recovery mode where you can clear caches or, as a last resort, perform a factory reset. iOS has recovery and DFU modes that allow a restore via a computer. In all cases, you must think about data. If the user's data is not backed up to the cloud or a computer, a **factory reset** will erase it. In a professional setting you should obtain explicit permission, explain the consequences, and where possible, attempt a backup before committing to destructive actions.

Connectivity and Sync Troubleshooting

Signal problems—Wi-Fi, cellular, Bluetooth, or cloud/app sync—sit in the **signal** portion of your mental model. They often present with very similar user descriptions, so you are looking for clues in status icons and context.

With **Wi-Fi complaints**, start by confirming the basics on the device itself. Make sure Wi-Fi is enabled and that airplane mode is not turned on. Check which SSID the device is connected to; users may accidentally join a neighbor's open network or a guest network with limited access and then assume "the Wi-Fi is broken." If the device will not connect to a specific network, have it forget that network and rejoin, re-entering the password. This clears corrupted credentials and is a common real-world fix. To separate device issues from network issues, try connecting the same phone to a different known-good Wi-Fi network, such as a hotspot or another access point. If the phone behaves well elsewhere, you likely have a router or ISP problem. If all devices in an area have intermittent Wi-Fi, tweaking one phone's network settings will not help; in that case you would troubleshoot the access point itself, which you will explore more deeply in the network troubleshooting section.

For **cellular data and voice problems**, the indicators at the top of the screen are your friends. "No Service," "Emergency calls only," or an exclamation mark on the signal bars tell you that the device cannot register normally with the network. Again, verify that airplane mode is off. Then, check whether the issue is location-specific: inside certain buildings or basements, coverage may simply be poor. Ask if other users on the same carrier have problems in the same area. If they do, you are probably facing a carrier or local tower issue. If only one device is affected, removing and reseating the **SIM card** is an effective step, as poor contact can cause registration failures. Some carriers also rely on **APN (Access Point Name)** settings for data; incorrect or missing APNs can lead to "bars but no data." On managed devices, APN settings may be controlled by profiles that you must not change without approval.

Bluetooth brings its own flavor of frustration. Users describe "won't pair," "keeps disconnecting," or "no sound in the car even though it says connected." The basic sequence is straightforward but must be followed deliberately. Confirm Bluetooth is enabled on the phone and that the other device (headset, car, speaker) is in pairing mode; many devices time out of pairing mode quickly, so you may need to trigger it again. If the phone shows a previously paired connection that no longer works, instruct it to forget that device and pair fresh. Range and interference matter too; Bluetooth is short-range, so walls, bodies, and competing signals can cause drops. Finally, be aware that not all Bluetooth connections support all functions. A car kit may support phone calls but not high-quality stereo music, which a user interprets as "Bluetooth audio is broken" even though the device is working as designed.

Cloud-based services and apps add one more dimension: **email and app sync issues**. When someone says, "My email isn't updating" or "my calendar on the phone doesn't match my desktop," the temptation is to immediately dive into server settings. Resist that. First, verify the device has general connectivity by loading a web page or another app that requires the internet. If the network is fine, then open the account settings. Check that the username and password are current; password changes on the server side are extremely common causes of sync failures. For corporate accounts, confirm that the server name, port, and security settings match the organization's documentation. Also review sync options: many platforms allow disabling background sync or limiting it to Wi-Fi to save data and battery, which users may toggle without realizing the side effects. In environments with multi-factor authentication, some services require app-specific passwords, and missing these can silently prevent sync.

A simple but powerful technique is comparative testing. See whether the same email or cloud account works correctly in a web browser or on another device. If the account works elsewhere but not on the phone, the problem is local to that mobile device. If it fails everywhere, the user's account or the remote service is at fault, and your role shifts from device troubleshooting to helping them contact the appropriate support channel.

Reset and Restore: Knowing When to Stop

Every troubleshooting path eventually reaches a decision point: you have tried simple, non-destructive steps and the problem persists. At that point, it becomes crucial to distinguish between **non-destructive resets**, which aim to preserve user data, and **destructive actions**, which intentionally wipe data and settings.

Non-destructive options include normal reboots, forced restarts, and targeted resets. For connectivity anomalies that do not respond to toggling radios and re-entering credentials, both Android and iOS provide a **reset network settings** function. This clears saved Wi-Fi networks, Bluetooth pairings, and sometimes cellular configuration, without touching user photos, apps, or messages. It is a strong next step when a device has chronic Wi-Fi or Bluetooth issues while other devices work fine. Similarly, you can reset individual app settings, clear caches, or log out and back in to a cloud account to refresh its tokens. These moves are reversible in the sense that data in the cloud or on external servers is not destroyed.

A **factory reset**, by contrast, returns the device to its out-of-box state, removing user data, installed apps, and many configuration changes. It is justified in cases of severe OS corruption, persistent malware, or when preparing a device for reassignment or disposal. Before performing a factory reset, you should help the user confirm that important data is backed up—either to a computer via synchronization software or to a cloud backup service. You must also ensure you are authorized to erase the device. In corporate settings, MDM platforms can trigger remote wipes, enforce encryption, and even block local resets to prevent data leakage. On the exam, you will often be asked to choose the **least invasive** effective step, so be careful not to jump directly to factory reset when a reboot, settings adjustment, or network reset would reasonably address the symptom.

Mobile troubleshooting is about pattern recognition and restraint as much as it is about technical skill. When you learn to map each new complaint into power, output/input, data/OS, or signal, and then walk the user through calm, methodical steps using the tools built into the device, you not only solve problems—you build trust.

5.5 Network Connectivity Troubleshooting

When you start working in IT support, it does not take long before someone says, "I can't get on the Internet." They usually cannot tell you more than that, and the problem might be anything from a loose cable under the desk to a DNS failure at the ISP. This is where network troubleshooting stops being theory and becomes a practical detective job. The same structured troubleshooting methodology you learned earlier still applies—you identify the problem, form a theory, test it, and so on—but now your clues are link lights, IP addresses, ping replies, and Wi-Fi signal bars. The goal is not just to make the connection work again, but to understand what failed, document it, and prevent the same thing from biting you later.

A useful way to frame your thinking is to walk through the connection from the ground up. I often use the **PLANS** idea in my head: physical, link, address, network path, and service. You start by asking, "Is anything physically connected or associated?" Then you confirm that the OS sees a live link. After that you look at addressing: IP, subnet mask, default gateway, DNS. Only once that looks sane do you ask whether packets can traverse the path to the router and beyond. Finally, you look at the specific application or service the user cares about. This keeps you from jumping straight to exotic explanations when the Ethernet cable is still dangling loose behind the tower.

From the user's point of view, most network problems look very similar. They say "the Internet is down," regardless of whether they lost all connectivity, can reach local printers but not websites, or are simply suffering from high latency. As a technician, you translate that vague complaint into more precise symptoms. No connectivity at all often shows up as a red X on the Windows network icon, messages like "Network cable unplugged," or "Not connected – no connections are available." Your first thoughts should immediately drop to the physical and link layers: Is the cable seated? Are the link LEDs lit? Is Wi-Fi enabled or did someone accidentally toggle airplane mode? A surprising number of "complex" incidents end here, with a reconnected cable or a function key that turns the wireless adapter back on.

Other times, the system thinks it is connected, but Windows shows a small yellow triangle and says "No Internet access" or "Limited." This is where **limited or local-only connectivity** comes into play. In this state, a device might be able to talk to itself or, in some cases, to other devices on the same local segment, but it cannot reach the default gateway or anything on the wider Internet. A classic clue is the **APIPA address**, a 169.254.x.x address with a 255.255.0.0 mask and no default gateway. When Windows or another OS cannot obtain an address from DHCP, it assigns itself an Automatic Private IP Addressing (APIPA) address so it can still do some very limited local communication. On the exam and in real life, seeing 169.254 is your red flag that DHCP failed or the device was never able to reach a DHCP server in the first place.

Intermittent connectivity symptoms feel different. Users say, "My Wi-Fi keeps dropping," "It works for a while and then everything times out," or "My VPN disconnects every few minutes." These issues can be some of the most frustrating, because they often depend on time and location. In wired networks, intermittence might hint at a marginal cable, a flaky port on a switch, or a speed/duplex mismatch causing retransmissions. On wireless, patterns are even more important: if the connection fails only in one room, you are thinking about weak signal and interference; if it happens whenever a lot of people come into the office, you suspect an overloaded access point or router.

Slowness introduces another dimension. Users complain that pages spin forever, online games lag, or remote desktops feel like they are moving through molasses. The key here is to scope the slowness. If a user can copy files quickly to a local server but web browsing is slow, the bottleneck is probably upstream—perhaps the ISP, maybe congestion on the WAN side of the router. If every device on the network is slow at the same time, you think about bandwidth saturation, a misconfigured switch, or a single user or system (sometimes malware) consuming all available bandwidth. On a single wired workstation, odd slowness paired with lots of errors in interface statistics often comes back to a speed and **duplex mismatch**, where one side is fixed at full duplex and the other is auto-negotiating incorrectly.

Then there are the subtle cases where "the Internet is fine, except for this one thing." You might see that users can browse most sites but cannot reach a particular internal web application. Or they can ping an IP address, but when they try the hostname, it fails. These are your **name resolution** and service-specific problems. If raw IP connectivity works but name-based access fails, DNS immediately moves to the top of your suspect list. Perhaps the device is pointed at a dead DNS server, or an internal DNS zone is misconfigured. Alternatively, if everything but one particular service (such as email or VPN) works, you start thinking about service outages on the server side, firewall rules blocking certain ports, or incorrect application configuration.

Underneath all of these symptoms lies the question of scope: is the problem on this device only, on a specific group of devices, or across the entire network and Internet connection? Before you touch the router, you should have clear evidence that more than one user is affected. If one laptop cannot connect but the others in the same office can, you focus on that laptop. If everyone on a particular switch is having trouble but users on another switch are fine, you suspect that switch or its uplink. If all users, wired and wireless, suddenly lose access to the Internet, now you consider the router, modem, or ISP. On the exam, CompTIA loves to see whether you pay attention to that scope and choose the most appropriate action for the impact described.

Once you have a symptom and a sense of scope, you start climbing what I like to call the **ping ladder**. This is a simple but powerful sequence that works in almost every IP network. At the first rung, you ping the loopback address, 127.0.0.1. This never leaves the host; it just confirms that the TCP/IP stack is functioning. If that fails, you know the problem is entirely local—corrupted TCP/IP, a misbehaving firewall driver, or a deeply broken OS. The second rung is pinging your own IP address. If loopback works but your own address does not respond, you are looking at a NIC problem, a driver issue, or an IP binding misconfiguration.

The third rung is your default gateway, usually the router interface on your local network. If you can ping yourself but not the gateway, then the trouble lies somewhere between your NIC and that router. On a wired client, that brings you back to cables, switch ports, and link status. On Wi-Fi, you think about association to the correct SSID, signal strength, and wireless security settings. The fourth rung is an external IP address, such as a well-known public DNS server. A successful ping to the gateway but not to an external IP strongly suggests an upstream issue: perhaps the modem is down, the ISP connection is out, or the router's WAN interface is misconfigured. Finally, the fifth rung is a hostname, such as www.example.com. If you can reach the external IP but name-based pings fail, you have effectively isolated the problem to DNS and can move on to checking DNS server settings or testing with nslookup.

Nearly every step of that ladder relies on understanding the device's IP settings. In Windows, **ipconfig/all** is your best friend here. When you run it, you are scanning several key items. You want to see whether the **IPv4 address** is in the expected range for that network, whether the **subnet mask** matches, and whether a **default gateway** and **DNS servers** are present and plausible. Seeing an APIPA address with no gateway confirms DHCP trouble. Seeing a static IP address that duplicates another machine's address gives you an **IP conflict**, which often manifests as flapping connectivity: the device works for a bit, then stops when ARP tables update or another system "wins" the address battle. A missing default gateway explains why a user can reach local resources but nothing on the Internet. Incorrect DNS entries mean that even though the ping ladder up to external IP succeeds, browsers and other applications that rely on names will still fail.

You also need to stay fluent in the basics of the physical and link layers. On wired connections, you always look to the link lights on both the NIC and the switch or router. A dark light means no link; a steady or blinking light usually indicates some level of connectivity. When you suspect the cable itself, a simple swap with a known-good patch cable can be the fastest test. In more persistent cases, or when you are building or validating cabling, a **cable tester** becomes important. A basic tester checks continuity and pinout, telling you whether each pair is wired correctly, whether any pins are open or shorted, or whether a cable is mis-terminated. For troubleshooting a single NIC, a **loopback plug** can help: you plug it into the port, and if the NIC can send and receive its own test traffic internally, the hardware is probably fine.

Speed and duplex issues tend to show up as unexplained slowness or excessive errors. Ethernet devices usually negotiate speed and duplex automatically, and in modern gear that generally works well. However, if one side is hard-set to full duplex and the other is auto-negotiating, they can end up mismatched. The side on half duplex will detect what it thinks are collisions, back off, and retransmit, dragging performance down. On a workstation, you can examine the adapter properties to see the negotiated speed and duplex, or check the switch port's statistics for errors and collisions. The preferred fix is usually to set both sides to auto unless you have a compelling reason to force specific values.

Wireless networks add another layer of nuance. The first question is always: are we on the right network, with the right settings? It is very easy, especially in dense environments like apartment buildings, for users to accidentally connect to the wrong SSID with a similar name. Incorrect passphrases or mismatched security types (trying to connect with WPA2 when the access point expects WPA3, for instance) produce symptoms like repeated password prompts or "Cannot connect to this network" errors. Having a user "forget" the network and then rejoin, carefully selecting the intended SSID and entering the correct passphrase, is often the simplest fix and should be tried before you engage in deep IP troubleshooting.

When the problem follows a particular location, you suspect **weak signal** and interference. Walls, floors, metal appliances, and even water in plumbing can attenuate a Wi-Fi signal. Other electronic devices—microwave ovens, cordless phones, baby monitors—can create interference in the 2.4 GHz band. Neighbors' access points using the same or overlapping channels can also crowd the airwaves. A **Wi-Fi analyzer** app on a phone or laptop gives you a visualization of signal strength and channel usage over time. By comparing the signal level in different rooms and noting which channels are congested, you can make informed decisions about relocating the router, adjusting antennas, or changing channels to avoid overlap.

Wireless access points and SOHO routers can also simply be overloaded. When a single consumer-grade device is handling dozens of clients streaming video, gaming, and downloading updates, it may struggle, leading to dropped associations or slow response. Here, watching the pattern is key. If one user is slow while everyone else near the same AP is fine, the issue is likely on that user's device. If everyone's connection degrades whenever more people arrive, the AP or the upstream Internet link may not have the capacity. Power management settings on laptops and mobile devices also play a role; some drivers aggressively power down the wireless adapter to save battery, causing intermittent disconnections that mysteriously resolve when the device is plugged in.

All of this theory becomes far more concrete when you walk through actual cases. Consider the "mysterious 169.254 address" incident in a small office. A user reports that their computer claims to be connected, but nothing loads. You sit down, see the yellow triangle on the network icon, and confirm that the Ethernet cable is firmly in place with link lights showing on both ends. That covers the physical and link parts of PLANS. Moving to address, you run **ipconfig** and see 169.254.32.5 with a 255.255.0.0 mask and no default gateway. Instantly, you recognize APIPA and infer that DHCP did not provide a lease. You check a neighboring PC and find it in the same state. Now the problem's scope has widened: it is not just one machine. Your theory shifts from "this NIC has an issue" to "the DHCP server, likely the router, is not working properly." Power-cycling the router restores normal 192.168.1.x leases for everyone, and a quick ipconfig /renew or a reboot on the affected PCs confirms full Internet access. You then note in your ticket that the router's DHCP service failed and was restored by a reboot.

Contrast that with a remote worker who says, "My Wi-Fi keeps dropping when I'm in the bedroom, but it's fine in the living room." Here, the problem is clearly location-specific and intermittent. There is little reason to suspect DHCP or DNS; the same device works perfectly in one place and poorly in another. You ask the user to check the signal bars in both rooms and hear that the living room shows full strength while the bedroom hovers at one bar or sometimes none. That alone points to weak signal, but you go a step further and have them run a simple Wi-Fi analyzer on their phone. It shows their network's signal dropping sharply in the bedroom and several neighboring networks competing on the same channel. Putting that together, you conclude that both distance/obstructions and channel congestion are at play. Guiding the user through changing their router's channel to a less crowded one, and suggesting they move the router to a more central, higher position, leads to a noticeable improvement in connection stability and speed in the bedroom.

Under exam conditions and in real environments, what separates an effective troubleshooter from a guesser is this disciplined, evidence-driven process. You start with the obvious physical and link checks, you read the IP configuration carefully, you use tools like **ping, tracert, nslookup,** cable testers, and Wi-Fi analyzers to answer specific questions, and you change one thing at a time based on a clear theory. Over time, the pattern recognition becomes second nature. You see APIPA and think "DHCP or link." You see "can ping IP but not hostname" and immediately focus on DNS. You hear "only in that room" and picture signal strength and interference. Network troubleshooting stops being a mysterious art and becomes a structured problem you know how to approach, one step at a time.

5.6 Printer Troubleshooting

If you hang around any help desk long enough, you eventually hear some version of "The printer is broken" at least once a day. Printers combine mechanical parts, consumables, firmware, drivers, and network connectivity in one device, which makes them incredibly useful and incredibly prone to problems. The good news is that printer issues follow patterns. Once you learn how to read those patterns and apply a structured troubleshooting approach, what feels like chaos starts to make sense. In this section, we'll take the concepts you learned in printer operation, configuration, and maintenance and turn them into a practical troubleshooting toolkit for the Core 1 exam and real-life support work.

A good place to begin is with mindset. Your goal is not to become an in-depth printer hardware repair technician; your goal is to restore service quickly, safely, and in a way that fits your role. That means you'll focus on symptoms that a frontline A+ technician is expected to handle: jams, misfeeds, ugly output, "nothing prints," and mysterious queue problems. Behind each complaint is a relatively small set of likely causes. Your job is to interpret vague user descriptions, connect them to technical symptoms, and then test your theory with low-risk, logical steps.

When a user says, "The printer's broken," you should immediately start clarifying. Which printer? From which computer? Does it fail for everyone or just you? Did anything change recently—new toner, new paper, a move to a different office, a Windows update? This is the **identify the problem** phase of general troubleshooting, applied specifically to printers. Often, just by asking whether the printer prints a self-test page correctly, or whether others in the office can print, you can separate hardware issues from driver, queue, or network issues before you ever touch the device.

Once you have a basic picture, you mentally categorize the problem. Is this about paper movement through the device, about the appearance of what's on the page, about the computer and printer communicating correctly, or about the underlying connection? Thinking in those broad buckets keeps you from jumping straight to "reinstall the printer" or "replace the toner" every time. From there, you **establish a theory**: for example, repeated jams right at the tray suggest worn rollers, while ugly output that is the same from every source suggests something in the imaging path rather than an application setting.

You then **test your theory** with targeted actions. If you suspect a driver problem, you might print a test page directly from the printer's control panel. If that page looks fine, the hardware is probably okay, and you turn your attention to the computer, driver, or network. If you suspect a network issue, you might ping the printer's IP address or print a configuration page to see whether it has a valid address. As you refine your theory, you **plan and implement** the least disruptive, safest steps first—clearing the queue before reinstalling drivers, reseating a toner cartridge before calling for on-site service, checking a paper setting before replacing a fuser.

When things appear to be fixed, you still are not done. You **verify functionality** by recreating the original problem scenario, not just printing any random test. If the complaint was "wireless printing from my laptop fails," then you should confirm that wireless printing from that laptop now works, not just that a self-test page prints. Finally, in a professional environment, you **document** what happened: error codes, root cause, and what you did. Over time, those notes reveal patterns such as a particular printer constantly jamming, which may justify a full maintenance kit or replacement.

One of the most common categories of printer calls involves the physical movement of paper. When paper doesn't move correctly, you see **paper jams**, misfeeds, multiple sheets feeding together, or skewed pages. A user might describe this as "It makes a horrible crunching sound and then stops" or "Every time I print, it says there's a jam." If the printer displays a "Paper Jam" message or an error code, you pay attention to whether it tends to happen at the same place every time. Consistent jams as paper leaves the tray point toward worn or dirty pickup rollers or incorrect paper loading. Consistent jams near the fuser suggest something catching or leftover scraps from a previous jam. Random jams all along the path, especially in humid environments or with very cheap paper, often relate to poor-quality or damp paper, an overfilled tray, or users mixing different paper weights in the same tray.

Clearing a jam is not just "yank the paper out." You must respect safety and the printer's design. If the vendor documentation says to power off before clearing, follow that guidance; the fuser can be very hot, and internal components can carry high voltages. Open the designated access doors and remove paper gently in the direction of the paper path rather than pulling backward. If you tear the paper, you leave scraps inside that cause recurring jams. After you clear the obvious jam, you visually inspect the path—rollers, guides, and corners—for torn bits, labels that have peeled off, or foreign objects like paper clips. Once everything is clear and covers are properly closed, you test again. If the same area jams repeatedly, you start thinking beyond user error and look toward maintenance items like roller cleaning or replacement.

Closely related to jams are issues where the printer feeds paper incorrectly. You might hear the pickup mechanism spinning while no paper moves, or see the printer grab several sheets instead of one. These symptoms often trace back to **pickup rollers** and **separation pads**. Over time, the rubber surface of rollers hardens or becomes slick with dust and paper residue, making it harder to grip the top sheet. Separation pads, which are meant to keep only one sheet feeding, also wear down. In many office printers, a first-line fix is to clean rollers and pads with approved tools—often a slightly damp lint-free cloth or vendor-provided cleaning kit. You also look for bad loading habits: users mixing sizes in one tray, overfilling trays, or failing to adjust the paper guides tightly against the stack. If careful cleaning and correct loading do not help and the printer has many thousands of pages on it, roller replacement may be required, which you might escalate to authorized service depending on your organization's policies.

Once paper is moving correctly, the next broad category of symptoms is **print quality problems**—the user's "It prints, but it looks terrible." Here, knowing how each printer type creates an image is essential, because the same symptom means different things on different devices. For laser printers, you think in terms of toner, imaging drum, fuser, and paper settings. For inkjets, your mind goes to print heads, nozzles, and ink behavior on paper. For thermal printers, you focus on the thermal paper and heating elements. For impact printers, you consider ribbons, pins, and alignment.

On a laser printer, faded or very light print across the entire page often points to low toner or an exhausted imaging drum. Before you replace anything, though, you check the printer's density or quality settings; someone may have switched it to an "eco" or toner-save mode. If the entire page is consistently light and the printer has many pages on the current toner cartridge, replacing or shaking the cartridge (if the vendor recommends that) is a reasonable step. Streaks or vertical lines down the page, especially at a fixed position, suggest something on a rotating component. A scratch or debris on the drum, toner caked on a corona wire (on models that use one), or contamination on internal rollers can all create this symptom. Many printers offer a built-in cleaning cycle that you can run through the control panel, and some have user-accessible parts of the imaging assembly you can gently clean. If the streaks repeat at a regular interval that matches the drum circumference, that further confirms a drum-related problem.

Ghosting—where a faint copy of the image appears further down the page—is particularly exam-relevant. When the same image appears again lower on the page, usually lighter, you suspect the fuser or drum not fully discharging. The fuser might not be heating to the correct temperature or may be worn, causing residual toner to transfer repeatedly. Alternatively, the drum may still hold part of the previous charge as it rotates. In either case, "replace toner" is not the best answer; the test expects you to recognize that the fuser and imaging system, not the toner itself, are at fault. Another laser-specific complaint is that the toner smears or can be wiped off easily with a finger. That again points to poor fusing: either the fuser is not hot enough, or the printer's media settings do not match reality. If a user is printing on heavy cardstock while the printer is set to "Plain Paper," the fuser will move the paper through too quickly and at a lower temperature than needed. Adjusting the paper type setting to "Cardstock" or another heavy media value often fixes smearing without replacing any hardware, as in the scenario where reports on thick paper suddenly began to smear.

Inkjet issues behave differently. Streaks, missing lines, or entire bands of color missing from prints usually come from **clogged nozzles** or nearly empty cartridges. Most inkjet printers include a nozzle check and cleaning utility accessible from the front panel or driver software. Running a nozzle check prints a pattern that shows which nozzles are firing correctly. If you see gaps, you run a cleaning cycle, test again, and repeat only as necessary. Every cleaning consumes ink, so you avoid doing it "just in case." When colors look wrong—muddy, shifted, or far from the screen—you look at paper type and color management. Wrong media settings can cause too much or too little ink to be deposited, and glossy photo paper tends to behave very differently from cheap office paper. Using third-party ink can also change how colors render or how long the print takes to dry. If ink never seems to dry or smudges easily, especially on coated or photo papers, suspect either the wrong paper type in the settings or environmental factors such as very high humidity.

Thermal and impact printers tend to show simpler, more distinctive symptoms. A thermal receipt printer that starts producing very light output or blank paper often is not "out of ink"—there is no ink. Instead, the thermal paper itself may be at fault. If the roll was installed backward, the printer is heating the wrong side, so nothing appears. If the paper is expired or stored in heat or direct sunlight, the coating degrades and prints faintly. Horizontal white lines across prints, where some text lines are missing, usually point to dirt or permanent damage on the heating elements. Cleaning with vendor-approved isopropyl swabs or cleaning cards is the first step. For impact printers, faded characters or missing columns typically betray a worn ribbon or damaged print head. If multi-part forms are misaligned, you consider platen or head alignment adjustments, which are usually done via knobs or menu options rather than disassembling the device.

So far we've been focusing on the output itself. But plenty of printer tickets are about nothing printing at all, even though the printer looks fine physically. This is where **software, drivers, and the print spooler** enter the picture. A classic driver problem is a page full of garbled symbols, random characters, or completely wrong layout. That strongly suggests that the computer is sending data in a format the printer does not understand because the wrong driver is installed or the driver is corrupted. Similarly, a generic driver might allow basic printing but hide features such as duplexing or stapling, leading users to report, "I can't choose two-sided printing anymore." The remedy is to confirm the exact printer model and the client operating system (including 32- or 64-bit) and install the correct driver from a trusted source, usually the manufacturer's website or a managed print server.

The **print spooler** acts as a traffic manager, receiving jobs from applications, storing them, and sending them to the printer in order. When it misbehaves, users see print jobs stuck in the queue with statuses like "Error – Printing" or "Spooling," and nothing emerges from the printer. On a single workstation, you typically open the queue, attempt to cancel or clear the jobs, and then restart the spooler service via the operating system's tools. In Windows, that might mean restarting the Print Spooler service through Services or using administrative command-line tools. If clearing and restarting resolve the issue for that one user, you have probably fixed a local queue corruption. If you discover that everyone printing to a shared printer experiences stuck jobs, you look at the print server instead. Logging onto the server, clearing the queue, and restarting the server-side spooler often restores printing, as in the scenario where multiple users saw "Printing" in their queues but nothing came out until the spooler service was restarted.

Finally, every printer is also a network or local device that must be reachable. For locally attached printers, your connectivity checks are basic but important: is the printer powered on and showing "Ready"? Is the USB cable firmly connected on both ends? Does the operating system show the device under printers or devices? Swapping to another known-good USB port or cable is a quick way to rule out a flaky connection. If the printer can print a self-test page but the computer cannot send jobs to it, your focus shifts to drivers, port configuration, or the local spooler.

Networked printers add another layer. Here, **scope of impact** is one of your most powerful tools. If only one user cannot print while everyone else can, the problem is almost always on the client side: that user's driver, their print queue, the specific application, or their permissions. If no one can print to that printer, but the device itself shows "Ready," you suspect the network path or print server. Printing a configuration page from the printer's panel verifies its IP address, subnet mask, and gateway. If the page shows an address in the 169.254.x.x range, you know it failed to get a DHCP lease, which explains why no one can reach it. You would then investigate DHCP scopes, static IP misconfigurations, or cabling. Basic network tests apply as usual: if you can ping the printer's IP from a client, but print jobs still fail, the network is probably fine and you focus on spooler or driver issues. If you cannot ping it, check cabling, switches, wireless signal, and IP settings.

Wireless printers bring their own quirks. A user might say, "It works sometimes but not others," especially when the printer is far from the access point or sitting in a Wi-Fi dead spot. Weak signal, incorrect SSID, wrong passphrase, or wireless isolation features on the access point can all interfere with wireless printing. Verifying that the printer is associated to the correct network and has a valid IP address is your starting point. In environments with centralized print servers, users might not connect directly to the printer at all; instead, they connect to a shared queue on the server. In those cases, "Access denied" or an inability to see the printer at all usually involves permissions or group policy, which you either adjust (if within your role) or escalate to the system administrator.

Throughout all of this, you have to respect safety and vendor guidelines. Laser printer fusers reach temperatures hot enough to cause burns, and many models retain high-voltage charges internally even after you power them off. Moving belts and gears can pinch fingers. As a junior technician, you focus on user-serviceable areas: clearing paper in documented access points, replacing toner or ink cartridges, swapping ribbons, cleaning rollers and heads using recommended methods. When a fix would require disassembling sealed assemblies, opening power supplies, or handling internal high-voltage components, you stop and escalate to authorized service or follow your organization's repair contract.

Once you restore printing, you always loop back to prevention and communication. If a jam was caused by users loading thick cardstock into a tray configured for plain paper, you might clearly label trays and show staff how to change media types. If ghosting appears every few months on a heavily used laser printer, you might recommend scheduling maintenance or planning for a fuser replacement during off-hours. When you resolve a network queue problem by restarting a hung spooler, you document the event, including the time and any patterns you notice, so that recurring issues can be linked to firmware bugs or resource constraints on the server. Over time, that combination of technical reasoning, user education, and careful documentation is what turns printer troubleshooting from a daily headache into a manageable, routine part of your support role.

5.7 Knowledge Check

Question 1: A desktop PC shows no lights, no fans, and no sounds when the user presses the power button. The outlet has not yet been checked. According to best troubleshooting practice, what should you do first?

A. Replace the power supply with a higher-wattage unit and retest the system's power-on behavior
B. Verify the wall outlet or power strip is providing power by testing it with another known-good device
C. Remove the motherboard from the case to check for shorts and inspect for any visible component damage
D. Replace the motherboard and CPU as a matched set and then attempt to power on the system again

Question 2: A user says their desktop "just died." You find both the PC and monitor are off, and plugging a phone charger into the outlet shows no power. What is the most appropriate next step?

A. Check the wall switch or circuit breaker controlling the outlet and restore power if it has been turned off or tripped
B. Replace the PC's power supply with a compatible unit and then attempt to power on the computer again
C. Boot the system from a diagnostic USB drive to test for operating system or storage-related problems
D. Reseat the RAM modules in their slots and run a memory diagnostic to check for faulty memory

Question 3: A newly built system powers on and the fans spin, but there is no POST, no beeps, and no video. You have confirmed the PSU switch is on and the 24-pin ATX connector is attached. Which simple internal check should you perform next?

A. Reinstall the operating system from scratch using a bootable USB drive and then retest the system
B. Verify the 4- or 8-pin CPU power connector is firmly seated in the motherboard's CPU power socket
C. Replace the graphics card with a higher-end model that supports more advanced video resolutions
D. Clear CMOS by removing the motherboard battery and resetting all BIOS/UEFI configuration settings

Question 4: A tower powers on and performs POST successfully but frequently blue-screens with various, non-repeating stop codes after a recent RAM upgrade. What should you try first?

A. Replace the motherboard with a new compatible model and then reinstall the operating system
B. Reseat or swap the new RAM modules, testing each module individually for stability and errors
C. Reinstall the video driver from the manufacturer's website to rule out graphics-related issues
D. Replace the CPU with a known-good processor and retest the system for further blue-screen errors

Question 5: A desktop powers on, you hear a repeating beep code, and there is no video output. The manufacturer's documentation says this pattern indicates a memory problem. What is your best next step?

A. Replace the power supply immediately with a known-good unit and then attempt to boot the system
B. Reinstall the operating system from recovery media to correct any corrupted system files
C. Disable onboard video in BIOS/UEFI and install a dedicated graphics card for video output
D. Power down, reseat the RAM modules, and test with one known-good DIMM installed at a time

Question 6: When troubleshooting a system that will not POST, you decide to use a "minimal boot configuration." Which of the following sets of components best describes this configuration?

A. Motherboard, CPU, RAM, all storage drives, and all installed expansion cards and peripherals
B. Motherboard, CPU with cooler, single RAM stick, PSU, and basic video output if the platform requires it
C. Motherboard, CPU, RAM, GPU, and all USB peripherals such as keyboard, mouse, and external drives
D. PSU, primary storage drive, and network card only, with all other components temporarily removed

Question 7: A user's PC fails to boot and displays "No boot device found." In BIOS/UEFI, the primary drive is not listed at all. What is the first, least invasive step you should take?

A. Power down the system and reseat the drive's data and power cables securely on both ends
B. Immediately replace the drive with a new unit and restore all user data from a recent backup
C. Run CHKDSK from Windows Recovery Environment to repair potential file system corruption
D. Change the boot mode from UEFI to Legacy in BIOS/UEFI and then attempt to boot again

Question 8: A system was recently moved to a new desk. Now it displays "Operating System not found," but in BIOS the SSD is not detected. You visually inspect the inside of the case. What should you do next?

A. Rebuild the boot loader using bootrec commands from Windows installation or recovery media
B. Reseat the SATA data and power connectors to the SSD and verify they are firmly attached
C. Perform a full low-level format of the SSD using the manufacturer's diagnostic utilities
D. Replace the motherboard's SATA controller by installing a new board or add-in controller card

Question 9: A technician installs a new 2 TB SATA drive as a data disk. The BIOS detects the drive, but Windows does not show it in File Explorer. In Disk Management, the drive appears as "Disk 2 – Unknown, Not Initialized" with all space unallocated. What should the technician do?

A. Replace the drive, as it is clearly defective and not usable by the operating system
B. Run CHKDSK /F against Disk 2 to attempt to repair any existing file system errors
C. Initialize the disk in Disk Management, create a new partition, and format it with a file system
D. Enable SMART monitoring in BIOS to track the drive's health and predict potential failures

Question 10: A three-disk RAID 5 array in a small office server shows as "Degraded" in the RAID management utility, with one disk marked as failed. All data is still available. Which of the following actions is most appropriate?

A. Delete and recreate the RAID 5 array from scratch, then restore all data from a verified backup
B. Verify current backups, replace the failed disk with a compatible one, and allow the array to rebuild
C. Add a fourth drive to the system and convert the existing array to RAID 10 for higher redundancy
D. Immediately power off the system and leave it offline until a vendor engineer can arrive onsite

Question 11: A high-performance workstation uses a two-disk RAID 0 array for speed. One of the disks fails and the array is marked as "Failed." What is the correct expectation and response?

A. Replace the failed disk and allow the RAID 0 array to rebuild automatically from the remaining disk
B. Run CHKDSK on the remaining disk to restore the striped volume and recover all user data
C. Convert the RAID 0 array to RAID 1 without data loss to regain redundancy and fault tolerance
D. Replace the failed disk, recreate the RAID 0 array, and restore all data from a recent backup

Question 12: After a BIOS update, a user's PC no longer boots into Windows and shows "No boot device found." In BIOS, the SATA mode has changed from RAID to AHCI. The disks are present but the array is missing. What should the technician try first?

A. Reinstall Windows on the first disk in AHCI mode and restore user data from backup copies
B. Initialize the disks in Disk Management and create new volumes to replace the missing array
C. Change the SATA mode back to RAID in BIOS/UEFI, save the settings, and reboot the system
D. Replace the RAID controller card with a new unit and then reconfigure the storage array

Question 13: A user's monitor shows "No Signal" even though the PC powers on, fans spin, and the power LED on the monitor is lit. Which of the following is the most likely and simplest cause to check next?

A. Corrupted operating system files preventing Windows from loading the desktop properly
B. Loose or incorrectly connected video cable, or the wrong input source selected on the monitor
C. Failed CPU that prevents the system from executing any instructions or displaying video
D. Bad RAM causing POST errors that always result in a "No Signal" message on the monitor

Question 14: A user connects their desktop to a new LCD monitor. The image appears stretched and slightly blurry, and text is not sharp. What is the best way to correct this?

A. Set the display resolution in the operating system to match the monitor's native resolution setting
B. Replace the video card with one that supports higher resolutions and additional display outputs
C. Reduce the refresh rate to 30 Hz so the monitor can more easily scale the incoming video signal
D. Enable night light mode and increase contrast to improve the clarity and readability of text

Question 15: A projector shows "No Signal" while a laptop displays the desktop on its own screen. The HDMI cable is firmly connected to both devices, and the projector is on. What should the technician have the user do on the laptop first?

A. Update the projector firmware to the latest version to improve compatibility with the laptop
B. Press Windows key + P and select Duplicate or Extend display mode to enable the external output
C. Boot the laptop into Safe Mode to load minimal drivers and test basic video functionality
D. Lower the laptop screen's brightness to encourage output to the external projector instead

Question 16: A gamer reports colored artifacts and random horizontal lines on the screen even during the motherboard POST logo, which worsen after a few minutes of use. Which of the following is the most appropriate first hardware-focused step?

A. Reinstall the operating system to eliminate any potential software or driver corruption issues
B. Power down, open the case, check that the GPU is fully seated, and ensure its fan and heatsink are clean
C. Lower the screen resolution to 800×600 to reduce the load on the graphics subsystem and monitor
D. Replace the monitor with a different display to rule out a defective LCD panel or backlight issue

Question 17: A user's phone "won't charge." You test the phone with your known-good charger and cable, and it begins charging immediately. What is the most likely problem?

A. Failed internal battery that can no longer hold a charge even when connected to external power
B. Faulty motherboard power circuitry that prevents the device from accepting any charging current
C. User's original charger or cable is defective and not providing proper power to the smartphone
D. Corrupted charging firmware that must be reflashed before the battery can charge correctly

Question 18: A user complains that their phone's battery drains very quickly and the device becomes hot even when idle. In the battery usage screen, one recently installed app shows unusually high background usage. What is the most appropriate next step?

A. Replace the phone's battery with a new one to restore normal capacity and operating temperature
B. Perform a factory reset immediately to wipe the device and reinstall the mobile operating system
C. Disable or uninstall the problematic app and then retest the phone's battery life and temperature
D. Put the phone in airplane mode permanently so that wireless radios do not consume any power

ANSWERS

1: Correct Answer: B

Rationale: With a completely dead system, start with the simplest external power check. Verifying the outlet or power strip with a known-good device is quick and non-invasive. Replacing internal components or pulling the motherboard (A, C, D) is premature before confirming basic power.

2: Correct Answer: A

Rationale: The outlet itself has no power, so you should check for a wall switch or tripped breaker controlling that outlet and restore power. Replacing the PSU (B), booting from USB (C), or reseating RAM (D) will not fix a dead circuit.

3: Correct Answer: B

Rationale: On new builds, "fans spin, no POST, no video" is often caused by a missing or loose 4-/8-pin CPU power connector. Verifying this connector is a simple, targeted next step. Reinstalling the OS (A) is irrelevant without POST, and replacing the GPU (C) or clearing CMOS (D) is less likely.

4: Correct Answer: B

Rationale: New, unstable RAM commonly causes varied blue screens. Reseating and testing each new module individually is the least invasive way to isolate a bad or incompatible stick. Replacing the motherboard (A) or CPU (D) is excessive, and video drivers (C) are unlikely given the timing.

5: Correct Answer: D

Rationale: The beep code explicitly indicates memory trouble. Powering down, reseating RAM, and testing with one known-good DIMM is the correct next step. Replacing the PSU (A), reinstalling the OS (B), or changing video settings (C) does not address the indicated memory fault.

6: Correct Answer: B

Rationale: A minimal boot configuration uses only components required for POST: motherboard, CPU with cooler, one RAM stick, PSU, and basic video if needed. Including all drives and cards (A, C) defeats the purpose, and PSU plus drive only (D) cannot POST.

7: Correct Answer: A

Rationale: A drive missing from BIOS is often due to a loose data or power cable. Reseating these cables is quick and non-destructive. Immediately replacing the drive (B), running CHKDSK (C), or changing boot mode (D) is premature before confirming connectivity.

8: Correct Answer: B

Rationale: Moving a system can loosen SATA or power connectors. If the SSD is no longer detected in BIOS, reseating its data and power connectors is the logical first step. Boot loader repair (A) or formatting (C) require the drive to be detected, and replacing the controller (D) is far more invasive.

9: Correct Answer: C

Rationale: A new disk showing as "Unknown, Not Initialized" with unallocated space simply needs initialization, partitioning, and formatting before Windows can use it. Replacing the drive (A) is unnecessary, CHKDSK (B) is for existing file systems, and SMART (D) is for health monitoring.

10: Correct Answer: B

Rationale: A degraded RAID 5 array with one failed disk still has data but no redundancy. Verify backups, replace the failed disk, and let the array rebuild. Deleting and recreating the array (A) is unnecessary, and adding drives or powering off indefinitely (C, D) does not resolve the failed disk.

11: Correct Answer: D
Rationale: RAID 0 has no redundancy; if one disk fails, all data in the array is lost. Replace the failed disk, recreate the array, and restore from backup. RAID 0 cannot rebuild from a single disk (A), CHKDSK (B) cannot restore a broken stripe, and you cannot convert RAID 0 to RAID 1 without data loss (C).

12: Correct Answer: C
Rationale: Changing SATA mode from RAID to AHCI can make an existing RAID array appear missing. Restoring the original RAID mode in BIOS/UEFI and rebooting often brings the array back. Reinstalling Windows (A), reinitializing disks (B), or replacing the controller (D) is unnecessary until this is tried.

13: Correct Answer: B
Rationale: "No Signal" with the monitor powered on usually means no valid video signal is reaching it, often due to a loose cable or wrong input selection. OS corruption (A), CPU failure (C), or RAM errors (D) can cause no boot, but the simplest, most common cause here is a connection/input issue.

14: Correct Answer: A
Rationale: A stretched, blurry image and fuzzy text on an LCD indicate it is not running at its native resolution. Setting the OS resolution to the monitor's native value corrects this. Replacing the video card (B), lowering refresh rate (C), or changing visual modes (D) does not address the root cause.

15: Correct Answer: B
Rationale: The laptop is likely only using its internal display. Pressing Windows key + P and choosing Duplicate or Extend enables output to the projector. Updating firmware (A), Safe Mode (C), or brightness changes (D) do not control external display usage.

16: Correct Answer: B
Rationale: Colored artifacts and lines appearing during POST indicate a likely graphics hardware issue, often caused by overheating, poor GPU seating, or failing VRAM. The most appropriate first step is to power down the system, reseat the graphics card, and ensure its cooling fan and heatsink are clean and functioning properly. Software reinstallations or resolution changes cannot affect POST-level display corruption.

17: Correct Answer: C
Rationale: If the phone charges normally with a known-good charger and cable, the most likely issue is the user's original charger or cable being defective. A failed battery (A) or motherboard power circuitry (B) would affect charging regardless of charger, and "charging firmware" (D) is not a typical field diagnosis.

18: Correct Answer: C
Rationale: High background usage and heat from a single recently installed app indicate that app is misbehaving. Disabling or uninstalling it and retesting is the least drastic, most targeted step. Replacing the battery (A) or factory resetting (B) is premature, and permanent airplane mode (D) is impractical.

Part II – Core 2 (220-1202)

Operating Systems, Security, Software Troubleshooting, and Operations

CHAPTER 6

Operating Systems

6.1 Operating System Types & Purposes

On a typical Monday morning at a help desk, you might see three tickets land almost at the same time. One user can't get a new USB printer to work with their Windows laptop. Another, working on a MacBook, is trying to access a shared folder on the company server and keeps seeing a strange authentication prompt. A third is a manager with a company-issued iPhone who wants to install an Android-only app they found online. Technically, these sound like separate problems: a printer issue, a file-sharing issue, and an app installation issue. In reality, they all revolve around the same core element: the operating system.

The **operating system**—the OS—is the fundamental layer of software that sits between hardware and applications. It decides how memory is used, how files are stored, how input and output devices are accessed, how users log in, and how programs talk to the network. When you troubleshoot anything in IT support, you are almost always interacting with the operating system, either directly or indirectly. Before you can be effective at solving problems or making recommendations, you need a clear mental map of the major OS families in use today, what they are designed for, and where their limitations lie. This chapter builds that map, so that in later chapters, when we zoom into Windows tools or macOS features or Linux commands, you already understand the "neighborhood" each one lives in.

Core Concepts Under Every OS

Despite all the branding and marketing around operating systems, the core job is remarkably similar across platforms. Every OS includes a **kernel**, the part that runs closest to the hardware and manages critical functions like process scheduling, memory management, and device access. On top of this kernel, the OS provides various interfaces. For users, the most visible is the graphical user interface, or **GUI**—the windows, icons, menus, and pointers you click and tap. There is almost always a **command-line interface** (CLI) as well, where you type instructions into a text-based shell. The balance between GUI and CLI varies: Windows heavily emphasizes GUI use but has command-line and PowerShell; Linux is perfectly happy as a text-only server; macOS combines a polished GUI with a full Unix-style terminal under the hood.

Another universal concept you will see repeatedly is system architecture, especially **32-bit versus 64-bit** operating systems. These terms describe, in part, how the CPU handles memory addresses and instructions. A 32-bit OS can address roughly 4 GB of RAM (and in practice often less), which was fine years ago but is a serious limitation today. A 64-bit OS can theoretically address far more memory than you will see in any desktop system and is now the standard. This distinction matters for compatibility: a 64-bit OS can usually run 32-bit applications through built-in compatibility layers, but a 32-bit OS generally cannot run 64-bit applications or 64-bit drivers. When you see a question about a user with an older 32-bit Windows system trying to install a "64-bit only" application or driver, you should immediately think about this architectural mismatch.

With these basic ideas in place—kernel versus interface, GUI versus CLI, and 32-bit versus 64-bit—you can start to categorize the major OS families you will support.

Desktop Operating Systems: The "Big Four"

Most of the time, when you think of a computer OS, you are thinking about a **desktop or client operating system**: the software a user interacts with on a laptop or workstation. In modern environments, four families dominate this space: Windows, macOS, Linux, and ChromeOS. They all perform the same basic functions, but they live in very different ecosystems and are chosen for different reasons.

Microsoft **Windows** is still the dominant desktop OS in business environments. It runs on hardware from many vendors, as well as on custom-built PCs, and supports an enormous range of applications and peripherals. A big reason Windows remains so common in organizations is backward compatibility: many companies rely on older, line-of-business applications that were written for earlier versions of Windows, and rewriting or replacing those applications is expensive. Windows also ties deeply into Microsoft's ecosystem—Active Directory for centralized authentication, Group Policy for configuration management, and cloud services such as OneDrive and Microsoft 365. As an entry-level support technician, a large share of your tickets will be for Windows client systems: installing or updating software, resolving driver and printing issues, handling malware infections, or troubleshooting domain logon problems. Later chapters in this book devote significant space to Windows for that reason.

Apple **macOS** occupies a different niche. It is a Unix-based OS that only runs, officially, on Apple hardware: MacBook Airs and Pros, iMacs, Mac minis, Mac Studio systems. This tight integration of hardware and software is a hallmark of Apple's approach. macOS is deeply tied into the Apple ecosystem: iCloud for storage and syncing, Handoff and Continuity for moving tasks between devices, iMessage and FaceTime for communication. You see macOS heavily in creative fields such as graphic design, video editing, and music production, and also among executives and managers who simply prefer Apple devices. From a support perspective, the limited hardware configurations mean fewer driver headaches than with Windows, but you must learn different terminology and workflows: users open Finder instead of File Explorer, use the Dock and Launchpad instead of the Windows Start menu, and search with Spotlight. In many organizations, macOS and Windows clients coexist, which means you will frequently help Mac users connect to Windows-based file shares, printers, and authentication services.

Linux is not a single OS in the way Windows or macOS is; it is a kernel that underpins many **distributions** (distros) such as Ubuntu, Debian, Fedora, and others. These distros package the Linux kernel with different desktop environments, utilities, and package managers. Linux can be run as a full desktop OS with a GUI, or as a headless server with only a CLI, and it scales from tiny embedded devices to massive servers. In the desktop space, Linux is more common among technically savvy users, developers, and in organizations that value open source and customization. On the server side, Linux dominates web and application hosting, and it is the foundation of many network appliances and NAS devices. As a support tech, you may not administer large Linux servers at first, but you will almost certainly encounter Linux-based devices in the field and need to be comfortable with the idea that these systems might present only a web interface or SSH shell, not a familiar Windows-style GUI.

ChromeOS rounds out the desktop "big four" as a lightweight, cloud-centric OS primarily used on Chromebooks. Built by Google, ChromeOS is designed around the Chrome browser, with tight integration to Google accounts and Google Workspace. Most applications are web-based, with support for Android apps on many models and some limited Linux application support on newer devices. Local storage tends to be minimal; the expectation is that documents live in Google Drive and other cloud services. ChromeOS shines in education, where schools need hundreds or thousands of inexpensive, easy-to-manage laptops, and in environments where users' work is almost entirely web-based. From a support angle, you will not be dealing with the same driver and system-level issues as in Windows; instead, your work will gravitate toward Wi-Fi and connectivity problems, account syncing issues, browser behavior, and managing device enrollment into Google's management console.

Mobile Operating Systems: Phones and Tablets

The OS on a smartphone or tablet solves the same fundamental problems as a desktop OS, but under different constraints. **Mobile operating systems** must be optimized for touch input, variable network connectivity, battery life, and built-in sensors such as GPS, cameras, and accelerometers. They also introduce a more controlled application distribution model, generally through curated app stores, and tend to enforce strong sandboxing so apps cannot freely access each other's data.

Android is the most widely deployed mobile OS globally. It is based on the Linux kernel but heavily customized by Google and by manufacturers such as Samsung and others. This creates a highly diverse ecosystem: Android devices vary widely in screen size, CPU and memory, and manufacturer "skins" like Samsung's One UI or Google's Pixel UI. Apps are primarily distributed through the Google Play Store, but some vendors add their own stores, and users can, on many devices, enable "unknown sources" and sideload apps. This flexibility and openness can be powerful for business use—field service apps, barcode scanning, specialized industrial tablets—but it also increases variation and potential security risk. In support, you need to be comfortable navigating different layouts and menu names to do similar tasks: checking OS and app versions, managing permissions, clearing app caches, or configuring corporate email and VPN access.

Apple's **iOS** (for iPhone) and **iPadOS** (for iPad) represent a more closed, tightly controlled mobile environment. These operating systems run only on Apple hardware, and apps are normally installed exclusively from Apple's App Store. Apple manages updates centrally, enforces strict sandboxing and permissions, and ties devices strongly to an Apple ID and iCloud services. In business, you often see iPhones and iPads in executive suites, sales teams, healthcare environments, and education, where the stability and consistent behavior of the platform are highly valued. Support work in these ecosystems commonly involves managing Apple IDs and iCloud storage, enrolling devices in mobile device management (MDM) systems, pushing configuration profiles, and troubleshooting access to corporate Wi-Fi, VPN, and email. When a manager asks why they can't install an Android-only app on their iPhone, understanding that these are entirely different OS ecosystems—different binaries, different app stores, different security models—helps you explain the limitation clearly and suggest alternatives.

Server, Thin Client, and Embedded Operating Systems

So far, we have focused on user-facing OSs, but much of IT infrastructure runs on operating systems that end users never log into directly. **Server operating systems** such as Windows Server and various Linux server distros are designed to provide services to many clients at once: file and print sharing, web hosting, directory and authentication services, databases, and more. They are optimized for stability, scalability, and remote management rather than for a polished end-user GUI. In an entry-level role, you might not be responsible for installing or administering these systems, but you must understand that many desktop problems trace back to them. When a user cannot log into their Windows computer on the domain, the underlying issue may be with a Windows Server domain controller or an LDAP service on a Linux system. If a shared folder suddenly becomes unavailable, the NAS or file server OS is a likely suspect.

In some environments, rather than giving each user a full, powerful PC, organizations deploy **thin clients** that run a very minimal OS—sometimes a stripped-down Linux, sometimes a locked-down Windows variant, sometimes a proprietary thin client OS. These endpoints handle basic input/output and network connectivity, but the actual desktop the user sees is running elsewhere, in a **Virtual Desktop Infrastructure** (VDI) or remote desktop session on a server. This centralizes management and can reduce hardware costs, since thin clients can be relatively low power. As a technician, you need to separate problems into two layers: if a user cannot even reach the login screen of the virtual desktop, the issue might be with the thin client device, its firmware, or local network. If they can connect but applications are slow or crashing, the issue is more likely within the server-side OS hosting the virtual desktops.

Another important category is **embedded and appliance operating systems**. These are OSs built into single-purpose or limited-purpose devices: routers, firewalls, smart TVs, industrial controllers, IoT gadgets, NAS units, and so on. Often they are based on Linux or on a real-time operating system, but they present themselves to you through a web interface, a dedicated management application, or a command-line over SSH or a serial console. Users rarely, if ever, see a desktop on these systems. Updates for these devices are usually called firmware updates rather than OS upgrades, but conceptually you are often updating the underlying operating system image. When someone reports, "The internet is down" or "Our shared storage is offline," your troubleshooting may lead you into these embedded OSs, where you will check interface status, logs, or configuration settings through whatever management interface they provide.

6.2 OS Installations, Upgrades & Deployment Methods

When most people think of "fixing computers," they picture exactly what this chapter is about: installing or upgrading an operating system and bringing a machine back to life. In reality, that process is less about clicking "Next" a bunch of times and more about planning, risk management, and choosing the right method for the situation. In a professional environment, you almost never "just reinstall Windows" without thinking carefully about data, downtime, licensing, and how this change fits into the bigger IT picture. An OS installation is a planned change, not a casual button press.

You will see OS installs and upgrades across the entire lifecycle of a device. A brand-new desktop arrives from the vendor and needs to be set up with the correct edition of Windows and company applications. A five-year-old laptop is being repurposed from engineering to sales and needs a clean slate. A drive fails and must be replaced, leaving you to reinstall the OS from scratch. A company decides to move from Windows 10 to Windows 11 across the organization. In every one of these situations, your technical skills matter, but so does your judgment about which installation or deployment method makes sense.

Before you touch installation media or change any firmware settings, you should develop the habit of pausing and planning. At a minimum, this means checking that the target hardware can actually support the OS you're considering, that you understand how the current data and applications will be handled, and that you know how much downtime is acceptable. Hardware compatibility is an obvious starting point. For a modern Windows client, that includes verifying CPU capabilities, the amount of RAM, available storage, and whether the graphics and other components have drivers for the target OS. The CompTIA A+ exam will not ask you to quote specific gigabyte numbers, but it does expect you to recognize that attempting to install a 64-bit Windows 11 on a system with 2 GB of RAM and no TPM is a non-starter.

That leads naturally into the distinction between **32-bit and 64-bit operating systems**, which remains important conceptually even though most new systems are 64-bit only. A 32-bit OS can only directly address around 4 GB of RAM and requires 32-bit drivers. A 64-bit OS can use much more memory and is the norm in business environments, but it needs 64-bit drivers and may not run very old 16-bit applications at all. When you are planning an installation or upgrade, you do not just pick 64-bit automatically; you ask whether the CPU supports it, whether the RAM amount justifies it, and whether any legacy software needs to be preserved. In most modern Windows scenarios, a 64-bit edition is the right answer, but the exam wants you to be aware of these trade-offs.

Also in the planning phase is a basic understanding of Windows editions and licensing. We will go into more detail on edition differences in the next section, but you should already know that Windows Home and Pro are aimed at different use cases. If a small business wants to join devices to an Active Directory domain and use features like BitLocker drive encryption, Windows 11 Home is not sufficient. That becomes a licensing and edition decision you must resolve before you decide on your installation path. An in-place upgrade from Home to Pro using a product key change might be fine for a single machine, but for twenty-five devices it may be more efficient to re-image them with a standard Pro image.

Data and applications bring another layer of constraints. You should always ask yourself: what data must be preserved, and how is it backed up? If a user has critical documents only on the local drive and no backup, you must treat that system differently from a machine where all data lives in a central file server or cloud storage. Some line-of-business applications may only support older versions of Windows or require complex licensing that is painful to reinstall. Those realities might rule out a clean install in favor of an upgrade or migration that preserves applications. It is this blend of technical and business thinking that turns you from a "reinstaller" into a real support professional.

Once you have that big-picture context, you can start choosing between the main types of installations. A **clean installation** is the most drastic but also the simplest from the OS perspective: you wipe the existing OS partition (and in many cases the entire disk) and install a fresh copy of Windows. This is the right choice when the system is heavily infected with malware, when the OS is so corrupted that repair tools fail, or when you are repurposing a machine and want no trace of the previous user. It is also often recommended when moving between major Windows versions, such as from an older, heavily modified Windows 10 to a fresh Windows 11, to avoid carrying forward years of accumulated problems. The downside is obvious: unless user data has been backed up and applications are well-documented, a clean install can cause data loss and a lot of user frustration. On the exam, any scenario that emphasizes "must preserve local data" should make you think very carefully before choosing a clean install.

An **in-place upgrade** takes almost the opposite approach. Here, you run the installation from within the existing OS, and the setup program attempts to upgrade to a newer version or edition while preserving user data, installed applications, and most settings. Upgrading from Windows 10 to Windows 11 on the same hardware, or from Windows 11 Home to Pro, are classic in-place upgrade scenarios. This method minimizes downtime and user disruption, which is attractive both in real life and on exam questions. However, the trade-off is that any underlying problems—registry corruption, misconfigurations, leftover malware—may be carried forward. An in-place upgrade can also fail partway through due to compatibility issues, in which case Windows will usually roll back to the previous version, but you may have lost valuable time.

There is also a middle-ground technique sometimes called a **repair installation** or repair upgrade, where you reinstall the same version of Windows over itself using installation media or recovery tools. The goal here is not to move to a new version but to repair missing or corrupt system files while leaving user data intact. This can help when the OS is unstable but still mostly bootable. You'll see this idea again when we dive deeper into Windows troubleshooting, but for now understand that repair installs are about fixing, not replacing, the current OS.

Beyond single-OS scenarios, you will occasionally support users who need to run two operating systems on the same hardware. A **multi-boot** or **dual-boot** configuration lets the user choose at startup between, for example, Windows and Linux. This is useful for developers, IT staff, or anyone who relies on software that only runs on a specific OS. Setting up a dual-boot requires careful partitioning of the disk so that each OS has its own volume, and you must be mindful of boot loaders and user confusion ("I installed my program, but I can't find it"—because they logged into the wrong OS). Alternatively, you might install an OS inside a **virtual machine**, where the "install" happens within virtualization software instead of on the physical hardware. That approach is especially valuable for testing, running older OS versions, or isolating risky software without affecting the host system.

Once you have decided on the type of install, the next challenge is simply convincing the machine to start the installer. Modern Windows installations typically begin from a bootable USB flash drive, from a DVD on older systems, from a virtual ISO image attached to a virtual machine, or from a network server using PXE (Preboot Execution Environment). Conceptually, creating a bootable USB involves downloading the vendor's ISO image and using a tool to write it to the USB in a way that makes it bootable, not just copying the file. When a system refuses to boot from your USB, the problem is often one of three things: the USB was not actually made bootable, the firmware boot order is still trying the internal drive first, or the firmware is in a mode (UEFI vs Legacy/CSM) that does not match how the USB was created.

Understanding firmware is essential here. A computer's **BIOS or UEFI** firmware controls which devices it tries to boot from and in what order. You typically access this setup with a key like F2, Del, F10, or Esc during startup, but the exact key varies by manufacturer. For a one-time installation, you might use a temporary boot menu to select USB without permanently changing the boot order. Modern systems also use Secure Boot, a UEFI feature that only allows signed, trusted bootloaders to run. If you try to boot an unsigned OS or older imaging tool, Secure Boot may block it until you adjust the firmware settings, which should always be done in line with your organization's security policies.

In larger environments, instead of relying on local media, you often see **PXE/network boot**. In this model, the PC is configured to boot from the network, contacts a deployment server, and receives either a full OS image or access to the standard installer over the network. This is the backbone of many corporate imaging systems and is a common answer to scenario questions involving dozens or hundreds of identical machines.

Once the installer is running, almost every Windows setup walks you through some variation of the same core decisions. One of the most important is where to install the OS, which means understanding disks and partitions. The installer will list available drives and existing partitions. Deleting a partition really does delete its data; there is no recycle bin at this level. On systems that have been previously used, you may see multiple partitions: the main Windows volume, a recovery partition, and on UEFI systems, an EFI System Partition. Novice technicians sometimes delete everything out of impatience and end up wiping out important recovery tools or a second OS. A clean installation onto an entirely new drive is straightforward; installing alongside an existing OS for dual-boot requires you to either use free space or shrink an existing partition to make room.

Underlying those partitions is the **partition style**, which for Windows is either MBR (Master Boot Record) or GPT (GUID Partition Table). The A+ exam expects you to know that GPT is the modern standard, supports larger disks and more partitions, and is required by UEFI for certain secure boot configurations, while MBR is older, supports fewer primary partitions, and has lower size limits. You do not need to memorize the exact terabyte limits, but you should recognize that new UEFI-based Windows installations will typically use GPT by default. On top of partitions, you must choose a file system. For Windows system volumes, **NTFS** is the default and almost always the correct choice on the exam, because it supports large files, permissions, and many security features. **FAT32** and **exFAT** show up more often on removable drives and simple storage devices; they lack the security capabilities needed for a Windows system partition and are not suitable choices for installing the OS.

So far we have been talking as if you are installing one machine at a time. In a home or very small office, that is often the reality. But if you are rolling out or refreshing dozens of systems, manually repeating the same steps is inefficient and prone to mistakes. This is where **unattended installations** and **image-based deployments** come into play. An unattended installation uses an answer file—essentially a configuration script—that preanswers the installer's questions about language, product keys, partitioning, and so on. Instead of a technician clicking "Next" and typing the same information over and over, the system reads the answer file and runs through most of the process automatically. Your role then shifts to creating and maintaining those answer files, and troubleshooting when the installer encounters a situation the file did not anticipate, such as unexpected disk layouts or missing drivers.

An even more powerful approach is **imaging**, sometimes called cloning. In this model, you build a single "golden" reference machine: install the correct edition of Windows, apply updates, install standard applications, configure settings and security baselines, but avoid machine-specific items like unique names or domain memberships until after deployment. You then capture that configured system as an image and deploy it to other identical or similar hardware using imaging tools, often over the network with PXE or from bootable media. This technique can turn a two-hour manual install into a 15-minute imaging process, which is exactly why exam scenarios involving "25 identical new desktops" almost always point toward imaging or unattended installations rather than configuring each device by hand.

Modern environments increasingly blend on-premises imaging with **cloud-based deployment**. For example, a device might come with a basic OEM Windows image but, once connected to the internet and enrolled in a cloud management platform, it automatically downloads corporate policies, applications, and configuration profiles. Some vendors offer cloud recovery or reset options where the OS image itself is pulled from the internet instead of local recovery partitions. From an A+ perspective, you do not have to be an expert in specific cloud tools, but you should be comfortable with the idea that your job may be to get the base OS installed, ensure network connectivity, enroll the device in the organization's management system, and then let the cloud finish the customization.

After installation, your work is not done. A freshly installed OS is more like a bare chassis than a finished car. You must verify that all hardware devices have appropriate drivers, paying particular attention to network, storage, and chipset drivers. If Device Manager shows unknown or malfunctioning devices, you may need to install manufacturer-supplied drivers before the system is fully usable. Once the system is online, running Windows Update to pull down the latest patches is not optional; it is a security requirement. You also need to check activation status, since unactivated Windows installations have functional and compliance limitations. In a business network, joining the machine to the correct workgroup or domain is essential so that it can receive group policies and access shared resources.

Security and user readiness are the final pieces. You should confirm that the Windows firewall is enabled, that antivirus or endpoint protection is installed and active, and that user accounts and permissions are set appropriately for the person who will use the system. If this was an upgrade or a reinstall on a user's existing machine, restoring their data from backup and reinstalling their required applications is critical. Before you walk away or close the ticket, it is good practice to have the user log in and verify that they can open their critical applications, access network shares and printers, and generally do their work. That quick "user acceptance" step often catches configuration gaps that a purely technical checklist might miss.

Of course, not every installation or upgrade goes smoothly. Installation media that will not boot often points you back to basics: confirm that the USB is truly bootable, that the firmware boot order and mode match your media, and that you are not fighting Secure Boot unintentionally. When setup refuses to continue because there is not enough disk space, or the CPU or TPM does not meet requirements, your only options are to change the hardware, free up space, or choose a different OS path—the installer is enforcing real constraints. And when an in-place upgrade fails and rolls back repeatedly, the professional response is not to keep trying the same thing, but to reassess: consider backing up data and performing a clean install, or investigating known compatibility blocks. Throughout these situations, the troubleshooting methodology you learned earlier still applies: identify the problem clearly, form a theory, test it, take action, verify the result, and document what you did so the next technician—and the future you—understands the history of that system.

6.3 Windows Editions & Feature Differences

If you ask most users what version of Windows they run, they'll often say "Windows 10" or "Windows 11" and leave it at that. From a support perspective, that answer is only half useful. For you as a technician, the more important question is, "Which **edition** of Windows 10 or 11 is installed?" The edition quietly decides what you can and cannot do on that system. It determines whether you can join it to a domain, encrypt its drive with BitLocker, manage it with Group Policy, host a Remote Desktop session, or run Hyper-V virtual machines. Two machines can look almost identical on the surface, but if one is running Home and the other Pro, your troubleshooting and configuration options are very different.

This chapter focuses on those desktop client editions you're most likely to see in the field: Home, Pro, Enterprise, and Education, mostly in their Windows 10 and Windows 11 forms. Windows Server has its own world of editions and roles, which we cover elsewhere; here we stay with end-user systems—laptops and desktops on desks and in backpacks. The CompTIA A+ exam expects you to recognize which features belong to which editions and, more importantly, to reason from business or user requirements to an appropriate edition. That's a different mindset from just memorizing a table of checkmarks. You're learning to think, "This organization needs centralized control and full-disk encryption, therefore they cannot run Home here," and to spot edition limitations during troubleshooting instead of chasing phantom bugs.

One Brand, Several Personalities

Modern Windows is really a **family of editions** that share the same basic interface and core components but are packaged for different types of customers. On one end, you have **Windows Home**, aimed at individual consumers who buy a laptop from a retail store or an online seller and just want to browse, stream, game, and do a bit of productivity work. On the other, you have **Windows Enterprise** and **Windows Education**, generally not sold as individual licenses, but delivered to large organizations and schools under volume licensing and managed by centralized IT departments. In between sits **Windows Pro**, which is the workhorse edition for small and medium businesses and many corporate environments that don't require every single advanced enterprise feature.

As a technician, you often first encounter this question indirectly. A user calls in and says, "My manager told me to enable BitLocker, but I can't find it anywhere," or "The instructions say to run gpedit.msc, but Windows can't find it." In these cases, you're not dealing with a misconfigured setting; you're hitting an edition wall. The system may be functioning exactly as designed for that edition. Your job is to recognize that, confirm the edition, and then either propose an upgrade path or an alternative solution. That's why becoming fluent in the differences between Windows editions is such a practical skill.

There is also a special twist you'll see occasionally: **Windows in S Mode**, such as Windows 11 Home in S Mode. S Mode isn't a separate edition in the same way that Home and Pro are; it's more like a locked-down operating state. When a system is in S Mode, it can only run apps from the Microsoft Store and is forced to use Microsoft Edge and some built-in security constraints. This matters because it sharply limits what you can install and troubleshoot. A user who says, "I can't install Chrome" or "The installer just won't run" might not be dealing with malware or broken permissions at all—they may simply be stuck in S Mode.

Home, Pro, Enterprise, and Education in Practice

It helps to think of each major edition in terms of who it was built for and what assumptions Microsoft made about how it will be used. **Windows Home** assumes a non-managed, standalone environment. The person buying this machine is not an IT department. They are not cloning standardized images, joining Active Directory domains, or deploying Group Policy objects. Windows Home still gives them the core Windows experience: familiar desktop, Windows Defender Antivirus, Windows Firewall, Windows Update, and support for local and Microsoft accounts. But Microsoft deliberately leaves out many of the tools you need for centralized management, enterprise security integration, or advanced virtualization. For most home users this is fine; they'd never touch those features anyway.

Move up to **Windows Pro**, and the assumptions change. Now Microsoft expects that many of these PCs will live in a business setting. They may be joined to an on-premises Active Directory domain or to Azure Active Directory. An IT team may be pushing policies to them and deploying software. Users may need to encrypt their drives in case of theft, connect into their work machines remotely, or run local virtual machines for testing. So Pro builds on Home by enabling those "professional" capabilities: domain join, Group Policy, BitLocker, Remote Desktop hosting, and Hyper-V, among others. When you see a small office with a server and a few dozen desktops, or a consultant with a laptop full of client data, Windows Pro is typically the baseline.

Above Pro you find **Windows Enterprise** and **Windows Education**. Functionally, you can think of these as "Pro plus more enterprise controls." They include everything in Pro, but add additional security, management, and deployment tools aimed at large networks—hundreds or thousands of endpoints rather than a handful. Features can include things like AppLocker for advanced application control, enterprise data protection, and deep integration with advanced Microsoft security and management platforms. For the A+ exam, you are not expected to memorize every unique Enterprise-only feature. It is more important to grasp the pattern: when a scenario talks about a large organization with centralized IT, strict compliance requirements, and volume licensing, Enterprise or Education is implied. When you need all of Pro's features plus even tighter control and reporting, those editions become the right choice.

The Education edition mirrors Enterprise closely but is licensed and sometimes slightly tuned for academic environments, such as school computer labs or student-issued laptops. From your perspective as a support technician, you can generally treat Enterprise and Education as functionally similar: they have at least the capabilities of Pro, often with additional centralized management possibilities.

Sitting slightly sideways to these is **S Mode**. Think of S Mode as a security and manageability shell around Home or Pro. Its purpose is to reduce the attack surface by eliminating traditional Win32 desktop apps and limiting users to Microsoft Store apps, which Microsoft can vet and sandbox more tightly. In schools, this helps keep students from installing games or malware. In some small businesses, it reduces support overhead. But for you, it presents a special kind of troubleshooting: if a user on Windows 11 Home in S Mode wants to install a traditional VPN client or a vendor's custom desktop software, they simply can't until the system is switched out of S Mode—a one-way operation that permanently converts it to standard Home or Pro behavior.

Key Business Features and Where They Live

Rather than trying to memorize a big comparison grid, it's more effective to link specific needs to specific features, and then to the minimum edition that supports those features. There is a simple mental shortcut that works well for the exam and for real life: the cluster of **domain join**, **BitLocker**, **Hyper-V**, and **Remote Desktop host**. If someone needs any of these, you need at least Pro.

Domain join is the starting point. In a workgroup, each Windows PC manages its own local accounts and settings. In a domain, user accounts and many security settings live in a centralized directory, most commonly Active Directory. A domain-joined PC can authenticate users against that directory and receive policies and login scripts from domain controllers. **Windows Home cannot join an on-premises Active Directory domain.** It also cannot be fully joined and managed the same way by Azure AD as Pro or higher can. By contrast, **Windows Pro, Enterprise, and Education** are all designed to join domains and participate in centralized authentication and management. When you see a scenario describing a company with domain controllers, group policies, and roaming user profiles, that environment assumes Pro or higher on the client side.

Connected with domain environments is **Group Policy**. Group Policy is the framework that lets IT administrators centrally enforce configuration settings across many computers and users: password complexity rules, lock screen timers, software restrictions, desktop wallpaper, firewall configuration, and much more. On a domain, Group Policy Objects are applied from the server side. Pro, Enterprise, and Education systems can both host a **Local Group Policy Editor** and process domain-based group policies. Home, on the other hand, does not include the normal Local Group Policy Editor, and even if you manage to hack something together, it is not intended to participate in domain Group Policy the way Pro machines do. So if you're asked to "configure a password complexity policy using Group Policy" on a standalone Home PC, the technically correct answer may be that this edition doesn't support what the manager is asking; you'd recommend an upgrade to Pro or a different management approach.

Security of data at rest is covered by **BitLocker**, Microsoft's full-disk encryption technology. BitLocker encrypts the entire drive, usually tying the encryption keys to a Trusted Platform Module (TPM) chip, so if the device is lost or stolen, the data remains unreadable without proper credentials. Full BitLocker is available in Pro, Enterprise, and Education editions. Some Home systems may show a feature called "device encryption" if the hardware supports it, but for exam purposes and practical support work, you should treat Home as lacking the full BitLocker feature set and central manageability. This matters in scenarios where a business laptop contains sensitive customer information: company policy may require that all such laptops run Windows Pro or higher specifically so BitLocker can be enabled and managed through Group Policy or mobile device management tools.

Remote access is another frequent point of confusion. Every modern Windows edition includes the **Remote Desktop client**, which lets you connect out to another system that is offering a Remote Desktop session. But the ability to be that host—that is, to accept incoming Remote Desktop Protocol (RDP) connections—is restricted. **Only Pro, Enterprise, and Education can act as Remote Desktop hosts.** Home editions cannot host standard RDP remote sessions; they can participate in more limited Remote Assistance scenarios, but that's not the same as RDP hosting. So if a user wants to leave their office desktop on and connect into it from home using Remote Desktop, that office desktop must be running at least Windows Pro.

Then there is **Hyper-V**, Microsoft's built-in hypervisor for running virtual machines. Hyper-V is useful for developers, IT pros, and power users who need to test software, run multiple operating systems, or create isolated lab environments. Hyper-V is available on Pro, Enterprise, and Education editions, provided the underlying hardware supports virtualization extensions and has enough resources. On Home, Hyper-V simply isn't there—the user must rely on third-party virtualization tools, if those will run on their edition. In a troubleshooting situation where someone insists they turned on hardware virtualization in the BIOS but still can't find Hyper-V in Windows Features, checking for Home edition is a key step.

Enterprise and Education also stack on additional **business security and management enhancements**. You'll hear about things like AppLocker, DirectAccess, advanced device guard features, and integration with enterprise-grade management platforms. You don't need to become a product catalog; what matters is recognizing that advanced, large-scale, or highly regulated environments usually lean on Enterprise or Education because Pro alone may not provide the granularity of control or the compliance reporting they require.

Finally, there is the quieter but important area of **update and deployment control**. Home systems have relatively limited options for deferring or fine-tuning Windows Update behavior. Users can choose reboot times and pause updates for short periods, but they can't easily participate in centrally scheduled update rings. Pro and higher editions introduce features such as Windows Update for Business and Group Policy settings that can defer feature updates, set patching schedules, and coordinate deployments across many machines. When a scenario describes an organization wanting to test patches on a pilot group before rolling them out broadly, or to prevent feature updates from immediately hitting all production machines, that is another subtle hint that Pro or above is required.

Matching Editions to Real-World Needs

When you put all these features together, the differences in editions start to feel less like a memorization exercise and more like natural consequences of who the operating system was made for. A typical **home user** wants to browse, watch movies, write documents, store family photos, and maybe play some games. They are not required to comply with PCI-DSS or HIPAA. No one is centrally pushing policies to their machine. They don't need domain join, Hyper-V, or Remote Desktop hosting. Their threats are more about phishing, malware, and unstable freeware than about targeted corporate espionage. For this person, Windows Home is usually sufficient, and it's what they'll get by default when they buy a consumer laptop at retail.

Contrast that with a **small business office** that has a local file server and a domain controller. Employees log into any office PC with the same domain credentials. The business owner wants to enforce screen lock policies, require complex passwords, and prevent staff from changing network settings or installing random software. They also want to encrypt staff laptops in case of theft and occasionally connect to their workstations remotely. Those needs map directly to domain join, Group Policy, BitLocker, and Remote Desktop host. Based on that set of requirements, Windows Pro becomes the natural choice. If you see an exam question describing a "small office with a domain that wants to centrally manage group policies and use BitLocker on all laptops," and it asks which edition to deploy, Pro is the answer you should land on.

Now imagine a **national corporation** with thousands of endpoints across many sites, or a **university** managing labs and faculty laptops. Here, IT needs not only what Pro provides, but also advanced app control, integration with large-scale deployment tools, possibly strict regulatory compliance, and detailed security baselines. They might need to precisely restrict which software runs where, capture forensic data, or respond to threats in a coordinated way. They would almost certainly be using **Enterprise or Education** editions, obtained through volume licensing and deployed using corporate imaging and provisioning tools. When a scenario layers in language like "strict compliance requirements," "centralized IT operations," "volume licensing," or "thousands of devices," you should think of those top-tier enterprise editions.

S Mode adds a final nuance to these decision points. You might see S Mode in a **school** that hands out Windows 11 laptops to students and wants to prevent them from installing arbitrary applications or browsers. You could also see it in a very small business that bought low-cost devices preconfigured in S Mode and now finds that a critical line-of-business app will not install. Your support role in these cases is partly technical, partly advisory: you confirm that the system is in S Mode, explain that it only permits Microsoft Store apps and Edge, and discuss the implications of switching out of S Mode. Because that switch is one-way, and because it removes certain security constraints, organizations may have policies specifying when and how it may be done.

Spotting Edition Limits While Troubleshooting

On the job and in the exam, edition awareness becomes especially important when you are dealing with "missing" features. A user reports that there is no option to join a domain in their Settings, or that searching for "BitLocker" yields nothing, or that gpedit.msc isn't found, or that the Remote Desktop options don't let them enable incoming connections. Those are all classic signs that you should check the edition before diving deeper. Windows makes this easy: in Windows 10 and 11, you can open Settings, go to System, then About, and look under Windows specifications to see both the edition and version.

Once you know the edition, you mentally map the user's request to the needed feature set. If they want encryption, you think BitLocker and know that means Pro or higher. If they want centralized policy enforcement, you think Group Policy and domain join, again Pro or above. If they want to host Remote Desktop sessions, you recall that Home cannot act as an RDP host. If they ask for local virtualization with Hyper-V, you remember that Hyper-V is not a Home feature even when the CPU supports virtualization. When the required feature is clearly tied to an edition they do not have, your resolution may be recommending an upgrade rather than trying to force a configuration that the edition is not designed to support.

This mindset not only saves you time but also keeps your troubleshooting grounded. Instead of reinstalling features, running DISM scans, or assuming malware every time something seems "missing," you pause and ask whether the operating system is actually capable of what is being requested. Over time, you will find that patterns emerge: Home is home; it omits business-class capabilities. Pro is the professional baseline, adding business support. Enterprise and Education extend those capabilities into highly managed, large-scale deployments. And any time you see requirements involving domain join, BitLocker, Hyper-V, or Remote Desktop hosting, you know instinctively that you are in Pro-and-above territory, and that Windows Home is not going to meet the brief.

6.4 Windows GUI Tools & Administrative Utilities

When you start doing real desktop support, you quickly discover that users rarely say, "My Device Manager shows a driver problem" or "I think a service failed to start." They say things like "My computer is slow," "My new drive isn't there," or "This program keeps crashing." Bridging that gap is one of the core skills of an A+ technician: you hear a vague symptom and you immediately think, "Which Windows tool will show me what's really going on?" This chapter is about those tools—the graphical utilities that act as your instrument panel and toolkit for a Windows system.

You have already seen the broad Windows environment: the desktop, the Start menu, the Settings app, and the legacy Control Panel. Those are the user-facing pieces. The tools in this chapter sit just behind that layer. They don't replace the troubleshooting methodology you learned earlier; they support it. You still start with the symptom, form a theory, and test it. The difference is that now, instead of guessing in the dark, you can open a specific console that shows hardware health, disk layout, performance metrics, log entries, or startup configuration. Over time you will build an almost reflexive mapping in your head: performance complaint—open Task Manager; missing device—check Device Manager; missing partition—check Disk Management; intermittent crash—open Event Viewer.

Task Manager: Your First Performance Window

The most common GUI tool you will use is **Task Manager**, and it helps to think of it as your first-responder utility. When a user says, "Everything is frozen" or "This app won't close," the most efficient initial move is often to open Task Manager and see what the system is actually doing. You can launch it with Ctrl+Shift+Esc, through Ctrl+Alt+Delete and choosing Task Manager, or by right-clicking the taskbar or Start button depending on the Windows version.

On a newer system, Task Manager usually opens in a simplified view at first, just listing running apps. For real troubleshooting, you switch to the **More details** view, which exposes multiple tabs: Processes, Performance, App history, Startup, Users, Details, and Services. The Processes tab is where you spend most of your time. It shows running apps and background processes, along with their CPU, memory, disk, and network usage. Watching these columns in real time lets you see whether high CPU, memory pressure, or constant disk activity is behind a "my computer is slow" complaint. If you see one application marked "Not responding" and pegging the CPU at 99 percent, you have a concrete culprit instead of a vague feeling.

Ending a process from Task Manager is one of the few aggressive actions CompTIA expects you to know at this level. If a user's word processor is frozen and unsaved work is already gone, using End task to close the unresponsive process is reasonable. What you do not do is start randomly ending system processes you don't recognize. Part of maturing as a technician is learning to distinguish between safe, targeted actions—like ending a clearly frozen application or disabling a non-critical startup app—and dangerous guesswork.

Task Manager is also your quick window into system-wide performance. The Performance tab shows graphs for CPU, memory, disk, and network. If a system feels sluggish and you see memory usage hovering near 100 percent, that steers your theory toward "not enough RAM" or a memory-hungry application. If disk usage is constantly maxed out, you might suspect an indexing task, antivirus scan, or background process thrashing the drive. From that same Performance tab, a link opens **Resource Monitor**, which drills down into exactly which processes are hitting the disk or network hardest. We will come back to Resource Monitor shortly; for now, remember that Task Manager gives you the first snapshot, and Resource Monitor gives you more detail when the snapshot shows a problem.

One more Task Manager capability matters for the exam: startup control. In modern Windows, the **Startup** tab lists applications that run automatically when the user signs in, along with a "Startup impact" rating. When someone complains about very slow boot times or a desktop that takes minutes to become usable, you use this tab to identify unnecessary startup programs and disable them. This is much safer than randomly disabling Windows services, and it is exactly the kind of basic corrective action the A+ expects you to recognize.

Device Manager: Where Hardware Meets Drivers

If Task Manager is your first stop for performance, **Device Manager** is your first stop for hardware and driver issues. You reach it by right-clicking the Start button and choosing Device Manager, by searching for it, or via the Computer Management console. When it opens, you see a tree of hardware categories: Disk drives, Display adapters, Network adapters, Sound, video and game controllers, and many others.

The real value of Device Manager is that it shows you whether Windows recognizes a piece of hardware and whether its driver is working properly. Visual cues matter here. A device with a small yellow triangle and exclamation mark has a problem—often a missing, incompatible, or corrupted driver. A device that appears greyed out or with a down arrow is disabled. On older versions of Windows, you might see a red X instead. CompTIA loves to describe these icons in exam questions and ask which tool you are in or what they mean.

When you open a device's properties, you gain access to several key tabs. The General tab provides a high-level status message such as "This device is working properly" or an error code. The Driver tab allows you to update the driver, roll back to a previous version, disable or enable the device, or uninstall it. At the A+ level, you are expected to know that if a new driver causes problems—say the user updated a graphics driver and now gets crashes—you can use the Roll Back Driver option to revert to the prior version. Likewise, if a wireless adapter has "vanished" from the user's perspective, Device Manager is where you would confirm whether the adapter itself is disabled, has a driver issue, or is missing entirely.

It is important not to confuse Device Manager with Disk Management. Both can show you something related to a hard drive, but from completely different perspectives. Device Manager cares about the **device** and its **driver**.

Disk Management cares about how that device is carved up into partitions and volumes. If the scenario is "Windows does not see the network card," you think Device Manager. If it is "New hard drive is not visible in File Explorer," you think Disk Management.

Disk Management: Seeing Disks, Partitions, and Volumes

When a storage-related problem comes up—new drive not showing, drive letter missing, unallocated space—you switch to **Disk Management**. You can open it by right-clicking the Start button and choosing Disk Management or by launching the Computer Management console and selecting it from there. Disk Management gives you two coordinated views: an upper pane listing volumes and a lower graphical pane showing physical disks and their partitions.

Understanding the basic language of this tool is crucial. A **disk** is the physical device. A **partition** is a defined region on that disk. A **volume** is what Windows mounts and gives a drive letter or mount point, usually corresponding to a partition. In Disk Management, you will see disks labeled "Disk 0," "Disk 1," and so forth, with their statuses such as Online or Offline. Each partition or volume has its own status as well: Healthy, Unallocated, or possibly Failed. If a user adds a new second hard drive and it does not appear in File Explorer, Disk Management might show that disk as Online but with all space Unallocated. In that case, you would create a new simple volume, format it with an appropriate file system such as NTFS, and assign a drive letter.

Another frequent use is resolving drive letter conflicts. A user might plug in an external drive and expect it to appear as E:, but it doesn't show up at all. Disk Management might reveal that the system tried to assign a letter already in use by a mapped network drive. By right-clicking the volume and choosing Change Drive Letter and Paths, you can assign a different, unused letter and restore access. Being able to think, "Drive is visible in Device Manager, but not in File Explorer, so I need Disk Management for drive letter or formatting issues," is exactly the sort of reasoning the exam looks for.

Disk Management also allows tasks like extending or shrinking basic volumes, provided there is contiguous unallocated space in the right place, and marking a partition as Active for boot purposes. You do not need to become a storage architect for A+, but you should be comfortable reading this layout, recognizing normal "Healthy" statuses, and identifying obvious configuration issues such as unallocated disks or offline volumes.

Event Viewer and Reliability Monitor: History and Patterns

Some of the hardest problems to diagnose are intermittent ones. A system that reboots "every so often," an application that crashes "once in a while," or a service that "sometimes doesn't start" cannot be captured easily with a snapshot tool like Task Manager. This is where **Event Viewer** comes in. Event Viewer is Windows' central log viewer, tracking significant events over time. You open it by searching for "Event Viewer" or via Computer Management.

Inside Event Viewer, you will encounter several log groups, but for A+ purposes the most important are under Windows Logs: Application, Security, and System. Each log entry has a time, a source, an event ID, and a level such as Information, Warning, or Error. When investigating a crash that just occurred, you would typically open the System or Application log, filter or sort for Errors around the time of the incident, and then open those entries to read their details. You are not expected to memorize particular event IDs for the exam, but you are expected to know that Event Viewer is the right place to correlate a user's report ("It crashed at 3:15") with a logged error from a driver, service, or application at that time.

Event Viewer itself does not fix anything. It does, however, point you in the right direction. If you see repeated disk-related errors in the System log, your next steps might involve Disk Management, backups, and possibly hardware diagnostics. If you see that a particular service is failing to start with an error, you may move over to the Services console to inspect and adjust that service. CompTIA likes this hand-off thinking: use Event Viewer to gather evidence, then choose the next tool based on what you find.

Closely related is **Reliability Monitor**, which you can open by searching for "Reliability Monitor" or via the Security and Maintenance area in Control Panel. It presents a timeline of the system's stability, scoring each day and marking application failures, Windows failures, and other critical events on a graph. While Event Viewer is detailed and dense, Reliability Monitor is more visual and high-level. If a user says, "This started a few weeks ago," you can quickly see whether that period aligns with a particular Windows update, driver installation, or repeated application failure. On the exam, recognizing Reliability Monitor as the tool that shows a graphical history of crashes and changes can help you choose it over more generic-sounding options.

System Configuration and Services: Controlling Boot and Background Behavior

While startup applications are managed in Task Manager, deeper boot behavior and service configuration are handled through **System Configuration** and the **Services** console. System Configuration, commonly referred to by its executable name **msconfig**, is opened from the Run dialog or search box by typing "msconfig." It presents several tabs, including General, Boot, Services, and, on older versions, Startup. In current Windows versions, the Startup tab simply points you to Task Manager; that is intentional and worth remembering.

System Configuration is primarily a troubleshooting tool. You can select a **Selective startup** mode to load only basic services and drivers, similar to a lightweight diagnostic mode, when you suspect that an added service or startup component is causing problems. The Boot tab allows you to enable options like Safe boot, which forces Windows to start in a reduced environment suitable for diagnosing driver or startup issues. The Services tab lists services with checkboxes, and you can hide all Microsoft services to focus on third-party ones. CompTIA wants you to know that you can temporarily disable non-essential services here while tracking down a start-up conflict, but it also wants you to understand this must be done thoughtfully, with documentation, not as a quick "speed up the PC" trick.

For more precise control over individual services, you use the **Services** console (services.msc). This tool lists all Windows services, showing their Status (Running, Stopped) and Startup Type (Automatic, Automatic (Delayed Start), Manual, Disabled). From here you can start, stop, or restart a service and change its startup type. If Event Viewer reveals that a particular service fails occasionally, you might come to the Services console to check its configuration or to restart it. On the exam, when you see phrases like "change a service from automatic to disabled" or "restart a specific background service," you should associate them with the Services console rather than with Task Manager or msconfig, even though Task Manager's Services tab gives you a shortcut link.

System Information, Computer Management, and Windows Security

Not all tools are about changing things; some are about quickly learning what you are dealing with. **System Information** (msinfo32) is a read-only utility that gives you a comprehensive snapshot of the system: OS version and build, BIOS or UEFI version, total and available physical memory, processor type, and an inventory of many hardware components. You can open it by searching for "System Information" or running msinfo32. When you are on a support call and need to verify whether a system meets the minimum requirements for an application, or when you are documenting a machine's specs in a ticket, System Information is far more efficient than hunting around in several different dialogs.

Another important "hub" is **Computer Management** (compmgmt.msc). Rather than being a single tool, Computer Management is a Microsoft Management Console (MMC) that hosts multiple snap-ins: Task Scheduler, Event Viewer, Shared Folders, Local Users and Groups (on some editions), Device Manager, Disk Management, and more. Many administrative tasks start here because it centralizes access. From an exam standpoint, recognize that Computer Management might be the portal you use to open a specific tool the question is really about. If the issue is with disks, you still think "Disk Management," but you might reach it via Computer Management in the workflow.

Finally, you should be aware of the **Windows Security** app (sometimes still called Windows Defender in older documentation), which centralizes Windows' built-in security features: antivirus, firewall, account protection, device security, and more. The security details belong in later chapters, but here you should simply recognize that when a user reports messages from Windows Defender or asks about virus scans, the Windows Security GUI is where those settings and reports live. CompTIA may expect you to distinguish between using a performance tool to investigate slowness versus using the security UI to initiate or review malware scans.

As you become more comfortable with these utilities, your troubleshooting starts to feel less like guesswork and more like a systematic investigation. A user's vague "it's acting weird" becomes a sequence in your mind: check Task Manager for obvious resource issues, glance at Device Manager if hardware is involved, verify storage in Disk Management, look at recent errors in Event Viewer or Reliability Monitor, and then, if needed, adjust startup or services through msconfig and Services. Over time, choosing the right GUI tool becomes automatic, and that is exactly the skill set the A+ exam is trying to measure.

6.5 Windows Command-Line Tools

In most day-to-day support work, you will live in the Windows graphical interface: Settings, Control Panel, File Explorer, Task Manager, and the other tools we explored in the previous section. But every technician eventually hits a wall where the GUI stops being helpful. Maybe the desktop never loads and you only get a blank screen and a mouse cursor. Maybe you are connected to a remote system over a slow VPN and opening graphical tools is painfully sluggish. Or maybe you are in a Windows Recovery Environment where only a barebones Command Prompt is available. In those moments, your comfort level with the command line often determines whether you can fix the problem or are forced to reimage the machine.

Windows actually gives you two main command-line environments. The older one, **Command Prompt** (the `cmd.exe` shell), is where most of the classic utilities you need for the A+ exam live: `ipconfig`, `chkdsk`, `dir`, and so on. The newer one, **PowerShell**, is more powerful and scriptable, using verb–noun "cmdlets" like `Get-Process` and `Get-Service`. From an exam perspective, you should recognize that `ipconfig`, `ping`, `robocopy`, and friends are traditional command-line tools and will generally be shown running in Command Prompt, although in real life you can run most of them inside a PowerShell window as well. When a question explicitly mentions a cmdlet such as `Get-Help` or `Get-EventLog`, that's your clue it is talking about PowerShell rather than the legacy shell.

However you access it—Windows Terminal, the Start menu, Safe Mode with Command Prompt, or a recovery environment—the first thing to remember is that many troubleshooting commands must run in an **elevated** context. If you are modifying disks, repairing system files, or changing system configuration, you must open Command Prompt "as administrator." On the job, you know you got this wrong when the command replies with "Access is denied" even though you typed everything correctly. On the exam, this is often hinted at rather than stated: a scenario will describe failure to run a tool like `chkdsk /f`, and the missing step is to launch an elevated shell.

Once you are inside Command Prompt, you will notice that nearly every tool follows the same basic structure: a **command**, followed optionally by switches and arguments. In abstract form, you can think of it as `command [options] [arguments]`. For example, `ipconfig /all` runs the `ipconfig` command with the `/all` switch to request detailed information, and `chkdsk C: /f /r` runs `chkdsk` against the C: drive with options to fix errors and locate bad sectors. Switches in Windows tools commonly start with a forward slash, drive letters are followed by a colon, and paths use the backslash as a separator, such as `C:\Windows\System32`. Commands are not case-sensitive, so `IPCONFIG`, `ipconfig`, and `IpConfig` are all equivalent.

The most important "meta-command" you can learn is the universal help switch, `/?`. Almost every command-line tool supports it. If you type `ipconfig /?` or `robocopy /?`, you get a short usage guide listing all the switches and their meanings. This is your built-in manual, and on the exam it is perfectly legitimate to think of it as part of your troubleshooting workflow: in a real environment, if you forget a switch, you check the `/?` help rather than guess. There is also the `help` command itself, which lists available commands, and in PowerShell you will see the `Get-Help` cmdlet serving a similar role. When your screen gets cluttered with output, a quick run of `cls` clears the window so the next command's output is easier to read—this might feel trivial, but when you are following a troubleshooting sequence and comparing different outputs, being able to see only the last run can keep you from misreading old data.

With those basics in mind, nearly everything else you do falls into a few functional categories. One of the most fundamental is simply **navigating the file system** and working with files and folders. Before you can copy logs, run tools stored in a particular path, or examine configuration files, you often need to get to the right directory. The command `dir` lists the contents of the current directory, similar to what you see in a File Explorer window. By default, it shows file names, sizes, dates, and attributes. If the directory contains many items, you can add `/p` to pause after each screenful of text, or `/w` for a wide format that packs more names on each line. When a user insists that a file "is definitely there," but your application cannot see it, running `dir` in the expected path quickly confirms whether the file really exists and whether it might have a slightly different name or extension.

To move around the directory tree, you use `cd`, short for **change directory**. Typing `cd C:\Windows\System32` takes you directly to that folder, regardless of your current location. If you need to move one level up, `cd ..` does exactly that, changing from, say, `C:\Users\Alice\Documents` to `C:\Users\Alice`. You will find yourself alternating between `dir` and `cd` frequently: list what is here, move to the next place, list again, until you reach the directory that contains the files you want to work with. When you need to create a new folder—for example, a temporary directory to hold copies of user data before a reimage—you use `md` or `mkdir`, as in `mkdir C:\Backup\Alice`. To remove a folder, you use `rd` or `rmdir`. Deleting an empty directory is straightforward, but if the directory contains files and subfolders you must specify additional options such as `/s` to remove the whole tree, and you need to be very certain you have the correct path before pressing Enter.

Copying and deleting files are where command-line work starts to have serious consequences, so you must slow down and think. The `copy` command is the simplest file-copying tool: you specify a source and a destination, such as `copy C:\Logs\app.log D:\Archive\app.log`. For a small number of files, this is usually enough. Once you need to deal with multiple directories or larger data sets, however, you quickly outgrow `copy`. The next level up is `xcopy`, which adds support for copying full directory trees and more control over what is included. A very common scenario is copying the entire contents of a user profile to an external drive before wiping and reimaging a computer. A command like `xcopy C:\Users\Alice D:\AliceBackup /s /i` can accomplish this, where `/s` includes subdirectories and `/i` assumes that the destination is a directory. As environments and data sizes grew, Microsoft introduced `robocopy`—**Robust File Copy**—which is now the preferred tool for more serious jobs. `robocopy` can mirror folder structures, resume interrupted copies, preserve permissions and timestamps, and handle very large directory trees efficiently. When you see a question about migrating large amounts of data between file servers, or keeping two directories in sync, `robocopy` is the tool that fits that description, not `copy` or `xcopy`.

On the destructive side, `del` and its synonym `erase` remove files. Unlike deleting through the GUI, which generally moves items to the Recycle Bin, `del` really deletes them from the perspective of the file system. There is no easy Undo button. This is especially dangerous when combined with wildcards, such as `del *.*` or `del *.log`, which delete many files at once. Before running a delete command, it is wise to run `dir` with the same pattern and visually confirm the list of affected files. Several exam questions are designed to test your understanding that some command-line actions are irreversible and must be used with caution. If the task you are performing could potentially wipe out important data—formatting, partitioning, bulk deletion—you should assume that double-checking the command and path is part of proper professional practice.

Beyond individual files, many of your most critical tasks involve assessing and repairing the **health of the disk and the operating system** itself. The core tool for checking a disk is `chkdsk`, which stands for **check disk**. Running `chkdsk C:` without switches performs a read-only scan of the file system structure on the C: drive and reports any problems it finds. When you add `/f`, such as in `chkdsk C: /f`, you are telling it to fix errors it encounters. If you add `/r` as well, as in `chkdsk C: /f /r`, it also looks for bad sectors on the physical disk surface, tries to recover readable information, and marks the bad areas so they will not be used again. Because the system drive is in use while Windows is running, `chkdsk` will often respond by asking if you want to schedule the scan for the next reboot. This is normal and something you should expect in practice. Returning to the earlier power outage scenario, if a user complains of frequent freezes and you suspect file system damage, the typical sequence is to run `chkdsk` first to repair the "floor" the files sit on, and then follow up with a system file repair.

For system files themselves, the key tool is `sfc`, or **System File Checker**. When you run `sfc /scannow` from an elevated Command Prompt, Windows scans all protected system files and compares them against known good copies stored in a cache. If it finds any that are missing or have been modified, it silently replaces them with the correct versions. This is particularly useful after malware removal, failed updates, or mysterious crashes that you suspect might be caused by damaged core components rather than user data. The exam loves to contrast `sfc` and `chkdsk`. A helpful way to keep them straight is to think of `chkdsk` as repairing the file system structure and the physical disk, while `sfc` repairs the Windows system files that live on top of that structure. When the scenario talks about missing DLLs, corrupted system libraries, or Windows components not functioning correctly, the right answer is `sfc`, not `chkdsk`.

Where the disk itself is concerned—not just file systems and files—you move into tools that can be extremely powerful and extremely dangerous if misused. `diskpart` is the command-line utility for managing disks, partitions, and volumes. It lets you list all disks, select one, view its partitions, create and delete volumes, and in some cases convert between partition styles such as MBR and GPT. The A+ exam does not expect you to memorize every `diskpart` subcommand, but it does expect you to know what kind of task it is used for and to recognize that it can destroy data if you choose the wrong disk or volume. Typically, you would use `diskpart` when preparing a new drive, troubleshooting partition table problems, or working in a recovery environment where the graphical Disk Management console is not available. Once you have a partition that is ready to store data, the `format` command is used to put a file system on it, most often NTFS in a modern Windows environment. Again, formatting erases existing data on that volume, so your instinct should be to treat it as a last resort or a step you only perform when you are absolutely sure there is nothing on that partition that needs to be preserved.

When a system will not even boot into Windows, the problem may be with the boot records themselves rather than with user files. In that case, you typically start from Windows installation media or recovery media, open a Command Prompt in that environment, and use `bootrec` to repair the boot process. At the A+ level, you should associate `bootrec` with commands like `/fixmbr`, `/fixboot`, and `/rebuildbcd`, which repair the master boot record, fix boot sectors, and rebuild the Boot Configuration Data store, respectively. You will not be asked to construct elaborate sequences, but you should recognize that `bootrec` appears in scenarios where the system shows messages like "Operating system not found" or loops endlessly without loading Windows, and that it is not the same thing as `chkdsk` or `sfc`.

While you are inspecting and repairing systems, you often need to gather **general system information** and manage processes. The `systeminfo` command outputs a detailed report that includes the Windows edition and version, build number, system manufacturer and model, BIOS version, total and available physical memory, and a list of installed hotfixes. This can be invaluable when verifying whether a machine meets the minimum requirements for an application, checking whether a particular update has been installed, or simply recording baseline information in a ticket. To identify the computer on the network quickly, the `hostname` command returns the system's network name, which is useful in remote sessions where the user might not know their computer name or when you are juggling multiple remote connections.

For running processes, `tasklist` and `taskkill` are the command-line counterparts to the GUI Task Manager. `tasklist` shows all running processes, along with their process IDs (PIDs), memory usage, and in some cases the user account under which they are running. When an application is hung and cannot be closed through the GUI, or when you suspect that a particular executable is consuming too many resources, tasklist helps you confirm whether it is still running. To terminate a process directly, you use taskkill. You can specify a process by image name—for example, taskkill /IM notepad.exe /F to force-close all instances of Notepad—or by PID using the /PID switch. It is possible to crash or destabilize a system by killing critical processes, so, as with other powerful commands, you should verify what you are targeting and prefer graceful closure when possible.

Control over shutdown and restarts also exists at the command line through the shutdown utility. This becomes especially important when you are managing remote systems, or when the graphical interface is not responding but the system itself is still alive. Using shutdown /s /t 0 initiates an immediate shutdown, /r triggers a reboot, and /t specifies a delay in seconds before the action occurs. You can also specify a remote computer by adding /m \\computername, assuming you have appropriate permissions and remote shutdown is allowed in the environment. In an enterprise, it is common to embed shutdown commands in scripts that roll out updates overnight and then reboot affected machines in a controlled way.

Another major category of command-line work, and one that appears very frequently on the exam, is **network troubleshooting**. When a user says, "I can't get online," the GUI network troubleshooter may or may not give you useful feedback, but the core command-line tools expose exactly what is happening. The most foundational is ipconfig, which displays the system's IPv4 and IPv6 addresses, subnet masks, default gateway, and other TCP/IP configuration data. The plain ipconfig output is fairly minimal, but ipconfig /all adds details such as the MAC address, DNS servers, whether DHCP is enabled, the address of the DHCP server, and the lease obtained/expiration times. One critical pattern to recognize is an address in the 169.254.x.x range. That is an **APIPA** address, assigned automatically when the system cannot reach a DHCP server. If you see this in ipconfig, it strongly suggests a DHCP issue or a connectivity problem between the client and the DHCP server.

ipconfig also gives you some active tools for refreshing network settings. ipconfig /release tells the system to give up its current DHCP lease, and ipconfig /renew requests a new one. If a machine has a valid-looking address but cannot reach resources, forcing a release and renew is a quick way to see whether the DHCP server responds and whether a new lease resolves the problem. Another handy subcommand is ipconfig /flushdns, which clears the DNS resolver cache on the local machine. When DNS records have changed on the network but your workstation still remembers the old IP mapping, flushing the cache often resolves "I can reach the server by IP but not by name" type symptoms.

Once you know the IP configuration, testing actual **connectivity** is the next step. The ping command sends ICMP Echo Request packets to a destination and reports whether it receives Echo Replies, along with round-trip time statistics. A classic troubleshooting sequence starts locally: ping 127.0.0.1 tests the local TCP/IP stack, and if that fails, you know the problem is inside the host rather than on the network. Pinging your default gateway tells you whether you can reach the local router, and pinging a known external IP address, such as a public DNS server, tells you whether you have general internet connectivity regardless of DNS. When pings to IP addresses succeed but pings to hostnames fail, you have a DNS resolution issue. It is important not to confuse ping with DNS tools; ping is primarily a reachability tester. For DNS-specific checks, you turn to nslookup.

If basic pings work but users report slowness or intermittent connectivity, tracert helps you see the path packets take through the network. Each line of tracert output represents a hop—usually a router or gateway—between the source and the destination. Long delays or timeouts at a particular hop suggest where congestion or failure is occurring. If your trace fails immediately at the first hop, the issue is likely with the local network or default gateway. If it gets several hops out before failing, you may be dealing with a WAN or internet provider issue rather than a local one. Technicians often use tracert in conjunction with ping results to decide whether to escalate a problem to the network team, to an ISP, or to continue troubleshooting the workstation.

For a view of current network activity on the host itself, netstat displays active TCP connections and listening ports. Running netstat -an shows raw IP addresses and port numbers, which can reveal whether an expected service is listening on the right port or whether there are unusual outbound connections that might indicate malware. While the A+ exam does not dive into deep interpretation of `netstat` output, it does expect you to recognize it as the tool you would use to list active network connections, as distinct from `ipconfig`, which shows configuration, or `ping`, which tests connectivity.

Returning to DNS, `nslookup` lets you query DNS servers directly. You can specify a hostname and see what IP address the DNS server returns, or specify a DNS server to query. This is very useful for verifying whether a DNS problem is local or systemic. For example, if `nslookup www.example.com` against your corporate DNS server fails but the same query against a public DNS server succeeds, that points to an issue with the corporate DNS infrastructure. If both fail, the problem may be with your connection to any DNS servers or with the domain's DNS records.

Windows also has a family of `net` commands covering various network-related tasks. At the A+ level, two that come up frequently are `net use` and `net user`. `net use` is used to manage connections to shared resources, such as mapping a network drive. A technician might use `net use X: \\fileserver\share` to map drive X: to a file server's shared folder, often supplying credentials when the logged-on user does not have direct access. When troubleshooting file share access, `net use` helps you see which connections exist and disconnect ones that are stuck or using the wrong credentials. `net user` focuses on user accounts, particularly local accounts. Running `net user` by itself lists all the local accounts on a machine; adding a user name, as in `net user alice`, displays detailed information about that account, including group memberships and whether the account is active. With appropriate privileges, you can also use it to change a local user's password. On the exam, you should be able to distinguish between `net use` for share connections and `net user` for account information and management.

All of these tools can be run from either Command Prompt or PowerShell, but it is worth pausing briefly on how PowerShell differs conceptually. PowerShell is built around **objects** rather than plain text, and it uses cmdlets with a consistent Verb-Noun syntax such as `Get-Process`, `Stop-Service`, or `Get-Help`. These cmdlets can pass structured data to one another in powerful ways, which becomes important when you start scripting. However, traditional commands like `ipconfig`, `ping`, `chkdsk`, and `robocopy` still behave essentially the same when you run them in a PowerShell window; they produce text output that scrolls by in the console. From an A+ perspective, the distinction you need is mostly recognition: if you see `Get-Process` or `Get-Service`, that means PowerShell. If you see the familiar utilities we have been discussing, they are the classic Windows command-line tools.

As you gain experience, you start to build mental associations between symptoms and these command-line utilities. A user cannot see network shares, so you instinctively think of `ipconfig`, `ping`, and `net use`. A system is sluggish after a power failure, and you reach for `chkdsk` followed by `sfc`. A particular program will not close and is eating CPU in Task Manager, so you picture `tasklist` to confirm and `taskkill` to end it. This is exactly the kind of reasoning the CompTIA A+ Core 2 exam is looking for: not that you can recite syntax from memory, but that you can look at a problem, place it into the right general category—file, disk, system, or network—and then choose the tool that fits that situation.

6.6 Windows Settings & Account Configuration

When you start supporting real Windows users, you quickly discover that most of your work does not happen in exotic admin consoles or obscure command-line tools. It happens in a single, very familiar place: the Windows Settings app. Users describe vague symptoms—"my screen looks weird," "it keeps asking for some admin password," "my computer keeps restarting for updates," or "my sound just disappeared"—and your job is to translate that everyday language into the right Settings area and the right change. This chapter is about building that translation skill: understanding how Windows Settings is organized, how user accounts and sign-in options are configured, and how to reason backward from a complaint to the underlying configuration that needs attention.

Core System Settings You Will Use Constantly

The System category is one you will visit constantly. Inside it, the **Display** page controls how things look on the screen: **resolution**, **scaling**, orientation, and multi-monitor layout. Resolution is the number of pixels being used to draw the desktop; scaling is how large text and interface elements appear at that resolution. LCD monitors are designed for a particular "native" resolution, and Windows usually labels that as "Recommended." If a user tells you "everything is huge and kind of blurry," that is often a sign that the resolution has been dropped below the panel's native value, or that scaling is set very high. Walking them to Settings > System > Display and checking that the resolution is set to the recommended value is a fast, exam-relevant troubleshooting pattern. If the resolution is correct but text is too small, you can adjust scaling upward in small steps—say from 100 percent to 125 percent—without sacrificing sharpness.

Display is also where you handle dual-monitor setups. On that page, Windows shows rectangles representing each monitor; you can drag them to match the physical arrangement, choose whether the desktop is extended across both or duplicated on each, and select which monitor is the **main display**. Users may say "my taskbar is on the wrong screen" or "I can only see my background on this second monitor, not my apps." In practice, that usually means the wrong monitor is marked as main, or the desktop is set to "show only on 1" instead of extend. Display is also where you turn on features like night light, which warms the color temperature in the evening and can help with eye strain.

Right next to Display in the System section is **Sound**, which underpins another very common set of complaints. Even when the physical speakers and cables are fine, users can end up with "no sound" because Windows is sending audio to the wrong place. On the Sound page, you see a list of **output devices**—built-in speakers, external speakers, USB headsets, HDMI or DisplayPort audio on a monitor—and **input devices** such as microphones. If a user plugs a new monitor in and suddenly cannot hear anything from their desktop speakers, it is very often because Windows automatically switched the default output to "HDMI display audio." Selecting the correct output device and testing it usually resolves the issue. You can also adjust per-app volume through the volume mixer from the same area, which helps when one application is muted while others are fine.

You will also spend time in **Network & Internet**. This is not for deep protocol troubleshooting—that comes in the networking chapters—but for basic connectivity and verification. On the main Network & Internet page, Windows shows the current status: connected via Ethernet, connected to a Wi-Fi network, or offline. From here you can choose Wi-Fi, view available networks, connect to one, or forget a problematic network so the system stops auto-connecting to it. Airplane mode toggles all wireless radios off and on. Clicking into the active network's properties lets you see IP settings, such as whether the system is using DHCP or a static address. When a user says "I'm not online" or "the Wi-Fi menu disappeared," your first stop should be this status overview to see whether Windows itself thinks it has connectivity.

Appearance and comfort settings are concentrated in **Personalization** and **Accessibility** (or Ease of Access, depending on version). Personalization controls the wallpaper, lock screen background, themes, and the behavior of the Start menu and taskbar. While these might not sound "technical," they matter to users. Someone who sits at the same computer eight hours a day may be genuinely distressed when a profile reset returns their desktop to the default theme. On the support side, knowing your way around themes and Start layout can let you quickly restore a familiar environment and reduce user resistance.

Accessibility is where you go when a user says "I can't read this text," "the colors are hard on my eyes," or "I have trouble using the mouse." Without touching monitor resolution, you can increase system-wide text size, turn on high-contrast color schemes, enable the Magnifier for on-demand zooming, activate Narrator screen-reading for visually impaired users, or adjust keyboard and mouse behaviors. Subtle adjustments here can make the difference between someone struggling all day and being able to work comfortably, and on the exam it is important to recognize that these are configuration options, not separate applications.

From a technical operations perspective, **Time & language** is more important than it first appears. On that page, you configure the system time, date, and time zone, and you choose language and region settings. When someone travels between time zones or a laptop's CMOS battery fails, the system clock can drift. That, in turn, can break authentication or cause SSL certificate errors, because many security mechanisms depend on correct time. Asking a user to glance at the clock in the taskbar is an easy first step, and correcting it through Settings > Time & language can instantly resolve mysterious "website not secure" warnings. Language and region matter as well; if a user complains that apps suddenly appear in another language, or date formats are wrong, it is often because the display language or region was changed here.

Managing Windows Update through Settings

Windows Update is important enough to deserve its own spotlight. In modern Windows, it has a dedicated category: **Windows Update**. This is where the operating system checks for new patches, feature updates, and many device drivers. You can see update status, manually trigger "Check for updates," view the update history to confirm that a particular patch installed successfully, and see pending restarts.

From a support perspective, one of the most frequent complaints you will hear is some variation of "my PC keeps restarting at the worst times." Users may interpret these as random crashes, but often they are scheduled reboots after updates. In Windows Update, you can configure **active hours**, which tell Windows when the user typically works so that automatic restarts avoid that window. You can also pause updates temporarily if someone is in the middle of critical work, though from a security standpoint you should not leave a machine unpatched indefinitely. On exam questions, disabling updates outright is rarely the correct answer; the safer, more realistic approach is to adjust timing and behavior, not to turn off protection.

In a corporate domain environment, you will sometimes find that Windows Update settings are marked as "managed by your organization." That means Group Policy or another management tool is controlling them centrally. In that case, Settings still serves as your dashboard for seeing what happened, even if you cannot change every option. On standalone home or small office systems, however, the technician is typically expected to manage updates directly through this interface.

Windows Accounts: Who the User Is and What They Can Do

Once you are comfortable adjusting the system, you need to understand who is allowed to make those changes. That takes us to the **Accounts** category. This is where Windows stores information about the current user, other users of the machine, and their relationship to Microsoft's online services or to a workplace or school environment.

A core distinction you must master is between a **local account** and a **Microsoft account**. A local account exists only on that specific computer. Its username and password are stored in the local SAM database, and it is not automatically linked to any online services. This is typical for kiosks, lab machines, or environments where you deliberately want to avoid cloud integration. A Microsoft account, by contrast, is an email-based online identity—often an Outlook.com or Hotmail address—that can sign in to multiple devices. When a user logs into Windows with a Microsoft account, certain settings, themes, and browser favorites can sync across machines, and they can access the Microsoft Store and OneDrive more seamlessly. Some features, like purchasing apps from the Store, essentially require a Microsoft account.

On top of the account type is the **permission level**: **administrator** or **standard user**. An administrator can install software and drivers, change system-wide settings, manage other accounts, and override certain restrictions. A standard user is limited mostly to their own data and personalization; installing many kinds of software or changing secure settings will prompt for administrator credentials. This structure enforces the principle of **least privilege**: users should have only the rights they need to do their jobs, and no more. It is tempting—especially when you are under time pressure—to solve every "access denied" problem by making the user an administrator. Both the exam and real-world security practices will punish that habit. A user who runs as admin all the time has far more power to accidentally break the system or to let malware run with full rights.

Consider a typical support call: a user says, "I'm trying to install this accounting application, and it keeps popping up a window asking for some admin password. I don't know it, and I can't click past it." What they are seeing is a User Account Control (UAC) prompt. Your job is not to tell them to just disable UAC; instead, you confirm what type of account they are using. You might guide them to Settings > Accounts > Your info and look for whether it says "Administrator" or "Standard user" under their name. If they are standard and this is a work machine, the correct response is usually to either remote in with IT admin credentials and perform the install for them or schedule a visit, following policy. On a personally owned home PC, you might help them log in as the local admin account or enter the admin password once, without permanently changing their account type.

Within the Accounts section, the **Family & other users** (or simply "Other users") page is where you add new accounts and adjust roles. From there, you can add another Microsoft account, create a new local account, and set whether that new user is an administrator or standard. Removing accounts from this page is possible as well, but you need to remember that deleting an account can remove that user's profile data from the local disk. For more granular control, such as disabling but not deleting accounts, later chapters will introduce Local Users and Groups (lusrmgr.msc). For A+-level work, however, you are expected to handle basic add/remove and role changes from within Settings.

You will also encounter **Access work or school**, which is where a device is joined to an organization's Microsoft 365 or Azure AD tenant. When an employee says, "I need to connect this laptop to the company so I can get email and Teams," you send them here to add their work account. Deep domain management and group policy configuration are beyond this chapter, but recognizing that this is the entry point for corporate resources is important.

Sign-In Options: How Users Prove Who They Are

Account type and permission level define what a user is allowed to do. Separate from that is **how** they sign in to prove they are that user. In Settings > Accounts > **Sign-in options**, Windows lets you configure several forms of authentication for the same underlying account. This distinction is a common exam trap: switching from a password to a PIN does not turn a standard user into an administrator. It only changes the method they use to authenticate.

The most basic sign-in method is the account **password** itself. On top of that, modern Windows offers a **Windows Hello PIN**, which is a numeric code tied to that particular device. Under the hood, a PIN can be considered safer in some ways, because compromising it does not automatically give an attacker access to the user's online Microsoft account on other machines. Where supported hardware is present, **biometric** options like fingerprint readers and facial recognition integrate into Windows Hello as well, letting users sign in quickly without typing anything. Some editions still support a **picture password**, where the user draws a pattern on an image, though this is less commonly used.

From the support perspective, you need to be ready for conversations like "I forgot my PIN." In that case, the solution is not recreating the Windows account; it is walking the user through resetting the PIN, which usually requires entering the underlying account password or performing Microsoft account recovery online. If the user no longer remembers their Microsoft account password either, you are now dealing with an account recovery issue, not just a Settings toggle. Understanding these dependencies helps you choose the right next step.

On the same Sign-in options page, you can configure when Windows requires the user to sign in again after sleep or when the screen is locked. In an office, company policy may require a short idle timeout so that unattended machines lock themselves automatically. As a technician, you should know how to adjust those timeouts in Settings when asked—and also when to say, "we have to keep this within policy." Teaching users to lock their own screens with Windows key + L is a simple but important security habit that connects this usability topic to the broader security discussions you will see later.

Privacy and App Permissions: When Hardware "Works" but Apps Cannot Use It

Another category worth understanding at a high level is **Privacy & security**. Here, Windows centralizes control over which applications are allowed to access sensitive capabilities like location, camera, microphone, contacts, notifications, and more. Many newer desktop apps respect these permissions, and if they are blocked here, they simply will not see the device, even if the driver is installed and the hardware is fully functional.

Imagine a user calling to say, "My webcam doesn't work in Zoom, but the little light comes on sometimes and it works in another app." Before condemning the camera, you should consider that this might be a permissions issue. In Settings > Privacy & security > Camera, you can verify that camera access is allowed for apps in general, and specifically for the type of app in question (Microsoft Store apps vs desktop apps). Similar controls exist for the microphone. On the exam, if you see a scenario where a single application cannot access a camera or mic while others can, Privacy & security is a more appropriate tool than Device Manager.

You do not need to memorize every toggle in this category for A+, but you should recognize that not every "device not working" complaint is a driver or hardware failure. Sometimes the fix is a single switch in Settings that grants the application permission to use the resource.

Thinking Like a Technician: Mapping Symptoms to Settings

What ties all of this together is your ability to listen to a user's description and quickly narrow down where in Settings to start. If someone says, "everything on my screen is tiny and hard to read," you think System > Display: check scaling and resolution. If they say, "I hear sound from the monitor but not my speakers," you think System > Sound: select the right output device. If the complaint is "I can't install this, it keeps asking for a password I don't have," that is Accounts: verify whether they are a standard user and decide how to handle administrative access safely. "My apps are all in Spanish now" points to Time & language: check display language and region. "My PC restarts in the middle of my work every week" suggests Windows Update: inspect active hours and restart behavior.

This habit of starting with Settings and simple configuration checks before assuming deep hardware or OS corruption is central both to success on the CompTIA A+ exam and to being effective on a help desk. As you practice, try to classify each new issue you see into a small number of Settings categories in your mind. Over time, opening the right page and applying the right adjustment will become second nature.

6.7 Windows Client Networking Features

When you start working in IT support, a huge percentage of your day will be spent dealing with some variation of "I can't connect." Sometimes that means no internet at all. Sometimes it means a user can browse websites but can't see a shared drive, or they can print to a local USB printer but not to a shared office printer. From the Windows client side, all of these problems are about the same core ideas: how the computer connects to the network, how it classifies that network, what it chooses to share, how it protects itself with the firewall, and how it allows remote access. Once you understand where those levers live and what they do, most "I can't connect" tickets become systematic puzzles instead of mysteries.

It helps to think of Windows networking on the client as four layers that stack on top of each other. At the bottom, you have **connectivity**: the network adapter, IP configuration, gateway, and DNS. On top of that is the **profile**, where Windows decides whether this network is public, private, or part of a domain, which in turn controls discovery and default sharing behavior. Above that sits the **firewall**, deciding what traffic is actually allowed into or out of the machine. And finally, at the top, you have the **services** and tools that ride on top of all that: file and printer sharing, mapped drives, Remote Desktop, Quick Assist, VPN clients, and so on. When you troubleshoot, you work up and down those layers: if Remote Desktop won't connect, for example, you don't jump straight into firewall rules without first confirming that the machine even has an IP address and can be reached.

Network Profiles and Discovery

The moment a Windows client connects to a new network—whether that's a wired office LAN, home Wi-Fi, or the free hotspot in a coffee shop—it quietly asks a key question: "How much do I trust this place?" Windows expresses the answer as a **network profile**. On standalone clients you'll see two main choices: **Public** and **Private**. In domain environments, a third one appears: **Domain**. The profile dictates default firewall behavior and whether the system is willing to advertise itself and its shared resources to others on that network.

On a **Public** network, Windows assumes the worst: this might be an airport, hotel, or any untrusted environment. By default, **network discovery** is off, so your computer will not announce its presence, and it will not go out of its way to find other PCs. File and printer sharing are also off by default, and the firewall is much more restrictive about inbound connections. This is the paranoid setting, and that's intentional. If you connect your laptop at a conference and everything "just works" in terms of others being able to browse your shares, that's a security failure, not a feature. On **Private** networks, Windows assumes you're on a trusted home or small office LAN. Discovery and file/printer sharing can be enabled, and the firewall relaxes enough to allow typical LAN traffic, so other devices can see your computer under the Network section in File Explorer and access properly shared folders or printers.

In a corporate environment with Active Directory, systems that are joined to a domain end up on the **Domain** profile whenever they are on the corporate network. You won't normally change that manually; it is governed by Group Policy and controlled centrally by administrators. For the A+ exam, it's enough to recognize that domain-joined computers can have profile behaviors dictated by the organization, which may differ from what you see on a standalone home system, even though the underlying concepts are the same.

On modern Windows 10 and 11 systems, you can view and change the network profile in the Settings app. You go to Settings, then Network & Internet, and choose either Wi-Fi or Ethernet depending on your connection. Selecting the name of the network brings up options where you can mark it as Public or Private. This is a deceptively powerful switch. Imagine you get a ticket from a user who says, "I can get to websites just fine, but I can't see the shared drive or the office printer that everyone else uses." They clearly have IP connectivity to the internet, so the bottom layer is probably okay. A very high-yield check is to look at that profile setting—often, Windows has set the network to Public, which is safer from a security standpoint but blocks discovery and sharing. Changing it to Private (when appropriate and safe) often makes the missing shares and printers suddenly appear.

Network discovery, which you might see referenced in the classic Control Panel under "Advanced sharing settings," is the feature that allows the computer to see and be seen on the local network. When discovery is off, the machine won't show up in other users' Network views, even if it technically has shared folders. On Public networks, discovery is off by default. On Private networks, you can choose to turn it on. The exam likes to test this relationship: for a computer to appear under Network in File Explorer, it not only needs to be reachable at the IP level and correctly profiled as Private or Domain, it also needs network discovery and file/printer sharing enabled for that profile.

Configuring Network Adapters and IP Settings

Underneath the profile layer are the raw adapter and IP configuration settings. Earlier in the book you saw the theory of IPv4, DHCP, default gateways, and DNS. Here you see how those concepts show up inside Windows itself. When you open the classic **Network and Sharing Center** in Control Panel and click "Change adapter settings," you see the list of network interfaces: Ethernet, Wi-Fi, maybe a "vEthernet" virtual adapter from Hyper-V, or a VPN adapter. In Windows 10 and 11's Settings app, a similar list appears under Network & Internet, then "Advanced network settings."

Each adapter has a status that you can view by right-clicking and choosing "Status." This window tells you whether the adapter is connected, the connection speed, bytes sent and received, and whether IPv4 and IPv6 have internet connectivity. From here, clicking "Details" shows the IP address, subnet mask, default gateway, and DNS servers that Windows is using. This is where you confirm whether the machine received an address from DHCP or fell back to an **APIPA** address (169.254.x.x), which means DHCP failed and the machine gave itself a link-local address that works only for limited local communication. If a user says they are connected to Wi-Fi but see "No internet" under the network icon, one of your first steps should be to look here. If you see 169.254.x.x, you know the DHCP conversation never completed, and you can start checking things like the router, the cable, or the access point rather than blaming the browser.

For many environments, IP configuration is automatic. In the adapter's properties, if you open the properties of **Internet Protocol Version 4 (TCP/IPv4)**, you'll usually see "Obtain an IP address automatically" and "Obtain DNS server address automatically" selected. That's DHCP doing its job. However, you can also configure static IP settings there. When you choose "Use the following IP address," you must fill in the address, subnet mask, and default gateway manually, and often DNS servers as well. Static addresses are common for devices that must be reachable at fixed addresses, like servers, shared printers, or NAS appliances. They're less common on normal workstations, but you will still encounter them.

Misconfigured static settings are a frequent source of trouble. Imagine a user complains that they can reach other computers in the office but not the internet. You check the IPv4 properties and find a static IP that doesn't match the rest of the subnet, or a missing default gateway, or DNS servers set to some old, internal address that no longer exists. From Windows' perspective, the NIC is "connected," but packets destined for the internet don't know where to go. In those cases, returning the adapter to DHCP or correcting the static configuration usually resolves the problem. As a support tech, you should get comfortable reading that IPv4 properties dialog and matching what you see to the expected network parameters.

The GUI isn't your only tool; later chapters explore command-line tools like `ipconfig` and `ping`, but you don't always need to go there first. For many basic connectivity tickets, simply confirming "Do we have a valid IP, gateway, and DNS?" from the adapter details will point you in the right direction.

File and Printer Sharing on Windows Clients

Once the computer is on the network, the next question is what, if anything, it should share. Windows clients can share folders and printers so other users on the LAN can access them, but this depends heavily on the profile and discovery settings you just learned about. If the network is set to Public or network discovery is disabled, you can configure shares all day and nobody will see them.

The high-level sharing switches live in the classic **Advanced sharing settings** in the Network and Sharing Center. There, each profile (Private, Public, and Domain if applicable) has its own options to turn network discovery on or off, and to turn file and printer sharing on or off. You might also see a separate control for sharing **Public folders**, which we'll come back to. For a home or small office LAN where users want to share files, you'd typically set the profile to Private and enable both discovery and file/printer sharing for that profile.

When you want to share a specific folder, you usually start in File Explorer. Right-click the folder, choose Properties, then open the Sharing tab. The "Share..." button launches a simple wizard where you can choose users or groups and assign basic permission levels like read or read/write. For more granular control, "Advanced Sharing..." lets you set the share name, limit the number of simultaneous users, and open the **permissions** dialog. This is where Windows' permission models overlap: there are **share permissions**, which apply only to network access, and **NTFS permissions**, which apply both locally and over the network. For this chapter, the main idea is that the user's effective access is the most restrictive combination of the two. Giving "Everyone: Read" at the share level doesn't magically override tight NTFS permissions, and likewise, generous NTFS permissions can still be blocked by restrictive share permissions.

From another computer on the same LAN, a user accesses a share by going to File Explorer and entering a UNC path like `\\COMPUTERNAME\Sharename`, or by typing that into the Run dialog. If everything is configured correctly, they see the folder contents. If they get "Windows cannot access" errors, your troubleshooting naturally works through the layers: can they ping the remote machine by name or IP, is the network profile appropriate and discovery enabled, is the firewall allowing file and printer sharing on that profile, and are the share/NTFS permissions correct for their account?

Windows also includes a set of **Public folders**, such as Public Documents and Public Desktop, under `C:\Users\Public`. These are designed as common drop-zones for file sharing on a local computer and, optionally, across the network. In Advanced sharing settings, you'll find an option to turn sharing of Public folders on or off. In some home setups, users don't realize that when they "just see other people's files" on the network, what they're really using are these Public folders with sharing enabled.

For frequently used shares, mapping a **network drive** gives users a friendly drive letter instead of a long UNC path. In File Explorer under "This PC," the "Map network drive" option lets you choose a drive letter (for example, Z:) and type the network path, such as `\\SERVER\Shared`. You can also choose to reconnect at sign-in and, if needed, specify different credentials. In many corporate environments, login scripts or Group Policy automatically map departmental shares for users, which means when a mapped drive stops working, they're confused. They may see the drive letter listed with a red X. That red X doesn't always mean the share is gone; often it simply means Windows hasn't yet re-established the connection. As soon as the user double-clicks the drive and the network path is reachable, the connection reactivates. If it stays disconnected, you again work the layers: does the client have network connectivity, is the VPN connected if they're remote, did the server name or user password change?

Printer sharing follows similar patterns. A locally installed printer—say, one connected by USB to a user's PC—can be shared so others on the LAN can print through that PC. In Windows 10 and 11, you open Settings, then Bluetooth & devices, then Printers & scanners, select the printer, and open its Printer properties (not just the settings page). On the Sharing tab, you check "Share this printer" and optionally give it a share name that others will use. There's also an option to "Render print jobs on client computers," which offloads processing from the host. Other users then add the printer by browsing the network (if discovery is working) or by specifying a path like `\\COMPUTERNAME\PrinterName`. If someone complains they can't see a shared printer, don't forget to check the host computer's profile and sharing settings; a printer shared from a machine on a Public network profile with sharing disabled simply won't be visible.

Windows Defender Firewall on the Client

Even if you have the right IP configuration and the right sharing settings, Windows still has one more major gatekeeper: **Windows Defender Firewall**. The firewall's job is to control network traffic based on a set of rules, and it has separate behavior for the Domain, Private, and Public profiles. From a support perspective, you mainly care about verifying whether the firewall is on for a given profile and whether it is allowing a particular app or feature.

You can reach the firewall in two main ways. The classic route is through Control Panel, under "Windows Defender Firewall," which shows you the status of each profile and offers links to change settings. Modern Windows also integrates this into the Windows Security interface, reachable through Settings under Privacy & security, then Windows Security, then "Firewall & network protection." There you will again see the three profile types, each of which can be enabled or disabled and configured separately. On Public networks, the firewall rules are strict by default: many inbound connections are blocked unless explicitly allowed. On Private and Domain networks, certain inbound services, like file and printer sharing or Remote Desktop, may be allowed when you enable those features.

When a new application first tries to accept inbound connections, you'll often see a prompt: "Windows Defender Firewall has blocked some features of this app." You're asked whether to allow it on Private networks, Public networks, or both. This prompt is where many less experienced users accidentally weaken security by checking every box. From a security-aware support perspective, you want to be intentional. Allowing an app on Private networks only is usually appropriate for home or office scenarios. Allowing it on Public networks means that whenever the laptop is sitting on open Wi-Fi in a hotel, that application is exposed—something you generally want to avoid unless there's a very specific business reason.

If you need to review or change these decisions later, you can use the "Allow an app or feature through Windows Defender Firewall" link in the firewall control panel. That opens a list of known applications and features, each with checkboxes under Private and Public. For example, you might see "File and Printer Sharing" or "Remote Desktop" in the list. If a user cannot connect to a share or RDP doesn't work, but everything else about the network looks healthy, checking whether those entries are allowed on the appropriate profile is a key step. A common but poor workaround is to simply turn the firewall off entirely to "see if it fixes it." On an exam question, that's almost never the correct answer. The proper fix is to enable just the necessary feature or app for the correct profile and leave the firewall otherwise active.

There is a deeper level, "Windows Defender Firewall with Advanced Security," accessible from the left pane of the firewall window. This exposes the full list of inbound and outbound rules, detailed port configurations, and profile-specific behavior. For A+ purposes, you mainly need to know that these rules exist and that enabling features like Remote Desktop automatically creates corresponding rules. If you ever see a scenario where connectivity works perfectly with the firewall disabled and fails as soon as the firewall is re-enabled, the right mental model is not "the network is broken," but "which specific inbound rule do I need to enable for this profile so I can leave the firewall on?"

Remote Desktop, Quick Assist, and VPN

Once you're comfortable with client connectivity, profiles, sharing, and firewalls, the next layer is remote access. In support work, there's a crucial difference between remote access tools that log you into a machine as if you were physically there, and assistance tools that let you see and control the user's current session to help them.

Remote Desktop Protocol (RDP) is the classic Windows feature that lets you connect to another Windows computer and get a full desktop session. To use it, the target computer must be running an edition that supports being a Remote Desktop host (for example, Windows 10/11 Pro or Enterprise, not Home), and Remote Desktop must be explicitly enabled. You can turn it on in Settings under System, then Remote Desktop, or via System Properties on the Remote tab. The user account you log in with must be allowed remote access, either by being an administrator or by being added to the Remote Desktop Users group. The machine must also be reachable over the network, and the firewall must allow Remote Desktop on the active profile.

On the client side, you start the connection with the Remote Desktop Connection program (`mstsc.exe`) or the modern Remote Desktop app. You supply the computer name or IP address, credentials, and off you go—if everything underneath is correct. When it fails, the troubleshooting is layered. First, can you even reach the machine via ping or by browsing its shares? If not, you might be dealing with basic connectivity or VPN issues. If you can, but RDP still fails, check whether the network profile on the host is set to Public, in which case RDP is often blocked, and whether the firewall is allowing Remote Desktop on that profile. On exam questions, when you see "Remote Desktop can't connect to the remote computer," you're generally expected to think about those prerequisites rather than, say, replacing network cables.

For helping end users directly, Windows provides **Quick Assist**, a remote assistance tool built into Windows 10 and 11. Unlike RDP, which typically logs you into a separate session, Quick Assist is designed for support: the user stays logged in, sees everything you do, and must consent to the connection. The basic workflow is simple. As the technician, you launch Quick Assist and choose to assist another person, which generates a one-time security code. The user on the remote PC launches Quick Assist on their end, selects that they want to receive assistance, and enters the code. Once they approve, you can either view their screen or request control to interact with their desktop. Quick Assist traffic usually traverses the internet using Microsoft's infrastructure, and in most cases it will punch through firewalls and NAT without you configuring anything special.

Understanding the difference between Remote Desktop and a tool like Quick Assist matters for both practice and the exam. If the goal is to support a user while they watch and learn, especially when they're working from home, Quick Assist (or similar remote assistance products) is the appropriate tool. If the goal is for you to remotely use a workstation as if you were sitting at it—perhaps to work on a lab machine after hours—Remote Desktop is more appropriate. The exam likes to test which tool you would choose for a scenario like "view and control the user's desktop while they are logged in."

Finally, many remote access stories involve a **VPN** connection in addition to these tools. A VPN client running on the Windows machine establishes a secure tunnel into the corporate network, effectively making the remote PC a logical part of the office LAN. On Windows, VPN connections are configured under Settings in the Network & Internet section, where users can add a VPN connection with the parameters provided by their organization. If a remote employee says, "When I'm in the office I can reach the S: drive and the internal printer, but from home I can't," one of the first questions you should ask is, "Are you connected to the VPN?" If not, Windows will happily talk to the internet but have no route to internal IP ranges, so mapped drives, internal websites, and RDP sessions to internal hosts will all fail. That distinction—public internet versus internal network via VPN—is a common exam angle.

In practice, when you troubleshoot any of these remote access issues, you come back to the same mental checklist. Does the adapter have a valid IP configuration and route to the destination? Is the network profiled correctly for what the user is trying to do? Is the firewall allowing the specific feature on this profile? And finally, is the particular service—file share, printer share, Remote Desktop, Quick Assist, VPN client—correctly configured and running? Once you train yourself to work that way, both the CompTIA A+ questions and real-world tickets about Windows networking become much more predictable.

6.8 macOS Features & Tools

If you've spent most of your time in Windows, macOS can feel a little unfamiliar at first glance, but underneath the surface it's dealing with the same problems: managing files, running processes, connecting to networks, and protecting users. For the A+ exam, CompTIA isn't trying to turn you into a Mac administrator. What they expect is that, when you see a Mac-related scenario, you can recognize the environment, know where to click, and choose the right built-in tool to solve common problems. Think of this section as learning a new accent of a language you already speak, rather than learning an entirely different language.

Apple names macOS releases after California locations—Sonoma, Ventura, Monterey, and so on—but the exam is much more interested in the **features and tools** than in specific version names. Across modern macOS versions, the key components you'll work with as an entry-level tech are consistent: the Menu Bar across the top, the Dock along the bottom (by default), Finder for file management, System Settings for configuration, and diagnostic tools like Activity Monitor and Disk Utility when things go wrong. Once you can mentally map "macOS word" to "Windows function" ("Finder is like File Explorer," "Activity Monitor is like Task Manager"), the interface stops being intimidating and starts becoming another environment you can support confidently.

Navigating the macOS Interface

Your tour of macOS starts at the very top of the screen with the **Menu Bar**. Unlike Windows, where each application window has its own menu, macOS has a global Menu Bar that changes depending on which app is active. On the far left is the Apple logo; clicking this opens the Apple menu, which is where you access options such as **About This Mac**, **System Settings**, **Sleep**, **Restart**, **Shut Down**, and **Log Out**. As a support technician, this menu is often your first navigation anchor when coaching users over the phone: "Click the Apple in the top-left corner" is an easy, reliable instruction.

To the right of the Apple menu, you see the menu for the currently active application—File, Edit, View, and so on. On the far right of the Menu Bar live status icons and quick controls: Wi-Fi, Bluetooth, battery level, date and time, Spotlight, Siri, and **Control Center**. Control Center is Apple's consolidated panel for toggling things like Wi-Fi, Bluetooth, Do Not Disturb, and brightness—conceptually similar to the quick actions section in the Windows notification area. When a user calls saying they "don't see their Wi-Fi icon" or "can't find Bluetooth," you'll often verify those from the Menu Bar or Control Center before diving into deeper settings.

Along the bottom of the screen (again, by default) sits the **Dock**, which plays a dual role as app launcher and window switcher. It's the closest conceptual equivalent to the Windows taskbar. Static icons in the Dock are shortcuts to applications; they stay there even if the app isn't running. Apps that are running typically have a small indicator dot under their icon, so when you're troubleshooting "my app disappeared," you can ask the user whether there's a dot under that app's icon to confirm it's still open. Users can customize the Dock by dragging apps in or out of it, and a common help-desk instruction is "right-click the icon, go to Options, and choose Remove from Dock" if you want to declutter it. The Dock also frequently holds the **Downloads** folder and a shortcut to **Trash**, both of which matter when you're helping users find newly downloaded files or clean up space.

File management in macOS revolves around **Finder**, which is the system's file manager and is always running in the background. Where Windows users would open File Explorer, Mac users open Finder. Its smiling-face icon is usually the first icon in the Dock. When you open Finder, you see a sidebar on the left with locations like Desktop, Documents, Downloads, iCloud Drive, and any attached external drives. The main pane on the right shows the contents of the selected location. In a support context, you'll frequently walk users through navigating to Downloads to locate an installer, checking the Desktop for a file they "lost," or making sure that an external USB drive is actually mounted and visible. To eject removable media properly, you either click the small eject icon next to its name in the Finder sidebar or right-click the volume and choose Eject. That small step is significant in troubleshooting disk issues; if the drive doesn't appear in Finder at all, you're likely moving toward Disk Utility instead.

macOS also gives you several tools for quickly finding things and managing multiple open windows. **Spotlight** is the system-wide search, and for a technician it's one of the most efficient entry points into any task. You open Spotlight with Command + Space, then start typing the name of an app, file, or system setting. When you're walking a user through opening a tool like Activity Monitor or Terminal, you almost never need them to hunt through folders; you can simply say, "Press Command + Space, type 'Activity Monitor,' and press Enter." That shortcut alone saves enormous time during remote support sessions.

For managing open windows, Apple offers **Mission Control**, typically invoked by pressing the Mission Control key (often F3) or swiping up with three or four fingers on the trackpad. Mission Control zooms out to show all open windows and desktops (Spaces). Users can create multiple desktops to separate workspaces—for example, one desktop for email and documents, another for a presentation. From an exam standpoint, Mission Control is the feature that "shows all your open applications and desktops and lets you switch between them," analogous to Windows Task View. If you see a question describing a Mac user who struggles with lots of overlapping windows, Mission Control is the feature you'd guide them to.

System Settings and Core Configuration Areas

Underneath the user interface, almost every configuration change you'd make on a Mac runs through **System Settings** (known as System Preferences on older macOS versions). Conceptually, this is the macOS answer to the combination of Windows Settings and Control Panel. You can reach it from the Apple menu, from its icon in the Dock, or even via Spotlight. Once opened, you see categories organized in a sidebar and detail panes on the right.

For networking, the crucial panel is **Network**. Here you configure Wi-Fi, Ethernet, VPN, and sometimes proxy settings. When a user complains that "Wi-Fi won't connect," you'll have them open System Settings, choose Network, and verify whether Wi-Fi is on, whether the correct SSID is selected, and whether there's a valid IP address. This is also where you'd forget and re-add a problematic Wi-Fi network or check whether the Mac is actually using Ethernet instead of wireless. The mental link to keep is "Network pane for connectivity issues," just as you'd go to Network & Internet in Windows.

Another key panel is **Users & Groups**. This is where you see all local accounts on the Mac, including which ones are administrators and which are standard users. You can change a user's password, enable or disable automatic login, and configure **login items**—apps that open automatically when the user signs in. Understanding the difference between an admin and a standard account is crucial in both security and troubleshooting: installing software, changing certain system settings, or unlocking some panels requires an admin username and password. On the exam, if you see a Mac scenario where the user cannot install an application or change a security setting, one of your first thoughts should be, "Is this user an administrator?" and the relevant location is Users & Groups.

Security and privacy options live under **Privacy & Security**. This panel centralizes several important behaviors that show up in real-world support work and on the exam. Here you'll find macOS permissions for camera, microphone, screen recording, location services, and **Full Disk Access**. When an application cannot access the camera or the microphone, or a screen-sharing tool can't record the display, the root cause is often that the app has not been granted permission in Privacy & Security. This is also where **Gatekeeper** settings live—the controls that determine whether macOS allows apps downloaded from the App Store only, or from the App Store and identified developers. If a user downloads an application from the web, installs it correctly, but sees an error that it "can't be opened because it is from an unidentified developer," you're dealing with Gatekeeper. You can resolve legitimate cases by going into Privacy & Security, scrolling to the security section, and using the "Open Anyway" option that appears for recently blocked apps, assuming your organization's policy allows that software.

Patching and upgrades are handled through **Software Update**, another important area within System Settings. This panel checks for available macOS updates and updates to built-in apps. For security and stability, Apple pushes regular updates, and keeping systems current is as important on macOS as on Windows. From a support perspective, when a user is experiencing strange behavior, checking whether there is a pending update or a half-applied update is a quick sanity step. On the exam, if you're asked how to keep macOS up to date, Software Update is the correct target, not some third-party utility.

Monitoring and Troubleshooting Tools

When things go wrong on a Mac, you rely heavily on a set of core tools that parallel what you know from Windows. At the top of that list is **Activity Monitor**, which is macOS's equivalent of Task Manager. You can open it via Spotlight or from the Utilities folder. Activity Monitor shows you running processes and their resource usage across several tabs: CPU, Memory, Energy, Disk, and Network. If a user reports that their Mac is "super slow" and they keep seeing the spinning beachball cursor, you'll likely have them open Activity Monitor and select the CPU tab. Sorting by CPU usage lets you see if a particular process is consuming an unusually high percentage of CPU, and the Memory tab shows you how much RAM each process is using and whether the system is under memory pressure.

From Activity Monitor, you can select a problematic process and click the Stop button to quit it. This is less disruptive than restarting the entire Mac and is exactly the kind of thinking the A+ exam wants to see you apply: identify the symptom, choose Activity Monitor as the tool, and terminate the specific misbehaving process. If a process is marked "Not Responding," that's a clear indication it may need to be shut down. You'll often use this in combination with another important feature: **Force Quit**.

The **Force Quit Applications** dialog is a quick way to kill unresponsive apps without digging into Activity Monitor. You open it with Command + Option + Esc, and it displays a list of currently running applications, flagging any that are not responding. You select the problematic app and click Force Quit, similar to using "End task" on the Applications tab of older Windows Task Manager. On a call, when a user says that "the spinning beachball won't go away and the app is frozen," guiding them to Force Quit just that one application is usually safer and faster than having them restart the entire system, especially if they have unsaved work open in other apps.

For issues related to storage and disks, macOS provides **Disk Utility**, found in the Utilities folder or via Spotlight. Disk Utility shows all internal and external storage devices, along with their containers and volumes. You don't need to be an expert in Apple's APFS structure for A+, but you should recognize Disk Utility as the place to confirm that a drive is detected, to mount or unmount it, and to run basic checks and repairs. The **First Aid** function in Disk Utility checks the file system on a volume and attempts to repair common issues. When a user complains that their external drive "doesn't show files" or seems corrupted, you might first check whether it appears in Finder; if it doesn't, Disk Utility is your next stop to see if the hardware is recognized at all. You can also erase and reformat disks from here, with the important caution that erasing a disk destroys its data—something you must be very clear about before proceeding, especially in a professional environment.

Another piece of the troubleshooting puzzle is **About This Mac** and the deeper **System Information** tool. When you click the Apple menu and choose About This Mac, you get a summary window that shows the macOS version, processor or chip type (Intel or Apple Silicon), memory, and a simple overview of storage usage. This is a quick way to verify whether a system meets the minimum requirements for an application or for a macOS upgrade. From this window, there's usually a button to open a more detailed **System Report**, which launches System Information. There you can drill down into hardware details (RAM configuration, storage devices, network interfaces), software, and connected peripherals. In a help-desk role, you might use this to confirm that a network adapter is present, to see what kind of GPU the system has, or to identify precise model identifiers when working with vendor support.

Finally, macOS includes **Terminal**, its command-line interface. Terminal gives you access to a Unix shell, and advanced administrators use it for scripts, configuration tweaks, and low-level troubleshooting. For the A+ exam, you are not expected to know lots of shell commands; what you need is the conceptual understanding that Terminal is the macOS equivalent of Windows Command Prompt or PowerShell. If a question describes a Mac technician using a command-line interface to modify system files or run diagnostics, Terminal is the component being referenced.

Application Management and Time Machine

Installing and removing applications on macOS has its own conventions, which often show up in exam questions. Many users obtain apps from the **Mac App Store**, where installation is as simple as clicking Get or Install, similar to mobile app stores. Outside the App Store, the most common packaging format you'll encounter is the **.dmg** file, which stands for disk image. A .dmg is not an executable installer like a Windows .exe file; instead, it behaves like a virtual disk. When you double-click a .dmg, macOS mounts it as a new volume, often opening a Finder window that shows the application icon and sometimes a shortcut to the Applications folder.

The typical installation pattern in this case is to drag the application icon from the disk image into the **Applications** folder. Once that's done, you can eject the mounted disk image and, if you want, delete the original .dmg file because it's no longer needed. Uninstalling an application is usually as simple as dragging the app from the Applications folder to the Trash, then emptying Trash. Some complex applications include their own uninstallers, but for many, this drag-to-Trash model is adequate. In managed environments, enterprise tools or mobile device management (MDM) platforms may handle deployment and removal centrally, but the exam will focus more on the basic local workflow and recognizing .dmg as a macOS format.

Backing up data in macOS is typically handled by **Time Machine**, Apple's built-in backup utility. Time Machine is designed to perform automatic, versioned backups to an external drive or a network share. Once configured in System Settings under Time Machine, the Mac periodically backs up the user's files, allowing them to restore previous versions or recover from data loss. As a support technician, you might need to confirm that Time Machine is enabled, that the backup disk is connected and not full, or help a user restore a mistakenly deleted file. You don't need to memorize every step of a full system recovery for A+, but you should associate Time Machine with backups and understand that its configuration lives in System Settings.

6.9 Linux Features & Tools

If you mostly live in Windows, Linux can feel like the mysterious operating system that developers and "server people" use. From an A+ technician's point of view, that mystery needs to disappear. You are not training to be a Linux administrator here, but you do need to be comfortable enough that, when someone hands you a Linux prompt, you can move around, look at the right places, run the right commands, and come back with useful answers instead of excuses. The exam reflects that same expectation: recognize Linux when you see it, know its basic structure, and be able to use a handful of core tools calmly and correctly.

Linux is best thought of as two layers working together. At the heart is the **Linux kernel**, which talks to the hardware, manages memory, handles processes, and provides the core services that make the system run. Around that kernel is a collection of tools, libraries, and utilities—things like shells, text editors, and network tools. When you bundle the kernel with these userland tools, plus a package manager and some default configuration, you get a **distribution** such as Ubuntu, Debian, Red Hat Enterprise Linux, Fedora, or CentOS. Distributions differ in their packaging systems, default configurations, and target audiences, but the basic commands you will use at the terminal—`ls`, `cd`, `cp`, `rm`, `ping`, `ps`, and so on—behave the same way almost everywhere.

Another defining feature of Linux is that it is **open source**. The kernel and most of the userland tools are licensed in a way that allows anyone to examine the source code, modify it, and redistribute changes under certain conditions. In practice, this means Linux has been adapted to an enormous variety of roles. In a business environment you might see it running web servers, file servers, network appliances, firewalls, storage devices, and virtual machines in the cloud. Developers often prefer Linux on their workstations, especially for programming, DevOps, and data science work. Some desktops and laptops run user-friendly Linux distros with full graphical environments, but many systems you will touch as a support technician are **headless**—no local monitor, no GUI—accessed over the network using SSH and administered entirely from a terminal.

That brings us to the **shell**. When you open a terminal window on a Linux desktop, or connect to a Linux server with SSH, you are usually interacting with a shell such as **bash** (Bourne Again Shell) or **zsh**. The shell is the command interpreter: it reads what you type, parses it into commands and arguments, and runs those commands. From the exam's perspective, you do not need to distinguish bash from zsh or other alternatives. You simply need to understand that the place where you type Linux commands is the shell prompt, not a Windows-style GUI interface. Typical prompts might look like `student@ubuntu:~$` or `root@web01:/etc#`, and elements like the forward slashes, the tilde (`~`), the presence of `root`, or the dollar sign versus hash symbol are clues that you are in a Linux environment.

Understanding the Linux File System

To get anything done on Linux, you first need to be comfortable with its file system layout. Windows divides storage into lettered drives like `C:\` and uses backslashes in paths. Linux uses a **single-root hierarchy**, where everything starts from the root directory, written simply as `/`. There are no drive letters; instead, different storage devices and partitions are "mounted" somewhere under this root. Paths use forward slashes, so you will see locations such as `/etc/hosts` or `/var/log/syslog`.

At the top of this hierarchy, several standard directories appear on almost every Linux installation. User data typically lives under `/home`, where each user has a subdirectory such as `/home/alice` or `/home/bob`. The root user, which we will explore more later, has its own home directory at `/root`. System-wide configuration files live under `/etc`; if someone tells you "edit the SSH configuration," they are probably referring to `/etc/ssh/sshd_config`. Variable data such as logs, spools, and queues are found in `/var`; a critical subdirectory here is `/var/log`, which holds many of the logs you will read during troubleshooting. Executable programs that ordinary users run are most often found in `/bin` and `/usr/bin`. Temporary data, which the system or applications may delete at any time, tends to go in `/tmp`. You may also encounter `/dev`, which contains device files representing hardware devices; you do not need to administer these for the A+ exam, but recognizing `/dev` as "devices, not regular documents" is helpful.

Once you know that everything hangs off `/`, you can distinguish between **absolute** and **relative** paths. An absolute path begins with `/` and tells you how to reach an item from the root of the file system, such as `/etc/hosts` or `/home/student/Documents`. A relative path is interpreted from whatever directory you are currently in. If you are in `/var` and someone tells you to check `log/auth.log`, the system will look for `/var/log/auth.log` because you are already "inside" `/var`. Two special entries help with relative paths: a single dot (.) means "this directory," and two dots (..) mean "the parent directory one level up." Another shortcut you will see often is the tilde (~), which the shell expands to the current user's home directory. If your user's home is `/home/student`, then `cd ~` and `cd /home/student` do the same thing.

Three commands form the core of navigation on a Linux system. The first is `pwd`, short for "print working directory," which simply tells you where you are in the tree. New technicians often forget to check this and then wonder why they cannot find a file; running `pwd` before you start moving around is a good habit. The second is `ls`, which lists the files and directories in your current location. You can add options to adjust the output, such as `ls -l` for a detailed long listing that includes permissions and sizes, or `ls -a` to show hidden files, which in Linux are any filenames that start with a dot. The third navigation command is `cd`, "change directory," which moves you to a different location. You might run `cd /etc` to go directly to the configuration directory, `cd ..` to move up one level, or `cd ~` to return to your home directory. When you first log into a trouble ticket's Linux host, one reasonable pattern is to run `pwd` to confirm where you are, `ls` to see what is there, and then `cd` to wherever you need to work.

Working with Files and Directories

With navigation under control, the next step is manipulating files and directories in a safe, predictable way. Imagine a simple scenario: a senior admin asks you to make a backup of a configuration file before she edits it, and then later check a log file for error messages. You do not need to know the application in depth; you just need the right file tools.

Linux provides `touch` as a quick way to create an empty file or update the timestamp on an existing one. For example, `touch test.txt` in your home directory will create `test.txt` if it does not exist. To copy files, you use `cp`. A simple `cp file1 file2` creates a copy of `file1` named `file2` in the current directory. When you need to copy directories and everything inside them, you usually add the `-r` (recursive) option, as in `cp -r /etc/myapp /home/student/backup_myapp`. Moving or renaming items is handled by `mv`. The system does not distinguish between "move" and "rename"; if you run `mv oldname newname` in the same directory, you have effectively renamed the file. If you include a path, such as `mv file.txt /tmp/`, then you have moved the file to a new directory.

Removing files is where you need to slow down and be deliberate. The `rm` command deletes files permanently; there is no Recycle Bin or Trash for the shell to recover them from if you change your mind. Deleting a single file, such as `rm old.log`, is straightforward. Deleting directories and their contents usually involves `rm -r directoryname`, and the `-r` flag can be very destructive if you mistype a path or run it in the wrong place. In day-to-day work and on the exam, you should train yourself to read an `rm` command twice before pressing Enter, especially when it includes `-r` or wildcards like `*`. For directory creation and removal, Linux offers `mkdir` to make a new directory and `rmdir` to remove an empty one. If a directory still contains files, `rmdir` will fail, which is often a useful safety net.

To read what is inside a file, you have a few different options. For short configuration files or scripts, `cat` is convenient; it prints the entire contents directly to your terminal. Running `cat /etc/hosts` will show you the local hostname mappings, for example. For longer files—most log files fall into this category—`less` is a better choice. `less /var/log/syslog` opens the file in a paging viewer where you can scroll with the arrow keys or the spacebar, search for strings, and press `q` when you are done. Another helpful tool for logs is `tail`, which shows you the end of a file. If you suspect an issue just occurred, `tail /var/log/auth.log` will display the most recent lines. Adding `-f` to `tail` puts it into "follow" mode, so `tail -f /var/log/syslog` will keep updating your terminal as new log entries are written. Watching a log in real time while a user reproduces a problem is a powerful troubleshooting pattern.

These basic tools combine into many common support workflows. Before editing a configuration file, you might use `cp` to create a backup with a `.bak` extension, such as `cp /etc/app.conf /etc/app.conf.bak`. After making changes (usually with an editor like `nano` or `vi` that we will mention but not cover in depth), you might check related logs under `/var/log` using `less` or `tail` to confirm whether the application is behaving as expected. If you accidentally create a useless test file, `rm` cleans it up. The commands themselves are simple; the professional skill lies in knowing when and where to use them and being cautious with anything that can delete or overwrite data.

Users, Groups, and Permissions

Linux's security model is built around **users**, **groups**, and **permissions**. Every file and directory has an owning user, an associated group, and a set of permissions that specify what the owner, the group, and everyone else can do with it. When you run `ls -l`, you see this information in a structured way. Take an example line like:

```
-rw-r--r-- 1 alice staff 1024 Dec 18 config.txt
```

The first character indicates the type; a hyphen means a regular file, while a `d` would indicate a directory. The next nine characters are grouped into three sets of three: `rw-`, `r--`, and `r--`. These correspond to permissions for the **user** (the owner), the **group**, and **others** (everyone else) in that order. Within each group, `r` stands for read, `w` for write, and `x` for execute. In this example, the owner `alice` can read and write the file but not execute it as a program, while members of the `staff` group and everyone else can only read it.

Permissions on directories are interpreted slightly differently. Read permission on a directory allows you to list its contents. Write permission lets you create or delete files within it. Execute permission on a directory means you can "enter" it and access files there, assuming you also have the appropriate permissions on the files themselves. This is why a directory may have `rwx` permissions even if the files inside are not executable; the `x` simply controls traversal.

The most powerful account on a Linux system is the **root** user. Root effectively bypasses normal permission checking and can read, write, or execute almost anything. That power comes with enormous risk; a careless command run as root can delete or overwrite key system files, render the OS unbootable, or expose sensitive data. For that reason, modern Linux practice favors using **sudo** instead of logging in directly as root. When a user is configured in the appropriate group, they can prefix a command with `sudo`, such as `sudo apt update` or `sudo cp file1 /etc/important.conf`, to run just that command with root privileges. The system will usually prompt for the user's own password and log the command usage for accountability.

Two commands allow administrators to adjust ownership and permissions when necessary. The `chmod` command changes the permission bits. You might see `chmod u+x script.sh`, which adds execute permission for the user on `script.sh`. There is also a numeric notation such as `chmod 755 file`, where `7`, `5`, and `5` represent particular combinations of `r`, `w`, and `x` for user, group, and others respectively. The A+ exam expects you to recognize what chmod does more than to memorize all numeric codes. The `chown` command changes the owning user and group. For example, `sudo chown bob:staff report.txt` would make `bob` the owner of `report.txt` and set its group to `staff`. In many practical support situations, you will not be the one deciding new permissions, but you will read `ls -l` output to understand why a user gets "Permission denied" and communicate clearly to the administrator what needs to change.

Imagine a user on a shared Linux workstation who cannot modify a configuration file in `/etc` even though they insist they need to. You connect, navigate to the directory, and run `ls -l filename`. The output shows that the owner is `root`, the group is `root`, and the permissions are `-rw-r--r--`. The user is not root and not a member of the root group, so they have only read access. From there you can explain that, under the principle of least privilege, they are correctly prevented from editing OS-level configuration, and either escalate the request or offer to make the edit yourself under the change management process.

Processes and System Status

When someone says "the Linux server is slow" or "the app is hanging," you need ways to inspect what is going on under the hood. On Linux, running programs are called **processes**, and several tools help you see and manage them. The simplest is `ps`, which by itself might show only the processes in your current shell. Variants such as `ps aux` or `ps -ef` (the exact flags can vary by distribution traditions) show a full list of processes, along with their process IDs (PIDs), CPU usage, memory usage, and the commands that started them. If an application is clearly misbehaving, an administrator might ask you to find its PID in `ps` output as a first step.

For a live, constantly updated view of the system, `top` is often the tool of choice. Running `top` brings up an interactive display that refreshes every few seconds, showing overall CPU and memory usage at the top and a sorted list of processes below. You can watch in real time which processes are consuming the most resources. On some systems you may also find `htop`, a more colorful and user-friendly version of `top`, but `top` itself is almost universally available and is what the exam is most likely to reference. If you discover a single runaway process pegging the CPU, or an application that is consuming an unreasonable amount of memory, that observation is exactly the kind of concrete detail you want to include when you escalate the ticket.

Sometimes you will be instructed to terminate a stuck process. The `kill` command sends a signal to a process ID, usually asking it to exit gracefully. For example, `kill 1234` would target the process with PID 1234. There are stronger signals that can force an immediate stop, but those are riskier and usually fall under more advanced administration. In an entry-level role, you should follow organizational policy closely before killing processes, because doing so can interrupt business services.

Performance problems often involve storage and memory as well as CPU. The `df` command (disk free) shows you file system usage; `df -h` uses human-readable units such as MB and GB. If a filesystem, especially the root filesystem `/`, is at or near 100% usage, the server may behave erratically, and writes may fail with "No space left on device." The `free` command reports memory usage; `free -h` similarly makes the numbers easier to interpret. On a busy application server, you might use `top`, `df -h`, and `free -h` together to form a quick picture: plenty of CPU but no disk space, or full memory but plenty of storage, and so on. This is often enough to narrow down the problem significantly.

Networking and Connectivity on Linux

Networking fundamentals do not change between operating systems—IP addresses, gateways, subnets, and DNS all work the same way—but the tools you use to see and modify them do. On modern Linux distributions, the primary tool for inspecting network interfaces is the `ip` command. To get a quick summary of addresses on all network interfaces, you can run `ip addr` or the common shorthand `ip a`. The output shows each interface, its IPv4 and IPv6 addresses, and its status. If a server has lost its IP address or is sitting in the wrong subnet, you will see that here. Older documentation and some systems still use `ifconfig`, and you may encounter that on the exam as well, but `ip` is the preferred tool going forward.

Connectivity tests also look familiar. `ping` behaves much the same way as it does on Windows: `ping 8.8.8.8` sends ICMP echo requests to a public DNS server run by Google, and responses indicate basic network connectivity. If pinging an IP works but pinging a hostname such as `ping www.example.com` fails, you have a hint that DNS resolution is the problem. The `ip route` command displays the routing table, including the default gateway, which is important if a host can reach local systems but not anything on other networks. On desktop-oriented distributions that use NetworkManager, a tool called `nmcli` provides command-line control over network connections, although you are less likely to need that in entry-level support scenarios.

For DNS-specific troubleshooting, some systems include `nslookup` or `dig`. With `dig example.com`, you can ask which IP address DNS resolves `example.com` to, providing more detail than a simple ping. These tools are not guaranteed to be installed by default, so do not be surprised if you receive a "command not found" error and have to install a DNS utilities package or ask an administrator to do so.

Consider a typical ticket: a web application running on a Linux server is not reachable by users. You SSH into the server, which already tells you that the machine is up and at least partly reachable. You run `ip addr` to confirm the server still has the expected IP address on the correct interface. Next, you `ping 8.8.8.8` to test outbound connectivity; if that works, routing and external access are likely fine. If inbound connections are the problem, you might ping a client or test access from another server. Having verified that the network stack is functional, you can shift attention to the web service itself or related logs, rather than blaming "the network" in the abstract.

Package Management and Software Installation

Where Windows uses standalone installers like `.exe` and `.msi` files, Linux typically uses **package managers** to install, update, and remove software in a standardized way. The two major families you should recognize for A+ purposes are Debian-based systems, such as Debian and Ubuntu, and Red Hat-based systems, such as Red Hat Enterprise Linux, CentOS, and Fedora. Debian-style distributions use tools like `apt` or `apt-get`, while Red Hat-style distributions use `yum` or its successor `dnf`.

On an Ubuntu server, for example, you might see an administrator run `sudo apt update` to refresh the package lists from configured repositories, followed by `sudo apt install packagename` to install a particular piece of software. On a CentOS server, similar tasks might be done with `sudo yum update` or `sudo dnf install packagename`. These commands automatically handle dependencies and keep track of what is installed. In a production environment, you should be cautious about applying updates or installing new software on your own initiative; many organizations require change management approval before altering server software. For the exam, the key idea is simply to recognize that `apt`, `yum`, and `dnf` are Linux package managers and to choose them appropriately over Windows tools when the scenario clearly involves a Linux system.

Logs and Command-Line Troubleshooting Patterns

Linux systems generate a rich set of logs, and knowing where to find them and how to read them is crucial for troubleshooting. Most system logs are stored under `/var/log`. The exact files vary by distribution, but you are likely to encounter files like `/var/log/syslog` or `/var/log/messages` for general system messages, `/var/log/auth.log` for authentication-related events, and application-specific logs in subdirectories such as `/var/log/apache2` for Apache web servers or `/var/log/nginx` for Nginx. When you are investigating an issue, one of your first moves should be to figure out which log is relevant and examine it with `less`, `tail`, or `grep`.

The `grep` command searches for patterns in text, which makes it ideal for filtering long log files. For example, `grep error /var/log/syslog` will print only the lines in `syslog` that contain the word "error." You can combine pipes and other shell features to create more sophisticated searches, but even simple use of grep is powerful at the A+ level. Suppose a user reports that they tried and failed to log in repeatedly around 10:15 a.m. You might run `grep "10:15" /var/log/auth.log` to find the relevant messages and confirm whether the failures were due to bad passwords, account lockout, or something else entirely.

A basic, repeatable troubleshooting pattern on Linux might look like this. You start by clarifying the symptom: maybe a developer says, "My Linux VM says 'No space left on device,' and the application stopped writing logs." You log into the VM and run `df -h` to check filesystem usage, confirming that `/` is at 100%. You navigate to `/var/log`, use `ls -lh` to spot very large log files, and perhaps use `du` (disk usage) to summarize directory sizes if you are comfortable with it. Before deleting anything, you make a backup copy with `cp`, then remove or truncate the offending log file according to policy. Finally, you rerun `df -h` to verify that space has been freed, and you document what you did in the ticket. At no point did you need deep Linux internals; you simply combined file system knowledge, a few commands, and systematic reasoning.

In another scenario, a Linux web server is reported as down. You SSH in successfully and immediately know the machine itself is alive. You check CPU and memory with `top`, disk space with `df -h`, and nothing is obviously wrong at the OS level. Then you move to the relevant logs in `/var/log/apache2` or `/var/log/nginx`, using `less` and `grep` to look for recent errors. You might see lines indicating that the service failed to bind to port 80 or crashed repeatedly. If you are authorized, you might restart the service with a simple `sudo systemctl restart apache2`; if not, you capture the exact errors and pass them to the administrator. Either way, you have used Linux tools to narrow the fault from "the website is down" to "the web daemon is failing to start because of a configuration or port conflict."

Across all of these examples, the mindset is consistent. Recognize that you are on Linux by cues like forward-slash paths and `sudo` in example commands. Use navigation and file tools to orient yourself. Inspect processes, resources, and network configuration to understand system health. Read logs and permissions output carefully. When the issue is beyond your authority or expertise, escalate with specific evidence instead of vague descriptions. This is exactly the level of Linux fluency the CompTIA A+ exam expects and the level that will make you a confident, effective support technician when Linux appears in your real-world tickets.

6.10 Installing Applications to Meet Requirements

When most people think about installing software, they picture double-clicking an installer and clicking Next a few times. In a home setting, that often works. In a professional environment, that attitude creates unstable systems, security gaps, and angry managers. For an entry-level technician, installing applications is less about "Can I get this to run?" and more about "Does this install meet all the requirements for this user, this device, and this organization?" Once you start thinking in those terms, every installation becomes a small technical and policy puzzle to solve, not just a mechanical task.

At a high level, every application you install has to satisfy several categories of requirements at the same time. There is the obvious **technical compatibility**: the operating system version and edition, the 32- or 64-bit architecture, CPU capabilities, RAM, storage, and any software dependencies like .NET or Java. Even if an installer will launch, that doesn't mean the app is supported or stable on that platform. Then there is the **functional and business fit** question: does this software actually solve the user's problem in a way that aligns with the organization's standards and workflows? A video editor might technically install on an office PC, but that does not mean it belongs in the accounting department. Layered on top of that is **licensing and compliance**. You need to know that there is a legitimate license available, that the license type matches how the software will be used, and that installing it on this device does not break company policy. Finally, there is **security and manageability**. An application that requires local admin rights to run, updates only when a user remembers to check the vendor's website, and was downloaded from an unknown mirror might "work," but it fails the security and operations test.

As you move into real support roles and into exam scenarios, it helps to build a small mental routine you run before any install. You check whether the device meets the requirements, whether there is an appropriate license, whether you have (and should have) the permissions to install it, and what platform or method you should use to deploy it. If you get into that habit now, you avoid the most common pitfalls that CompTIA likes to test: mismatched architectures, ignored OS minimums, unauthorized software, and unsafe shortcuts around security controls.

A large part of this routine is simply learning to slow down and read system requirements properly instead of assuming "if I can download it, it must work." Vendor download pages and app store listings are full of critical clues. You will see lines such as "Windows 10 64-bit or later," "macOS 12+," "Android 10 and above," or "requires a 64-bit processor with AVX2 support." The "or later" and "+" phrasing is telling you the minimum supported version, not a suggestion. If a desktop is still on Windows 8.1, an application marked "Windows 10 64-bit or later" is not supported, no matter how fast the hardware feels. The same is true in the other direction: an older 32-bit operating system cannot run a 64-bit-only application; Windows will simply refuse to launch it. On the other hand, a 64-bit edition of Windows can usually run 32-bit applications thanks to the WoW64 subsystem, which is why you often see separate "x86" and "x64" download links on vendor sites.

You also need to distinguish between **minimum** and **recommended** specifications. Minimum RAM or CPU requirements typically represent the absolute floor at which the application will open at all, not the level at which it will be pleasant or productive to use. If a graphics application lists 4 GB RAM as minimum and 8 GB as recommended, and you install it on a 4 GB system that also needs to run a browser, email, and antivirus, the user will feel like the PC is "broken" even though it technically meets the vendor's minimum. The same goes for storage. Many installers will check that there is enough free space for the installation itself, but they cannot predict how much user data will be generated. If a database client claims to need 2 GB and you have 3 GB free on the C: drive, you should already be thinking about cleaning up, expanding storage, or choosing a different target disk.

Dependencies are another area where new technicians get caught. A line that says "requires .NET Framework 4.8 or later" or "Java 11 runtime required" is not a suggestion. If you miss this and rush the install, you might get through the wizard only to find error messages the first time you launch the program. Some installers will attempt to download and install needed components for you; others will simply fail with a vague error message. In many exam scenarios, the right answer involves recognizing that a missing dependency, not the OS itself, is preventing a successful install.

Along with requirements comes the question of where you get the software. In a corporate environment, you are rarely choosing software on your own. Most organizations maintain an approved software list and have standardized on particular versions and license models. Before you grab an installer, you should know whether the software is **per-device** or **per-user**, whether it uses a **subscription** model, and how many licenses are available. Per-seat or per-device licenses typically allow installation on a fixed number of systems; concurrent licenses allow a certain number of simultaneous users regardless of how many copies are installed. Subscription models, especially for Software as a Service (SaaS) offerings, are usually linked to accounts in platforms such as Microsoft 365 or Adobe Creative Cloud. You may be responsible for installing the client application, but the actual access is controlled by the user's identity in the vendor's cloud. Installing the same per-user subscription on five different office PCs does not magically give five people legal access, and exam questions may ask you to recognize that.

You also need to distinguish among **OEM**, retail, and various free software categories. OEM licenses are tied to the hardware they ship with and are not meant to be transferred to another device. Retail licenses are generally more flexible. Some software is freeware with no cost but possibly significant usage restrictions, some is time-limited trial or shareware, and some is fully open source, where you can inspect and even modify the code under the terms of an open-source license. From a support perspective, the safety of the **source** matters just as much as the license terms. Official vendor sites and platform-specific stores such as the Microsoft Store, Mac App Store, Google Play, and the Apple App Store are safer defaults than random third-party download portals. Pirated or "cracked" software is out of bounds: besides the obvious legal violations, you are effectively trusting unknown attackers with full access to the system.

Once you understand what you are installing and whether you're allowed to install it, you decide how to install it. For a single user on a standalone PC, an interactive local installation may be entirely appropriate. On Windows, that usually means running an **EXE** or **MSI** installer, following the prompts, and choosing options such as installation location and whether the app should be available to "just me" or "all users." The "all users" choice writes application files into system-wide locations such as Program Files and creates Start menu entries visible to everyone; it generally requires administrative rights. Installing "just for me" often stores files under the user's profile and may not require elevation, but it also means that if another user logs into the same computer, they may not even see that the application exists. Many exam questions subtly hinge on recognizing that kind of scoping issue.

For macOS, you often encounter **DMG** disk images or **PKG** installers. A DMG will mount like a virtual disk, revealing the application bundle. The usual pattern is to drag the application into the **/Applications** folder for system-wide availability or into **~/Applications** inside the user's home folder for a user-specific install. PKG files behave much like traditional installers, stepping through a wizard and writing files into their proper locations. Both patterns may trigger macOS **Gatekeeper**, which enforces policies about whether apps can run depending on where they came from and whether the developer is identified. When macOS warns that an app "can't be opened because it is from an unidentified developer," it is not challenging your ego as a technician; it is enforcing policy. If your organization explicitly allows that vendor, the correct response is to verify that the file truly came from the official site, confirm it supports the running macOS version, and then use the approved method to open it, such as right-clicking the app and choosing Open or adjusting the Security & Privacy settings as permitted. Simply disabling Gatekeeper system-wide would be the wrong answer in both the exam and real life.

On Linux systems, especially in server or developer environments, application installation is more often done through **package managers** than standalone installers. On a Debian- or Ubuntu-based distribution, that means using tools like `apt` to install packages from repositories: `sudo apt install package-name`. On Red Hat, CentOS, or Fedora, you might use `dnf` or `yum`. These repositories are curated sets of software that the distribution maintainers support. Installing from them is generally safer and easier to maintain than grabbing a random `.deb` or `.rpm` file from the web. When you must use third-party packages or compressed archives, you should be aware you are stepping outside the usual trust boundary and potentially taking on extra work around updates and security. Again, the principle is the same: meet requirements, respect policy, and choose the safest, most manageable method available.

Mobile platforms look different, but the underlying decisions are the same. On Android and iOS, the primary method of installation is through the official app stores. Here, app listings will specify minimum OS versions, required device features (like GPS, camera, or gyroscope), storage needs, and requested permissions such as access to contacts, microphone, or location. In a corporate environment, smartphones and tablets may be enrolled in a **Mobile Device Management (MDM)** system. Instead of the user freely installing apps, you might be pushing apps to devices from a centralized console or making them available through a company portal. Sideloading—installing apps from outside the official store—is typically disabled by policy because it bypasses a major security control. If you see an exam scenario where an employee wants to install a third-party APK file on a managed Android device, the expected answer is not to show them how to enable developer options, but to follow policy: either deny the request or escalate it for formal review and packaging through the MDM platform.

Throughout all of these platforms, security and permissions considerations are woven into every step. In Windows, many installers will trigger **User Account Control (UAC)** prompts because they need to write into protected areas of the file system or the registry. Treat those prompts as a deliberate pause, not an annoyance. Before entering admin credentials or clicking Yes, verify that the installer is expected, that the publisher listed matches the vendor, and that the user's request has been approved. If a standard user cannot install an application because they do not have administrator rights, that is usually by design. The correct approach is to use an authorized admin account or a software deployment mechanism, not to weaken UAC settings. The same principle of **least privilege** applies everywhere: only grant the rights necessary for installation, and do not leave behind elevated privileges for everyday app use unless the software truly requires it, in which case you may need to reconsider the software choice.

Even when you have the right installer, the right permissions, and the right hardware, things still go wrong. A disciplined troubleshooting approach will save you time and match exactly what the exam expects. Start by paying attention to error messages rather than immediately trying random fixes. "This app can't run on your PC" in Windows, "not a valid Win32 application," "requires macOS 12.0 or later," "package not found," or "insufficient storage available" on a mobile device are not mysteries; they are clues. Once you have the symptoms, circle back to requirements and constraints. Confirm the OS version and architecture, check available disk space, verify that you are online if the installer needs to download components, and consider whether group policies, application whitelisting, or MDM restrictions are blocking the process.

From there, form a simple theory and test it. If an installer refuses to run because the OS is too old, the solution is not to force the install; it is to either upgrade the operating system (if supported and approved) or select an older version of the application that still supports that platform. If a package manager cannot find a package, perhaps the repository is disabled or the system's package lists are outdated. If a macOS app will not open due to Gatekeeper, check whether it has the proper signature or if policy requires a different distribution channel. After each change, try the install or launch again and see if the behavior improves. Only when you have a successful installation should you consider the job done, and even then you should take a moment to verify that the application not only opens but can perform a basic task relevant to the user.

These installation decisions, and the reasoning behind them, are exactly what later chapters on documentation and change management build on. Many organizations require you to log what was installed, on which device, under which license, and for which user or department. That might feel bureaucratic, but when you need to troubleshoot a performance issue, investigate a security incident, or count licenses during an audit, those records are invaluable. In the exam, this often appears as a final step in the troubleshooting process: after resolving an installation issue or deploying new software, the correct last step is to update documentation or close the ticket with clear notes. Thinking about application installation as a requirement-driven, policy-aware process now will make those later topics feel like a natural extension rather than new burdens added on top.

6.11 Knowledge Check

Question 1: A user with a 32-bit version of Windows 10 is trying to install a "Windows 10 64-bit only" accounting application and gets an error that the app cannot run on this PC. Which underlying issue best explains this problem?

- **A.** The system does not have enough free disk space for the installer to complete successfully
- **B.** The CPU does not support virtualization extensions required by the accounting application
- **C.** The OS architecture cannot run a 64-bit-only application on a 32-bit Windows installation
- **D.** The user does not have local administrator rights on the computer to install the software

Question 2: A user in a small office needs to join their Windows laptop to the company's on-premises Active Directory domain and enable BitLocker drive encryption. Which minimum Windows edition do they need?

- **A.** Windows 11 Home, which supports local accounts but not domain join or BitLocker
- **B.** Windows 11 Pro, which supports both domain join and BitLocker drive encryption
- **C.** Windows 11 Home in S Mode, which restricts apps to the Microsoft Store only
- **D.** Windows 11 Education, which is typically licensed for academic institutions only

Question 3: A school wants inexpensive laptops that are easy to centrally manage, used mostly for web apps and Google Workspace, with minimal local storage and automatic enrollment into Google's management tools. Which client OS is the best fit?

- **A.** Linux Mint, a general-purpose desktop Linux distribution for individual users
- **B.** ChromeOS, a web-centric OS tightly integrated with Google Workspace and management
- **C.** Windows 11 Home, a consumer OS without native Google Workspace management
- **D.** macOS, a premium desktop OS designed primarily for Apple hardware users

Question 4: A user says their Windows 11 PC is "very slow" and the desktop takes several minutes to become usable after sign-in. You suspect too many nonessential apps are starting with Windows. Which tool should you use first to safely disable unnecessary startup applications?

- **A.** Services (services.msc) to stop and disable background Windows services globally
- **B.** System Configuration (msconfig) Services tab to turn off system and third-party services
- **C.** Local Group Policy Editor (gpedit.msc) to create policies that block startup programs
- **D.** Task Manager Startup tab to review and disable nonessential startup applications

Question 5: A Windows 10 system frequently reports file system errors after a recent power outage. You want to scan and repair logical file system problems and check for bad sectors on the C: volume. Which single command is most appropriate?

- **A.** chkdsk C: /f /r to fix file system errors and locate bad sectors on the volume
- **B.** sfc /scannow to verify and repair protected Windows system files only
- **C.** diskpart /fixfs to modify disk partitions and low-level disk configuration
- **D.** bootrec /rebuildbcd to repair the boot configuration data for startup issues

Question 6: A user complains that their Windows 11 laptop connects to Wi-Fi and can browse the internet, but they cannot see any shared folders or printers on the office LAN. You discover that the network profile is set to Public. What is the best next step?

- **A.** Disable Windows Defender Firewall entirely so that all network traffic is allowed
- **B.** Assign a static IP address instead of using DHCP to reach the shared resources
- **C.** Change the network profile to Private and ensure network discovery and file/printer sharing are enabled for that profile
- **D.** Run ipconfig /flushdns and reboot the wireless access point to refresh name resolution

Question 7: A MacBook user reports that a video conferencing app can't access their webcam, even though the camera works in other apps. Which macOS area should you check and adjust first?

- **A.** Finder preferences to change how files and folders are displayed on the desktop
- **B.** Users & Groups login items to control which apps start automatically at login
- **C.** Dock & Menu Bar settings to customize icons and menu bar appearance only
- **D.** Privacy & Security camera permissions to allow the app to use the built-in webcam

Question 8: A user running Ubuntu Desktop over SSH asks you to "see what's eating all the CPU right now." Which Linux command provides an interactive, continuously updating view of real-time CPU and memory usage by process?

- **A.** top, which shows a live, updating list of processes and their resource usage
- **B.** ps aux, which lists running processes in a static snapshot of current activity
- **C.** free -h, which summarizes overall memory usage in human-readable units
- **D.** df -h, which reports disk space usage on mounted filesystems only

Question 9: A user upgraded their graphics driver and now experiences frequent crashes in Windows 10. In Device Manager, which action is the most appropriate to return to the previous stable driver version?

- **A.** Disable the device so that Windows stops using the graphics adapter entirely
- **B.** Uninstall the device and scan for hardware changes to reinstall the same driver
- **C.** Update driver and search automatically online for a potentially newer driver
- **D.** Use Roll Back Driver on the Driver tab to restore the previously installed version

Question 10: A Windows 11 PC will not boot and displays "Operating system not found." You boot from Windows installation media, open the Recovery Command Prompt, and determine that the boot records are likely corrupted. Which command-line tool is specifically intended to repair the MBR and boot configuration?

- **A.** bootrec, which repairs the MBR, boot sector, and Boot Configuration Data (BCD)
- **B.** chkdsk, which scans disks for file system errors and bad sectors on volumes
- **C.** sfc, which verifies and repairs protected Windows system files within the OS
- **D.** diskpart, which manages disk partitions and volumes but not boot records directly

Question 11: A user running Windows 10 reports that their screen text is very small and hard to read, even though they are using the monitor's native resolution. Which setting should you adjust first to make text larger without lowering resolution?

A. Display scaling percentage in Settings > System > Display to enlarge text and UI
B. Color calibration in Control Panel to adjust color balance and gamma levels
C. Monitor refresh rate in advanced display settings to change how often the screen updates
D. Font smoothing options in Performance Settings to improve text anti-aliasing only

Question 12: A Windows 11 Home user wants to enable BitLocker and join their laptop to an on-premises Active Directory domain, but the options are not available. You confirm they are running Windows 11 Home, not in S Mode. What should you recommend?

A. Disable UAC and enable Domain Services in Windows Features to unlock enterprise options
B. Upgrade the OS to Windows 11 Pro to gain BitLocker and on-prem domain join capabilities
C. Reinstall Windows 11 Home from scratch to unlock hidden encryption and domain features
D. Enable Hyper-V and use a VM to connect to the domain instead of the host system

Question 13: A Linux admin asks you to confirm how much free disk space remains on each mounted filesystem of a server. Which command is best suited for this, with human-readable output?

A. free -h, which shows memory and swap usage in human-readable format
B. df -h, which displays disk space usage for mounted filesystems in human-readable units
C. ls -l, which lists directory contents with detailed file information only
D. du -h /, which summarizes disk usage per directory starting from the root

Question 14: A user on Windows 10 reports that they receive repeated prompts that Windows Defender Firewall is blocking features of a new application on public Wi-Fi. They need the app to accept incoming connections only on their trusted home network and not in public places. How should you configure the firewall?

A. Turn off the firewall for the Public profile only so that all apps work on public Wi-Fi
B. Turn off the firewall completely for all profiles to avoid any future prompts
C. Allow the app through the firewall on both Public and Private networks for convenience
D. Allow the app through the firewall only on Private (and/or Domain) networks, not on Public

Question 15: A technician must verify detailed hardware and OS information (such as BIOS version, total RAM, and Windows build) on a Windows 11 PC to check compatibility with a new application. Which built-in GUI tool provides a comprehensive, read-only overview of this information?

A. System Information (msinfo32), which summarizes hardware resources and system details
B. Task Manager Performance tab, which shows real-time CPU, memory, and disk usage graphs
C. System Configuration (msconfig), which manages boot options and startup selections
D. Device Manager, which lists hardware devices and their drivers without full system summary

Question 16: A Windows user complains that a specific program crashes "every few days," but they can't remember exactly when. You want a visual history of application failures and system changes to correlate patterns over time. Which Windows tool should you use?

A. Reliability Monitor, which displays a timeline of crashes, warnings, and key events
B. Performance Monitor, which tracks performance counters and resource usage trends
C. Resource Monitor, which shows real-time CPU, disk, network, and memory activity
D. Computer Management, which consolidates several administrative tools in one console

Question 17: A Windows 10 user says they can open websites but cannot access a shared folder using its hostname (for example, \fileserver), while accessing it by IP address works. Which command is the best first step on their workstation to address potential stale DNS entries?

A. ipconfig /release to drop the current IP address lease from the DHCP server
B. ipconfig /flushdns to clear the local DNS resolver cache on the workstation
C. nslookup /clearcache to remove cached entries from the DNS server database
D. net use /purge to remove existing mapped network drive connections only

Question 18: A help-desk technician needs to remotely view and control a user's Windows 11 desktop over the internet so they can walk the user through troubleshooting, with the user watching everything the technician does. Which built-in Windows tool is specifically designed for this scenario?

A. Remote Desktop Connection (mstsc), which connects to unattended remote hosts only
B. Quick Assist, which allows interactive remote assistance with user consent
C. Windows PowerShell Remoting, which provides command-line remote management only
D. Event Viewer Remote Management, which lets admins view remote event logs only

Question 19: A company uses thin clients that connect to a virtual desktop infrastructure (VDI) hosted on Windows Server. A user reports that their thin client powers on but cannot reach the login screen of the virtual desktop at all. Which layer is the most likely area of initial focus for troubleshooting?

A. The user's Windows domain profile and roaming settings inside the virtual desktop
B. The performance of the VDI host hypervisor and virtual machine resource usage
C. Application crashes inside the remote Windows desktop session after login
D. The thin client device, its firmware configuration, or its local network connectivity

Question 20: A Windows 11 Pro laptop frequently drops its Wi-Fi connection after waking from sleep, while other devices on the same network are fine. You want to check and update the wireless adapter's driver and power management settings. Which tool is the best starting point?

A. Device Manager, to manage drivers and hardware power settings for the adapter
B. Disk Management, to partition and format local storage drives on the system
C. Task Scheduler, to configure automated tasks and scripts based on triggers
D. Event Viewer, to review system logs but not directly change driver settings

ANSWERS

1: Correct Answer: C
Rationale: A 32-bit Windows OS cannot execute 64-bit-only applications because the OS architecture does not support 64-bit binaries. Disk space, virtualization support, or admin rights would cause different issues, not a specific 32-/64-bit incompatibility error.

2: Correct Answer: B
Rationale: Domain join and BitLocker require at least a Pro or business edition. Windows 11 Pro supports both. Home and Home in S Mode lack these features; Education can support them but is not the minimum and is for academic licensing.

3: Correct Answer: B
Rationale: ChromeOS is optimized for web apps, integrates with Google Workspace, supports centralized management, and auto-enrolls in Google Admin, matching the school's requirements. The other OS options lack this tight Google management focus.

4: Correct Answer: D
Rationale: The Task Manager Startup tab is the recommended place to review and disable nonessential startup apps without risking critical services. Services, msconfig, or Group Policy are more intrusive and not the first choice for this symptom.

5: Correct Answer: A
Rationale: chkdsk C: /f /r scans the C: volume, fixes logical file system errors (/f), and checks for bad sectors while attempting recovery (/r). sfc repairs protected system files, diskpart manages partitions, and bootrec fixes boot data, not full file system checks.

6: Correct Answer: C
Rationale: A Public profile disables network discovery and file/printer sharing by default. Changing the profile to Private and enabling discovery and sharing for that profile allows access to LAN resources while keeping stricter rules for public networks.

7: Correct Answer: D
Rationale: Camera access is controlled in System Settings > Privacy & Security > Camera. If the app is denied there, it cannot use the webcam even if others can. Finder, login items, and Dock settings do not manage camera permissions.

8: Correct Answer: A
Rationale: top provides an interactive, continuously updating list of processes with CPU and memory usage, ideal for seeing what is "eating CPU" in real time. ps aux is static, free -h shows memory totals, and df -h shows disk usage only.

9: Correct Answer: D
Rationale: Roll Back Driver in Device Manager restores the previous driver version, appropriate when a new driver causes crashes. Disabling the device stops it from working, uninstalling usually reinstalls the same driver, and updating may not revert to the known good version.

10: Correct Answer: A
Rationale: bootrec from the recovery environment repairs the MBR, boot sector, and BCD, addressing "Operating system not found" due to corrupted boot records. chkdsk checks file systems, sfc repairs system files, and diskpart manages partitions, not boot records directly.

11: Correct Answer: A
Rationale: Increasing display scaling in Settings > System > Display enlarges text and UI elements while keeping native resolution, preserving clarity. Color calibration, refresh rate, and font smoothing do not significantly increase text size.

12: Correct Answer: B
Rationale: BitLocker and on-prem AD domain join are not available in Windows 11 Home. Upgrading to Windows 11 Pro (or another business edition) is required. Reinstalling Home, changing UAC, or using Hyper-V does not add these host OS features.

13: Correct Answer: B
Rationale: df -h shows disk space usage and free space for mounted filesystems in human-readable units, matching the admin's need. free -h shows memory, ls -l lists files, and du -h / reports per-directory usage, not overall filesystem free space.

14: Correct Answer: D
Rationale: Allowing the app through Windows Defender Firewall only on Private (and/or Domain) networks lets it accept incoming connections on trusted networks while remaining blocked on Public networks, which is the secure behavior for public Wi-Fi.

15: Correct Answer: A
Rationale: System Information (msinfo32) provides a detailed, read-only summary of hardware and system details, including BIOS version, RAM, and Windows build. Task Manager, msconfig, and Device Manager do not offer as complete a compatibility overview.

16: Correct Answer: A
Rationale: Reliability Monitor shows a graphical timeline of crashes, warnings, and key system changes, helping correlate intermittent app failures with dates and events. Performance Monitor and Resource Monitor focus on performance, and Computer Management is a general console.

17: Correct Answer: B
Rationale: ipconfig /flushdns clears the local DNS resolver cache, resolving issues where hostnames like \fileserver map to stale IPs. Releasing the IP, clearing DNS server caches, or purging mapped drives do not directly clear the workstation's DNS cache.

18: Correct Answer: B
Rationale: Quick Assist is built into Windows for remote assistance, allowing a technician, with user consent, to view and control the user's desktop while the user watches. Remote Desktop is for unattended sessions, and PowerShell remoting and Event Viewer are non-GUI admin tools.

19: Correct Answer: D
Rationale: If the thin client cannot reach the virtual desktop login screen, initial troubleshooting should focus on the thin client hardware, firmware/configuration, and its local network connectivity. Profile, hypervisor performance, or in-session app issues occur after login.

20: Correct Answer: A
Rationale: Device Manager is the correct tool to view and update the wireless adapter's driver and adjust its power management settings. Disk Management handles storage, Task Scheduler automates tasks, and Event Viewer only logs events.

CHAPTER 7

Security

7.1 Physical & Logical Security Measures

Imagine this: a sales rep leaves a company laptop on a table at a coffee shop, runs to the counter to grab an order, and by the time they turn around, the laptop is gone. As a support technician, you'll eventually hear some version of this story. When that call comes in, your first concern is not the hardware cost—though that hurts too. The real question is, "What did that laptop have access to, and how well was that access protected?" The answer depends on two broad categories of defenses: **physical security**, which failed when the thief walked away with the device, and **logical security**, which may still stand between the attacker and the data if the laptop was configured properly.

Security in IT support is really about managing risk through layers. You'll see this described as **defense in depth**: multiple, overlapping controls so that if one fails, others still limit the damage. With that stolen laptop, a cable lock would have made it harder to grab in the first place. A strong login password and full-disk encryption would help keep the data confidential even after the device is lost. Central account controls could allow the user's credentials to be disabled. None of these measures is perfect alone, but together they give you a very different outcome than a completely unsecured machine.

Underneath those layers is a simple framework you'll see throughout the exam and your career: the **CIA triad**. Security controls are ultimately there to protect **confidentiality**, **integrity**, and **availability**. Confidentiality is about keeping information secret from people who are not supposed to see it. Locking an office door, encrypting files, or using strong authentication all support confidentiality. Integrity is about making sure information stays accurate and unaltered except through authorized changes. File permissions that prevent users from overwriting critical data, or change control processes that track who modifies configurations, are integrity protections. Availability is about making sure systems and data are reachable when needed: here, protecting equipment from theft or damage, providing redundant systems, and managing power and environment are key. As you work through physical and logical controls, it helps to keep asking, "Which part of CIA is this mainly protecting?"

Physical Security: Controlling the Real World

New technicians sometimes think of security only as firewalls and passwords, but physical security is often more fundamental. If an attacker can walk into a room, sit down at a machine, plug in a device, or carry equipment out the door, many logical controls become much easier to bypass. For that reason, organizations put a lot of effort into controlling access to spaces and protecting the devices themselves.

At the facility level, you will encounter **secure areas** such as locked offices, server rooms, and network closets. Critical infrastructure—servers, switches, backup devices—should never be in public or easily accessible spaces. Access to these rooms is usually controlled by mechanical keys or, more often in modern environments, by electronic systems such as badges, keycards, or key fobs. These electronic systems are preferred because they can be centrally managed: a lost badge can be deactivated, access can be logged and audited, and permissions can be changed without rekeying locks. Some environments add PIN pads or **biometric readers** for high-value areas, combining "something you have" (a card) with "something you know" (a PIN) or "something you are" (a fingerprint) to strengthen control.

Part of physical security is managing people who are not regular employees. **Visitor management** is where you'll see sign-in sheets or electronic visitor logs at reception, temporary visitor badges, and policies requiring visitors to be escorted in restricted zones. As a support tech, you might be the person who escorts a vendor into the server room or verifies that someone asking for access is actually on the approved list. It's not glamorous, but it's a critical part of keeping strangers from wandering into sensitive spaces and potentially tampering with equipment or viewing confidential information.

Physical security is not only about keeping people out; it's also about being able to see and respond when something happens. Organizations deploy surveillance cameras, often referred to as **CCTV** systems, in hallways, entrances, and server rooms. These are **detective** and **deterrent** controls more than preventive ones—cameras do not stop a theft by themselves, but the knowledge that an action is recorded can discourage casual misbehavior, and recordings provide evidence after incidents. Alarm systems, motion sensors, and appropriate lighting around entrances and parking lots all contribute to making it harder to attack or steal from the facility without being noticed.

As you move closer to the devices you work with every day, the physical controls get more hands-on. In open offices, libraries, training rooms, or public kiosks, you'll see **cable locks** attached to laptops or small desktops. These locks thread through a metal security slot on the device and anchor it to a desk or cart. A determined thief with tools could eventually defeat a cable lock, but it greatly increases the effort and time required, which is often enough to prevent opportunistic theft. Network equipment and servers are commonly mounted in locking racks or cabinets so that even someone who makes it into the room cannot simply unplug and walk away with a switch.

A related class of physical controls focuses on ports and visibility. **Port locks** can block unused USB ports, network jacks, or video connectors so that casual users cannot plug in unauthorized devices. In some workplaces, security policies explicitly restrict the use of personal USB drives or phones for data transfer, and port locks help enforce that. **Privacy filters**—those dark, polarized screens you may have seen on laptops or monitors—limit the viewing angle so that only someone directly in front of the screen can read it. In reception areas, hospitals, call centers, or any place where screens face public spaces, privacy filters help protect against "shoulder surfing," where someone glances at sensitive information on a screen as they pass by.

Even data that is not currently online needs protection. Backup tapes, external drives, and printed reports often contain highly sensitive information. These should be stored in locked, and ideally fire-resistant, cabinets or safes. From an availability standpoint, those storage areas should also be environmentally appropriate: dry, temperature-controlled rooms rather than hot closets or damp basements. Physical and environmental protections meet here—if your backups are stolen or destroyed, data may be both unavailable and no longer confidential.

The important habit to build is matching the control to the threat. When the risk is "unauthorized person gets near the equipment," you should think first in terms of physical measures: doors, locks, badges, cameras, cable locks, visitor logs. When the risk is "authorized person misuses or overuses access," you lean more on logical controls and policies.

Logical Security: Who You Are, What You Can Do

Physical controls are about controlling the real-world environment around systems. **Logical security** builds on top of that to control how systems are accessed and what users can do once they are in. Even in a perfectly secured building, someone can still cause damage if they log in with weak credentials or have more privileges than they need. Logical controls are where your daily configuration work as a technician will often focus.

It helps to separate three closely related ideas: **identification**, **authentication**, and **authorization**. Identification is the act of claiming an identity: typing a username into a login prompt, presenting a badge to a card reader, or entering an email address into a cloud service. Authentication is proving that claim, usually by providing a credential such as a password, a PIN, a fingerprint, a smart card, or a one-time code. Authorization is what happens after you're successfully authenticated: the system decides which files, applications, settings, or network resources you're actually allowed to access. A server might authenticate you as "jsmith," but whether "jsmith" can open a payroll spreadsheet or modify a firewall rule is an authorization decision.

You will often hear these ideas grouped into the **AAA model**: **authentication**, **authorization**, and **accounting**. Accounting in this context means logging and auditing—tracking who did what and when. When you later troubleshoot failed logins or suspicious activity, those logs become critical for understanding whether credentials were misused, accounts were attacked, or permissions were misconfigured.

The strength of authentication depends largely on the factors used. Security professionals talk about **factors** as categories of proof. The most common are "something you know," "something you have," and "something you are." **Something you know** includes passwords, passphrases, and PINs. These are convenient and inexpensive to implement but are also vulnerable to guessing, reuse, and phishing. **Something you have** is a physical or virtual object in your possession: a smart card, a hardware token, a mobile phone receiving SMS codes, or an authenticator app generating one-time codes. **Something you are** refers to biometrics: fingerprints, facial recognition, iris patterns, and similar traits.

When you combine factors from at least two different categories, you have **multifactor authentication (MFA)**. A common example is a password (something you know) plus a code from an authenticator app on your phone (something you have). A badge plus a PIN at a door is another MFA combination. It's important to notice that using multiple items from the same factor category does not make it multifactor. A password plus a security question is still just "something you know," even if it feels like two steps. On the exam, when a question asks for a "stronger authentication method" than a password alone, the better answer is usually to add another factor, such as a hardware token or phone app, rather than just making the password more complex.

Accounts, Permissions, and Least Privilege

Once you can reliably identify and authenticate users, the next job of logical security is to control what they are allowed to do. This is where **accounts**, **groups**, and **permissions** come in. You worked with accounts when you learned about operating systems, but security pushes you to think more carefully about how they're used.

On a standalone machine, users log in with **local accounts** that exist only on that system. In a business environment, most accounts will be domain or directory accounts managed centrally, allowing a single username and password to apply across many systems and making it easier to disable or update access when someone changes roles. Regardless of where the account lives, there is a key distinction between general **standard user accounts** and elevated **administrator** (or root) accounts. The principle of **least privilege** says that each user should have only the minimum rights necessary to perform their job. That means using a standard account for day-to-day work and only invoking administrator rights when there is a specific, approved need, like installing software or changing system-wide settings.

Permissions are how those rights are implemented. At a conceptual level, typical file and folder permissions include the ability to read (view contents), write (modify contents), execute (run as a program), modify (change or delete), and take full control (change permissions themselves). Rather than assigning permissions one user at a time, administrators often organize users into **groups** based on job function—such as "Sales," "HR," or "Help Desk Level 1"—and then assign permissions to the groups. This model, sometimes called role-based access control, simplifies administration and supports least privilege: new employees are placed into the right groups, and their access aligns with their role automatically.

A subtle but important point is that **deny** permissions are usually stronger than allow permissions. If a user is a member of two groups, one that allows access and one that explicitly denies it, the deny will typically win. In practice, explicit denies are used sparingly and carefully, but you need to be aware of this behavior when analyzing scenarios. When someone complains that they cannot access a resource they believe they should see, part of your troubleshooting is to check both group memberships and any explicit denies.

You will often face pressure from users who want administrator rights "just to install this one program" or "because it's easier." Granting those rights broadly can feel like it reduces your short-term workload, but it dramatically increases the risk of malware infections, accidental misconfigurations, and data loss. Sticking to least privilege, even when it means you or a senior tech must perform certain actions on behalf of users, is one of the most effective everyday security measures you can support.

Passwords, Sessions, and Everyday Defenses

For most users, the login password is the most visible part of security. The way password policies are designed and enforced has a huge effect on both usability and risk. Traditional guidance focused on high complexity and frequent changes: short passwords full of symbols, rotated every 30 or 60 days. Modern best practice, reflected in newer standards, emphasizes **length** and memorability over arbitrary complexity, and changing passwords primarily when there is evidence of compromise. An organization might require at least 12 characters with a mix of character types, but allow passphrases that are easier to remember and harder to guess than something like "P@ssw0rd1."

Whatever the exact rules, your role often includes enforcing password policies through system settings and educating users about safe habits. That means discouraging obvious choices such as birthdays, pet names, or simple patterns, and warning against reusing the same password across many different sites. On corporate systems, **lockout policies** usually kick in after a certain number of failed login attempts, temporarily disabling the account or requiring help desk intervention. These controls slow down brute-force guessing attacks but also generate tickets from legitimate users who mistype their passwords several times in a row, so you'll see both the security and the operational side of them.

Beyond initial login, session security is just as important. An unattended workstation with an unlocked session is a disaster waiting to happen. Anyone walking by can sit down, read email, copy files, send messages as that user, or change settings, and all of it will appear to come from the legitimate account. To reduce this risk, systems are typically configured with **screen lock and timeout** settings: after a few minutes of inactivity, the display locks and requires the password again. As a tech, you will often be responsible for confirming that these timeouts are set appropriately and for showing users how to manually lock their screens when they step away, especially in areas where visitors or other staff can approach the workstation.

This risk is easy to visualize in a lobby or reception scenario. Picture walking past the front desk at lunchtime and seeing the receptionist's computer sitting unlocked and unattended, with a calendar and internal contacts visible. Visitors are seated within a few steps of the keyboard. In that moment, both physical and logical security are failing. In the short term, you might lock the workstation if policy allows, or find the receptionist or a supervisor to do so. In the longer term, you would look for missing logical controls (perhaps the inactivity timeout is set too long or not enforced by policy) and consider physical and visual protections like repositioning the monitor or adding a privacy filter. Antivirus and complex network tools are irrelevant here; recognizing the session and physical exposure is the key.

Firmware and Boot Security: The Bridge Layer

Some of the most powerful safeguards sit at a layer between physical and logical security: the system firmware and boot process. Modern computers use **BIOS** or, more commonly now, **UEFI** firmware to initialize hardware and hand control to the operating system. If an attacker with physical access can alter firmware settings or boot from a malicious USB drive, they may be able to bypass operating system logins entirely. That's why many organizations protect firmware configuration itself.

You can usually set a **setup password** (also called a supervisor or administrator password) in BIOS/UEFI. This does not prevent the system from booting, but it does prevent unauthorized users from changing firmware settings such as the boot order or turning off security features. In some cases, there is also an optional **user or boot password** that must be entered for the system to start at all, providing a second barrier if someone tries to use the machine without permission. From the exam perspective, it is important to distinguish these: one protects access to settings, the other to the boot process itself.

Another key control is the **boot sequence**. By default, many systems will attempt to boot from removable media such as USB drives or DVDs before booting from the internal drive. Attackers can exploit this by booting a live operating system from removable media to access files on the internal disk without knowing the main OS password. Disabling boot from external devices, or at least moving the internal drive to the top of the boot order and protecting firmware with a setup password, makes this much harder. In enterprise deployments, **Secure Boot** can also be enabled to ensure that only operating systems and bootloaders signed by trusted authorities are allowed to start, blocking some types of rootkits and unauthorized OS images.

These firmware controls illustrate how physical and logical security meet. The threat starts with physical access to the machine, but the defense is implemented through logical configuration. On exam questions, when you see a scenario describing an attacker booting from a USB stick to bypass Windows logon, the appropriate countermeasures involve the boot order, firmware passwords, and potentially Secure Boot, not malware tools or user account changes.

Controls, Policies, and Your Role

Finally, it is worth emphasizing that technical controls do not exist in a vacuum. Every lock, timeout, and permission setting should tie back to an organizational **policy**. Policies such as acceptable use, password standards, clean desk requirements, badge display rules, and visitor handling define what the organization expects from employees. **Administrative controls** like these are then enforced by the **physical controls** we've discussed—doors, locks, badges, cameras—and by **logical controls** like permissions, authentication, and timeouts.

A **clean desk policy**, for instance, supports confidentiality by requiring that sensitive documents not be left out where others can see them. Logical measures such as screen locks and secure printing features, and physical measures like locked drawers and shredders, help staff comply. A badge policy that insists employees wear ID visibly is backed by locked doors and badge readers; your job may include troubleshooting those badge readers when they fail. An acceptable use policy that forbids personal USB drives for data transfer is enforced through a mix of port locks, group policy settings that disable USB storage, and user education.

As an entry-level technician, you usually will not be the person writing these policies, but you will be the one who implements and supports many of the controls they describe. That means configuring user accounts according to least-privilege principles, setting password and lockout policies, deploying cable locks and privacy screens, adjusting BIOS/UEFI security settings when systems are imaged, and helping users understand why MFA or screen locking is not just an inconvenience but a core part of keeping systems and data safe. It also means recognizing when something you see in the environment—like that unlocked workstation in reception or a stack of backup drives sitting on an open shelf—violates policy or exposes risk, and knowing how to respond appropriately within your role.

These foundational concepts of physical and logical security are the base layer for everything else you will study in security. When you move into Windows-specific security settings, wireless authentication, malware defenses, workstation hardening, and mobile device security in the upcoming sections, you will be applying the same ideas—controlling who can get near systems, who can log in, what they can do, and how their actions are tracked—just in more specialized and detailed ways.

7.2 Windows Security Settings & Built-In Protections

If you think about a Windows PC as a house, most of the tools you use to keep that "house" safe are already built in. You have locks on the doors, alarms on the windows, smoke detectors, maybe even a camera over the front door. In Windows 10 and Windows 11, those "locks and alarms" are collected into a single place called

Windows Security, and as a support technician, that is where you will spend a lot of your time when it comes to protecting systems and answering security questions.

You can open Windows Security in a couple of ways, and on the exam they expect you to at least recognize where these settings live. From the Start menu you can search for "Windows Security," or you can move through Settings: in Windows 10 that path is Start, then Settings, then Update & Security, then Windows Security; in Windows 11 it is Start, Settings, then Privacy & Security, then Windows Security. However you get there, what you see is a dashboard made up of tiles. Each tile corresponds to a different "layer" of protection. Virus & threat protection covers malware, Account protection deals with how users sign in, Firewall & network protection focuses on network traffic, App & browser control wraps in reputation-based checks like SmartScreen, Device security exposes hardware-based protections, and you may also see Device performance & health and Family options. A helpful way to think about this is that each tile answers a different question: "Am I protected from malware?", "Is my sign-in secure?", "Is my network traffic controlled?", "Are apps and sites being checked before I run or visit them?", and "Is the underlying hardware running security features properly?"

Once you have that mental map of the dashboard, it becomes much easier to decide where to go when a user reports a security-related symptom. If they are seeing malware alerts or want a manual scan, you head into Virus & threat protection. If an application suddenly cannot reach a server, you suspect Firewall & network protection. If a laptop has been lost and you need to verify whether the drive was encrypted, you look at BitLocker status in device encryption or BitLocker management tools. This habit of mapping problems to the correct security "layer" is exactly the kind of reasoning CompTIA builds into A+ scenarios.

At the core of Windows' built-in protections is **Microsoft Defender Antivirus**, which lives under the Virus & threat protection tile. Defender is the anti-malware engine that ships with Windows; unless a third-party antivirus suite has taken over that role, it quietly runs in the background on every modern Windows client. Its job is to watch what the system does in real time—files being opened, programs launching, scripts running, downloads arriving—and compare that activity against its malware definitions and behavior analysis. If it detects something suspicious, it can block the operation immediately, quarantine a file so it cannot run, or remove it entirely. Definitions and the scanning engine are kept up to date primarily through Windows Update, though you can also trigger a manual update from inside the Virus & threat protection interface if you suspect the system has missed some updates.

When you open Virus & threat protection, Windows will show you the current status in plain language, something like "No current threats" along with the time of the last scan. For an A+ candidate, it is important not just to recognize that this screen exists, but to feel comfortable choosing the right type of scan when needed. A **Quick scan** focuses on the most common locations malware tends to use—system folders, startup areas, loaded processes. This is often your first step if the user reports suspicious behavior but is still able to work. A **Full scan** walks every file on every drive and can take hours; this is appropriate when you suspect deep infection or after you have removed something and want to be confident nothing is left behind. A **Custom scan** is useful when you only want to check a specific folder or drive, such as a USB flash drive a user is worried about. The scan history on this page lets you review what has been found over time and what Defender did with it, which is invaluable when a user tells you "something popped up last night but I clicked it away."

Defender's real-time protection setting is another area you will see on the exam. Real-time protection intercepts operations as they happen; turning it off means you are relying only on periodic or manual scans, which is almost always a bad idea. Windows lets you temporarily disable real-time protection from Virus & threat protection settings, and occasionally you may have to do that for a specific troubleshooting case, such as installing an older, unsigned internal tool that Defender keeps blocking even though you have verified it is safe. In that situation, the professional approach is to turn real-time protection off only long enough to complete the task, immediately turn it back on, and, if necessary, configure a narrow exclusion for that specific file or folder instead of leaving a gaping hole in protection.

Exclusions are another important concept. In Virus & threat protection settings, you can define exclusions for specific files, folders, file types, or processes. This tells Defender not to scan those items. Exclusions can be a lifesaver when you have a legitimate program that Defender keeps flagging as malware, or when constant scanning of a massive development directory is hurting performance. But exclusions are also a liability if they are applied too broadly. Excluding an entire drive or a high-level folder structure gives malware a safe haven if it ever lands there. As a support tech, you aim for the smallest, most targeted exclusion that solves the immediate business problem, and you always document what you changed so it can be reviewed later. On the exam, any answer that says "Turn off antivirus entirely to stop the warnings" should raise red flags in your mind; a better answer usually involves a scan, quarantine review, or a narrowly scoped exclusion.

Many of your real-world tickets will involve interpreting Defender's alerts. A user might call in saying a pop-up claimed a file was quarantined and now their program will not open. Your workflow is to open Virus & threat protection, check Protection history, and identify exactly what was blocked. If the detection name clearly indicates known malware and the path points to a Downloads folder or temporary directory, the answer is usually to leave it quarantined, reassure the user that Defender did its job, and perhaps educate them about not opening unknown attachments. If instead you see that a long-standing line-of-business executable in Program Files has suddenly been flagged right after a Windows update, that could be a false positive. In that case you research the detection name, compare hashes with a known-good copy, and only if you are confident it is not malicious do you restore it and consider adding a small exclusion. The exam expects you to distinguish between these kinds of situations.

Closely allied with antivirus is **Windows Defender Firewall**, accessed through the Firewall & network protection tile. While antivirus focuses on what code runs on the system, the firewall governs who can talk to the system over the network and what the system can talk to. By default, Windows Defender Firewall is enabled for all network profiles and quietly blocks unsolicited inbound traffic unless you or an application have explicitly allowed it. Outbound traffic is mostly allowed by default, which means applications can initiate connections out to the internet or other systems unless there is a rule blocking them.

Windows uses three firewall profiles: Domain, Private, and Public. These are not different networks physically; they are different security attitudes the firewall adopts based on how you classify the connection. When a PC is joined to an Active Directory domain and connected on that corporate network, the Domain profile applies, and many settings are controlled by central Group Policy. When a user connects to their secured home Wi-Fi, they will typically choose it as a Private network, indicating it is somewhat trusted; file and printer sharing and device discovery are more likely to be allowed in that profile. When they open a laptop in a coffee shop and connect to public Wi-Fi, that network should be marked as Public, which is the most restrictive. The system will not advertise itself for discovery, and inbound connections will generally be blocked. A classic exam question will describe a user on hotel Wi-Fi unable to access file shares from their coworker's laptop; recognizing that the Public firewall profile is likely preventing file and printer sharing is part of thinking like a technician.

From the Firewall & network protection screen, you can see at a glance whether the firewall is on for each profile and whether it is blocking incoming connections. There is also a link to "Allow an app through firewall," which opens a Control Panel interface listing applications that have requested firewall access. Each entry shows whether the app is allowed on Domain, Private, or Public networks. Many programs that need network access will create their own rules on installation and then prompt the user to confirm. You have probably seen the dialog that asks "Allow this app to communicate on private networks?" with checkboxes for private and public networks. For line-of-business applications that should not be available on coffee shop Wi-Fi, the correct choice is often to allow them on Domain and Private only. Opening wide access on Public networks unnecessarily increases attack surface.

For more complex situations, you can open the Windows Defender Firewall with Advanced Security console by searching for it or using tools like wf.msc. There you can create granular inbound and outbound rules based on program path, port number, protocol, or source and destination IP addresses. While A+ does not expect you to memorize every possible rule option, you should know that this is where to go when a new service needs a specific port opened or when you must troubleshoot why a program cannot reach a remote server even though DNS and routing work. A good practical sequence is to verify connectivity with simple tools like ping or a web browser, then check firewall status and allowed apps, and only then experiment with a temporary rule or temporary firewall disable to confirm whether the firewall is involved. Whatever you change, you restore protections afterward and refine the rule rather than leaving the firewall off.

Security at the network edge is only part of the story; you also have to control who can sign in to the machine and what credentials are at stake. The **Account protection** tile in Windows Security brings together sign-in options and identity-related alerts. Windows supports both **local accounts** and **Microsoft accounts**. A local account is defined only on that machine, with its username and password stored locally. This is simple and works well for standalone PCs that are not tied into Microsoft cloud services. A Microsoft account uses an email address as the username and is part of Microsoft's cloud identity system; it unlocks features like OneDrive sync, Store purchases, and easier password recovery, and it often supports multi-factor authentication by default. From a security standpoint, a Microsoft account with multifactor is generally harder to compromise remotely than a lone local account with a weak password.

Modern Windows also encourages the use of **Windows Hello** sign-in methods. These include a PIN, fingerprint reader, and facial recognition, depending on what hardware the device has. A PIN may look less secure because it is often shorter than a password, but it has an important property: it is tied to that specific device. Compromising the PIN does not let an attacker sign in to your Microsoft account on another machine. Biometrics like fingerprints and facial recognition provide convenient, fast unlocks while still requiring that the user be physically present. From a support perspective, you will frequently guide users through adding or changing Hello options in Settings under Accounts, then Sign-in options. The Account protection tile may show alerts such as "Set up Windows Hello for faster and more secure sign-in," which are not errors but recommendations for stronger authentication.

User accounts can also be protected through basic password and lockout behavior. In domain environments, administrators control password length, complexity, and lockout policies with Group Policy, but on standalone systems you can still configure some of these in Local Security Policy or through account properties. The security principle is straightforward: more complex passwords and shorter lockout thresholds make brute-force guessing attacks harder, but they increase the likelihood that a legitimate user will lock themselves out after a few mistyped attempts. On the exam, if a scenario describes repeated login attempts from an unknown source, increasing account lockout sensitivity or requiring stronger passwords will often be the recommended countermeasure.

Even if you do a perfect job on accounts and apps, you still face a critical question: what happens if someone simply steals the device? Without encryption, an attacker can remove a laptop's drive, plug it into another computer, and read data regardless of Windows account passwords. That is where **BitLocker** and related features come in. BitLocker Drive Encryption is Microsoft's full volume encryption system; when enabled, it encrypts every bit on the drive and ties the keys to the system's Trusted Platform Module (TPM) and boot configuration. As long as the system has not been tampered with, the TPM silently releases the key at boot, and Windows starts normally. If the hardware significantly changes or the drive is moved to another machine, BitLocker will require a recovery key, and without that, the data remains unreadable.

On many business-class Windows Pro or Enterprise systems, you will see a Manage BitLocker link in Control Panel or by right-clicking a drive in File Explorer. There you can turn BitLocker on for the operating system volume and for data volumes. When you enable BitLocker, Windows insists you create and store a **recovery key**. This can be saved to a file, printed, stored in a Microsoft account, or, in corporate environments, backed up to Active Directory or Azure AD. Losing that key can mean permanent data loss, so part of your role is to help users store it in a safe but accessible place, not on the same laptop you are encrypting. BitLocker To Go extends this concept to removable media such as USB flash drives and external hard drives. These drives can be configured to require a password or smart card to unlock; once mounted on a supported Windows system and unlocked, they behave like normal drives, but if lost, their contents remain protected.

Consumer-oriented Windows Home systems often replace full BitLocker with **Device Encryption**, which is a simplified form of full-disk encryption that may be automatically enabled if the hardware meets certain prerequisites, such as having a TPM and being signed into with a Microsoft account. You can usually find its status under Settings, Update & Security, then Device encryption. For A+ purposes, it is enough to understand that whether the label is BitLocker or Device Encryption, the goal is the same: protect data at rest so that physical access to hardware does not automatically mean access to information. Verifying that laptops, especially those used outside the office, have encryption enabled is a basic compliance check you will perform regularly.

Beyond antivirus, firewall, accounts, and encryption, Windows includes a set of additional protections that live mostly under the **App & browser control** and **Device security** tiles. One of the most visible is **SmartScreen**, part of what Windows calls reputation-based protection. SmartScreen monitors websites you visit in Microsoft Edge and the executables you download or run, and compares them against Microsoft's online reputation service. If you try to visit a known malicious site, Edge will display a red warning page. If you attempt to run a downloaded program that is rare or unsigned, you may see a "Windows protected your PC" dialog, with an option to run it anyway under "More info." The key for you, both in the field and on the exam, is to recognize that SmartScreen is making a decision based on the reputation and characteristics of the file or site, not on a malware signature. When a non-technical user gets that warning, the safest guidance is usually "If you were not expecting this, or you do not fully trust the source, do not override it."

App & browser control is also where you will find **reputation-based protection settings** more broadly, and, on some builds, access to **exploit protection** configuration. Exploit protection applies process-level mitigations such as Data Execution Prevention (DEP) and Address Space Layout Randomization (ASLR) to make common exploit techniques harder. At the A+ level, you mostly need to be aware that these exist and that they can occasionally cause compatibility problems with legacy applications or drivers. When a low-level driver or virtualization tool fails to load and Device security reports an issue with **core isolation** or **memory integrity**, you might need to toggle those options or update the offending driver. Core isolation uses virtualization-based security to isolate certain critical processes and memory regions from the rest of the OS, helping to thwart kernel-level attacks, but older unsigned drivers do not always cooperate.

Ransomware has pushed another built-in feature into the spotlight: **Controlled folder access**. This option, available under Virus & threat protection's ransomware protection settings or under App & browser control depending on the version, lets Windows designate certain folders—like Documents, Pictures, and Desktop—as protected. Only trusted, allowed applications can write to these locations. If an unknown program suddenly tries to encrypt or modify large numbers of files there, Windows will block the activity and alert the user. This can significantly blunt many ransomware attacks, but it can also disrupt legitimate software that saves files into those directories, particularly custom business applications. When that happens, your job is to review the block events, confirm the application is legitimate, and add it to the allowed list for controlled folder access, rather than turning the entire feature off permanently.

Seen together, these tools implement what is sometimes called a layered defense, or "defense in depth." You can even organize them using a simple mental model like **LANEN**: Login protected by account settings and Windows Hello; Antivirus with Microsoft Defender scanning code and files; Network control via Windows Defender Firewall; Encryption guarding data at rest with BitLocker or Device Encryption; and Network services and apps supervised by SmartScreen, exploit protection, and controlled folder access. When you troubleshoot a security-related complaint, walking through those layers in your head helps you quickly narrow down where to look. If a user cannot access a site but can ping it, is it firewall, DNS, or SmartScreen? If an application suddenly cannot save to Documents, is controlled folder access blocking it? If a stolen laptop is reported, can you confirm BitLocker was enabled so you can confidently report that the data was protected?

As you move into later chapters on malware removal, workstation hardening, and troubleshooting security issues, these same Windows Security components will keep reappearing. The better you understand how to configure them from the local client, how to verify their status, and how to recognize when they are the cause of a symptom rather than evidence of an attack, the more effective you will be both in the exam environment and in a real help desk role.

7.3 Wireless Security Protocols & Authentication

If you spend any time on a help desk, you quickly discover that "Wi-Fi problems" are often "Wi-Fi security problems" wearing a disguise. Users complain that the network "forgets" their password, a new phone connects fine but an old printer refuses, or the guest network feels "unsafe." Underneath those symptoms are decisions about which wireless security protocol the access point is using and how clients are authenticated. To be effective in support—and to pass the A+ exams—you need more than a list of acronyms. You need to be able to look at a router's wireless settings, understand what they mean, pick the right options, and reason through what happens when they don't match what a device expects.

At a basic level, wireless security has to solve two problems at once. First, it must control who is allowed to join the network, which is the **authentication** side. Second, it must protect the actual data flying through the air, which is the **encryption** side. On a wired network, an attacker usually has to be inside the building to plug in; on Wi-Fi, they just need to be within radio range. That is why the wireless standards evolved so quickly from very weak protections to the much stronger mechanisms you see on modern WPA2 and WPA3 networks. Understanding that evolution will help you immediately identify which options are obsolete, which are acceptable, and which you should prefer when you have a choice.

From WEP to WPA3: The Security Ladder

The story starts with **WEP (Wired Equivalent Privacy)**, the first widely used Wi-Fi "security" mechanism. The name tells you the goal: make wireless "equivalent" to wired privacy. The reality turned out very different. WEP relied on the RC4 stream cipher with small initialization vectors and static keys. In practice, this design made it trivial for attackers to capture enough wireless traffic and mathematically derive the key. Free tools can crack a WEP key in minutes. For you, the key takeaway is that WEP is effectively no security at all. On both the exam and in real networks, if WEP appears as an option alongside WPA2 or WPA3, you can treat it as "broken" and not acceptable for production use.

As WEP's weaknesses became obvious, vendors needed something they could roll out quickly to existing hardware. That stopgap was **WPA (Wi-Fi Protected Access)**. WPA introduced **TKIP (Temporal Key Integrity Protocol)**, which tried to fix some of WEP's problems by changing encryption keys dynamically and adding integrity checks. It was a significant step up at the time, but TKIP still inherited weaknesses from the underlying RC4 approach and is now considered legacy and weak. You will still see configuration options like "WPA/TKIP" or "WPA/WPA2 mixed (TKIP+AES)" on older routers. In modern deployments, TKIP should be treated as a compatibility mode for very old devices, not as a secure default.

Real improvement arrived with **WPA2 (Wi-Fi Protected Access 2)**. WPA2 replaced TKIP with **AES-based CCMP** (Counter Mode with Cipher Block Chaining Message Authentication Code Protocol). You don't need to understand the math, but you should recognize "AES/CCMP" as the strong, modern cipher pair that became the baseline for secure Wi-Fi. For more than a decade, WPA2 with AES/CCMP has been the workhorse of home and business networks. When you see a SOHO router offering "WPA2-PSK (AES)" as a security mode, that is generally the minimum you should choose. WPA2 can technically still use TKIP in some configurations, but "WPA2-TKIP" is not the secure combination the exam expects you to recommend.

The latest step on the ladder is **WPA3.** Where WPA2 focused on strong encryption of the data once you were on the network, WPA3 also improves how devices prove they know the password in the first place and how open networks behave. In **WPA3-Personal**, the old pre-shared key handshake is replaced with **SAE (Simultaneous Authentication of Equals)**. SAE is far more resistant to offline password-guessing attacks, which matters in the real world because users continue to choose weak passphrases no matter how nicely you ask them not to. In **WPA3-Enterprise**, the standard strengthens encryption further for business environments, while still using the same overall enterprise authentication model you will see with WPA2-Enterprise.

You will also encounter WPA3's "Enhanced Open" mode, based on **OWE (Opportunistic Wireless Encryption)**. Traditional "open" Wi-Fi sends traffic in the clear, with no encryption at all; OWE provides encryption for each client session even though there is no shared password. To the user, it still feels like an open network—they tap, it connects without a passphrase—but behind the scenes, the link is protected from eavesdropping. This is especially relevant for public hotspots, though in practice many open networks you see today still use older, completely unencrypted behavior.

In both exam questions and real configuration decisions, it helps to visualize a simple ranking: WEP at the bottom, then WPA/TKIP, then WPA2 with AES, then WPA3 at the top. When a scenario asks you to "choose the most secure wireless configuration," you mentally climb that ladder and select the highest rung that your devices can realistically support.

Personal vs Enterprise: Two Approaches to Authentication

So far we have focused on how the network encrypts traffic. Equally important is how it decides who is allowed to join. Here, the key distinction is between **Personal (pre-shared key)** and **Enterprise (802.1X/RADIUS)** authentication models.

In **WPA2-Personal** or **WPA3-Personal**, every device uses the same Wi-Fi password, also called a **pre-shared key (PSK)**. This is what you see in almost all home routers and many small offices: the "Wi-Fi password" is printed on a sticker, or the office manager has chosen a phrase and written it on a whiteboard. From a support perspective, Personal mode is simple to set up. You log into the router, choose WPA2- or WPA3-Personal with AES, type in a strong passphrase, and then distribute that passphrase to users. Every client that knows the PSK and supports the right protocol can join.

The simplicity of Personal mode is also its main weakness. If you have ten employees and one leaves angrily, they still know the Wi-Fi password. If they shared it with a friend, that friend can still join months later. If you change the password to lock them out, you have to update it on every remaining device, which can be disruptive and time-consuming. There is also no per-user accountability; from the network's standpoint, all devices that know the PSK look the same.

In business and institutional environments, those limitations are unacceptable, which is where **WPA2-Enterprise** and **WPA3-Enterprise** come in. In Enterprise mode, the wireless network uses **802.1X** to integrate with a central authentication system, most commonly a **RADIUS** server. Instead of entering a shared Wi-Fi password, users authenticate with individual credentials—usually their domain username and password, or sometimes a certificate or smart card. The access point acts as an **authenticator**, passing the user's credentials to the RADIUS server. The client device is the **supplicant**, and the RADIUS server is the final authority that decides whether to accept or reject the login.

Within this 802.1X framework, the actual credential exchange is carried by the **Extensible Authentication Protocol (EAP)**. EAP is more of a container than a single protocol; there are many EAP types that specify how to handle passwords, certificates, and so on. For the A+ exam, you do not need to memorize those flavors, but you should recognize that when you see "EAP" and "RADIUS" in a question, you are firmly in Enterprise Wi-Fi territory.

For a support technician, Enterprise mode changes the workflow. When a user complains they cannot join the corporate Wi-Fi and the connection dialog asks for a username and password instead of a simple network key, you know they are dealing with WPA2- or WPA3-Enterprise. At that point, basic checks include verifying they are using the correct SSID, confirming their domain account is active and in the right authorization group, and making sure the RADIUS server is reachable and not misconfigured. The advantage for the organization is clear: when an employee leaves, disabling or removing their account from the "WiFi users" group instantly cuts their access, with no impact on anyone else's devices.

Choosing between Personal and Enterprise comes down to scale and control. A three-person home office does not need the complexity of 802.1X and RADIUS; WPA2-Personal with a strong passphrase is perfectly reasonable. A university campus with thousands of users and constant account churn cannot live with a single shared Wi-Fi password; WPA2- or WPA3-Enterprise is the only sane choice.

Open Networks, Guests, and Captive Portals

Not all wireless access is intended to be tightly controlled. Coffee shops, hotels, and even many offices offer some kind of guest wireless access that trades convenience against security. A completely **open network** has no password at all; users just select the SSID and connect. On traditional open networks, there is also no encryption, which means that traffic can be observed by anyone else on the same network segment who is running the right tools. HTTPS and application-level encryption mitigate some of that risk, but from an infrastructure standpoint, open Wi-Fi is considered high-risk.

WPA3's **Enhanced Open** option, built on OWE, addresses that risk by giving each client its own encrypted session even though no shared password is configured. To the user interface, it still behaves like an open network—no passphrase prompt—but the radio traffic is not easily sniffed. However, adoption of Enhanced Open is still in progress; for the A+ exam, you should assume that "open network" typically means no password and no encryption, unless the scenario explicitly mentions WPA3 or OWE.

Then you have **guest networks**, which sit somewhere in between open and fully secured. Many routers support a separate guest SSID that isolates guest devices from the main internal LAN while still providing internet access. You might configure that guest SSID as open or protected with a simple PSK that changes occasionally. Hotels and some offices layer a **captive portal** on top of this: after the device associates with the Wi-Fi, the first web request is intercepted and redirected to a login or terms-of-service page. The user might enter a room number, a voucher code, or just click "Accept" to continue.

It is important to distinguish the role of a captive portal from the wireless security protocol itself. WPA2 or WPA3 controls the low-level radio connection and encryption. A captive portal operates at a higher network layer, after the wireless link is already established. This distinction shows up in troubleshooting: if a user says, "I can connect to the Wi-Fi but nothing loads in the browser," you may suspect a captive portal page not appearing correctly. If they say, "I get 'incorrect password' and never connect at all," the problem lies in the wireless security and authentication stage, not the portal.

WPA3 Details and Mixed-Mode Reality

Although WPA3 is the modern target, its deployment is constrained by legacy devices. Many consumer and even some business access points offer a **transition mode**, often labeled "WPA2/WPA3-Personal," where devices that support WPA3 use its stronger handshake, and older WPA2 devices are still allowed to connect using the older mechanisms. This is a practical compromise, but it also means that if you truly want all clients to benefit from WPA3's protections, you eventually have to retire the older hardware.

Two WPA3-related ideas are worth holding in your mental toolkit. First, **SAE** provides a much more robust handshake for WPA3-Personal. In older WPA2-PSK networks, an attacker could capture the four-way handshake and perform an offline dictionary attack against the PSK. With SAE, that kind of offline guessing is dramatically harder, which is especially valuable in environments where end users insist on using weaker passwords. Second, **Protected Management Frames (PMF)**, required for WPA3 and available with newer WPA2 implementations, protect management traffic such as disassociation frames from being spoofed. That reduces the effectiveness of some denial-of-service attacks that try to kick clients off the network by forging management frames.

From a support standpoint, you are more likely to encounter WPA3 indirectly through symptoms than through deep crypto details. A user buys a new router, leaves it in WPA3-only mode, and then discovers that their older streaming stick or smart thermostat cannot connect. Or an enterprise enables WPA3-Enterprise on newer access points and starts seeing issues with particular models of barcode scanner that have outdated wireless chipsets. In these cases, your job is to map the symptom—"connects fine here but not there"—back to the underlying security mode and client capability.

Being comfortable with that mapping is ultimately what the A+ exam is looking for. When a question describes a user being prompted for a username and password instead of a network key, you should immediately think "Enterprise, 802.1X, RADIUS." When it describes a small office wanting to avoid reconfiguring every device whenever someone leaves, you should weigh the pros and cons of staying with WPA2-Personal versus investing in an Enterprise setup. When it gives you a list of security options including WEP, WPA-TKIP, WPA2-AES, and WPA3, you should know exactly how to rank them without hesitation.

The more you practice connecting those dots—protocol name to security strength, Personal versus Enterprise to authentication behavior, open versus secured to user risk—the more wireless "mysteries" start to look like straightforward configuration puzzles that you know how to solve.

7.4 Malware Types & Prevention Methods

If you work in IT support for any length of time, you will deal with malware. Some days it will be obvious and dramatic, like a user calling in a panic because every document on their desktop has been renamed and they're staring at a ransom note. Other days, it will be subtle: a slightly sluggish system, a browser that "just started acting weird," or an antivirus alert that keeps reappearing. To make sense of these situations—and to pass the A+ exam—you need a solid mental model of what malware is, how different types behave, and what practical steps keep it out of your environment as much as possible.

At its core, **malware** is simply software that has been intentionally designed to cause harm, steal information, or provide unauthorized access or control. It targets the three pillars you've seen before: confidentiality, integrity, and availability. Some malware focuses on stealing data (confidentiality), some on corrupting or modifying it (integrity), and others on locking you out of your own systems (availability). Not every unwanted program is a catastrophic threat, but if it undermines those security goals, it belongs in the malware family from a security perspective. That definition is broader than "virus," which many users still use as a catch-all term; viruses are just one species in a much larger ecosystem.

It helps to separate malware from two closely related concepts that appear throughout this domain: social engineering and vulnerabilities. A **phishing** email that tricks users into clicking a link is not itself malware; it's a delivery technique. It often serves as the vehicle to get the malicious code onto the system, but the code and the trick are different things. Likewise, a missing security update in Windows or a misconfigured permission on a network share is a **vulnerability**—a weakness that malware can exploit, but not malware by itself. In most real incidents, all three appear together: a vulnerability in unpatched software, a phishing email to convince a user to open an attachment, and a ransomware payload that actually does the damage. When you're reading exam questions, train yourself to mentally separate the trick (social engineering), the weakness (vulnerability), and the payload (malware), even though they all work as a team.

A good place to start the tour of malware types is with the classics: **viruses** and **worms**. A virus is malicious code that attaches itself to a **host file** or program. It doesn't usually appear as a standalone application on the desktop. Instead, it may insert its code into an executable, a document with macros, or even a boot sector. It typically requires user action to spread: someone runs the infected program, opens the tainted document, or shares that file with another user, and the virus executes and replicates. Imagine a user receiving a spreadsheet from a colleague, opening it, and unknowingly triggering a macro that silently infects all their other spreadsheets. In that scenario, the virus is "hitchhiking" on files as they move between systems.

A **worm**, by contrast, is like a virus that learned to drive. It does not need a user to copy or open files. Instead, it spreads automatically over networks by exploiting vulnerabilities in services or protocols. A classic pattern is a worm that scans IP ranges looking for unpatched systems with a specific open port, then uses a software flaw to copy and execute itself on each vulnerable host. You might see symptoms like sudden network congestion, high CPU usage on multiple machines at once, or thousands of log entries showing repeated connection attempts on a given port. From an A+ standpoint, the key distinctions you want to keep straight are that a virus needs a host and usually some user interaction, while a worm is self-propagating across networks and often targets unpatched systems directly.

Next, consider **Trojans**, which take their name from the Trojan Horse myth for a reason. A Trojan is malicious software disguised as something the user wants. Unlike worms, Trojans generally do not spread on their own; the attacker relies on the user to willingly install the program, believing it's legitimate. This might be a "free game," a "system optimizer," a pirated software crack, or even a fake antivirus tool claiming to have found hundreds of infections. Once installed, the Trojan can do almost anything: drop additional malware, open backdoors, or give remote control of the system to an attacker. A very common and exam-relevant subcategory is the **Remote Access Trojan (RAT)**, which quietly provides persistent remote access. In a small business, a RAT infection may first appear as a mysterious remote login alert or suspicious changes to configuration files that none of the staff admits to making.

Ransomware has become the public face of malware over the last decade because of its dramatic impact on availability. Ransomware's hallmark behavior is encryption or locking of data or systems, followed by a demand for payment—often in cryptocurrency—to restore access. A user might report that all their documents now have a strange, uniform extension and no longer open in Word, and that a text file or wallpaper message instructs them to pay a ransom to recover their files. On the exam and in real life, the combination of sudden file inaccessibility plus a payment demand should immediately suggest ransomware. Delivery often occurs through phishing attachments that use macros, malicious links, or Trojans masquerading as legitimate downloads. Prevention here involves more than just antivirus; robust and tested backups, restricted macro execution, and good email filtering all play critical roles.

While ransomware loudly announces its presence, **spyware** tries very hard not to be noticed. Spyware's goal is to observe and report on user activity without consent. It may track websites visited, capture screenshots, record credentials entered into web forms, or harvest system information and send it to a remote server. Symptoms can be vague: a browser that seems to redirect to odd search engines, unexpected toolbars, or an unusual number of background network connections. A special case of spyware is the **keylogger**, which focuses on capturing keystrokes. Keyloggers are particularly dangerous because they can record passwords, credit card numbers, and private messages in plain text as the user types. Many keyloggers run as simple background processes that don't display any user interface at all, which is why up-to-date endpoint protection and careful monitoring are so important.

If spyware spies, **adware** shouts. Adware is software that aggressively displays advertisements, often in pop-up windows or injected into web pages. It may change the browser's home page, install multiple toolbars, and redirect searches to ad-heavy or malicious sites. Users will usually complain about constant pop-ups, annoying banners, or very slow browser performance. Closely related are **Potentially Unwanted Programs (PUPs)**. PUPs tread a gray area: they may not be overtly malicious, but they are installed in deceptive ways, such as bundled with another application or pre-checked in an installer, and they often collect data or degrade performance. The classic story is a user who downloads a "free video converter" from a random site and the next day has three new toolbars, a "PC cleaner," and a "shopping assistant" that no one recalls explicitly approving. On the exam, adware and PUPs are still treated as security concerns, not just annoyances, because they can weaken the system and open doors for more serious threats.

Some of the most challenging malware to deal with falls under the **rootkit** category. A rootkit is designed to hide: it often buries itself deep in the operating system, sometimes at the kernel level, and may manipulate system calls and logs to conceal its presence and the presence of other malware. You may see signs such as system files mysteriously changing, antivirus tools that refuse to run or update, or logs that appear incomplete or tampered with. Because rootkits operate at such a low level, they can be very difficult to detect with normal tools, and removal often involves significant measures like offline scanning or complete OS reinstallation. For an entry-level technician, the important takeaway is that if you suspect a rootkit—especially on a critical system—you escalate according to incident response policy rather than casually trying a few quick fixes.

When many infected machines are coordinated together, you have a **botnet**. Each compromised device becomes a **bot** (or zombie) that quietly waits for instructions from a command-and-control (C2) server. The botnet's operator can then use this distributed army to send massive spam campaigns, conduct distributed denial-of-service (DDoS) attacks, or brute-force user accounts across the internet. From the perspective of a single workstation, symptoms might include high outbound network traffic at odd hours, the machine's IP address being blacklisted by email providers, or firewall logs showing repeated attempts to connect to suspicious external addresses. A single bot isn't always obvious to the end user, which is why centralized monitoring and properly configured firewalls are so valuable in larger environments.

Newer attack techniques have popularized **fileless malware**, which changes how you think about infection. Traditional malware relies on malicious files written to disk. Fileless malware, on the other hand, operates primarily in memory and often abuses legitimate administrative tools like PowerShell or Windows Management Instrumentation (WMI). An attacker might exploit a browser vulnerability, then run a PowerShell script directly from memory to download and execute further payloads, leaving very little behind on disk for classic antivirus to scan. For the A+ exam, it is enough to recognize that fileless malware is harder to detect with purely signature-based tools and that good prevention involves limiting script execution, enabling logging, patching aggressively, and using security products that include behavioral and memory-based detection.

A more targeted and less common but exam-relevant threat is the **logic bomb**. A logic bomb is malicious code that lies dormant until a specific condition is met, such as a particular date, a certain number of logins, or the disabling of a specific user account. These are often associated with insider threats; for example, a disgruntled administrator might plant code that will delete critical data 30 days after their account is removed. Logic bombs can be extremely damaging because they are usually discovered only after they have done their work, and normal antivirus scans may not flag them if the code appears inert until the trigger condition occurs.

Understanding the malware categories is only half of what you need; the other half is recognizing how these threats get into systems in the first place. Common **infection vectors** show up over and over in scenarios. Email attachments remain a major route: a user receives what appears to be an invoice, resume, or delivery notice, opens the document, and clicks "Enable Content" when prompted about macros. That single click can launch a ransomware attack or drop a Trojan. Malicious links work similarly, sending users to compromised websites that exploit browser vulnerabilities or trick them into downloading "updates" that are actually malware.

Drive-by downloads represent another pattern, where simply visiting a compromised site causes code to run, especially if the browser or plugins like Java or Flash (in legacy systems) are unpatched. Removable media, such as USB drives left in public places or handed around the office, can carry infected executables or autorun scripts. Pirated software and key generators are notorious Trojan carriers; users who go looking for "free" versions of expensive tools often end up installing far more than they bargained for. Even advertisements delivered by ad networks can be weaponized, a technique called malvertising, where clicking or even just loading a banner triggers malicious code.

Prevention methods, therefore, need to address both the technical weaknesses and the human behaviors that malware relies on. At the technical level, **endpoint protection** remains a cornerstone. Traditional antivirus relies on **signatures**—digital fingerprints of known malware—to detect threats. Modern endpoint protection platforms (EPP) go further, combining signatures with heuristic and behavioral analysis to spot suspicious actions, such as a process suddenly encrypting large numbers of files or injecting code into other processes. As an IT support technician, you are often responsible for verifying that endpoint protection is installed, licensed, running, and updating properly on every workstation. In managed environments, you may check a central console to confirm that all endpoints have current definitions and that scheduled scans are running as intended.

Firewalls provide another critical layer. A host-based firewall on each workstation can restrict unsolicited inbound connections and detect unusual outbound traffic, such as a bot trying to contact its C2 server. Network firewalls can block known malicious IP ranges, filter traffic by port and protocol, and enforce segmentation so that a worm infecting one subnet cannot easily spread everywhere. In a SOHO network, even a basic router firewall with properly configured rules can make it significantly harder for external attackers and worms to reach internal hosts directly.

Patch management is arguably one of the most powerful, and most underappreciated, malware prevention measures. Many worms and fileless attacks depend on known vulnerabilities in operating systems, browsers, and popular applications. Keeping systems updated shrinks the attack surface dramatically. In practice, that means enabling and monitoring Windows Update or the equivalent for macOS and Linux, ensuring third-party applications (browsers, office suites, PDF readers) receive updates, and following organizational change management procedures when applying patches to critical systems. On the A+ exam, when you see a scenario involving a worm rapidly spreading across a network by exploiting a service like SMB, patching and disabling unnecessary services are key preventive answers.

Account configuration and **least privilege** principles also play a big role. If users run as local administrators by default, any malware they accidentally execute inherits those powerful rights, making it easy to install rootkits, change system settings, and disable defenses. By contrast, when users operate as standard users and only elevate privileges when necessary (using tools like User Account Control in Windows), many types of malware find it harder to persist or cause deep system changes. As a support technician, you will help create and manage user accounts, decide who needs admin rights, and configure local security policies in line with company standards.

Secure browsing practices tighten things further. Browser configuration choices—such as disabling or limiting plugins, blocking pop-ups, and enabling warnings for dangerous sites—directly affect exposure to drive-by downloads and malvertising. Content filtering and DNS filtering services can prevent users from reaching known malicious domains, even if they click on a bad link. Later, when you study browser security configuration in more detail, you will see how specific settings and add-ons reinforce the malware prevention picture you're building here.

None of these technical controls work well if user behavior constantly undermines them. **User awareness** and informal training are therefore a central part of prevention, and this is an area where entry-level techs have more influence than they might think. Each time you handle a ticket about a suspicious email, a slow PC, or strange pop-ups, you have an opportunity to reinforce safer practices: verifying the sender and intent of attachments, hovering over links before clicking to inspect the actual URL, downloading software only from trusted sources such as official vendor sites or approved app stores, and reporting anything that "feels off" instead of ignoring it. You might not be the one designing formal training sessions, but the small conversations you have with users add up and can significantly reduce the number of incidents you see.

Finally, tie these ideas back to your day-to-day responsibilities. In a small business or SOHO environment, you may be the person who installs and maintains endpoint protection, configures firewalls on both routers and individual systems, enables automatic updates, and sets up standard user accounts. You will review incidents to see where things broke down—perhaps a user fell for a cleverly designed phishing attachment, or an important patch wasn't applied on time—and then adjust configurations or remind users accordingly. When you later learn the formal malware removal process, remember that prevention and removal work together: the more effectively you can keep systems hardened and users informed, the fewer emergency cleanups you will face, and the more time you can spend proactively improving the environment instead of constantly reacting to the latest infection.

7.5 Malware Removal Process (SOHO)

In a small office or home office environment, malware incidents are not an "if," they are a "when." Users install things they shouldn't, click things they shouldn't, and plug in devices they shouldn't. As the entry-level technician, you are often the one person who plays help desk, security, and "local IT department" all at once. That can feel intimidating, especially when a panicked user is standing over your shoulder insisting that "everything is broken" and "this has never happened before." The key to handling these situations professionally is not having an exotic toolkit or deep forensics skills; it is following a calm, consistent process in the correct order.

CompTIA treats malware removal as a defined workflow, not a random set of tricks. The exam writers love to shuffle the steps and see if you notice what is out of order. In real life, jumping straight to your favorite scanner, or browsing around a clearly infected system while it is still fully connected to the network, can make the situation worse. The sequence you are about to see is all about three priorities: limiting the spread of the infection, protecting data, and then restoring normal operations in a way that reduces the chance of a repeat incident. Once you internalize this sequence, malware questions on the exam start to feel less like puzzles and more like following a familiar checklist in your head.

Seeing the Problem: Identifying and Researching Symptoms

Everything starts with recognizing that you may be dealing with malware in the first place. You have already seen common **malware symptoms** in earlier sections: browser home pages that suddenly change to shady search engines, constant pop-up ads even when no browser is open, unexpected toolbars, or fake "antivirus" programs that seem more interested in your credit card than in your safety. Sometimes the symptoms are subtle, like a system that becomes sluggish over a few days, a fan that is constantly spinning at high speed, or an antivirus service that appears to be mysteriously disabled after each reboot.

When a user reports "weird behavior," your first mental question is, "Is this likely malware, or could it be something else?" That is where a bit of quick research comes in. Instead of guessing, you look up process names, error messages, or unusual program titles using trusted resources: vendor knowledge bases, a company wiki, or a known-clean system with a web browser. You might find that a scary-sounding process is actually a legitimate part of a new application the user installed, or that the "security optimizer" flashing red alerts is a widely known rogue program. This research step is important enough that CompTIA calls it out explicitly. Acting too aggressively before you have a reasonable level of confidence can destroy data or waste time chasing the wrong problem.

In a SOHO environment, you may not have formal logging or centralized detection tools, but you can still be systematic. Pay attention to when the symptoms started, whether other systems show similar behavior, and what changed recently on the affected device. An accountant who says the pop-ups began "right after I installed that free PDF editor" is handing you a major clue. Those early details help you choose the right tools and anticipate how widespread the issue might be.

Containment First: Quarantining the System

Once you have enough evidence to suspect malware, your next priority is not "run a scan." Your next priority is containment. This is where a lot of beginners slip up, both on the exam and in real life. While you poke around, the malware may be sending data out to a command-and-control server, scanning the local network for other vulnerable systems, or encrypting more files in the background. You want to stop that as quickly as possible.

In practice, **quarantining** the system means isolating it from anything else it can harm or communicate with. In a SOHO setting, this usually starts with disconnecting the device from the network: unplugging the Ethernet cable, turning off Wi-Fi, or even instructing a remote user to toggle airplane mode on a laptop. If the system has access to shared network resources, like a NAS device or a mapped file share, you want to prevent it from writing to those locations until you are confident the infection is under control. This is especially urgent if you suspect ransomware or worms that spread laterally.

It is worth drawing a clear line between two uses of the word "quarantine." At this stage, you are network-quarantining the machine—cutting it off from other systems and the internet. Later, security tools will talk about quarantining specific files, which means moving them into a secure area where they cannot run. CompTIA expects you to keep these concepts straight. If an exam question suggests downloading antimalware tools or running an online scanner before disconnecting, that is almost always the wrong choice. Stop the spread first; then you can think about tools.

Dealing with Restore Points: Disabling System Restore

With the machine safely isolated, you can start planning the cleanup. One piece that frequently trips up candidates is **System Restore** in Windows. System Restore captures snapshots of critical system files and some configuration settings, allowing you to roll back after a bad driver installation or misconfiguration. The problem is that malware can be present in those snapshots as well. If you leave existing restore points in place, you risk either the user or another technician later restoring the system right back to an infected state.

That is why one of the early steps in the CompTIA sequence is to disable System Restore on an infected Windows system, or to otherwise clear existing restore points. The order matters here. If you remove the malware first and only remember System Restore afterward, the system may already have stored additional, contaminated snapshots. By turning it off before you scan, you ensure that those infected points are discarded. Later, once the system is clean, you will turn it back on and create a fresh, known-good restore point.

On the exam, you are unlikely to be asked about the mechanics of System Restore in macOS or Linux in this context; the focus is very Windows-centric. What matters is recognizing that restore points are double-edged: a fantastic recovery tool when clean, and a way to resurrect malware if you are not careful.

Gaining the Upper Hand: Safe Mode and Offline Tools

The next tactical question is how you are going to run your cleanup tools without the malware fighting back. Many modern threats are quite aggressive about protecting themselves. They may kill antivirus processes, block the Task Manager, or reinstall themselves at startup using deeply buried services or scheduled tasks. Trying to remove them while the operating system is in its normal state is like trying to evict someone from a house while they are barricading the doors from the inside.

This is where **Safe Mode** and bootable recovery environments come in. Safe Mode in Windows starts the OS with a minimal set of drivers and services. Third-party applications, including many types of malware, are less likely to load. This gives your scanning tools a cleaner shot at the problem and makes it easier for you to disable suspicious startup items or services. In previous OS chapters, you saw how to reach Safe Mode using Advanced Startup options, Shift+Restart, or other methods. Exam scenarios expect you to know that when normal mode is unstable or clearly infected, Safe Mode is the next logical boot choice.

You also have to decide whether to allow networking in Safe Mode. From a security standpoint, Safe Mode without networking is safer because it limits the malware's ability to communicate while you work. However, in a SOHO environment you may not have antimalware installers or definition updates handy on local media. If you have another clean computer available, a best practice is to download tools and updates there, put them on a USB drive that you will later scan, and keep the infected machine offline. If that is not feasible, you may be forced to use Safe Mode with networking briefly to update definitions, but you should understand the trade-off.

Sometimes even Safe Mode is unusable because the malware has corrupted boot files or actively interferes with startup. In those cases, a **bootable antivirus or rescue environment** created on a clean system can be invaluable. These tools boot from USB or optical media into a self-contained OS, often Linux-based, that can scan the system disks without loading the installed Windows environment at all. Because the malware processes never start, they have no chance to hide or defend themselves.

The Core Task: Scanning and Removing with Updated Definitions

Once you have the machine in a controlled state—isolated from the network where practical, with restore points disabled, and preferably in Safe Mode or a recovery environment—you are finally ready for the step most people mistakenly try to start with: running your antimalware tools.

Two principles dominate this phase. The first is that your scanners must use **updated definitions**. Malware signatures evolve constantly; a tool that has not updated in months is only effective against yesterday's threats. Whether you are updating in Safe Mode with networking or pre-loading the latest definitions on a USB stick from a clean machine, you do not want to rely on stale data. The second principle is that you should favor comprehensive scanning over quick, superficial passes. Full system scans that include all local drives and any attached external storage catch items that might otherwise linger and reinfect later.

During scanning, you will see different options for dealing with detected items. Quarantine is usually the safest default: the tool moves the suspect file into a secure, isolated area where it cannot execute, but it is still available for analysis or, in rare cases, restoration if it turns out to be a false positive. Delete or remove is appropriate for clearly malicious files, but once they are gone, they are gone. Some scanners offer a "repair" or "clean" option that attempts to disinfect an infected file, preserving the original data while stripping out the malicious code. That can be helpful when the infected file is a critical system component or an important document, but it is not always possible.

In stubborn infections, one pass with a single product may not be enough. A common SOHO practice is to run a reputable antivirus suite first, then follow up with a second tool that specializes in adware or potentially unwanted programs, and finally a third that checks for rootkits or boot-sector modifications. The A+ exam does not expect you to memorize brand names, but it does care that you understand the idea of multiple layers of scanning. Manual techniques—such as hand-editing the registry, deleting files from obscure system directories, or disabling services you do not fully understand—should be your last resort. They can be effective, but they are also an easy way to render a system unbootable if you make a mistake.

After each cleanup pass, you should reboot and run another scan. The goal is to keep scanning until tools consistently report no active threats. If malware keeps reappearing, that is a sign you missed a component or that the infection has deeper persistence mechanisms than your current tools can handle. At that point, in a professional setting you might escalate the case or even consider a full backup-and-reinstall approach if time and data allow.

Moving from Crisis to Prevention: Updates and Scheduled Scans

Once you are confident the system is clean, your focus shifts from firefighting to resilience. Part of that is making sure your antimalware protection is not just present, but actually working day to day. That includes verifying that **real-time protection** is enabled if your product supports it, and configuring scheduled scans during off-hours so that new or dormant threats have fewer chances to hide indefinitely. A weekly full scan is common in SOHO environments, though high-risk systems may justify more frequent checks.

The other piece is patching. Whatever weakness allowed the malware to take hold, you want to close it. That means checking that Windows Update is functioning properly and set to install security updates promptly, not "whenever I remember." It also means looking at the usual suspects: web browsers, browser plugins, office suites, PDF readers, and any software that directly handles untrusted content from the internet. Many SOHO infections trace back to outdated software that has long-known vulnerabilities. On the exam, if you are asked what to do after successfully removing malware, "update the operating system and applications" is often a better answer than "tell the user to be more careful." Both matter, but patching removes the technical foothold.

Resetting the Safety Net: Re-enabling System Restore

At this point, the system should be stable, updated, and scanning cleanly. Now you can go back and restore your safety net. In Windows, that means re-enabling **System Restore** and immediately creating a new manual restore point. Giving it a descriptive name like "Post-malware cleanup – March 2025" helps anyone who looks later understand its context.

Again, timing is critical. You do not want to capture a restore point until you are as sure as you reasonably can be that the system is free of infection. If you rush and create the restore point too early, you might just be freezing a compromised state in amber to be re-used later. CompTIA questions love to place this step either too early or omit it entirely; in a well-ordered answer, you will always see restore re-enabled after cleanup and patching, not before.

The Human Side: User Education, Documentation, and Special Cases

The final part of the process is about people and process, not just technology. When you hand the system back to the user, taking a few minutes to explain in plain language what happened and how to avoid a repeat can be more valuable than all the scanning you just did. Blame and shame are counterproductive; instead, emphasize practical behaviors. Encourage them to download software only from trusted vendors or official app stores, to be skeptical of unexpected email attachments or links, and to pay attention to browser and operating system warnings rather than clicking past them out of habit. In the scenario with the home-based accountant and the "free PDF editor," that conversation would explicitly cover the risks of "free" utilities from unknown sites and rogue security pop-ups demanding payment.

At the same time, you should be documenting the incident. In even a tiny SOHO, a simple log or ticket system helps you track what you saw, what you did, and what the outcome was. That record should include observed symptoms, the suspected infection vector, tools used, scan results, and any changes made to settings or accounts. Over time, these notes become a mini knowledge base: patterns emerge, such as a particular user who keeps falling for the same phishing trick, or a certain website that seems to precede infections. Later chapters will expand on documentation and knowledge management, but malware cleanup is a place where those habits start.

Some infections raise additional questions you need to think through. If ransomware has encrypted files on a NAS, cleaning the ransomware off the originating PC is only half the job; you also need to determine whether you have **known-good backups** from before the encryption began. Backups taken during the infection period must be treated with suspicion and scanned offline before use. If you have no clean backups, your options become much worse, and in many cases the correct professional answer is to escalate rather than promising miracles. Similarly, if you suspect that the malware captured keystrokes or exfiltrated browser passwords, part of your post-cleanup checklist should be advising the user to change passwords and, where possible, enable multi-factor authentication on important accounts.

Throughout all of this, the CompTIA malware removal process gives you a mental script. You start by identifying and researching symptoms so you know what you are dealing with. You quarantine to stop the bleeding. You neutralize the risk from restore points, then boot in a way that gives you the advantage. You scan and remove with up-to-date tools, then patch and schedule protection so you are not back in the same place next week. You restore your recovery options with a clean restore point, and you finish by educating the user and recording what happened. That same sequence you practice in real SOHO incidents is exactly what you will be tested on in exam scenarios.

7.6 Workstation Hardening & Security Configuration

When you strip away the buzzwords, workstation hardening is really about this question: "If someone sits down at this computer, or attacks it over the network, how much damage can they do?" As an entry-level technician, you may not design company-wide security policies, but you will absolutely be the person who prepares and supports individual PCs. The choices you make when you build, rebuild, or tune a workstation—what accounts exist, which protections are enabled, how "locked down" the system feels—have a direct impact on how easy it is to compromise that machine.

Most operating systems, especially Windows, ship with their defaults tilted toward convenience and compatibility, not maximum security. Vendors want things to "just work" for the average home user. Hardening is the process of reviewing those defaults and tightening them so that the system exposes less of itself to attackers. A hardened workstation follows three big ideas you saw earlier in the security chapters: **least privilege**, **attack surface reduction**, and a **secure baseline**. In this section, you'll see how those concepts turn into very practical configuration steps and day-to-day decisions.

Least privilege means that users, applications, and services run with only the permissions they actually need. Attack surface reduction is about shrinking the number of ways an attacker can interact with the system—fewer open ports, fewer unnecessary services, fewer random programs installed. A secure baseline is simply the minimum standard you expect every workstation to meet before it goes into use: updates current, firewall on, malware protection active, accounts configured properly, and core security settings in place. Whether that baseline is applied by hand on a couple of SOHO PCs or through group policy in a large domain, the underlying configuration items are the same. For the A+ exam and for most entry-level roles, you focus on the local, workstation-level view.

Implementing Least Privilege on the Workstation

The most visible way least privilege shows up on a Windows workstation is through account types. A **local administrator** account can install software, change system-wide settings, manage other users, and bypass many protections. A **standard user** account can run applications and change most of its own environment, but cannot make system-wide changes without elevation. In a hardened environment, everyday work happens in standard user accounts. Administrator accounts exist, but they are used intentionally and sparingly.

In practice, that means avoiding the very common temptation to make everyone an admin "so they can install what they need." Imagine you are supporting a small accounting office. The owner insists on being a local administrator on her Windows 11 PC because "I don't want to call IT every time I install something." You know that she processes sensitive customer financial data, regularly opens email attachments from clients, and sometimes downloads utilities from random websites. Giving her full-time admin rights might make her feel more independent, but it also makes every mistake and every malware encounter far more dangerous. In both real life and on the exam, the better approach is to keep her as a standard user and use an admin account only when needed for legitimate installs or configuration changes.

User Account Control, or **UAC**, is one of the main tools Windows uses to enforce this boundary. UAC monitors actions that require elevated rights—installing drivers, writing to certain parts of the registry, modifying system files—and interrupts with a consent prompt. When you are logged on as a standard user, UAC asks for administrator credentials; when you are logged on as an admin, it still asks you to confirm that you want to elevate that particular action. From a hardening point of view, UAC is not an annoyance; it is a security tripwire.

If you see unexpected or frequent UAC prompts when you are just browsing the web or opening email, that is a sign something is trying to make system-level changes behind the scenes. The correct response is to investigate or block it, not to disable UAC.

On the exam, you will often see disabling UAC proposed as a "fix" for software that complains or prompts too much. That is almost never the right answer. A hardened Windows baseline leaves UAC on, with its default or stricter setting, and you solve application issues by updating the software, reinstalling it properly with admin privileges, or replacing it with a better-behaved alternative. If a scenario describes a user who cannot install software because UAC keeps asking for admin credentials, the solution that aligns with least privilege is typically to perform the install using an admin account, then let the user continue to run the program as a standard user.

Beyond the basic split between standard and admin accounts, Windows offers finer-grained control through tools like Local Users and Groups (lusrmgr.msc on Pro/Enterprise editions) and the **Local Security Policy** snap-in (secpol.msc). These are where you can see which users belong to which local groups, and which rights those groups have. For instance, you can configure who is allowed to "Log on locally," who can "Access this computer from the network," or who can "Install device drivers." On a shared kiosk PC in a lobby, you might allow only a restricted group to log on interactively and block network logons entirely, while still permitting remote management from IT. On a lab PC, you might prevent students from installing drivers, keeping them from plugging in unauthorized USB devices.

You do not need to memorize every individual policy for the A+ exam, but you should recognize the pattern: when the question is about limiting what a user can do on that specific machine, the answer usually involves changing the account type, adjusting local group membership, or modifying an appropriate local security setting. The principle remains the same: give the user just enough rights to perform their role, and nothing more.

Building a Secure Workstation Baseline

If you imagine building a PC from scratch for a new employee, a secure baseline is the checklist you mentally run through before handing over the keyboard. At the top of that list are updates. **Operating system** and application updates close known vulnerabilities. Almost every major ransomware or worm outbreak you read about exploited systems that had been missing patches for months, sometimes years. In a hardened configuration, Windows Update is enabled and set to install updates automatically on a regular basis. On a single home or SOHO machine, you generally leave automatic updates on and encourage users to reboot promptly when prompted. Turning off updates just to avoid reboots is a tradeoff heavily biased toward risk.

The same philosophy applies to key applications like browsers and productivity suites. Many modern programs update themselves, but you should verify that this is happening and not blocked. A support ticket that mentions repeated malware infections, pop-ups, or exploit warnings on a particular machine is a hint that its software is outdated. In an exam scenario, enabling or enforcing updates is almost always considered a strengthening, not a weakening, of security.

Next in the baseline is **endpoint protection**. A hardened Windows workstation needs an up-to-date antivirus/antimalware product with real-time protection enabled. On a standalone Windows 10 or 11 system, that is often Windows Security (Defender). In some environments, a third-party security suite replaces it. The important detail is that only one real-time antivirus engine runs at a time, because multiple products can interfere with each other and actually reduce protection. From a hardening perspective, you check that protection is on, virus definitions are current, and periodic scanning is scheduled. If a scenario describes a system with expired trial antivirus software or with antimalware manually disabled "because it slowed things down," your hardening response is to enable, update, or replace that protection.

The **firewall** is another baseline element. Windows Defender Firewall monitors incoming and optionally outgoing traffic and blocks unsolicited connections based on rules. A hardened workstation leaves the firewall enabled for at least private and public network profiles. The default configuration already allows most client activities like web browsing and email, while blocking inbound attempts unless an application has explicitly opened a port or you have created a rule. When a user wants to run something that truly requires inbound access, such as a remote assistance tool or a small local web server, you adjust the firewall to allow that specific traffic, rather than turning the firewall off.

This distinction shows up frequently on the exam. You might see two answer choices that both appear to fix a connectivity issue: one suggests "Disable the firewall," and another suggests "Create an inbound rule for the required port." The hardened, security-aware option is the one that preserves the firewall and just carves out the minimum exception necessary. Disabling the firewall system-wide is effectively removing a guardrail from every other application and service on that machine.

Secure login behavior is a quieter part of the baseline, but just as important. In a shared home or office environment, you should require some form of sign-in—password, PIN, or biometric—to access a user account. Configuring Windows to autologon to a privileged account means that anyone who turns on the PC has that level of access without challenge, which is clearly not hardened behavior. You also want the system to lock automatically after a period of inactivity, especially in an office where users might walk away from their desks. A five- to fifteen-minute idle timeout is common. On some systems, enabling the "Ctrl+Alt+Delete to log on" requirement can help prevent fake login screens, because that key combination is reserved for the real Windows logon process.

Reducing Attack Surface: Software, Services, and Remote Access

Once accounts, updates, AV, and firewall are in good shape, hardening turns to the question: "What else is running on this machine, and does it really need to be?" Every installed application is another piece of code that could contain vulnerabilities. Every background service is another process that might be exploitable. Attack surface reduction is about trimming away the unnecessary.

One of the easiest and most effective steps is uninstalling software that is not needed. New PCs often arrive with trial versions of programs, vendor utilities, browser toolbars, and promotional apps that the user will never touch. Over time, users may install peer-to-peer file sharing tools, "free" system optimizers, or browser extensions of dubious origin. Each of these increases risk. In a real support call, when you see a machine that is slow, full of ads, and prone to weird behavior, part of your remediation is to remove this clutter. But in a hardening context, you aim to prevent the problem in the first place by keeping the software set lean and purposeful.

Startup items and background processes are closely related. Windows provides multiple ways to control what launches at boot or login—Task Manager's Startup tab, the Apps > Startup area in Settings, and, for more advanced cases, System Configuration (msconfig). Malware, adware, and legitimate but unnecessary utilities all like to embed themselves here to run constantly. A hardened workstation runs only those startup items that truly need to be present all the time. This improves both performance and security, because there are fewer long-lived processes and less code in memory that an attacker could target.

Sharing and remote access deserve particular attention because they open the system to the network. Features like file and printer sharing and Remote Desktop can be very useful, but on a hardened workstation they are enabled only when there is a clear requirement. Consider a home PC used primarily for banking and email. There is no good reason for that machine to be sharing its entire C: drive or accepting Remote Desktop connections from the internet. Disabling unused sharing roles and remote access services closes entire classes of attack without affecting the user's normal workflow.

This is where the firewall and system settings work together. For example, enabling Remote Desktop on a Windows machine also opens the necessary firewall rules by default. If the user later decides they no longer need remote access, turning off Remote Desktop in System Properties closes that door. A support ticket from a user who "couldn't get Remote Desktop to connect so I just turned off the firewall, now it works" is a perfect illustration of poor hardening. The correct approach is to re-enable the firewall and then verify that Remote Desktop is configured correctly and that the needed ports are allowed, not to leave the machine exposed.

Data Protection and Local Privacy Settings

While encryption and data handling get deeper treatment in later sections, you should see how they fit into workstation hardening. On laptops and desktops that may contain sensitive information, enabling full-disk encryption such as **BitLocker** on supported Windows editions or FileVault on macOS is a major hardening step. It does not prevent someone from attacking the system while it is running, but it protects data if the device is lost or stolen. In some small business or home scenarios, you might be the person who explains to a user that if their unencrypted laptop is stolen, whoever has it can remove the drive and read their data, even if they do not know the Windows password.

At the application level, browser and office suite settings add another layer. Web browsers are prime attack vectors, so a hardened workstation uses built-in protections like safe browsing, pop-up blocking where appropriate, restricted permission prompts for camera and microphone, and limited or no use of risky plug-ins. Office applications often support macros, which are small bits of code embedded in documents. Because macro malware is a common attack path, a secure configuration either disables macros by default or warns loudly before running them, especially from documents downloaded from the internet. You will explore browser and application hardening more deeply in later chapters, but conceptually they are extensions of the same workstation-hardening mindset.

Balancing Security and Usability

The tricky part of workstation hardening is not knowing the theoretical "most secure" configuration; it is finding the point where the system is secure enough without being unusable. If you made passwords expire every seven days, locked accounts for an hour after a single failed login, and required users to call IT for every minor configuration change, you might feel virtuous as a security person, but your users would quickly find ways around your controls—or they would stop calling you and start doing dangerous things on their own.

As a technician, you learn to think in terms of requirements, risks, and alternatives. Suppose a junior developer, like in the earlier example, files a ticket complaining about UAC prompts and asks for permanent admin rights. The requirement is clear: they need to install development tools and update them frequently. The risk of granting permanent admin is also clear: developers download lots of code, scripts, and utilities from the internet, and an admin-level compromise would be severe. A reasonable alternative might be to keep their day-to-day account as a standard user but have a documented process where IT temporarily uses an admin account for authorized installs, or deploys approved tools centrally. That solution respects least privilege while still letting the developer do their job.

Similarly, when a remote worker disables the firewall to "get Remote Desktop working," the requirement is remote access, but the chosen solution creates a broad new risk. Instead, you re-enable the firewall and adjust only the specific rules needed for Remote Desktop, perhaps limiting access to connections from the corporate VPN. In an exam question, this kind of reasoning translates into choosing answers that maintain layered protections—updates, firewall, antimalware, least privilege—while tweaking configuration to meet the user's needs, rather than answers that throw away protections entirely in the name of convenience.

Over time, you will come to see workstation hardening not as a one-time checklist, but as a baseline you keep returning to. When troubleshooting strange behavior or security alerts, one of your first instincts should be to compare the machine in front of you to that mental baseline: Are updates on? Is there exactly one working antivirus solution? Is the firewall enabled? Are users running as standard accounts with UAC active? Each "no" you turn into a "yes" shrinks the attack surface and makes that workstation a little harder to compromise, without needing any flashy tools or complex enterprise infrastructure.

7.7 Securing Mobile Devices

If you think back a few years, a "phone" was just a way to make calls and send the occasional text. Today, that same device is a full-fledged computer that just happens to fit in a pocket. It holds corporate email, synced documents, VPN credentials, cloud storage apps, password managers, and often the multi-factor authentication codes that protect other systems. When a modern smartphone or tablet goes missing, you are not dealing with a lost gadget; you are potentially dealing with a data breach. As an entry-level support technician, your job is not only to know where the security settings live on Android and iOS, but also to understand why each one matters and how to explain those choices to nontechnical users in business and home environments.

The first layer of mobile security is brutally simple: keep other people from getting into the device in the first place. Unlike a desktop tucked into an office, phones and tablets are constantly traveling through airports, coffee shops, rideshares, and conferences. They are easy to misplace and easy to steal. That puts the focus on the **screen lock**, because whatever follows—encryption, app sandboxing, remote wipe—depends on preventing quick, casual access when the device falls into the wrong hands. Both Android and iOS offer a range of lock options. At one extreme is the "no lock" or simple swipe-to-unlock configuration, which might feel convenient but is essentially the same as leaving a laptop logged in on a park bench. From a security point of view, any device that accesses email, stores personal information, or touches corporate data should never operate this way.

On most devices, users can choose among PINs, passwords, patterns, and biometrics. A **PIN** is a numeric code—four digits used to be common, but many organizations now insist on six or more digits to slow down guessing attacks. This is a classic usability-versus-security trade-off: a longer PIN is harder to brute force, but also slightly more annoying to type dozens of times a day. A **password** can mix letters, numbers, and symbols, and is usually the most secure option in a traditional sense, but many people find long, complex passwords frustrating on a small touchscreen. Android's **pattern lock** lets users trace a shape across a grid of dots, which feels fast and intuitive but is easier to "shoulder surf" in public and sometimes leaves visible smudge patterns on the glass. Then there are **biometrics** such as fingerprint sensors, facial recognition (Face ID and its Android equivalents), and in some cases iris scanners. Biometrics are popular because they reduce the friction of using a strong PIN or password; under the hood, the device still ties the biometric unlock to a passcode that serves as a fallback when the environment or sensor fails. In certain regulated or high-security environments, you may encounter policies that prefer passcodes to biometrics for legal or privacy reasons, so it is important to remember that "strong lock" does not always mean "biometric allowed."

On the exam, you will see scenarios that test your ability to match lock types to risk levels. A shared clinical tablet used to access patient charts on hospital rounds should not be protected by a simple pattern swipe; a strong passcode, shorter auto-lock timeout, and enterprise control through Mobile Device Management (MDM) would be a more appropriate combination. A traveling salesperson who constantly unlocks a device in crowded spaces may be better served by a long numeric PIN combined with fingerprint or face unlock rather than a complex alphanumeric password or a pattern that can be watched and copied by someone nearby. The key is to read each scenario and ask, "How sensitive is the data, how likely is public use, and what policy applies?"

Once you have a reasonable screen lock in place, the next question is what happens if an attacker bypasses the operating system or simply removes the storage chip from the device. That is where **encryption** comes in. Full-disk or full-device encryption scrambles the data stored on the phone or tablet using a cryptographic key that is effectively tied to the user's passcode. Without that key, dumping the storage to another computer just yields unreadable ciphertext. On current iOS and most modern Android devices, enabling any nontrivial passcode typically turns on storage encryption automatically. However, as a technician, you should know where to verify this, how to explain it to a concerned user ("If someone steals the phone and tries to read the chip directly, your email and photos are still protected"), and why a device with no passcode is effectively unencrypted even if the setting claims otherwise.

It is also useful to separate the idea of whole-device encryption from **app-specific encryption** or secure containers. Some messaging apps, for example, provide end-to-end encryption for conversations; they are protecting data in transit and sometimes within the app's own storage, but that does not replace the need for OS-level encryption. In business environments using MDM, you may also see a "work profile" or encrypted container that isolates corporate data from personal apps. In those cases, the organization can remotely wipe that managed container without touching the user's private photos and messages, which becomes important in bring-your-own-device scenarios.

Even with good locks and encryption, people still lose devices. That is why both major platforms include "find my device" services that combine tracking, locking, and data destruction as needed. Apple's **Find My iPhone** and Google's **Find My Device** can show a last known location on a map, force a loud sound to help you find a phone lost under a couch cushion, display a custom message on the lock screen, remotely lock the device, and as a last resort, remotely wipe all its data. These features have to be configured and associated with the user's Apple ID or Google account ahead of time, which is where your configuration guidance matters. When an employee calls the help desk from an airport saying they left their phone in a rideshare, the correct action is not to tell them to "wait and see." If the phone is enrolled in an MDM system, IT can immediately issue a remote lock and then decide, based on how recoverable the device appears, whether to trigger a wipe and revoke access to corporate email, VPNs, and cloud apps. If there is no MDM, you would walk the user through signing in to the platform's web-based "Find My" service to lock or erase the device themselves, then assist them in changing account passwords and verifying multi-factor authentication settings.

Choosing between **remote lock** and **remote wipe** depends on the scenario. A misplaced phone likely sitting in a trusted environment, like somewhere at home, might simply be locked and located. A phone believed stolen, or lost in an uncontrolled environment like a taxi or public venue, should usually be wiped once it becomes clear it will not be recovered quickly. The exam will often include distractor answers that focus on physical recovery efforts or changing passwords alone; remember that the strongest control, when the device is gone, is to use these remote capabilities promptly.

So far, we have focused on protecting data at rest and responding to loss. The next layer is to reduce the attack surface by keeping the software itself up to date and controlling where that software comes from. **Operating system updates** and **app updates** are not just about new features; in many cases, they patch active vulnerabilities that malware authors are already exploiting. Android and iOS both support automatic updates, which home users are usually encouraged to keep enabled. In corporate environments, IT might delay or stage these updates to test compatibility with critical apps. That control is commonly exercised through MDM, which can specify when devices may install updates, require a particular minimum OS version, or block devices that fall too far behind.

Application source is another important variable. The official Apple App Store and Google Play Store perform a degree of vetting and can remove or disable malicious apps after the fact. Some Android devices, however, allow **sideloading** of apps—installing an APK directly from a website or third-party store—if the user or an admin enables "unknown sources" or "install unknown apps" in settings. From a security standpoint, this bypasses much of the ecosystem's built-in protection and is a common vector for malware and spyware. That is why many organizations use MDM policies to completely block installation from unknown sources and to maintain a **managed app catalog** or "managed Play Store" containing only approved apps. When a marketing user insists that they "need" a free PDF editor from a random website, your role is to explain that policy, point them to approved alternatives, and if necessary, submit the app for security review rather than disabling protections on their device.

Even when an app comes from an official store, you still need to think about what it can see and do. Mobile OSes rely heavily on **sandboxing**, which isolates apps from each other and from the core system, and on a permission model that forces apps to ask before accessing sensitive data like location, contacts, microphone, camera, SMS, and storage. Those permission prompts you reflexively tap through are actually critical security controls. A simple utility, such as a flashlight or calculator, has no legitimate reason to access your contact list or send SMS messages. If it requests those permissions, that is a red flag for data harvesting or fraud. From a support standpoint, you should be comfortable opening the permissions screen for a given app, reviewing what it can access, and tightening or revoking permissions that exceed what the app truly needs. On the exam, watch for scenarios where the best response to a privacy concern is not "uninstall antivirus" or "block Wi-Fi," but instead reviewing app permissions and potentially removing a suspicious app.

Another piece that often gets overlooked until it is too late is backup. Backups live at the intersection of security and availability. When a device is lost, stolen, or corrupted by malware, the situation is far less dire if recent data has been safely copied elsewhere. iOS devices can back up to **iCloud** or to a computer via iTunes/Finder, while Android devices can use Google's backup services, manufacturer-specific clouds, or local tools. For security purposes, these backups should be encrypted, and the accounts that control them should themselves be protected with strong authentication and, ideally, multi-factor authentication. In corporate environments, MDM can enforce whether corporate data may be backed up to consumer cloud services at all, or require backups to be stored only in approved, enterprise-controlled locations. As an A+ candidate, you should be able to distinguish between syncing data (for example, email syncing to an IMAP server) and true backup of device state, and recognize that both can play roles in recovery planning.

You will sometimes be asked about **mobile anti-malware** or endpoint protection apps. The reality is that iOS and Android are designed around sandboxing, signed apps, and controlled app stores, so they are less reliant on traditional antivirus than desktop platforms. However, organizations still deploy mobile security agents in many cases. These tools can scan for known malicious apps or URLs, detect jailbroken or rooted devices that have been deliberately weakened by the user, enforce web-filtering policies, check that required security settings are enabled, and feed compliance information back into the MDM system. For the exam, you should treat these as one component in a layered defense, not as a magic fix that replaces good configuration. If the root problem in a scenario is that a user is sideloading untrusted apps or ignoring updates, the correct answer will usually be to stop that behavior or enforce policy centrally, not simply to "install antivirus."

Zooming out, the enterprise answer to "How do we keep hundreds of phones and tablets configured correctly without touching each one?" is **Mobile Device Management**. MDM platforms allow IT staff to push Wi-Fi profiles, VPN configurations, email accounts, and certificates; enforce security baselines like minimum passcode length, maximum number of failed unlock attempts before wipe, auto-lock timeouts, and encryption requirements; and selectively enable or disable hardware features such as the camera, screen capture, NFC, or USB tethering. They also manage the app lifecycle, making certain apps mandatory, blocking others entirely, and granting or revoking access to a curated app store. Through MDM, support staff can trigger remote lock and wipe operations centrally and verify compliance across the entire fleet.

The way MDM is used in practice depends on the ownership model. In **corporate-owned** devices, the company typically applies strict controls and may lock the device down to business functions only. With **COPE** (Corporate-Owned, Personally Enabled), users are allowed personal use but within boundaries defined by IT. In true **BYOD** (Bring Your Own Device) environments, the device belongs to the employee, but the organization requires enrollment in MDM to access corporate resources. Modern Android and iOS can create a logical separation between work and personal data, often called a "work profile" on Android or a managed area on iOS. That lets IT wipe corporate apps and data if the user leaves the company or loses the device, without deleting family photos or personal apps. On the exam, whenever a question mentions needing to "enforce security settings across all employee smartphones without configuring each individually," or to "separate work and personal data on employee-owned devices," MDM or a related enterprise mobility management solution is almost always the expected answer.

Finally, it is worth circling back to basic physical practices and user behavior, because even the best technical controls cannot compensate for carelessness. Rugged cases and screen protectors are not security devices in the strict sense, but they reduce the chance that a cracked screen or broken button will lead a user to disable security features "until they can get it fixed." Users should be reminded not to leave devices unattended in cars, restaurants, or conference rooms, and to be wary of plugging into unknown USB charging stations where a compromised kiosk could attempt to extract data or install malware—a concern often called juice jacking. When connecting to public Wi-Fi from a mobile device, using a VPN and avoiding sensitive transactions is part of the broader network security picture you will explore in later sections, but it interacts closely with the configuration work you do here.

In practice, when you are handed a new phone to "secure," the mental checklist you build from this chapter will guide you: verify a strong screen lock and that encryption is active; ensure locate, lock, and wipe services are configured with a known account; set OS and app updates to an appropriate mode; confirm that app sources are restricted to approved stores and that obvious permission abuses are not present; check that backups are in place and protected; and determine whether an MDM policy should be enforced. That is the same mindset the exam will test, expressed through short scenarios that force you to choose the control that best addresses the specific risk described.

7.8 Securing SOHO Networks

If you work in IT support today, you will almost certainly be asked at some point to "secure my home Wi-Fi" or "lock down our office router." For many remote workers and small businesses, that single plastic box in the corner is the only thing standing between their internal devices and the entire internet. In enterprise environments you might have layers of firewalls, intrusion prevention, and centralized management. In a small office/home office, you usually have one **SOHO router** doing everything: routing, NAT, firewalling, wireless access, DHCP, and often DNS forwarding. Learning how to turn that off-the-shelf device into a reasonably secure "edge" is one of the most practical skills you can bring to an entry-level support role—and CompTIA A+ expects you to know it cold.

When we talk about the **network edge** in this context, we mean the boundary where a private LAN meets the public internet. In a typical SOHO setup, that edge is either a combined modem/router from the ISP, or a separate modem connected to a wireless router. Behind it, you find laptops, phones, tablets, smart TVs, game consoles, maybe a network printer or a NAS device. Some connect via Ethernet, most via Wi-Fi. In front of it is everything you do not control: the ISP's network and the larger internet. The job of that SOHO router is to use NAT to translate internal private IP addresses to a single public IP, and to act as a basic **stateful firewall**, allowing outbound traffic and related replies while dropping unsolicited inbound connections by default.

The threats to this environment are very real even if they are less dramatic than full-blown nation-state attacks. An attacker parked outside can try "drive-by" Wi-Fi attacks—probing for open or weak wireless networks. Malware on an infected device inside the LAN can use UPnP to punch holes in the firewall, or it may try to reach a command-and-control server on the internet. Botnets constantly scan public IP ranges looking for routers that still have default admin passwords or unpatched firmware vulnerabilities. A neighbor might not be malicious but will happily use your open Wi-Fi to stream HD video, dragging down your bandwidth and potentially exposing you to liability if they do something illegal. Your job when securing a SOHO network is to reduce this exposure at the edge, especially by strengthening wireless security and hardening router configuration.

Getting into the Router the Right Way

The first task for any technician asked to secure a SOHO network is simply getting into the router's management interface safely. That starts with identifying the router's **management IP address**, which is almost always in a private range such as 192.168.0.1, 192.168.1.1, or 10.0.0.1. Many devices have this printed on a label along with the default username and password. You can also find it by checking the default gateway on a connected system using ipconfig in Windows or the network settings on macOS or Linux. Once you know the address, you point a browser at it to bring up the web management interface.

Whenever possible, you should make these changes from a **wired Ethernet** connection rather than over Wi-Fi. That avoids the risk of losing your connection halfway through when you change wireless settings, and it reduces the chance that someone nearby can sniff unencrypted management traffic. Once you reach the login screen, you'll use whatever credentials are currently configured. In many real-world and exam scenarios, the router has never been hardened and still uses the default admin username and password printed on the sticker, or something predictable like "admin/admin." The moment you realize you can log in with that, you should treat it as a major red flag; attackers know these defaults too, and there are automated tools that do nothing but try common credential combinations across large blocks of addresses.

It is also important to keep straight the difference between **admin credentials** and the **Wi-Fi passphrase.** The admin credentials control who can change router settings. The Wi-Fi passphrase (sometimes called the network key) controls who can join the wireless network. These are often confused in exam questions. If a scenario describes someone changing the Wi-Fi password to keep neighbors off the network, that does nothing to prevent an attacker from logging in to the router itself if the admin password is still "admin." When you are asked to secure the router, think first about who can access the management interface, and only then about who can join the Wi-Fi network.

Hardening Router Management and Firmware

Before you touch any wireless settings, it makes sense to secure the management plane of the router itself. That starts with changing the default admin credentials. A secure **administrator password** should be long, not reused from any other service, and distinct from the Wi-Fi passphrase. Some devices let you change the admin username as well, which is a useful extra obstacle against automated attacks that assume "admin" is the account name. As a technician, you also have to think practically: document that new credential somewhere safe, such as a password manager or a secure note in a ticketing system, so you or the client are not locked out later and tempted to reset everything to defaults.

Once the admin account is no longer an easy target, your next step is to update the router's **firmware**. Firmware is the embedded operating system that runs the router's features. Like any software, it can have vulnerabilities, and vendors release updates to patch security holes, fix bugs, and sometimes add support for newer standards such as WPA3. On many consumer devices, you will find a firmware or "Software Update" section under an Administration, System, or Advanced menu. Some modern routers can check and download updates automatically; others require you to download a file from the manufacturer's website and upload it through the web interface. From a security standpoint, this step is critical. If an exam question mentions a known vulnerability in a specific router model or that the device is several years out of date, "update the firmware to the latest version" is often the correct remedial action before you fine-tune other settings.

With updated firmware, you can focus on securing how management traffic reaches the router. Ideally, access is limited to the internal network and secured with **HTTPS**. Using HTTPS for the management interface encrypts your login credentials and configuration commands, preventing someone on the same network from sniffing them in transit. Many routers still expose both HTTP and HTTPS for management; in that case, you should disable HTTP and force HTTPS where possible. Equally important is the setting often labeled "Remote Management" or "WAN Administration." When this is enabled, the router can be managed from the internet, not just from inside the LAN. That might be convenient for an advanced administrator with a VPN, but for a typical SOHO user it dramatically increases attack surface. In most small environments, the secure choice is to disable remote management entirely. If an exam scenario describes a user managing their router from a coffee shop over plain HTTP, you should immediately think "disable remote administration" or, at minimum, require secure channels such as VPN and HTTPS.

Some SOHO firmware allows you to change the management port or restrict management to certain internal IP addresses. Changing the port from 80/443 to something nonstandard will not stop a determined attacker, but it can reduce noise from generic internet scans. IP-based restrictions are stronger but can be overkill for a very small network. The key principle for the exam is that router management should not be exposed to the world, should not rely on defaults, and should use encryption when possible.

Designing Secure Wi-Fi Settings

Once management is locked down, you can move to the wireless side. Here the A+ exam expects you to be fluent with SSIDs, encryption modes, and pre-shared keys. The **SSID** is the wireless network name that clients see when they go to connect. From a security perspective, you should avoid SSIDs that directly identify the owner's name, address, or business, such as "SmithFamilyWiFi" or "ACME-Accounting." Those make targeted attacks easier and can expose more personal information than necessary. A neutral name like "OfficeNet-24" or "Home-5G" discloses less.

Most routers broadcast the SSID by default so devices can discover and display it. Some offer the option to "hide" the SSID. It is important not to overvalue this feature. A hidden SSID does not provide real security. Wireless traffic still contains information that allows an attacker with the right tools to identify the network name, and determined attackers can watch probe requests from legitimate clients to learn it. All hiding the SSID really does is make it slightly more annoying for legitimate users to connect. On the exam, SSID hiding might appear as a minor obscurity measure, but it is never a substitute for strong encryption and should not be treated as a primary control.

The real core of Wi-Fi security lies in the **encryption and authentication mode** the router uses. You will see options like Open, WEP, WPA, WPA2, and WPA3. For A+ you need to recognize their relative strength: Open means no encryption at all and is completely inappropriate for a SOHO environment except in very rare, controlled cases. WEP is an obsolete standard with well-known flaws; it should be considered insecure even if it is available. Original WPA is better than WEP but also outdated and no longer recommended when alternatives exist. Today the minimum you should configure on a SOHO router is **WPA2-Personal**, and where supported, **WPA3-Personal** is stronger still due to improvements in how keys are derived and how resistant it is to offline brute-force attacks.

Routers may also offer "Enterprise" variants such as WPA2-Enterprise or WPA3-Enterprise. These rely on 802.1X authentication and a **RADIUS** server to validate each user, often with usernames and passwords or certificates. That is appropriate for larger organizations with centralized directory services, but almost never for a small office or home which lacks such infrastructure. On the exam, if you are told this is a five-person office using an ISP-provided combo modem/router and there is no mention of RADIUS or Active Directory, you should assume the correct answer involves WPA2-Personal or WPA3-Personal, not an enterprise mode that the environment simply cannot support.

Equally important is the quality of the **Wi-Fi passphrase**. In a SOHO setting, the passphrase is often the primary security control: whoever has it can get on the network. Weak, short, or predictable keys like "password123," the owner's phone number, or the business name plus a year are trivial for attackers to guess or crack once they have captured a handshake. Since WPA2-Personal and WPA3-Personal rely on a pre-shared key, length and randomness matter. Long passphrases based on randomly generated words or characters are best. For a small business, you might choose something like four unrelated words with numbers and symbols mixed in, and then document it securely. It is also wise to train users not to share this key casually. If visitors need internet access, the better solution is usually to give them a **guest network** rather than reveal the main network's passphrase.

Segmenting SOHO Networks: Guest and IoT Isolation

One of the most effective but underused security techniques in small environments is **network segmentation**. Instead of putting every device—workstations, smartphones, printers, security cameras, and visitors' laptops—on the same LAN, you separate them logically so that compromise in one area does not automatically grant access to everything else.

Most modern SOHO routers make this easy through a built-in **guest Wi-Fi** feature. When enabled, the router broadcasts an additional SSID, often with its own passphrase and its own IP subnet. Clients that join the guest network get internet access but, if configured correctly, are blocked from reaching devices on the main LAN. Some routers also apply client isolation so guests cannot see each other's systems either. For a small business that occasionally hosts customers or contractors, putting those visitors on a guest SSID is far safer than giving them your primary Wi-Fi credentials. If an exam scenario describes guests being able to browse shared folders on office PCs or send jobs to internal printers, that is a cue that the guest network is either not being used or not properly isolated, and the appropriate fix is to enable LAN isolation for guest Wi-Fi or adjust guest settings so it only provides internet access.

A similar idea applies to **IoT and smart devices**. Many of these products—smart thermostats, cameras, light bulbs, TVs—receive few or no firmware updates and have a long history of security issues. If a camera is compromised, you do not want that attacker to be able to pivot directly into accounting workstations or a file server containing sensitive data. In a SOHO environment without VLANs, the simplest mitigation is to place such devices on a separate SSID or even reuse the guest network for them, as long as that network does not allow access back to internal resources. As a technician, you might configure "OfficeMain" for company devices and "Office-IoT" or the built-in guest SSID for cameras and smart TVs, then verify that routing between those segments is blocked.

Extra Controls: Firewall Behavior, UPnP, WPS, and MAC Filtering

Beyond Wi-Fi and management settings, most SOHO routers expose a handful of additional controls that have significant security implications. One of the most fundamental is the built-in **firewall**, which typically works hand-in-hand with NAT to block unsolicited inbound traffic. In default configuration, outbound connections initiated from inside are allowed, and return traffic is permitted because it is part of an established session. Random inbound packets from the internet that do not match an existing session are dropped. Users sometimes disable this firewall in desperation to "fix" a connectivity problem, but this removes a key layer of protection. On both the exam and in practice, you should be reluctant to disable the firewall; instead, troubleshoot the specific application or, if truly necessary, use more controlled mechanisms such as port forwarding.

Port forwarding itself is another area A+ expects you to reason about. When you create a **port forward**, you tell the router to accept inbound connections on a specific port and forward them to an internal IP address. This is how people expose services like game servers, IP cameras, or remote desktop to the internet. While it can be necessary, every open port is an exposure. Many exam questions are written to test whether you understand that security-focused tasks should reduce or audit such forwards, not create more of them. If the question is "How can the technician better secure this SOHO router?" the correct choice will almost never be "place the workstation in a DMZ" or "add a port forward," because those increase exposure.

Two convenience features that often appear in consumer routers are **UPnP (Universal Plug and Play)** and **WPS (Wi-Fi Protected Setup)**. UPnP allows internal devices to ask the router automatically for port forwards, without user involvement. That makes multiplayer games and some applications easier to use, but it also means malware running on a PC or IoT device can silently open inbound ports for itself. If a scenario mentions unexpected open ports or services reachable from the internet even though no one configured port forwarding, you should think of UPnP and recommend disabling it as a security measure.

WPS was designed to simplify connecting new wireless devices through a push-button method or an eight-digit PIN, so users would not need to type complex passphrases. Unfortunately, the **WPS PIN** method has well-known weaknesses that make it vulnerable to brute-force attacks. Many security best-practice guides now recommend disabling WPS entirely and relying on strong WPA2/WPA3 passphrases instead. On the exam, if you are given a choice between enabling WPS or using a long WPA3-Personal key, the secure answer is always the latter.

Finally, you may encounter **MAC filtering**, a feature that allows you to maintain an allowlist or blocklist of device MAC addresses permitted on the wireless network. While it sounds attractive—only known devices can connect—it has serious limitations. MAC addresses are visible in wireless frames and can be trivially **spoofed** by an attacker who knows what they are doing. That means MAC filtering may stop a casual neighbor but will not withstand someone with basic hacking tools. CompTIA wants you to recognize MAC filtering as a weak, supplemental measure at best, not a replacement for proper encryption. If a question asks how to secure Wi-Fi, and the options are "enable MAC filtering" or "change from WEP to WPA2-Personal," the correct answer is always to strengthen the encryption.

Many SOHO routers also provide simple **logs** and client lists. As a technician, you should get into the habit of checking the DHCP or "connected devices" list for unfamiliar devices, especially when users complain about slow Wi-Fi or suspect someone is "stealing" their internet. A long list of unknown smartphones and laptops on a home network is a sign that the Wi-Fi passphrase has been shared too widely or that the network was previously open. Administrative logs that show repeated failed login attempts, particularly from external IP addresses, may indicate that remote management is enabled and under brute-force attack. Even though these tools are basic compared to enterprise monitoring, they are valuable signals you can use to assess whether your hardening steps are working and where additional changes might be needed.

7.11 Knowledge Check

Question 1: A company wants to ensure that if a laptop is stolen from a coffee shop, the thief cannot access the data by removing the drive and connecting it to another computer. Which security measure best addresses this risk?

- **A.** Configure a strong BIOS/UEFI setup and boot password on the laptop to restrict unauthorized startup attempts
- **B.** Attach a privacy filter to the laptop display to prevent shoulder surfing by nearby individuals
- **C.** Implement full-disk encryption such as BitLocker or Device Encryption on the drive to protect all data at rest
- **D.** Disable all USB ports in the operating system to block external devices from connecting to the laptop

Question 2: A technician wants to improve authentication security for users logging into Windows laptops without buying additional hardware. Which change most effectively implements multifactor authentication (MFA)?

- **A.** Require a password plus a one-time code from an authenticator app installed on the user's smartphone for each login
- **B.** Require a longer and more complex password that must be changed every 30 days for all user accounts on the laptops
- **C.** Add multiple security questions that users must answer in addition to entering their existing password at sign-in
- **D.** Require users to press Ctrl+Alt+Delete before logging in to bring up the secure Windows sign-in screen

Question 3: A visitor asks to be let into the server room to "check something for the facilities team" and does not have a badge. What is the technician's most appropriate response from a security standpoint?

- **A.** Allow the visitor into the server room but remain present and observe them closely while they perform their stated work
- **B.** Ask the visitor to sign the physical visitor logbook at reception, then permit them to enter the secure server room area
- **C.** Deny entry to the server room and contact a supervisor or security to verify the visitor's identity and authorization status
- **D.** Permit entry to the server room if the visitor presents a business card that shows the company's logo, name, and phone number

Question 4: A user reports that they can see someone else's confidential information on a nearby monitor when walking past a reception desk. Which single control best mitigates this specific risk?

A. Installing a BIOS/UEFI user or boot password on the receptionist's workstation PC to prevent unauthorized startup
B. Enabling full-disk encryption on the receptionist's workstation to protect stored data if the system is stolen
C. Shortening the Windows automatic screen lock timeout to approximately 30 seconds of inactivity on the workstation
D. Installing a privacy filter on the receptionist's monitor to limit the viewing angle and block side views of the display

Question 5: A help desk technician needs to create user accounts for new employees on a Windows 11 PC that is joined to a domain. To follow the principle of least privilege, which type of account should users receive for day-to-day work?

A. Local administrator accounts so users can install any required software and change system settings on their own
B. Standard user accounts that provide only the permissions needed for normal daily tasks and business applications
C. A shared local power user account that multiple employees can use when elevated permissions are necessary
D. Domain administrator accounts so users have full control over domain resources and network-wide configurations

Question 6: A user's Windows PC repeatedly prompts for administrator approval (UAC) when installing software from unknown websites. The user wants the prompts disabled. From a workstation hardening perspective, what should the technician do?

A. Disable User Account Control (UAC) entirely so the user can install applications without any security interruptions
B. Leave UAC enabled and perform only approved software installations using an administrator account when required
C. Make the user a local administrator and reduce the UAC notification level to the lowest setting available in Windows
D. Enable automatic login using the local administrator account to avoid UAC prompts and elevation requests at startup

Question 7: A Windows user complains that a line-of-business application has stopped working after Microsoft Defender Antivirus quarantined one of its files. What should the technician do first?

A. Turn off real-time protection permanently so the application can run without further interference from Defender
B. Immediately restore the quarantined file and add a full-drive exclusion for that system in Microsoft Defender
C. Uninstall Microsoft Defender Antivirus and install a different third-party antivirus solution on the computer
D. Review the Protection history to identify the detection event and research whether it is a legitimate threat or false positive

Question 8: A company wants to provide wireless access for visitors but ensure guests cannot access internal file shares, printers, or management interfaces. Which router feature should the technician configure?

- **A.** Enable Wi-Fi Protected Setup (WPS) to allow faster onboarding and easier connection of guest wireless clients
- **B.** Use WEP security with a unique guest passphrase that is changed on a regular schedule for visiting users
- **C.** Disable DHCP for wireless clients so guests must configure static IP addresses manually on their own devices
- **D.** Configure a separate, isolated guest SSID that provides internet-only access and blocks access to internal resources

Question 9: A technician needs to ensure that only authorized employees can access a secure wiring closet, and that access attempts can be logged and revoked centrally. Which solution best meets this requirement?

- **A.** Install a mechanical door lock that uses a single shared physical key for all authorized staff members
- **B.** Mount a security camera above an unlocked door to record anyone entering the secure wiring closet area
- **C.** Implement an electronic badge reader on the door with centrally managed access control and audit logging
- **D.** Place a visitor sign-in sheet at the front desk to record names of people entering the office building

Question 10: A user receives an email that looks like it is from the company's cloud storage provider, stating their account will be disabled today unless they click a link and log in. The sender address is slightly misspelled, and the link points to an unfamiliar domain. What type of attack is this?

- **A.** Phishing attack attempting to steal credentials through a fraudulent email message and spoofed log-in website
- **B.** Tailgating attack where an unauthorized person physically follows someone into a secure or restricted area
- **C.** Logic bomb attack where malicious code triggers and executes after a specific event, date, or time condition
- **D.** Vishing attack where the attacker uses a voice phone call to trick the victim into revealing sensitive data

Question 11: A technician is asked to secure a company smartphone that contains corporate email and uses SMS for MFA codes. Which configuration change is most important to implement first?

- **A.** Disable Bluetooth on the smartphone so it cannot pair with or connect to nearby wireless Bluetooth devices
- **B.** Enable a strong screen lock (PIN or password) and verify that device encryption is turned on for stored data
- **C.** Turn off Wi-Fi on the smartphone and require the user to rely only on cellular data connections for access
- **D.** Remove all personal applications from the smartphone to limit non-business usage and personal activities

Question 12: A user's browser home page has changed to an unfamiliar search engine, multiple new toolbars have appeared, and pop-up ads display even when the browser is closed. Which malware type best fits this description?

A. Rootkit that hides deep in the operating system to conceal its presence and other malicious activity
B. Ransomware that encrypts user files and demands payment from the victim to restore access to data
C. Worm that self-replicates across networks and systems without requiring direct user interaction
D. Adware or potentially unwanted program (PUP) that injects ads and makes unwanted browser configuration changes

Question 13: A small office uses a Wi-Fi network secured with WPA2-Personal. The owner wants to avoid giving visitors the same passphrase used by employees. What is the best recommendation?

A. Enable MAC address filtering and add only employee devices to the allowed list of permitted wireless clients
B. Configure a separate guest SSID with its own passphrase and enable LAN isolation to keep guests off the internal LAN
C. Hide the primary SSID so that only employees who already know the network name can see and connect to it
D. Change the network to WPA2-Enterprise with a RADIUS server for all wireless authentication, including guests

Question 14: A Windows PC in a SOHO environment shows symptoms of malware: fake antivirus alerts, slow performance, and unwanted toolbars. According to the recommended malware removal process, what should the technician do immediately after identifying and researching the symptoms?

A. Run a full antivirus scan from normal mode with networking enabled on the infected system
B. Create a new System Restore point so the system can be rolled back to this state after cleanup is complete
C. Quarantine the system by disconnecting it from the network to prevent further spread or external communication
D. Reinstall the operating system from scratch right away to guarantee that the malware is completely removed

Question 15: A home user wants to "make the Wi-Fi really secure" and asks about enabling MAC address filtering as the only protection. What should the technician explain?

A. MAC filtering cannot be used at the same time as WPA2 or WPA3 wireless security modes on a home router
B. MAC filtering can be easily bypassed by attackers who can observe allowed MAC addresses and spoof them
C. MAC filtering is stronger than WPA2-PSK security if it is configured correctly on the wireless router
D. MAC filtering automatically encrypts all wireless traffic between clients and the access point by default

Question 16: A technician is configuring a new Windows 11 Pro laptop that will leave the office frequently and may contain sensitive client files. In addition to a strong login password, what should the technician enable to best protect data if the laptop is lost or stolen?

A. Enable the built-in Guest account so temporary users can access the laptop when needed without restrictions
B. Configure local administrator autologon so the system signs in automatically at startup for user convenience
C. Disable the Windows firewall on public networks to avoid potential connectivity issues when traveling
D. Enable BitLocker full-disk encryption (or Device Encryption if BitLocker is not available on the system)

Question 17: A small office environment wants to use wireless authentication tied to individual usernames and passwords stored in their Active Directory domain, rather than a shared Wi-Fi passphrase. Which wireless security mode should they implement?

A. WPA2-Enterprise using 802.1X authentication with a RADIUS server and integration with the directory service
B. WPA2-Personal using a long, complex pre-shared key that is shared among all wireless users in the office
C. WEP security with a rotating shared key that is changed on a regular schedule for all wireless clients
D. WPA3-Personal with MAC address filtering enabled for all authorized wireless clients on the network

Question 18: A user calls the help desk stating that "Microsoft support" phoned them and requested remote access to fix a virus, asking them to disable their antivirus and provide their credit card. What type of threat is this?

A. Worm that spreads automatically across the network to other systems without user interaction
B. Social engineering (quid pro quo / tech support scam) attempting to gain access and payment from the user
C. Logic bomb that triggers malicious activity when a specific date, time, or condition is met on the system
D. Insider threat where a trusted employee intentionally misuses their authorized access to company resources

Question 19: On a Windows PC, a virus has been removed but keeps returning after the user restores the system to a previous state. Which step was most likely missed during the malware removal process?

A. Running a full antivirus scan instead of relying only on a quick or partial scan of the system
B. Rebooting the computer into Safe Mode before performing the malware scan and cleanup procedure
C. Disabling and clearing System Restore points before cleanup, then re-enabling them afterward for future use
D. Updating the system's BIOS/UEFI firmware to the latest available version from the motherboard vendor

Question 20: A user's smartphone used for corporate email has been lost in a taxi. The device is enrolled in the company's MDM. What should the technician do first to protect company data?

A. Immediately change the user's Windows desktop password on their office workstation computer
B. Disable Bluetooth on the lost smartphone remotely using the MDM management console or policy
C. Issue a remote lock and, if recovery is unlikely, perform a remote wipe of the device via the MDM system
D. Remove the user's email account from the company's mail server configuration and address list

ANSWERS

1: Correct Answer: C

Rationale: Full-disk encryption protects data at rest so that, even if the drive is removed and connected to another system, the contents remain unreadable without the decryption key. BIOS passwords, privacy filters, or disabling USB ports do not stop direct access to a removed drive.

2: Correct Answer: A

Rationale: MFA requires at least two different factor types. A password is something you know, and a one-time code from an authenticator app on a phone is something you have, so together they provide MFA. The other options only strengthen or modify a single factor.

3: Correct Answer: C

Rationale: The technician must not allow unverified individuals into secure areas. Denying entry and contacting a supervisor or security to verify identity and authorization follows proper physical security practice. The other options allow access without proper verification.

4: Correct Answer: D

Rationale: A privacy filter narrows the viewing angle of the monitor, mitigating shoulder surfing and preventing passersby from seeing the screen. BIOS passwords, disk encryption, and short lock timeouts do not prevent viewing while the screen is actively in use.

5: Correct Answer: B

Rationale: Standard user accounts provide only the permissions needed for normal work, following least privilege. Local or domain administrator accounts grant excessive rights, and a shared elevated account is insecure and lacks accountability.

6: Correct Answer: B

Rationale: UAC is an important protection against unauthorized changes and malware. It should remain enabled, with installations performed by an administrator when approved. Disabling UAC, granting admin rights, or using admin autologon would significantly weaken security.

7: Correct Answer: D

Rationale: The technician should first review Protection history to see what Defender detected and quarantined, then research whether it is a real threat or a false positive. Disabling protection, restoring files, or replacing the AV without analysis can reintroduce or miss threats.

8: Correct Answer: D

Rationale: A separate, isolated guest SSID configured for internet-only access allows visitors online while blocking access to internal resources. WPS, WEP, or disabling DHCP do not provide proper isolation and can weaken security or usability.

9: Correct Answer: C

Rationale: An electronic badge reader with centrally managed access control supports per-user authorization, logging, and easy revocation, which is ideal for a secure wiring closet. Shared keys, cameras alone, or sign-in sheets do not provide granular control or detailed audit trails.

10: Correct Answer: A

Rationale: The email is a phishing attempt: it impersonates a trusted provider and uses a fraudulent link to trick the user into revealing credentials. Tailgating is physical, vishing uses phone calls, and a logic bomb is code triggered by a condition.

11: Correct Answer: B
Rationale: A strong screen lock plus device encryption protects corporate email and SMS MFA codes if the phone is lost or stolen, securing data at rest and blocking casual access. Disabling Bluetooth, Wi-Fi, or personal apps does not directly address data exposure from loss.

12: Correct Answer: D
Rationale: Changed home pages, unwanted toolbars, and persistent pop-up ads are typical of adware or PUPs that modify browser settings and inject advertising. Rootkits hide deeply, ransomware encrypts files, and worms self-replicate, which do not match the symptoms.

13: Correct Answer: B
Rationale: A separate guest SSID with its own passphrase and LAN isolation lets visitors access the internet without exposing the internal network or sharing the employee PSK. MAC filtering and hidden SSIDs are weak controls, and WPA2-Enterprise is more complex than needed here.

14: Correct Answer: C
Rationale: After identifying and researching symptoms, the next malware removal step is to quarantine the system by disconnecting it from the network to prevent spread or external communication. Scanning, restore points, or OS reinstall come in later steps if needed.

15: Correct Answer: B
Rationale: MAC addresses can be observed and spoofed, so MAC filtering alone is easily bypassed and not strong security. It does not provide encryption and should only supplement proper wireless security such as WPA2 or WPA3, not replace it.

16:Correct Answer: D
Rationale: BitLocker or Device Encryption protects data at rest so that, if the laptop is lost or stolen, the drive contents remain unreadable without the key. Enabling guest accounts, autologon, or disabling firewalls weakens security and does not protect stored data from theft.

17: Correct Answer: A
Rationale: WPA2-Enterprise with 802.1X/RADIUS authenticates users individually using directory credentials, matching the requirement for per-user authentication tied to Active Directory. WPA2/WPA3-Personal use shared passphrases, and WEP is obsolete and insecure.

18: Correct Answer: B
Rationale: This is a social engineering tech-support (quid pro quo) scam: the attacker offers "help" in exchange for access and payment, trying to trick the user into disabling protections and providing sensitive information. It is not a worm, logic bomb, or insider threat.

19: Correct Answer: C
Rationale: If infected restore points remain, using System Restore can reintroduce malware. Best practice is to disable and clear System Restore before cleanup, then re-enable it afterward to avoid reinfection from old restore points.

20: Correct Answer: C
Rationale: With MDM, the technician should remotely lock the device and, if recovery is unlikely, perform a remote wipe to protect corporate data on the lost smartphone. Changing desktop passwords, disabling Bluetooth, or removing the mailbox from the server does not secure data already on the device.

CHAPTER 8

Software Troubleshooting

8.1 Troubleshooting Windows OS Issues

When Windows "just isn't working," most users won't give you a clean technical description. You'll hear things like "it's broken," "it keeps restarting," or "it's so slow I can't do anything." Your job, both on the A+ exam and in real support work, is to turn that vague frustration into a clear problem statement, a reasonable theory, and a controlled fix that doesn't make things worse. That means treating Windows troubleshooting as a process, not as trial and error.

The same general troubleshooting methodology you learned earlier applies directly here. You start by identifying the problem, which in Windows usually means asking targeted questions and observing the system yourself. You then form a theory—sometimes more than one—about what might be wrong, test that theory using Windows tools, and implement the least-disruptive fix that matches your findings. Once applied, you verify that the system is actually stable and the user's real work is back to normal, then you document what you saw and what you did. For exam questions, CompTIA loves to hide this process inside short scenarios: the "best next step" is almost always the one that moves you logically along this path, rather than jumping immediately to extreme measures like reinstalling Windows.

A useful way to begin narrowing down Windows OS problems is to mentally sort them into a few broad categories as you listen and observe: **boot and startup problems**, **performance issues**, **stability problems**, and **error or access issues**. Sometimes more than one category is involved—for example, a system might boot slowly and then crash randomly—but having this mental sorting helps you pick the right tools and the right starting point. A user complaining "my computer doesn't turn on" leads you one way; a user saying "I can log in, but everything freezes" leads you somewhere very different.

Boot and Startup Problems

Boot problems feel urgent to users because they can't get to anything at all. From an A+ perspective, the important thing is to recognize where in the startup process the failure occurs and then choose an appropriate environment to work from. It helps to think in stages: firmware and basic hardware checks, the point where Windows actually starts loading, the login phase, and the desktop right after login.

If the error is along the lines of "Operating system not found" or "No bootable device," you are dealing with a very early failure, usually before Windows even gets involved. On Core 2, your focus is on the OS side of the picture, but you still need to recognize that this kind of message can indicate a broken or missing boot configuration, a misconfigured boot order, or a storage drive that Windows cannot see. If the hardware is fine and the BIOS/UEFI boot order looks correct, your next move is to try Windows' recovery tools, because the boot files themselves may be damaged.

More often, you'll see problems where the Windows logo appears but the boot never completes. Maybe you get a spinning circle forever, or the system goes into an automatic repair loop and reboots over and over. In those situations, your first goal is not to "fix everything" from the start; it is to get to a stable environment where you can work—either **Safe Mode** or the **Windows Recovery Environment (WinRE)**. Safe Mode loads a minimal set of drivers and services, which is perfect for undoing a bad driver update, removing problematic software, or running scans. WinRE, reached through Advanced Startup Options, is where tools like **Startup Repair** and **System Restore** live.

On modern systems, you can often reach Advanced Startup by interrupting the normal boot three times in a row, or by holding Shift while selecting Restart from within Windows (if you can still log in). In WinRE's menu you'll find options to continue to Windows, troubleshoot, or shut down. Under troubleshoot you get access to Startup Repair, System Restore, command prompt tools, and sometimes "Uninstall latest quality update" or "Uninstall latest feature update." Being comfortable with that menu is essential for the exam and for real-world work.

Imagine a user who tells you, "Windows updated last night and now I get a blue screen every time it restarts." That description points directly at a startup failure triggered by a recent change. Following a structured process, you would first confirm the symptom, then boot to WinRE. Instead of wiping the machine, you would try either Safe Mode, if it will load, or the "Uninstall latest update" options if Windows cannot boot at all. If you can get into Safe Mode, you might use Device Manager to roll back a graphics driver installed the night before. If you cannot reach Safe Mode, you might run Startup Repair or use **System Restore** to roll back the system state to a restore point from before the update.

A simple decision framework for startup issues can keep you organized: determine the **stage** of failure (before Windows starts, at the logo, at the login screen, or right after login), decide what **boot mode** you can reach (normal Windows, Safe Mode, or WinRE), and then choose the **least-destructive fix** that matches what you know. For example, if the system fails right after login only when a certain user signs in, the problem could be with that user profile or a startup application tied to that account, not with Windows itself. Creating a new local profile or disabling per-user startup apps is far less disruptive than resetting the entire PC.

You should also recognize when Windows boot files themselves might be damaged. A system stuck in a "Preparing Automatic Repair" loop or reporting that it can't find a boot device even though the disk shows up in firmware might need its boot configuration rebuilt. In the A+ context, it is usually enough to know that Startup Repair in WinRE can attempt to fix boot configuration data and that more advanced command-line tools exist if automated repair fails. The key, again, is to try that sort of targeted repair before deciding that the only option is a full reinstall.

Performance Problems: When "Slow" Could Mean Ten Different Things

Performance complaints are probably the most common Windows issues you will see. They are also some of the most misunderstood, because "slow" could refer to slow boot times, applications taking forever to open, lag only when browsing the web, or a system that starts fast but bogs down after an hour of usage. Your first task is to clarify what "slow" really means for that user and when it happens.

Once you have a clearer description, you can turn to Windows' real-time tools. **Task Manager** is the primary one, and you should be able to use it almost reflexively. On the Processes and Performance tabs, you can see how heavily the CPU, memory, disk, and network are being used and by which processes. If the CPU is constantly maxed out, you might find a single application or background process consuming most of it. High memory usage with frequent disk activity often shows that the system is paging heavily because it does not have enough RAM for the workload. Near-100% disk usage on a mechanical hard drive can cause the entire system to feel unresponsive, especially if Windows is running updates, indexing, or antivirus scans in the background.

Consider a user who says, "Every day around 1 p.m., the computer basically freezes." You check Task Manager and see that the antivirus engine and Windows Update are both very active at that time, consuming disk and CPU. That correlation suggests a benign but inconvenient cause: scheduled tasks competing for resources. The solution is not to replace hardware or reinstall the OS; instead, you might reschedule the scan or adjust update windows so they run outside that user's working hours. This is a good example of using observation and tools to match a pattern, rather than assuming the worst.

When performance issues are more constant, low disk space is often overlooked. If the system drive is nearly full, Windows can struggle to create temporary files, manage virtual memory, and apply updates. Disk Cleanup (or Storage Sense in Settings) can help remove temporary files, old update files, and other clutter. Removing unused applications and moving large personal data to another drive or network share can also restore breathing room. On systems with older spinning hard drives, fragmentation may still be a factor; Windows includes a disk optimization tool, but on modern SSDs fragmentation is not the performance concern it once was.

Startup bloat is another frequent culprit. Many users install apps that quietly insert themselves into the startup process, so by the time the desktop appears, a dozen unnecessary programs are already consuming memory and CPU cycles. Using the Startup tab in Task Manager or the older **System Configuration** (msconfig) utility, you can disable nonessential startup entries. This often yields dramatic improvements in boot and login times with minimal risk, as long as you avoid disabling critical security or system services.

You should also keep malware and outdated software in mind, but avoid making them your first assumption without evidence. If Task Manager shows unknown processes consuming resources, or if you see suspicious behavior like unexplained network activity, launching a scan with Windows Security or the organization's approved antivirus is appropriate. Likewise, if performance suffers only when a specific driver or application is in use, checking for updates from the vendor can resolve inefficient or buggy code. The SLOW mental checklist—clarifying Scope, checking Load, ruling out Obvious causes like low disk space or too many apps, and then using Windows tools—is a simple way to avoid jumping to conclusions.

Stability Issues: Crashes, Hangs, and Blue Screens

Some systems are not slow, but unreliable. They may run fine for a while and then freeze, reboot spontaneously, crash certain applications repeatedly, or display the dreaded Blue Screen of Death. These are stability issues, and resolving them usually requires looking not just at what is happening now, but at what has been happening over time.

Windows records a great deal of diagnostic information in **Event Viewer**. In the System log you will find operating system and driver events, including many of the errors that lead to blue screens or failed services. In the Application log you will see records from applications that have crashed, hung, or thrown significant errors. You are not expected to memorize specific Event IDs for the exam, but you should be comfortable navigating to these logs and filtering or sorting by error and critical events that occurred around the time of a reported problem.

Because Event Viewer can be dense, Microsoft also includes **Reliability Monitor**, which sits on top of those logs and presents them as an easy-to-read timeline with a stability index. Opening Reliability Monitor allows you to see a daily score from 1 to 10 and see at a glance when critical events, application failures, or hardware errors have occurred. If a user says, "It's been crashing for about a week," you can usually see that pattern immediately. For example, you might notice that "Program X has stopped working" appears every day since it was installed, or that Windows has recorded multiple hardware error events.

Blue screens are worth discussing briefly, because they are a common exam scenario. A **BSOD** occurs when Windows encounters a serious error it cannot safely recover from, often related to drivers, faulty hardware, or corrupted system files. Modern versions of Windows show a stop code and sometimes reference a specific driver. The exact numeric codes are less important for A+ than the reasoning pattern: if blue screens started right after a new graphics card driver was installed, or right after a new USB device was added, that change is suspect. If they occur under heavy load, such as during gaming or video editing, you might suspect that hardware is being stressed, exposing marginal RAM or overheating.

Your main Windows-level tools for stability problems include Device Manager, System Restore, and the same Safe Mode and WinRE environments used for boot issues. Rolling back a driver in Device Manager, uninstalling a newly added application, or applying a restore point from before problems began can often stabilize a flaky system. For application-specific crashes, you might use Programs and Features (or Settings -> Apps) to run a repair or reinstall that application, checking at the same time whether it is officially supported on the installed edition and version of Windows.

There will be times when Windows' own logs point you back toward hardware, which technically belongs more to Core 1. Repeated errors referencing disk timeouts, for example, or S.M.A.R.T. warnings in the logs, suggest a failing drive that no amount of OS tweaking can save. Likewise, frequent blue screens with varying stop codes might indicate bad memory. In those scenarios, a professional approach is to recognize that the OS is reporting underlying hardware trouble and either run the appropriate hardware diagnostics or escalate to a hardware-focused technician, rather than repeatedly reinstalling Windows.

System and Application Errors, Profiles, and Access Issues

Not every Windows problem is dramatic. Often you will deal with more mundane but equally disruptive issues: applications that refuse to launch, "Access denied" messages when opening files, or users being logged into temporary profiles with none of their usual settings. These are all cases where taking Windows' messages seriously pays off.

When an application will not start, crashes immediately, or produces a specific error message about a missing component such as a DLL, it is usually telling you that its installation is incomplete, corrupted, or incompatible with the current environment. You should avoid the instinct to simply "click away" the dialog and hope it goes away. Instead, note the exact wording and any error code. Checking Event Viewer's Application log or Reliability Monitor often confirms that this particular program has been failing regularly. From there, a repair install using the app's own installer or the "Modify/Repair" option in Programs and Features can restore missing files. If that fails, a full uninstall and reinstall is appropriate, while verifying that the version you are installing supports the current Windows edition and architecture.

Permission problems are another common category. A user might report that they cannot open a folder, save a document to a shared location, or modify a configuration file. In those cases, the "Access denied" message is not vague at all; it is telling you that the current account's rights or the NTFS permissions on the file system are not sufficient. On a stand-alone machine, you might check the user's group membership and the Security tab on the file or folder to confirm that their account has the needed permissions. In a domain environment, you might need to coordinate with an administrator, but the principle is the same: distinguish between a true permissions issue and other causes such as a file being locked because another process is using it.

Profile and login problems can be particularly confusing to end users. One classic scenario is the "temporary profile" issue, where a user logs in and sees a blank desktop, missing documents, and a notice that they have been signed in with a temporary profile. This usually indicates that Windows could not load the user's usual profile folder, possibly due to corruption or a permissions problem. The professional response is not to panic or delete anything immediately, but to check Event Viewer for profile service errors and confirm that the original profile folder still exists with the user's data. A pragmatic fix for persistent profile corruption is to create a new user profile, test it, and then migrate the user's data (documents, desktop items, browser favorites) according to organizational policy. That preserves productivity without risking additional damage to the corrupted profile.

Throughout all of these system and application errors, the habit you want to build is simple: read what Windows is telling you, correlate it with user reports and logs, and act in a way that fits the pattern. Do not ignore error codes, and do not immediately assume that every odd behavior is malware or "the network." Windows includes multiple layers of diagnostics; the exam expects you to use them instead of guessing.

Choosing the Right Repair Path

Once you have identified the category of problem and gathered evidence from tools like Task Manager, Event Viewer, Reliability Monitor, Safe Mode, and WinRE, you face a decision: how far do you go with repairs? CompTIA's scenarios often test this judgment. The best answers follow a hierarchy from least to most disruptive, always with user data and business impact in mind.

Inside normal Windows or Safe Mode, you have many low-impact options: closing resource-hungry apps, disabling unnecessary startup programs, rolling back or updating drivers, uninstalling recent applications or updates, and running malware or system file scans. When changes are recent and specific, these are usually where you start. If problems clearly began after a known change and you have restore points available, **System Restore** lets you roll back system files, drivers, and many configuration settings to a previous state without touching user data. It is more disruptive than simply rolling back a single driver, but far less drastic than wiping the system.

When the system will not boot properly, Startup Repair and related WinRE tools can try to repair missing or corrupted boot files without affecting the rest of the installation. If the core OS is badly damaged or deeply infected, but the hardware and user data are otherwise fine, options like "Reset this PC" or an in-place repair install of Windows can replace system components while offering the choice to keep user files. These should be reserved for situations where targeted fixes and restore points fail, and where you have verified backups or copied critical data off the system in accordance with policy.

Only at the far end of the spectrum does a full reinstall of Windows become the right answer. That might be appropriate when the installation is beyond repair, when malware is so extensive that trust in the system is lost, or when a clean deployment is required for other reasons. On the exam, answers that jump straight to "reinstall Windows" without trying less-destructive steps first are usually wrong, unless the stem makes it clear that prior attempts have already failed or that the installation is unrecoverable.

At every stage, think like a professional rather than a button-clicker. Before you trigger anything that could affect files or settings, communicate clearly with the user, confirm what data matters most to them, and ensure that appropriate backups exist. After any significant change, reboot as needed, test the user's typical workflows, and only then consider the issue resolved. That combination of structured reasoning and respect for the user's environment is exactly what the A+ Core 2 exam is designed to measure, and it is what will make you effective when Windows inevitably misbehaves in the real world.

8.2 Troubleshooting Mobile OS & Application Issues

If you compare your experience troubleshooting Windows to working on phones and tablets, you'll notice something interesting: the tools and menus look different, but the thinking is almost exactly the same. On a Windows desktop you identify the problem, form a theory, test the least disruptive fix, and only then move toward more drastic actions like reinstalling software or resetting the OS. Mobile OS troubleshooting follows that same methodology; the difference is that you access your tools through Settings screens and app stores instead of Control Panel and command-line utilities. For the CompTIA A+ Core 2 exam—and for real help desk work—you're expected to apply that disciplined, stepwise thinking when users hand you their iPhones and Android devices and say, "This just stopped working."

In day-to-day support, most mobile issues you see are not about shattered screens or failing batteries; they're about the operating system and apps behaving badly. An executive's email app stops syncing, a field tech's mapping app hangs on startup, a user's cloud storage app keeps saying it can't upload, or someone complains that their phone is suddenly "uselessly slow." Underneath those vague complaints are a handful of common root causes: misbehaving apps, low storage, connectivity problems, permission settings, or OS-level instability. Your job is to listen carefully, interpret the symptom pattern, and then choose the smallest hammer that will reasonably fix the problem.

App Crashes, Freezes, and Misbehavior

The most frequent tickets involve a single mobile app that "won't behave." Users usually describe this in very non-technical language: "The app just closes," "It won't open," "It freezes on the logo," or "It just spins and never loads." On Android, an app crash might show as an "App isn't responding" or "App has stopped" message, or the app may simply disappear and return the user to the home screen. On iOS, you often see the app briefly appear and then vanish, again taking you back to the home screen with or without an error pop-up.

Your first diagnostic decision is to distinguish between a **single-app problem** and a **system-wide problem.** If the user says, "My banking app crashes every time I log in, but everything else is fine," that's a strong indicator that the issue is isolated to that specific app or its data. If instead they say, "Mail, the browser, and my chat apps all keep crashing," you should broaden your suspicion to the OS, storage, or connectivity. This distinction is important on the exam: when only one app misbehaves, CompTIA expects you to start with app-level fixes, not OS resets.

When you do focus on a specific app, the least invasive step is to restart it. That usually means **force closing** the app rather than just tapping the home button. On Android, you can bring up the recent apps view and swipe the app away, or go into the app's information screen in Settings and tap Force stop. On iOS, you double-press the Home button or swipe up from the bottom (depending on device), open the App Switcher, and swipe the app off the top of the screen. Force stopping an app terminates its process and clears it from memory without touching its installed files or user data. Many "it's frozen" complaints are resolved with nothing more than a proper force close and reopen.

If restarting the app doesn't help, the next step is to consider its stored data. On Android, this is where you see the critical difference between **clearing cache** and **clearing data.** Cached data is temporary content the app keeps to speed up performance, such as images, thumbnails, or pre-fetched data. Clearing cache is usually safe; it may cause the app to reload content more slowly the next time, but it does not normally erase logins, settings, or user-created content. Clearing data (sometimes labeled "storage" or "app data") is far more destructive; it often resets the app to its first-run state, logging the user out, wiping preferences, and potentially deleting offline content. You must understand this distinction for the exam and in real life, and you should warn users explicitly if you're about to clear data.

iOS does not expose cache-clearing in the same way, but it offers options like **offloading** an app, which removes the app binary while preserving its data, or fully deleting and reinstalling the app. If you suspect corruption within the app itself, uninstalling and reinstalling is usually effective on both platforms. Again, communicate clearly: reinstalling can remove locally stored files for that app, even if cloud-synced data will return once the user signs back in. From a troubleshooting methodology standpoint, force close, then update the app from the app store, then clear cache or reinstall—with the most invasive options reserved for when lighter touches fail.

Sometimes the app itself is fine, but the back-end service is having trouble. For example, a streaming app that "spins forever" might be affected by a service outage rather than anything on the device. On the exam, hints like "other users in the office report the same problem" or "a system status page shows degraded performance" should nudge you toward suspecting a server-side issue. In practice, quickly checking store reviews or the vendor's status page can save you from unnecessary local troubleshooting.

Slowness, Lag, and General Performance Problems

Performance complaints on mobile are often vague: "My phone is laggy," "Everything takes forever," or "It used to be fast but now it's not." Your first task is to sharpen that description. Ask whether the slowness occurs everywhere or just in certain apps. If the browser and email are fine but a particular game stutters, you treat that as an app-level resource issue. If the entire device feels unresponsive—slow to unlock, sluggish when switching apps, delayed keyboard input—you look more broadly at OS performance, background processes, and storage.

On both Android and iOS, low free storage can have a dramatic impact on speed. The OS depends on having working room to manage app files, updates, and temporary data. When that space disappears, you see slow app launches, update failures, and sometimes spontaneous app closures. A smart first check is simply to open Settings and look at storage usage. If internal storage is nearly full, you've likely found at least a major contributing factor to the performance complaint.

Background apps and poorly written third-party apps also consume CPU and memory. Battery or performance settings on modern phones often show which apps are using the most resources. If you notice a single social media app using an outsized share of CPU and battery, that's a good suspect for performance degradation. Closing unnecessary apps, disabling overly aggressive widgets and live wallpapers, and rebooting the device are all low-impact steps that often yield big improvements. A full **power cycle**, or soft reset, clears temporary glitches, refreshes memory allocation, and restarts background services in a clean state.

Android offers an especially valuable diagnostic mode here: **safe mode**. When you boot an Android device into safe mode, the OS loads only its core services and preinstalled apps; most third-party apps are disabled. If the device performs normally in safe mode but is slow in regular mode, you've effectively proven that a downloaded app is causing the problem rather than the OS itself. From there, you can uninstall recently added apps or those with suspiciously high resource usage. iOS does not have the same named safe mode, but you can approximate the process by removing or disabling recently installed apps and limiting background app refresh to see whether behavior improves. On the exam, if you're given a scenario where "after installing a new third-party app, the phone is constantly freezing and rebooting," a good next step would be to reboot into safe mode (Android) or remove that app and retest. Jumping straight to factory reset in this situation would be considered an unnecessarily drastic action.

Storage Constraints and Their Side Effects

Storage issues are easy to underestimate, yet they are behind a huge percentage of complaints users describe as "bugs." When internal storage is nearly full, you often see a cascade of symptoms: apps fail to update, new apps won't install, photos and videos won't save, messaging apps can't download attachments, and the system may pop up "Storage almost full" or "Insufficient storage available" warnings. Even when users dismiss those warnings, the OS doesn't.

Troubleshooting starts with verifying how much storage is available and what categories are consuming it. On Android, you may see breakdowns for apps, images, videos, audio, and cached data, along with any **SD card** storage if the device supports removable media. On iOS, storage settings similarly show top offenders and suggestions such as offloading unused apps or optimizing photo storage. Remember that iOS devices lack expandable storage; when they're full, your main options are removing data or moving content into cloud services such as iCloud, OneDrive, or Google Photos.

Cleaning up storage is another area where the difference between cache and data matters. Clearing cached data across apps can immediately free some space with relatively little impact on the user experience. Deleting offline map packs, downloaded movies, or large messaging media folders can reclaim gigabytes. Next you can look at apps themselves, prioritizing large games or rarely used apps for removal. Users often prefer deleting apps to deleting personal photos or videos, so it helps to show them which apps are occupying the most space. On Android devices with SD cards, you may be able to move certain media or app data to the card, but you should be aware that not every app supports this and that removable storage is generally slower and less reliable than internal flash.

For the exam, pay attention to clues that point to storage as the root cause. If a scenario mentions "cannot update any apps" alongside "storage almost full" warnings, you should think about freeing space before trying to clear app caches individually or resetting network settings. Many app-store error codes essentially boil down to "not enough room to proceed."

Update Failures for Apps and OS

Update problems are another common class of tickets and A+ questions. Users might show you a device saying "Unable to install update," "Download failed," or "This app requires a newer version of iOS/Android." There are three recurring requirements for successful updates: sufficient battery, sufficient storage, and stable connectivity.

Most mobile operating systems refuse to apply major **OS updates** unless the device has a healthy battery charge or is plugged in. This is protective: losing power in the middle of an OS upgrade can brick the device. So if a user says, "It keeps telling me it can't install the update," it's worth confirming battery level and whether they are connected to reliable Wi-Fi rather than an unstable cellular connection. You should also verify that there is enough free storage for the update package and its temporary files.

For **app updates**, the process is similar. In the Google Play Store or Apple App Store, the user can manually trigger updates and may see specific error messages when they fail. Common causes include being signed into the wrong account (for example, trying to update an app purchased under a different Apple ID), having content filters or parental controls in place, or experiencing network timeouts. On Android, clearing the Play Store's cache or data can resolve some stubborn update errors, but as always, check connectivity and storage first. On iOS, signing out and back into the App Store account or rebooting the device often addresses update glitches.

A subtle exam point is device compatibility. Older phones eventually reach a point where they cannot install the latest OS. Some apps then require a minimum OS version, leading to "This app is not compatible with this device" messages. In those cases, no amount of resetting or cache clearing will help; the limitation is hardware and OS support, not a transient fault.

Connectivity Problems Masquerading as App Failures

Many app complaints are really network complaints in disguise. A user may say, "My email app stopped working," when, in fact, they lost Wi-Fi connectivity. Another might report that chat messages only send at home but never on cellular data. When you hear problems involving cloud-based apps—email, messaging, streaming, storage, collaboration tools—you should have connectivity on your mental short list immediately.

A methodical approach starts with the obvious state indicators. Check whether **Airplane mode** is accidentally enabled, which disables Wi-Fi and cellular data. Confirm that Wi-Fi is on, connected to a network with decent signal strength, and that cellular data is enabled where appropriate. A quick test with a browser or another known-good app is often useful: if nothing on the device can reach the internet, the problem is not with the individual app. If the app works fine on Wi-Fi but fails on cellular, then the culprit could be a carrier data restriction or per-app cellular data setting. Both Android and iOS allow you to restrict specific apps to Wi-Fi only, which can cause confusion if the user doesn't remember enabling that.

VPNs also frequently complicate app behavior. An always-on VPN that routes traffic through a corporate network might block certain external services, or might require particular DNS or certificate settings. Temporarily disabling the VPN as a test can quickly tell you whether it's contributing to the symptom. Again, you want to start with low-impact changes: toggle Airplane mode, disconnect and reconnect to Wi-Fi, test another app, and then look into app-specific settings such as "download on Wi-Fi only" or background data restrictions.

Account credentials and service status round out this category. When an email app reports "cannot connect to server," double-check that the username, password, and server settings are correct, and that the cloud service itself is not down. For enterprise apps, an expired password or disabled account can produce errors that look like connectivity failures. On the exam, references to "other users can connect without issue" or "login works on the web but not in the app" help you distinguish between user-account, device, and network causes.

Permissions, Notifications, and Account Issues

Modern mobile operating systems are very strict about what apps can access. Features like the camera, microphone, location services, contacts, photos, and even local network access are governed by explicit **permissions**. This is great for privacy but can create subtle troubleshooting puzzles. A user might say, "My banking app won't take a picture of my check," when in reality the app has been denied camera permission. Another person might complain that "maps never finds my location," because location access is disabled for that app or across the system.

On both Android and iOS, you can inspect and modify an app's permissions in Settings. The key is to map the symptom to the likely permission. If an app cannot save files locally, check its storage or files permission. If it cannot detect GPS location, verify location services first. If a voice chat app cannot hear the microphone, inspect microphone access. For the exam, you should be comfortable with the idea that permission misconfigurations are common reasons for specific in-app features failing while the rest of the app works.

Notifications introduce another layer. When users say "My calendar reminders don't pop up" or "I get no alerts from this messaging app," start by checking notification settings. App-level notification toggles, Do Not Disturb or Focus modes, and per-app sound/badge settings can all affect how, or whether, alerts appear. A muted app can feel "broken" to a user who expects audible pings.

Finally, account-related issues frequently masquerade as app defects. A cloud storage app may open fine but refuse to sync because the login token has expired or because the user signed in with the wrong account. App stores may block updates or paid content downloads if the Apple ID or Google account does not match the one originally used to obtain the app. Subscription-based services may disable functionality when billing fails, leading to vague "cannot complete request" messages. In both exam questions and real tickets, confirming correct credentials and active subscriptions is a core part of troubleshooting.

Resets, Safe Modes, and When to Start Over

Sometimes, despite all your focused efforts on individual apps, storage, connectivity, and permissions, a device remains unstable. At that point, you start thinking in terms of OS-level fixes. Here it becomes critical to use the right terms. A **soft reset** is essentially a normal restart or power cycle—turning the device off and back on using the standard power controls. A **hard reset** often refers to forcing a restart using hardware button combinations, useful when the OS is completely frozen and unresponsive. Neither of these should erase user data; they simply clear memory and restart services.

A **factory reset**, by contrast, is a last-resort option that erases user data and returns the device to its original, out-of-the-box state. The OS is reinitialized, settings revert to default, and apps and local data are removed. This is powerful and often highly effective for fixing deep OS corruption, severe performance problems, or lingering issues after malware removal—but it comes with the cost of data loss if you are not careful. Both the exam and professional practice demand that you **back up** important data before performing any factory reset. That means using iCloud, Google account backups, or your organization's mobile device management tools to capture contacts, photos, app data, and configuration where possible.

The decision to reset should follow a clear progression. You start with the simplest actions: force stop and reopen apps, check storage and connectivity, update apps and OS, reboot the device. If you suspect a rogue third-party app, you use Android safe mode or selectively uninstall suspicious apps. Only when the device remains unstable after these steps, or when malware has deeply compromised the system, do you move to a factory reset with the user's informed consent. After the reset, part of your troubleshooting responsibility is to restore backups, re-add required accounts, reinstall necessary applications, and verify that the original problem does not reappear before returning the device to the user.

Throughout all of this, remember that mobile OS troubleshooting is as much about communication and judgment as it is about technical skill. You're weighing the impact of each action on the user's data and time while trying to resolve the issue efficiently. The CompTIA A+ scenarios are designed to test exactly that mindset: can you read the clues, think in terms of likely causes—app, storage, permissions, connectivity, OS—and choose the least disruptive, technically sound next step?

8.3 Troubleshooting Mobile Security Issues

When users say, "My phone has a virus," what they really mean is, "My phone is doing something I don't trust." In mobile support, your job is less about naming the exact malware family and more about recognizing patterns of risky behavior, deciding whether the underlying cause is security-related or not, and then choosing a response that fixes the issue without destroying the user's digital life in the process. You already know the general troubleshooting methodology; in this section we're going to apply it specifically to mobile security incidents on Android and iOS/iPadOS, where evidence is more subtle and tools are more limited than on a typical desktop system.

A useful way to think about mobile security troubleshooting is that the "identify the problem" and "establish a theory of probable cause" steps are where you spend most of your effort. You often don't have deep system logs, kernel messages, or full-featured antivirus consoles. Instead, you rely on symptoms that users report—battery problems, mysterious charges, strange texts, pop-ups—and you correlate those with what you can observe directly on the device: app lists, data usage, security settings, and account activity. Once your theory is solid, the actual remediation steps tend to follow a predictable pattern: isolate, clean up apps and settings, protect accounts, and escalate to backup and reset only when necessary.

Recognizing Signs of Compromise or Risk

Imagine following a mobile device through a day in the life after it has been compromised. The first thing many users notice is not a scary alert; it is a subtle change in how the device feels. A phone that used to last all day on a charge now dies by mid-afternoon. The back of the device feels warm, even when the user is just reading email. These are classic signs that something is consuming excessive CPU and radio time in the background. Legitimate causes certainly exist—maybe the user just installed a major OS update and the phone is indexing photos, or they started playing a graphics-heavy game. As a security-minded troubleshooter, you look for patterns: if the battery drain coincides with the appearance of new, unknown apps, or if the battery statistics show large usage from a shady "System Service" that is actually an app in disguise, your theory shifts toward malware, such as crypto-miners or aggressive adware.

Data usage tells a similar story. Many mobile malware strains make money by pushing ads or exfiltrating data over the network. On Android and iOS, you can view data usage per app and see which processes are consuming the most bandwidth, especially in the background. When a user complains, "My monthly data just tripled and I barely use my phone," and you notice that a recently installed "free movie" or "free VPN" app is responsible for gigabytes of background transfer, that is a strong indicator of compromise or at least of a very risky app. In contrast, heavy usage from a legitimate streaming app during a road trip may look scary on the bill but is not a security issue; it is simply user behavior.

Network and communication anomalies often provide the most obvious red flags. Contacts may complain they are receiving strange SMS messages or instant messages from the user's number that contain only a short phrase and a suspicious link. Sometimes the user sees messages in their "sent" folder that they never wrote. This could be **smishing** (SMS phishing) in progress, potentially driven by an app that has permission to send and view SMS. Similarly, pop-up ads that appear when the browser is closed, full-screen interstitials that show up while the user is on the home screen, or redirects to unfamiliar search engines usually mean more than a poorly designed website. Ad-heavy sites certainly exist, but they only misbehave inside the browser. When ads follow the user across multiple apps, you should suspect an adware component installed as an app or profile at the system level.

Unknown apps and unexpected system changes are another category of warning signs you cannot afford to ignore. Users will sometimes say, "I didn't install this," but in practice they may have tapped through an installation prompt without reading it. As a technician, you don't need to argue with them; you just need to verify. Browsing the app list, you might see generic-sounding utilities, icons that don't match known vendors, or duplicate apps with extra spaces or characters in the name. If the user recalls tapping a link and "something downloaded" rather than going through the official app store, that strengthens the theory that these are side-loaded or malicious. On Android in particular, if an app resists removal, or the "Uninstall" button is grayed out, it may have been granted device administrator or device management rights; that is not normal for a flashlight or wallpaper app and is a significant security red flag.

Account and financial anomalies round out the picture. A phone that seems otherwise normal but is associated with unexpected app store receipts, unrecognized in-app purchases, or premium SMS charges suggests that either the device is executing unauthorized transactions, or someone with access to the account is. The CompTIA exam loves these scenarios because they force you to distinguish between malware and basic account or physical security. If the user admits they turned off the screen lock because it was annoying and also lets their children use the device, your working theory often shifts away from "virus" and toward unauthorized but technically legitimate purchases. On the other hand, if the user has a strong lock screen and is seeing password reset emails or new login alerts from cloud services used on that device, you should treat the device itself as potentially compromised and the account credentials as exposed.

You should also pay close attention to the security configuration itself. Sometimes the first sign of trouble is that core protections have mysteriously weakened. The user may discover that their PIN or biometric unlock has been replaced with a simple swipe, or that automatic screen lock now takes minutes instead of seconds. You might find an unfamiliar **device administrator**, configuration profile, or VPN listed in settings, installing its own certificate authority to intercept or redirect traffic. In a corporate context, a mobile device management (MDM) system might flag the device as non-compliant because it detects a **rooted** or **jailbroken** state. Rooting on Android or jailbreaking on iOS removes manufacturer restrictions and opens the door to deeper customization, but it also downgrades or bypasses the OS's built-in sandboxing and code-signing protections. When you see persistent malware that keeps coming back after uninstall attempts, or the presence of unofficial app stores and system-tweaking tools, suspect a rooted/jailbroken environment.

The challenge in all of these examples is separating security-relevant indicators from normal quirks. A hot phone right after setting it up from backup is probably just indexing. A brief battery drop on a long navigation session is expected. But when you see patterns—battery drain plus unknown apps plus unsolicited ads—the story starts to look like compromise rather than coincidence.

Risky Apps and Insecure Settings

Once you've collected symptoms, your next move is to look for root causes, and on mobile, **risky apps** and insecure configurations are at the top of the list. A large portion of mobile incidents begin with a user installing something they should not have installed, or changing a setting they did not fully understand.

On Android, **sideloading** is a common pathway. By default, the OS encourages users to install software from the official Google Play Store, where apps undergo at least basic screening. However, users can enable "Install unknown apps" for a browser or file manager and then install APK packages downloaded from the web. Not all sideloaded apps are malicious—enterprises and beta programs use this mechanism legitimately—but it bypasses an important layer of protection. If the timeline shows that the user's problems began shortly after following a link and installing a "free" version of a normally paid app, or a hacked game, that app becomes your primary suspect. On iOS, the equivalent is trusting an enterprise or developer profile to allow an app outside the App Store to run. If that profile was provided by the user's company, it may be legitimate; if it arrived via a random website promising free movies, it is almost certainly not.

Even apps from official stores can be problematic when they are granted more permissions than they deserve. This is where the concept of **least privilege** becomes practical. A simple wallpaper app that wants access to your contacts, SMS, microphone, and location is asking for far more than is needed for its stated purpose. When troubleshooting, you should review permissions for apps that align suspiciously well with the symptoms: an app with SMS permission on a device that is sending strange texts, or an app with phone and contacts access on a device showing unauthorized calls. It is not always outright malware; sometimes a legitimate app abuses permissions for aggressive data collection or ad tracking. Nonetheless, your remediation path is the same: reduce permissions to only what is required, or remove the app entirely if you cannot justify its access.

The underlying security posture of the device also matters. A rooted or jailbroken phone is inherently more susceptible to persistent malware because malicious code can escalate privileges, modify system partitions, and cloak itself more effectively. The exam may hint at this without using the words "root" or "jailbreak," describing instead a phone that can install apps from nonstandard stores, apply custom themes that alter system files, or run tools that modify core OS behavior. In organizational environments, these devices often violate policy outright and must be either reimaged to a stock state or removed from corporate access. In any case, if you are troubleshooting a rooted or jailbroken device, you should lower your expectations for how well traditional remediation steps will work and raise your suspicion level about every installed app.

It is important to remember that not every mobile security problem is the result of malware. Insecure settings, left alone, can be just as damaging. Disabling the screen lock, leaving Bluetooth permanently discoverable, connecting regularly to open, unsecured Wi-Fi, or turning off automatic OS and app updates all increase risk without any malicious software being present. When a child purchases in-game items on a parent's unlocked phone, the app is not at fault; the lack of a lock screen and purchase controls is. When a user complains about credential theft after routinely logging into sensitive sites over random café Wi-Fi with no VPN, the problem lies in their network practices. As you troubleshoot, always ask: "Is there any way normal behavior plus weak settings could explain this incident?" If the answer is yes, you may be dealing with a configuration issue rather than infection.

Remediation: From Minimal Impact to Full Reset

Once you have a solid theory, you can start planning remediation. A good mental model is to begin with the least disruptive actions and escalate only when needed. At the high end of severity, where malware is actively sending messages or exfiltrating data, your first task is isolation. Putting the device into airplane mode or disabling mobile data and Wi-Fi stops further communication while you investigate. This is especially important if the device is sending out phishing messages; you want to stop the spread before more contacts click on malicious links.

Next, you move into app-level cleanup. On both Android and iOS, reviewing the full list of installed apps and sorting by most recently installed is a quick way to identify potential culprits. Compare the list with what the user remembers installing. For anything that appears around the time the symptoms started, inspect its permissions, data usage, and battery usage. If an app is clearly suspicious—perhaps a "free streaming" app that has consumed gigabytes of data and holds device administrator rights—your first step is to remove its elevated rights and then uninstall it. On Android, that means going into the device admin or device management settings and revoking its status; on iOS, it may mean deleting an associated configuration profile before you can successfully remove the app. Sometimes, for borderline cases where an app seems legitimate but misbehaves after an update, clearing its cache or storage data, or resetting its permissions, resolves the issue without requiring full removal.

Beyond individual apps, you must restore a secure baseline configuration. That usually includes re-enabling or strengthening the lock screen with a PIN, password, or biometrics; confirming that automatic OS and app updates are turned on; disabling installation from unknown sources once any necessary enterprise apps are in place; and removing any unknown VPNs, profiles, or administrators. For Android devices, running a scan with a reputable mobile security solution, if permitted by your organization, can help identify known threats. For iOS, traditional antivirus is much more limited due to sandboxing; your focus is on profiles, certificates, and apps with unusual behavior.

If the symptoms suggest that account credentials have been compromised—such as repeated password reset emails or sign-in alerts from unknown locations—you need to address account security from a separate, trusted device. That means changing passwords, enabling multi-factor authentication, reviewing recent sign-ins, and revoking any suspicious sessions or connected apps. From a support perspective, you might also need to help the user contact their carrier or app store provider to dispute unauthorized charges and enable purchase protections, such as requiring a password or biometric confirmation for every transaction. Notice that in this entire sequence, you have not yet erased the phone; you are targeting the specific risky components first.

A factory reset becomes appropriate when your less invasive approaches fail, or when the compromise is severe enough that you cannot trust the integrity of the system. Malware that reappears after uninstall, non-removable malicious profiles, or a rooted/jailbroken phone involved in a significant security incident are good examples. Before resetting, you are responsible for preserving the user's legitimate data. That usually means backing up photos, contacts, and documents to a trusted cloud or to a computer, checking that the backup completed successfully, and then performing the wipe. Afterward, you should encourage the user to restore only essential apps from official sources, rather than blindly reinstalling everything from a previous, possibly contaminated backup. In a managed environment, MDM can help by pushing a known-good configuration and app set after the reset.

Security Issue or Something Else?

A key exam skill—and a key job skill—is resisting the urge to blame malware for every problem. Many of the same symptoms we have discussed can result from completely benign causes. Slow performance on a four-year-old budget phone used heavily for gaming is not suspicious; it is physics. Lag on a device with nearly full storage can be solved by freeing space. Pop-ups that appear only on one particular news site are ad design, not an infection. Battery drain that happens only while the screen is set to maximum brightness and navigation is running is a workload issue, not compromise.

Your process should always involve comparing at least two plausible theories: one security-related and one not. When a user complains of pop-ups, ask whether they appear only in the browser or system-wide. When data usage spikes, check the app usage breakdown; if it is all Netflix and YouTube, malware is unlikely. When financial anomalies arise, review whether the device is shared and whether the lock screen is enabled before assuming the worst. Tools like battery usage, data usage, storage stats, and the installed app list exist precisely to help you refine your theory instead of resorting to drastic measures every time.

Prevention and User Education

Every troubleshooting session is also an opportunity to reduce the odds of seeing the same problem again. Once you have cleaned up a device, you should take a moment to explain, in plain language, how the issue likely occurred and what the user can do differently. Encouraging users to install apps only from official app stores or authorized enterprise portals is one of the highest-impact recommendations you can make. Teaching them to pause and question apps that request broad permissions unrelated to their purpose reinforces the principle of least privilege in a way they can act on.

You can also frame basic hygiene—keeping the OS and apps updated, using a strong screen lock, turning on multi-factor authentication for key accounts, and avoiding unknown links in SMS and social media—as simply "making your phone harder to mess with." For users who ask about rooting or jailbreaking, especially in a business context, you can explain that while it might enable extra customization, it also disables many of the safety nets that kept them out of trouble this time, and often violates company policy. When you handle these conversations without judgment, users are far more likely to call you early the next time something feels off, giving you more time to respond before a minor issue becomes a major incident.

8.4 Troubleshooting PC Security Issues

When a desktop or laptop has a security problem, users almost never describe it in security language. They don't tell you, "I suspect a trojan with persistence via a scheduled task." They say things like, "My browser is acting weird," "This fake antivirus thing keeps popping up," or "My computer suddenly got really slow and the fan never stops." Troubleshooting PC security issues is about translating those vague, sometimes anxious complaints into a clear picture of what is happening, then responding in a way that fixes the problem without making the situation worse.

You have already seen the general troubleshooting methodology and the core security concepts in earlier chapters. Here, you put those pieces together in a very practical way. Instead of thinking just in terms of "What kind of malware is this?" you begin to think in terms of "What symptoms am I seeing? What's most likely causing them? And what is the safest, most efficient way to respond on this particular system, for this particular user?" That mix of pattern recognition and procedural discipline is exactly what the A+ exam expects, and it's exactly what makes you valuable in a real support role.

From User Complaint to Security Diagnosis

The first step in troubleshooting a possible security issue is simply to listen carefully. The user's description of the problem is often your best early clue, especially if you ask a few targeted follow-up questions. When someone says, "My web browser keeps opening random pages," you want to know whether that happens in all browsers or just one, whether it still happens if they disconnect from the network, and when it started. If a user complains that the computer is "slow and noisy," you might ask whether it happens all the time or only when they're using certain applications, and whether they've seen any error messages or strange windows.

As you listen, you mentally sort possibilities. You've probably been trained to think "could this be malware?" but you must balance that with the equally important question, "could this be a benign misconfiguration or normal system behavior?" A homepage that changed once after a browser update is different from a homepage that you fix repeatedly and that keeps changing back after every reboot. A busy CPU right after Patch Tuesday is different from a busy CPU all the time, driven by a process with a random name sitting in a temp folder.

Security troubleshooting requires more caution than other types of troubleshooting because your actions can widen the damage. If you start freely browsing from an infected system to "research the problem," you might be spreading malware or leaking data. If you reboot a system that is in the middle of being encrypted by ransomware, you might interfere with forensics or backup recovery. You're not just trying to make the symptoms go away; you're trying to contain and neutralize a threat in a way that protects the user, the machine, and often the rest of the environment.

Recognizing Security-Related Symptoms

Most security issues on PCs show up in a few familiar categories of symptoms. One of the most common categories is browser-related behavior. Users might complain that their homepage suddenly points to a search site they've never heard of, that their default search engine has changed, or that they are seeing far more pop-ups than usual, even when visiting mainstream sites. Sometimes they notice that when they click a legitimate search result, they are silently redirected to a completely different site. You will also see extra toolbars, side panels, or extensions that the user claims not to have installed. All of these are classic signs of **browser hijackers**, adware, or other **potentially unwanted programs (PUPs)** that often arrive bundled with "free" software installers.

Another category is performance and resource usage. The complaint here is usually "my PC is suddenly really slow" or "the fan is running all the time." When you dig deeper, you might find high CPU, disk, or network usage even when the user thinks nothing is running. Malware that mines cryptocurrency, participates in a botnet, or exfiltrates data will often consume noticeable resources in the background. However, legitimate causes can look similar: an antivirus suite running a full scan, a large Windows update, or a scheduled backup can all produce short-term spikes. Your job is to distinguish between a transient, explainable load and a persistent, unexplained one.

A particularly telling set of symptoms involves the system's own security tools. When users report that Windows Defender, a third-party antivirus program, or the firewall has mysteriously turned itself off and won't turn back on, your suspicion should go up. Malware often tries to disable the very tools designed to detect it. You might see error messages when trying to start an antivirus service, updates that fail repeatedly, or protection that shows as "off" in the Security Center with controls grayed out. That said, some security suites intentionally disable Windows Defender to avoid conflicts, so you must confirm whether what you're seeing is actually malicious or simply the behavior of a legitimate product.

The operating system itself can also give you signals. Unexpected User Account Control (UAC) prompts asking for administrator credentials to run unknown programs, new desktop icons or Start menu entries that appeared without the user installing anything, and applications that open at startup with names like "PC Cleaner Pro 2024 – Trial" can all indicate security issues. Ransomware tends to be obvious: files suddenly have strange extensions, users can't open documents that worked yesterday, and a ransom note appears on the desktop or in every folder demanding payment. Another pattern you will see on exams and in the field is **rogue security software**—fake antivirus or optimizer tools that insist they've found "thousands of problems" and demand payment to fix them.

At the same time, you need an eye for false positives. A user might interpret a legitimate browser pop-up about cookies or notifications as "a virus." A toolbar might actually have been installed intentionally months ago. A one-time freeze after a big application install is not necessarily "a hacker." What the exam often does is give you just enough detail to lean you toward one interpretation or another. The homepage that resets itself every time you fix it is more suspicious than the homepage that changed once. A fake antivirus that prevents you from opening Task Manager is more clearly malicious than a legitimate product that simply shows renewal reminders.

Malware, PUPs, or Misconfiguration?

Once you've gathered symptoms, you mentally sort what you're seeing into broad buckets. **Malware** in the classic sense—viruses, worms, trojans, ransomware, keyloggers, rootkits—is clearly malicious and usually persistent. It tends to interfere with security tools, re-create itself after deletion, and perform obviously harmful or unauthorized actions. If you see encrypted files, multiple backdoors, or tools that refuse to run, you are likely in this territory.

PUPs, adware, and simple browser hijackers are often more annoying than destructive. They may have been "consented to" in a legal sense via a bundled installer that the user clicked through too quickly, which is why not every antivirus suite blocks them by default. Their behavior includes unwanted ads, changed search engines, and injected offers into web pages, but they might not disable security tools or corrupt user files. That doesn't mean you ignore them; they are still security and privacy risks, and they erode user trust in the system.

Then there are pure misconfigurations or user-driven changes. A user may have changed their own homepage and forgotten. An organization may have deployed a proxy server or VPN that changes how websites resolve or look. A third-party security suite might be legitimately managing the firewall in a way that hides certain options in the Windows interface. Before you jump to full-scale malware removal, it's wise to ask whether any software was recently installed, whether IT deployed any new tools, and whether the issue affects one user profile or all accounts. If a problem is limited to one browser in one profile, it often points to a local setting or extension rather than a deep system infection.

Containing and Assessing a Suspected Security Incident

Once you suspect a security problem, your first concern is containment. If you strongly suspect ransomware—for example, numerous files are suddenly unreadable and have extensions you don't recognize, and a ransom note is displayed on screen—do not casually reboot, and do not start randomly clicking "fix" buttons. In an organization, the best move is usually to disconnect the system from the network, leave it powered on if instructed by policy (to preserve volatile evidence), and escalate to your security or incident response team. The A+ exam expects you to recognize that ransomware and large-scale compromise are not "just clean it and move on" situations.

For more routine malware suspicions, it is generally wise to disconnect the system from the network before you begin in-depth work. Physically unplugging an Ethernet cable or disabling Wi-Fi helps prevent the system from continuing to communicate with command-and-control servers, spreading to other hosts, or leaking more data. In a small office or home environment, you might isolate just the one PC; in a larger environment, you should also notify a supervisor, because similar symptoms might begin appearing on other machines.

Data preservation has to be weighed against risk. If the user has no backups and is desperate to save critical documents, you might consider copying essential data to clean, organization-controlled removable media before running aggressive cleanup or reimaging—understanding that if the system is heavily infected, some malware might hitch a ride. This is one reason many organizations maintain standard backup and imaging solutions: it allows you to prioritize security without feeling forced to take unsafe shortcuts to save data.

Using Built-In Tools to Investigate

With the system contained, you can start to investigate using tools built into the operating system. Task Manager in Windows (or Activity Monitor in macOS, System Monitor in many Linux environments) is often your first window into what is happening. Unusual processes consuming high CPU, memory, or disk are worthy of attention, especially if their names look random or unfamiliar and they are running from suspicious locations. In Windows, opening the file location of a process and seeing it living in a temporary directory or a user profile's obscure subfolder is a red flag. At the same time, you avoid killing processes blindly; some oddly named processes are actually legitimate system components, and terminating the wrong one can crash the system or cause data loss without actually addressing the malware.

Persistence mechanisms are another focus. Malware often ensures it runs at every boot by inserting itself into startup entries or scheduled tasks. The Startup tab in Task Manager, the System Configuration tool, and Task Scheduler can show you what programs and scripts are configured to run automatically. A scheduled task that launches a script from a temp folder every hour, for example, is suspicious. Removing such tasks after confirming they are malicious is an important part of lasting remediation.

Because so many security issues show up in the browser, you will often spend time in browser settings. Checking the homepage, default search engine, and proxy settings can quickly reveal hijacking. Reviewing extensions and add-ons often uncovers the culprit behind unexpected pop-ups or injected ads. If problems persist or if settings keep reverting after you fix them, it is often simplest to reset the browser to its default state, which usually removes extensions and custom configurations while leaving bookmarks and stored passwords intact, depending on the browser.

Event Viewer in Windows is sometimes useful for security troubleshooting, although more as supporting evidence than as your primary tool. You might see repeated application errors tied to a particular executable, or warnings about services failing to start. These can help you correlate user reports with underlying processes and guide you to what needs attention, but they rarely replace proper antivirus and anti-malware scanning.

A Structured Removal Workflow

Once you have a sense that malware or a PUP is present, you follow a structured removal process. You start by confirming what you are dealing with as best you can. If the installed antivirus is still functional, you can attempt an initial quick scan from within normal Windows. If it refuses to run, crashes, or says it cannot update, those failures themselves reinforce the suspicion of infection. In many stubborn cases, your next move is to restart the system into **Safe Mode**.

Safe Mode loads Windows with minimal drivers and services, and in many cases, that means the malware does not start. With fewer obstacles, your tools stand a better chance of running successfully. Safe Mode with Networking can allow you to update antivirus definitions or download trusted on-demand scanners if your organization's policies permit, though you still want to avoid unnecessary web browsing from an infected host. When Safe Mode is not usable—either because the malware interferes with boot options or because the system is too unstable—you might rely on bootable rescue media from a reputable antivirus vendor or a Windows PE environment to scan the system from outside the normal OS.

In any case, updated definitions are critical. Running a scan with outdated signatures is almost as bad as not scanning at all; new threats appear constantly, and detection logic evolves. You typically run at least one full-system scan with the existing antivirus and often an additional scan with a dedicated anti-malware tool to catch PUPs and other threats that the main product might ignore. Detected items are usually quarantined, which moves them into an isolated location where they cannot run, or removed entirely. Quarantining gives you a safety net if you later discover a false positive; deleting frees up space but is irreversible.

After the scanners have done their work, you still need to clean up residual components. This is where you go back to Programs and Features (or the equivalent) and uninstall any suspicious or unwanted software that appeared around the time of the problem, especially toolbars, download managers, and "optimizers." You revisit startup items and scheduled tasks to confirm that nothing related to the malware remains. In the browser, you remove unwanted extensions and consider a full reset of settings, then clear cache and cookies to get rid of injected scripts and tracking components.

When you are reasonably confident the system is clean, you can reconnect it to the network and immediately focus on updates. Applying the latest operating system patches and application updates—especially for the browser and common plug-ins—closes the vulnerabilities that may have been exploited. You also confirm that antivirus and firewall protection are enabled and updating properly. Part of verification is functional: you check that the symptoms are gone, that the browser no longer redirects or pops up strange ads, and that performance and resource usage have returned to normal. Part of it is procedural: you document what you found, what tools you used, and what you changed, so that anyone reviewing the ticket later understands the incident and the resolution path.

Hardening After Cleanup and Knowing When to Escalate

Cleanup is also an opportunity to harden the system against future problems. Ensuring that only one primary antivirus product is active avoids conflicts that can reduce protection. Verifying that the Windows or third-party firewall is on and properly configured, and that automatic updates are enabled, raises the baseline security level. In some environments, you might also tighten browser settings by disabling unnecessary plug-ins, restricting pop-ups, or turning on built-in tracking and phishing protection features.

If the infection involved credential theft, keylogging, or account compromise, password hygiene becomes critical. You may recommend or enforce password changes for email, banking, and corporate accounts accessed from the affected machine. You might also inspect local user accounts and group memberships for unauthorized additions, especially if the malware could have created backdoor administrator accounts.

Finally, you spend a moment on user education, delivered in a calm, non-judgmental way. If you can connect the incident to a specific behavior—installing a free game that bundled adware, clicking a fake "Download" button on a website, or opening a suspicious attachment—you can explain that link and suggest safer habits. Many A+ exam scenarios weave this interpersonal aspect into the technical question: not just "what tool do you run next?" but also "how do you explain the issue in terms the user understands, while maintaining professionalism?"

There are situations, though, where manual cleanup is not the best answer. If you see ransomware, evidence that sensitive data has been exfiltrated, or signs of a sophisticated rootkit with multiple backdoors, you should escalate according to policy. In some environments, that may mean handing the case to a security team; in a small office, it may mean informing management and recommending that all systems be checked. Sometimes the most secure and efficient course is to wipe and rebuild the system from a known-good image rather than fighting a deeply embedded infection. The A+ exam expects you to recognize when the time and risk involved in continued tinkering outweigh the benefits, and when a clean slate—properly patched and hardened afterward—is the right call.

8.5 Knowledge Check

Question 1: A user reports that after a Windows update overnight, the system now blue screens on every boot. What is the BEST next step following CompTIA's preferred troubleshooting methodology?

- **A.** Immediately perform a full reinstall of Windows using clean installation media
- **B.** Boot into WinRE and use Safe Mode or "Uninstall latest update" options for targeted repair
- **C.** Replace the system's hard drive and restore from a recent full system backup image
- **D.** Disable automatic updates in BIOS/UEFI and attempt to restart the operating system

Question 2: A Windows PC shows "Operating system not found" on startup, but the drive is detected correctly in UEFI. Which OS-focused action should you try FIRST?

- **A.** Boot to WinRE and run Startup Repair to automatically fix boot-related problems
- **B.** Repartition and reformat the system drive, then perform a clean OS installation
- **C.** Replace the SATA cable and power connector before attempting any software repairs
- **D.** Run Disk Cleanup from within Windows to remove temporary files and old updates

Question 3: A Windows system gets stuck in a "Preparing Automatic Repair" reboot loop. What is the most appropriate environment to work from NEXT?

- **A.** Normal boot into the standard Windows desktop environment for user access
- **B.** Windows Recovery Environment (WinRE) for advanced startup and repair tools
- **C.** BIOS/UEFI setup utility to adjust firmware settings and boot sequence options
- **D.** PXE boot from a network installation server to deploy a fresh OS image

Question 4: A user logs in and the desktop appears, but within 30 seconds the system freezes and becomes unresponsive. What is the BEST initial step?

- **A.** Perform a full system reset while keeping user files and reinstalling Windows
- **B.** Immediately run a factory restore from vendor media to return to defaults
- **C.** Replace the motherboard and RAM to eliminate potential hardware faults
- **D.** Attempt to boot into Safe Mode for further targeted troubleshooting and testing

Question 5: A Windows PC boots successfully but runs extremely slowly all day. Task Manager shows RAM is nearly full and disk activity is constantly high, with the page file being heavily used. What is the most likely cause?

A. Boot configuration data corruption preventing proper startup parameters
B. Temporary profile in use causing missing settings and desktop shortcuts
C. Insufficient physical memory for the current workload, causing heavy paging
D. Incorrect NTFS permissions on the system partition blocking file access

Question 6: A user complains that their Windows PC "freezes every day around 1 p.m." In Task Manager you see antivirus and Windows Update consuming CPU and disk at that time. What is the MOST appropriate solution?

A. Reinstall Windows and disable all scheduled tasks to prevent background activity
B. Replace the hard drive and increase RAM to improve overall system resources
C. Disable Windows Update permanently so that updates never run automatically
D. Adjust scan and update schedules to non-working hours to reduce disruption

Question 7: A Windows 10 system with a traditional HDD frequently becomes unresponsive right after login. Task Manager shows disk usage at 100% while Windows Search indexing and an antivirus scan are running. What is the BEST first action?

A. Run System Restore to revert to an earlier configuration before the issue
B. Reset this PC while keeping user files to refresh the operating system
C. Allow the tasks to complete, then reschedule or tune them for future logins
D. Disable all services using msconfig to prevent background processes from starting

Question 8: A user says, "My computer is so slow, I can't do anything." You clarify that only startup is slow; once the desktop is ready, performance is acceptable. Which tool should you use FIRST to address the likely cause?

A. Task Manager's Startup tab to review and disable unnecessary startup items
B. Disk Management to modify partitions and change drive letter assignments
C. Local Users and Groups to adjust user accounts and group memberships
D. Event Viewer's Application log to review application error and warning events

Question 9: A user reports that a specific Windows application "stops working" several times a day. Reliability Monitor shows repeated critical events for that application starting on the day it was installed. What is the BEST next step?

A. Perform a full OS reinstall to completely refresh Windows and all settings
B. Replace the system's storage drive to rule out underlying disk problems
C. Disable all startup items using msconfig to reduce background processes
D. Repair or reinstall that application from Programs and Features/Settings

Question 10: A Windows system shows random reboots and different blue-screen stop codes under heavy load. Event Viewer logs indicate disk timeout and S.M.A.R.T. warnings. From a Core 2 troubleshooting perspective, what should you do NEXT?

A. Run System Restore to a point before the errors started appearing
B. Escalate or run hardware diagnostics focusing on the drive's health and errors
C. Disable S.M.A.R.T. in BIOS/UEFI to stop the disk warning notifications
D. Rebuild the boot configuration data (BCD) using command-line repair tools

Question 11: A user logs in to Windows and sees a blank desktop with a message that they've been signed in with a temporary profile. Their documents appear missing, but you confirm the original profile folder and files still exist on disk. What is the MOST appropriate remediation?

- **A.** Create a new user profile and migrate the user's data from the old profile folder
- **B.** Delete the original profile folder and rely on the temporary profile going forward
- **C.** Reinstall Windows without attempting any recovery of the existing user data
- **D.** Disable the user's account in Local Users and Groups to prevent future logins

Question 12: A user cannot save documents to a shared folder and receives an "Access denied" error. Other users can save to the same share without issue. What should you check FIRST?

- **A.** The system's page file configuration for adequate virtual memory allocation
- **B.** Disk fragmentation on the user's local drive using the defragmentation tool
- **C.** The user's permissions and group membership for that folder and network share
- **D.** The user's browser cache and cookies for possible corrupted web data

Question 13: A Windows 11 PC is stuck at the spinning circle with the Windows logo and never reaches the login screen. You need a stable environment to troubleshoot. What is the BEST next move?

- **A.** Reinstall Windows from scratch using bootable media and wipe the system
- **B.** Force several failed boots to trigger Advanced Startup and enter WinRE tools
- **C.** Boot to normal mode and run Disk Cleanup to remove temporary files
- **D.** Log in as a different local user account to test profile-specific issues

Question 14: After you disable multiple nonessential startup programs through Task Manager, a user's Windows PC boots faster and runs more smoothly. This is mainly an example of addressing which category of issue?

- **A.** Stability problem causing frequent crashes and blue-screen errors
- **B.** Profile and access problem related to user accounts and permissions
- **C.** Performance problem affecting speed and responsiveness of the system
- **D.** Boot configuration corruption involving invalid BCD or boot loader entries

Question 15: You suspect a recent application install is causing instability in Windows. The user wants minimal impact on their data. Which built-in tool provides a system-wide rollback of drivers and system files while preserving user documents?

- **A.** Disk Cleanup for removing temporary files and old update components
- **B.** Task Scheduler for managing and modifying scheduled task execution
- **C.** Startup Repair for fixing boot issues that prevent Windows from loading
- **D.** System Restore for reverting system state to a previous restore point

Question 16: A user's complaint of "random crashes" prompts you to open Reliability Monitor, which shows a sharp drop in stability index with frequent failures of a newly installed app. How does this tool MOST help your troubleshooting process?

- **A.** It provides a timeline view correlating failures with recent software and update changes
- **B.** It automatically uninstalls problematic applications without user interaction
- **C.** It defragments the disk to improve system stability and file access performance
- **D.** It blocks OS updates that could cause crashes and prevents them from installing

Question 17: An Android user reports that a single app "just closes" every time they open it, but all other apps work fine. What is the BEST first troubleshooting step?

A. Force close the app from Settings and reopen it to see if the issue persists
B. Perform a factory reset on the device and reconfigure all user settings
C. Replace the device's battery to rule out power-related application issues
D. Enable airplane mode permanently to reduce network-related interruptions

Question 18: On Android, a streaming app frequently freezes. You want a low-impact step that may resolve the issue without removing user logins and settings. What should you try FIRST?

A. Clear the app's cache in Settings to remove temporary data and buffers
B. Clear the app's data/storage in Settings to reset it to default state
C. Perform a factory reset of the device and restore from a cloud backup
D. Remove and reinsert the SIM card to refresh the mobile network connection

Question 19: An Android user complains that after installing a "free game" from a third-party website, the phone is now slow and displays ads even on the home screen. What is the MOST likely initial cause?

A. Sideloaded app containing adware or potentially unwanted software components
B. Insufficient battery charge after the installation causing power throttling
C. Incorrect APN configuration from the mobile carrier affecting connectivity
D. Bluetooth being left turned on and consuming additional system resources

Question 20: An Android phone is extremely sluggish, and you discover that internal storage is almost completely full. Apps are failing to update. What is the BEST first action?

A. Disable background data for all apps to reduce network and battery usage
B. Enable airplane mode and reboot to clear temporary network connections
C. Free up storage by deleting unnecessary files, media, and unused applications
D. Turn off automatic brightness in display settings to conserve device power

ANSWERS

1: Correct Answer: B
Rationale: The failure started right after an update and now blocks normal boot. CompTIA's methodology favors least-disruptive steps first. Using WinRE to enter Safe Mode or uninstall the latest update targets the likely cause without immediately wiping or replacing hardware.

2: Correct Answer: A
Rationale: The drive is visible in UEFI, so basic hardware detection is working. The next step is OS-level repair of boot files. Startup Repair from WinRE is designed to fix boot problems before destructive actions like repartitioning or reinstalling.

3: Correct Answer: B
Rationale: A "Preparing Automatic Repair" loop indicates startup failure. You need WinRE to access tools such as Startup Repair, System Restore, and Safe Mode. Normal boot is not available, and a PXE reinstall is more disruptive than necessary at this stage.

4: Correct Answer: D
Rationale: Windows reaches the desktop but quickly freezes, suggesting a driver or software issue. Safe Mode loads minimal drivers and services, allowing targeted troubleshooting. Full resets or hardware replacement are premature and more disruptive.

5: Correct Answer: C
Rationale: High RAM usage, constant disk activity, and heavy page file use show the system is relying on virtual memory. This is typical of insufficient physical RAM for the workload, not boot data corruption, profiles, or NTFS permissions.

6: Correct Answer: D
Rationale: The freezes correlate with scheduled antivirus scans and Windows Update. Adjusting their schedules to off-hours is a focused, low-impact fix that preserves security while reducing disruption, unlike disabling updates or reinstalling.

7: Correct Answer: C
Rationale: On an HDD, intensive indexing and antivirus scans at login can cause 100% disk usage. Letting them finish, then tuning or rescheduling them, follows least-disruptive troubleshooting. System Restore, reset, or disabling all services is excessive.

8: Correct Answer: A
Rationale: Slow startup with normal performance afterward usually points to too many startup programs. Task Manager's Startup tab is the correct first tool to identify and disable unnecessary startup items.

9: Correct Answer: D
Rationale: Reliability Monitor shows failures isolated to one application starting from its installation. Repairing or reinstalling that app addresses the problem directly while leaving the OS and other apps intact.

10: Correct Answer: B
Rationale: Disk timeouts and S.M.A.R.T. warnings indicate likely drive hardware failure. The next step is to run or escalate hardware diagnostics on the drive and plan for backup/replacement, not OS rollbacks or boot configuration repairs.

Question 11: Correct Answer: A
Rationale: A temporary profile with the original profile still on disk indicates profile corruption. Best practice is to create a new profile and migrate the user's data, preserving files while resolving the corrupted profile.

12: Correct Answer: C
Rationale: One user gets "Access denied" while others can use the share, which points to a permissions or group membership issue. Checking that user's share and NTFS permissions is the correct first step.

13: Correct Answer: B
Rationale: The system hangs before the login screen, so you need recovery tools. Forcing several failed boots triggers Advanced Startup and WinRE, where you can run Startup Repair, System Restore, or Safe Mode, before resorting to a full reinstall.

14: Correct Answer: C
Rationale: Disabling unnecessary startup programs improves boot time and overall responsiveness. This is addressing a performance issue, not stability, access, or boot configuration corruption.

15: Correct Answer: D
Rationale: System Restore rolls back system files, drivers, and many settings to a previous restore point while preserving user documents, matching the requirement for minimal data impact. The other tools do not provide this type of rollback.

16: Correct Answer: A
Rationale: Reliability Monitor's main value is its timeline that correlates crashes and warnings with software installs, updates, and changes. This helps you identify likely causes, such as a newly installed app; it does not automatically uninstall or block updates.

17: Correct Answer: A
Rationale: For a single misbehaving app, the least-invasive first step is to force close it and reopen it. Factory reset or hardware changes are far too drastic, and airplane mode is unrelated to a single app crashing.

18: Correct Answer: A
Rationale: Clearing the app's cache removes temporary data that may be causing freezes while preserving logins and settings. Clearing data or factory reset would remove more user information than necessary for an initial step.

19: Correct Answer: A
Rationale: Installing a "free game" from a third-party site is sideloading, a common source of adware and potentially unwanted software that can slow the device and show ads on the home screen.

20: Correct Answer: C
Rationale: Critically low internal storage causes sluggish performance and prevents app updates. The correct first action is to free space by deleting unneeded files and apps. The other options do not address the storage shortage.

CHAPTER 9

Operational Procedures

9.1 Documentation, Ticketing & Knowledge Management

If you talk to experienced support technicians about what surprised them most when they started in IT, many will say it wasn't the technology—it was how much writing they had to do. In a professional environment, fixing the issue is only half your job. The other half is proving what happened, how you handled it, and how others can learn from it. That proof lives in documentation: tickets, asset records, change logs, and knowledge base articles. None of this is "extra admin work." It is the backbone of how IT support operates, how teams coordinate, how managers plan, and how auditors verify that the organization is following its own rules.

You can think of documentation as the nervous system of IT operations. Every contact with a user, whether by phone, email, chat, walk-up, or a remote session, should connect back into that system as a record. When documentation is good, patterns jump out: the same printer model failing across offices, a patch that keeps breaking a line-of-business app, or a department that clearly needs more training. When documentation is bad—or missing entirely—those patterns stay invisible, issues repeat, and people start guessing and blaming. CompTIA wants you to see documentation as a core operational procedure, tied directly to the troubleshooting methodology you learned earlier: you identify the problem, you test and implement a solution, and you document what you learned so the organization doesn't have to pay for the same problem twice.

Types of Operational Documentation

As a new technician, you will be surrounded by different types of documentation, and it helps to know what each one is for. The document you will live in most often is the **service ticket**. Tickets are created in a ticketing or service desk system whenever something needs IT's attention. Some of these tickets represent **incidents**—something is broken, degraded, or behaving abnormally. Others are **service requests**—nothing is broken, but a user needs access, a software installation, or some other standard service. Both flow through the same system, but they often follow slightly different paths and priorities.

Within a typical ticket you will see a set of standard fields. There is basic **contact information** so you know who the user is and how to reach them, often pulled from a directory like Active Directory. There is usually an **asset** or **configuration item** field that links the ticket to a specific device, such as a workstation, laptop, or printer, recorded in an asset database or configuration management database (CMDB). You will see a free-text **description** where the initial problem or request is described, often in the user's own words. You choose a **category** and possibly a **subcategory** that describe the type of issue—hardware versus software, network versus access, and so on. You will set or at least contribute to an **impact** and **urgency**, which combine to determine a **priority**. The system tracks **status** (new, in progress, on hold, resolved, closed), assigns the ticket to a group or named technician, and adds **timestamps** for all key changes. As you work, you add **work notes**, and when you are done, a short **resolution** description that explains fix and outcome.

Separate from tickets but closely related are **configuration and asset records**. These exist to answer questions like "Which PC is that?" or "Who is assigned this laptop?" Typical fields include hostname, serial number, model, physical location, department, installed operating system, and primary user. A good CMDB or asset inventory allows you to move beyond one-off fixes and think in terms of systems. If you discover that a specific NIC driver causes network drops on a particular laptop model, you can quickly identify every device with that model before the problem spreads. When you see a ticket linked to an asset, you immediately know what hardware and software you are dealing with, instead of asking basic questions every time.

Then there are **change and maintenance records**, which we will explore in much more detail in the next section on change management. For now, it is enough to understand that any planned modification to systems—such as patching, hardware replacements, network reconfigurations, or major software updates—should be captured in a change record rather than hidden inside an incident ticket. Change records track what is supposed to happen, when, and who approved it. Often, incident tickets are later linked to change records for root cause analysis. Imagine that immediately after a scheduled Windows update window, you see multiple tickets from the finance department about an accounting application failing to launch. Linking those incidents to the change record that drove the patch deployment makes it much easier to identify the true cause and decide what to do next.

Finally, there is the world of **knowledge base (KB) articles.** Unlike tickets, which are about one specific occurrence, KBs are meant to be reusable building blocks: how-to procedures, troubleshooting guides, FAQs, and known-issue workarounds. Many organizations have separate internal KBs for IT staff and public-facing KBs for end users. An internal KB article might explain in technical detail how to rebuild a corrupted Outlook profile, while a public article for users might show, step by step, how to connect to the corporate VPN. A good support culture constantly takes what it learns from tickets and formalizes those lessons into KB content so that future tickets can be resolved more quickly or avoided altogether.

The Ticket Lifecycle in Practice

It helps to follow a typical ticket from birth to closure. Picture a user calling the service desk and saying, "My screen is weird and I can't get to my files." Your first move should not be to guess at the fix; it should be to anchor this interaction in a ticket. Either you create a new ticket or you search to see if one already exists for the same user and problem. As you talk to the user, you collect the basics: their name, department, and best contact method; the device they are using; when the problem started; and what "weird" means in more precise terms. Maybe it turns out that icons are huge and the mapped network drive is missing. You record this in the description, ideally using the user's wording and then adding your translation.

Once intake is done, you categorize the ticket. Perhaps this is "Hardware > Desktop" if it looks like a display setting problem, or "Network > File share" if access issues seem more serious. Categorization is not just bookkeeping. The category often determines which queue receives the ticket, what service-level agreement (SLA) applies, and how managers later report on trends. If you lazily select the first category in the list, tickets get misrouted and statistics become unreliable. At this point, you also decide on impact and urgency. One user with a slightly off-resolution is low impact and low urgency; a sales floor that cannot use its point-of-sale terminals is high impact and high urgency. Priority typically reflects that combination. Even as an entry-level technician, your judgment here affects how the whole team responds.

After creation and categorization, the ticket is either automatically or manually assigned. If you are the one working it, you update the status to "In Progress" and begin your troubleshooting. Every meaningful step you take should be reflected in work notes. These notes are usually time-stamped and visible to other technicians and often to managers; sometimes a user-friendly version is visible to the user. Your notes might show that at 10:05 you connected via remote support, at 10:10 you verified that network connectivity was normal, at 10:15 you found that the display scaling was set to 200% and corrected it, and at 10:20 you confirmed the user could see their files again. The key is that the notes are factual, clear, and professional. You never write "user is clueless" or guess at motives. You also avoid storing sensitive information such as passwords, full credit card details, or unnecessary personal data, because tickets often live for years and can be audited.

Some tickets will move smoothly from intake to resolution with one technician. Others will require **escalation**. Suppose you are handling a VPN issue, and after confirming the basics—network connectivity, credentials, client version—you realize the problem lies in a firewall configuration that only the network team can modify. Instead of closing your notes with "Not my area, sent to networking," you assemble a concise but complete picture for the next team. You summarize the original user report, list the steps and tests you performed, attach relevant log snippets or screenshots, and explain why you believe the issue requires their expertise. Without that handoff quality, Tier 2 or Tier 3 teams must redo all your groundwork, wasting time and frustrating the user who has to answer the same questions repeatedly.

When a fix is finally in place, closure is not just flipping the ticket status. You document the **resolution** clearly. Rather than writing "fixed" or "resolved," you record the specific action and outcome: "Updated Intel NIC driver from 9.2.0 to 10.0.5 and disabled power management on adapter; user confirmed stable connection for 20 minutes." You then reach back to the user, confirm that their issue is resolved and no new problems have appeared, and only then move the ticket to a resolved or closed state according to your organization's process. These final steps matter because many organizations track metrics like **first-contact resolution** and **average resolution time**, and they rely on accurate status and timestamps to calculate them. Your documentation feeds those metrics, which in turn feed staffing decisions, training plans, and even budget justification.

Writing Effective Notes and Documentation

Once you appreciate that tickets are used by more than just you, your approach to writing changes. Good notes are **accurate and complete** enough that another technician who has never spoken to the user can read them and understand exactly what happened, what was tried, and where things stand. They should include key system details such as operating system version, application version, important error codes, and relevant configuration settings when those details matter to the issue. Vague entries like "rebooted" or "changed setting" offer almost no value; they don't help someone diagnose a recurring problem or verify that a particular configuration step is safe.

Clarity is just as important as completeness. Many technicians find it helpful to maintain a clear chronological structure in their notes. The sequence of events can reveal patterns—such as an error that appears only after a particular change—that would be hard to spot otherwise. You can think in terms of three natural segments: what was reported, what you observed and did, and what resolved the problem or why it remains unresolved. When you describe your actions, you can use precise technical language, because your primary audience is other IT staff. When you communicate directly to users through the ticket interface or email, you switch to user-friendly language, avoiding unnecessary jargon while still being honest and specific.

Tone and confidentiality round out professional documentation. Tickets can be audited by managers, HR, security teams, and sometimes even external regulators. They may be disclosed in legal proceedings. That means sarcasm, frustration, and personal commentary have no place in them. Instead of writing "user waited a week to report this obvious issue," you might record "user reports issue began last week; today is first reported occurrence." Similarly, organizational security policies typically forbid recording passwords, shared secrets, or sensitive personal identifiers in tickets or KBs. You might note that you "reset the user's password per policy and had them enter it directly," rather than pasting the actual string into the record. These habits protect both the user and you.

Knowledge Management and the Role of the KB

If tickets are the record of what has already happened, the **knowledge base** is the library that helps you handle the next occurrence better. In many environments, your first step after understanding a problem is not to start randomly trying things; it is to search the KB. By using relevant keywords from error messages, application names, device models, and symptoms, you can often find a documented solution or at least a structured troubleshooting path. This is especially powerful at Tier 1: with a solid KB, an entry-level technician can resolve issues that would otherwise have required escalation, simply by following a proven procedure.

As you gain experience, you will see patterns and realize that some of the solutions you are using regularly are not yet captured in the KB, or existing articles are outdated or incomplete. That is your opportunity to contribute. Good KB articles share certain characteristics. They have a clear, specific title that matches what someone would search for, such as "Configuring VPN Client X on Windows 11" rather than "VPN Stuff." They define their scope so readers know which systems and versions are covered. They describe symptoms or prerequisites concisely—what you should see when this article applies. They then walk step by step through the procedure, including commands, settings, and, when appropriate, screenshots. Finally, they explain how to verify success and mention common pitfalls or variations.

Writing KB content is different from writing ticket notes. You are not documenting a one-time story; you are designing instructions that a peer who has never seen the problem can follow reliably. That means no assumptions about unwritten steps and no "do some basic checks" placeholders. If a step requires administrative privileges, say so. If a change might disrupt service, include a warning. Over time, organizations usually apply some sort of review and versioning process to KB content. When an operating system reaches end of life, or a major update changes a UI, corresponding KB articles may need revision or retirement. As a front-line technician, you are often the first to notice when an article is misleading or obsolete; flagging that through the proper channel keeps the KB trustworthy.

There is a natural feedback loop between tickets and the KB. A cluster of similar tickets might indicate that an existing KB article needs to be promoted or made easier to find. A tricky incident that finally yields to a creative workaround might deserve a brand-new article so others don't have to reinvent the solution. You might handle an especially complex restore operation, document it thoroughly in the ticket, and then later expand that into a standardized recovery procedure in the KB. Thinking this way moves you from being purely reactive—fixing whatever appears—to being part of how the organization builds consistent, repeatable service.

Documentation, Security, and Professional Judgment

All of this documentation also plays a quiet but important role in security and compliance. Tickets and change records together form an **audit trail**, showing who did what, when, on which system, and often why. When there is a security incident or data breach, investigators will examine these records to reconstruct events. When auditors check whether the company is following its own change and access control policies, they often start with ticketing and change management data. If the records show that people routinely make changes "off the books" or grant access without approval, that is a serious finding.

Because of this, you will often face small judgment calls about what to document, where to put it, and how much detail to include. Suppose you help a user whose laptop keeps blue-screening. In the incident ticket, you capture the specific stop code, the OS build, the driver you updated, and the result. In the asset record, you update the device's hardware replacement history if you swapped RAM or a disk. If you realize this model has a recurring firmware issue, you might propose a KB article or add to an existing one with the exact firmware version that resolves it. If the fix involved a significant planned outage or system-wide risk—for example, updating the BIOS on hundreds of machines—you would also expect to see a linked change record that describes the scope, approvals, and schedule.

At the same time, not every keystroke belongs in a ticket. Writing novels for minor password resets would slow you down and bury what matters. A useful mental filter is to ask: if another technician inherits this ticket tomorrow, what do they need to know so they can avoid repeating the same tests, avoid making unsafe changes, and continue the work confidently? If the user calls back in two weeks with a related problem, will your notes be enough to give you context without starting from scratch? If the answer is yes, you have probably hit the right balance between detail and efficiency.

When you approach documentation, ticketing, and knowledge management with this mindset, you stop seeing them as bureaucratic chores. Instead, they become tools for making your own work easier, enabling your colleagues, and demonstrating professionalism. Over time, the quality of your records will quietly distinguish you as someone others can rely on—not just to fix problems, but to help the whole environment run in a controlled, predictable way.

9.2 Change Management Fundamentals

Imagine you're on the help desk and notice that the company's main file server looks overloaded. Users are complaining that saving documents takes forever. You search online, find a blog that suggests turning off a particular Windows service and tweaking a few registry keys to improve performance. You know you can do it in five minutes, and you're pretty sure it will help. You remote into the server, make the change, and reboot. For a few minutes, everything seems fine. Then the calls start. Accounting can't access the finance application. HR can't open personnel files. Your manager appears at your desk asking, "What changed?" In that moment, it's very clear why **change management** exists.

Change management, in an IT support context, is simply a controlled way of making changes to systems so that you avoid surprises, minimize risk, and always know who did what, when, and why. It is the opposite of "just try this and see what happens." Instead of improvised fixes, change management gives you a repeatable process for everything from small configuration tweaks on a production server to rolling out a new wireless network. The goal is not to slow you down for the sake of bureaucracy; the goal is to protect the business, the users, and frankly, you as the technician, from the fallout of uncontrolled change.

Unmanaged change causes three predictable kinds of pain. First, it causes outages. A "simple" firewall rule change can suddenly block a cloud service your sales team depends on. A firmware update on a switch can cut off an entire floor. Second, it creates security exposure. Turning off a security control "temporarily" to solve a problem might never get turned back on, or a misconfigured rule might open an unexpected path from the internet into internal systems. Third, it destroys accountability. If no one recorded the change, no one can easily prove what happened, investigations drag on, and blame tends to fall on whoever touched the system last. A formal change process addresses all three issues with one mindset: think before you act, act in a controlled way, and leave a clear trail.

For the CompTIA A+ exam, this mindset shows up again and again. You'll see scenarios where a technician is tempted to do something right away—upgrade a server, modify group policies, change a router configuration—simply because they know how. The better answer is usually to pause, check policy, and route the action through the correct change process. In other words, you're not being tested only on technical skill; you're being tested on whether you behave like a professional working inside an organization that depends on its IT systems to survive. Before you can manage changes well, you need a clear sense of what actually counts as a **change**. Many new technicians think of "change" as large projects or big upgrades, but from an operational perspective, it's much broader. Installing an operating system update on a file server is a change. Modifying a group policy that affects how users authenticate is a change. Updating firewall rules on the edge router, changing DNS entries, or pushing out a new version of a business-critical application are changes. So is replacing the company's main router, adding RAM to a critical virtualization host, or swapping a failing disk in a RAID array that supports production data. Even altering user permissions on a shared drive—especially in a regulated environment—can be a significant change to the organization's security posture.

Most organizations spell this out in policy: which things require a formal change request with approvals, which things are handled as routine tasks, and which might be explicitly prohibited without senior oversight. As a rule of thumb, anything that can affect multiple users, production systems, or the organization's security stance should go through change control. Replugging a monitor cable, helping a single user change a local printer default, or adjusting a screen resolution on a standalone workstation typically falls into "standard support actions" that are either pre-approved or too low risk to require formal change approval each time. But the minute a task touches shared infrastructure, server-side settings, or security controls, you should assume that some form of change management applies.

Even though organizations vary in how formal they are, the **core change management workflow** tends to follow the same basic pattern. First, someone identifies a need for change and records it. That might be you noticing that a server is low on disk space, or a department asking for new software, or the security team notifying

IT about a critical vulnerability. Instead of just acting, you open a ticket or submit a change request. That record should include the purpose of the change, what systems are involved, which users or departments might be impacted, and the desired timing. On the exam, when you see a scenario where a change is needed but nothing is written down yet, the "what should you do next?" answer is often to create that formal request.

Once the request exists, the next step is **impact and risk assessment**. At the A+ level you're not expected to do a full-blown risk analysis with scoring, but you should understand the key questions. Technically, what systems and services will this touch? Could it affect authentication, network connectivity, storage, or core applications? From the business side, which departments rely on those systems? Will this affect revenue-generating activities, customer-facing services, payroll, or anything with legal or compliance implications? From a security perspective, does the change alter firewalls, access permissions, encryption settings, or logging? And what dependencies might be involved—does another team need to adjust their system to match, or is something else likely to break if you move ahead? As a junior technician, your part in this assessment is often to provide accurate details about the systems involved and to flag potential risks you can see from your vantage point.

Only after that assessment does **approval** come into play. Very few meaningful changes are self-approved by the person doing the work. Routine workstation-level changes might just need a supervisor's okay. Infrastructure changes—servers, core switches, VPN gateways—often require sign-off from a change manager or a **Change Advisory Board (CAB)**. Changes that affect a particular application or business process might need approval from the business owner for that system, such as the finance director for the accounting system. What matters for your role is the habit: if the change is bigger than a trivial local fix, you do not assume you can just do it because you know how. You check the process, you seek approval, and you document who authorized it. With approval secured, the focus moves to **planning and scheduling**. This is where you decide when and how the change will be done. You work out a maintenance window that avoids peak business hours—late evening, early morning, or a weekend. You build a step-by-step implementation plan: what commands will be run, in what order, what tools and credentials are required, and who needs to be present or on call. Just as important, you define a rollback plan. If the new firmware causes instability, if the patch breaks authentication, or if the new configuration does not behave as expected, how will you get back to the previous working state? That might mean restoring from a backup, reverting a snapshot, or reapplying an old configuration file. A key aspect of good change management is not just "we have backups," but "we have verified, recent backups and a clear procedure to restore from them." This is where change management ties directly into the backup and recovery practices you'll see in the next section.

Planning is not complete without **communication**. Before implementation, affected users need a heads-up. A short, clear message—"Email will be unavailable Saturday from 1–3 PM while we apply security updates"—helps set expectations and reduce angry calls. Other IT teams, such as security or network operations, should be informed if the change touches their domains. The help desk needs to know that a particular service will be down or altered, so that when users call, they can respond with accurate information instead of starting from zero. For A+ questions, answers that include notifying users, coordinating with other teams, or updating the help desk are often the ones that show proper professional behavior.

Only then do you reach **implementation**. This is the part technicians tend to focus on, but in a mature environment it is just one phase of a larger process. When you implement, you follow the plan you laid out. You avoid improvising in production, especially if the idea wasn't discussed in the assessment phase. You make one controlled change at a time rather than stacking unrelated changes together, so that if something goes wrong, it's easier to trace the cause. As you go, you note relevant console messages, errors, or unusual observations in the change record. As an entry-level tech, you may perform the hands-on work under a senior admin's supervision, but your responsibility to stick to the approved plan is the same.

After the change is applied, you move into **testing and validation**. You don't assume success just because the system comes back up. You verify that services work as intended: users can log in, printers respond, shared drives mount, web applications load, and so on. You check that performance seems normal and that no obvious new errors appear in system or application logs. You confirm that security controls—firewalls, antivirus, access permissions—are operating as expected. Often, you'll ask a sample user from an affected department to confirm that their normal tasks work. Only when this validation is complete do you declare the change successful.

The last phase is **documentation and closeout**. This is where you update the ticket or change request with what actually happened: the steps you took, any deviations from the plan and why, the time the change began and ended, and the results of your testing. If the change altered something that's part of your official documentation—network diagrams, asset records, configuration baselines, standard images, or knowledge base articles—those sources need updating so that future troubleshooting and planning are based on reality. For larger or more impactful changes, there may also be a short post-implementation review meeting to discuss what went well, what went wrong, and how to improve the process next time.

Not every change goes through the full, heavy-weight version of this cycle. Organizations commonly distinguish between **standard changes**, **normal changes**, and **emergency changes**. Standard changes are low-risk, routine tasks with well-understood outcomes and documented procedures. Think of imaging a new workstation using the company's standard image, onboarding a user with a checklist the team follows every time, or pushing a minor, vendor-approved application update through a central management tool that has been tested repeatedly. These changes are essentially pre-approved as long as you follow the documented steps, but they are still documented through tickets or automatic logs.

Normal changes are the everyday non-emergency changes that use the full process: request, assessment, approval, planning, scheduling, communication, implementation, testing, and documentation. Upgrading a server operating system, changing firewall rules to support a new external web application, or migrating file shares to a different storage system would all be normal changes. In exam scenarios, when you see something that isn't routine and doesn't require immediate action to stop an outage or a security incident, you should mentally put it in the "normal change" bucket and look for options that involve approval and scheduling rather than acting on the spot.

Emergency changes are the exceptions reserved for situations where delay would cause serious harm. If a critical vulnerability is being actively exploited and your VPN servers are at risk, or a key production database server is down and the business is losing money every minute, waiting for the next scheduled CAB meeting is not reasonable. Emergency change processes allow for accelerated approvals—perhaps an on-call manager authorizes the work over the phone—and for immediate action. However, even in an emergency, process is not abandoned. You still document the change, you still confirm that backups exist if time allows, you still test as best you can, and you still conduct a post-change review afterward. On the exam, it's important not to treat convenience or impatience as an emergency. "I don't want to come in this weekend" is not an emergency; "the production site is down" is.

As an A+ technician, your role in all of this is very practical. You are often the one opening the initial ticket or change request when you see a need. You collect and record accurate details about which systems are affected, what users are impacted, and what symptoms are occurring. You follow the approved procedures and checklists rather than making undocumented changes on the side. When a proposed action starts to look bigger or riskier than it initially seemed—for example, you discover that the "small file server" is actually hosting data for a critical application—you pause and escalate, asking a supervisor or senior admin to reassess the change and possibly reroute it through a more formal process.

This is also where your understanding of documentation and ticketing from the previous section ties into change management. Tickets are often where changes are born, tracked, and closed. Good tickets contain enough information for someone else to understand the rationale for the change, the risks and impacts, and the exact actions that were taken. Configuration baselines—records of how a system is supposed to be configured—are maintained by closing the loop after changes and updating those baselines accordingly. When there is an incident later, being able to say, "Here is exactly what changed last week and who authorized it," is invaluable.

When you face change-related questions on the A+ exam, a simple reasoning pattern can help. First, decide whether the action described is really a change or just a local, low-risk support task. Then consider the scope and risk: one user or many, workstation or server, minor preference or security-relevant setting. Next, think about organizational process: would this normally go through formal change management, or is it a standard change? Based on urgency, classify it mentally as standard, normal, or emergency. Finally, notice which parts of the process are missing in the scenario: has anyone requested approval, scheduled downtime, notified users, checked backups, or documented the work? The correct answer will usually move the scenario toward completing those missing pieces instead of jumping straight into doing the technical work.

Learning to see your work through this lens is part of transitioning from "someone who knows computers" to "an IT professional." In the short term, it might feel like change management slows you down. In reality, it allows your entire organization to move faster with fewer disasters, fewer late-night emergencies, and fewer mysteries about why something broke. More importantly, it protects your users, your systems, and your own reputation every time you touch a production environment.

9.3 Backup & Recovery Methods

If you spend enough time in IT support, you discover that the scariest problems are rarely about a blue screen or a noisy fan. Those are annoying, but usually fixable. The real disasters happen when data disappears. Someone's entire client list is suddenly gone after a sync mishap, or a small office's accounting system is locked up by ransomware the week before tax filings are due. These are the moments when users look to you not just as a "computer person," but as the person who can save their work, their time, and sometimes their business. In those moments, your real power is not a fancy command-line trick; it is whether there is a usable backup and whether you know how to restore it correctly.

Backup and recovery is where operational procedures, security, and troubleshooting all intersect. From an A+ perspective, you are not expected to design complex enterprise disaster recovery environments, but you are expected to think clearly about workstation and small-office backups, configure them sensibly, verify that they are actually working, and use them properly when something goes wrong. That includes knowing what to back up, where to put it, how often to run the backup, and how to choose the right restore point when time is short and pressure is high. It also means being able to explain to a non-technical user what is and is not possible based on the protection that was in place before the incident.

Thinking About Risk: RPO, RTO, and What Truly Matters

Before you click any backup wizard, you need a mental model for why you are backing up and what risk you are trying to reduce. Two ideas guide this planning: **Recovery Point Objective (RPO)** and **Recovery Time Objective (RTO)**. You will see these terms more often in enterprise contexts, but the logic behind them is just as useful when you are setting up backups for a single workstation or a small office.

RPO answers the question, "How much data can we afford to lose?" If a one-person law office only works with documents that change once a day, they might be able to tolerate losing one day of work. In that case, a nightly backup could be enough. If you support a design shop where people are editing large projects all day, they may not be willing to lose more than an hour of work; that implies much more frequent backups or continuous synchronization with versioning. Whenever you see an exam question stating that "the company cannot afford to lose more than X of work," your brain should translate that directly into RPO and backup frequency.

RTO is about time rather than data. It asks, "How long can this person or system be down?" A warehouse manager's PC used mostly for reports might be allowed to be offline for half a day while you reinstall Windows and applications, then restore data from a file backup. Meanwhile, a front-desk workstation in a medical clinic may be critical for checking in patients; they might only accept a downtime of minutes. That situation pushes you toward backups that let you restore the entire system image quickly rather than rebuilding piece by piece. The shorter the RTO, the more you care about fast restore methods, even if they require more storage or more effort to maintain.

Once you understand how sensitive a user or small business is to data loss and downtime, you can decide what needs to be protected. User data is almost always at the top of the list: documents, spreadsheets, databases, photos, email archives, and sometimes browser favorites and other small but important items. System files and applications usually come second, not because they are unimportant, but because you can often reinstall them from media or downloads if you have to. For systems that would be very time-consuming to rebuild or where a specific configuration is mission-critical, you may choose to protect the entire system with an image so you can get back to exactly the state you had before a failure.

Backup Types: How Data Gets Copied Over Time

Once you know what you are protecting and how much loss and downtime are acceptable, you can choose how to structure the backups. The exam leans heavily on your understanding of **full**, **incremental**, and **differential** backups, because each one represents a trade-off between backup time, storage usage, and restore time.

A **full backup** is the simplest conceptually: it is a complete copy of all the selected data at one moment in time. If you back up an entire user profile as a full backup on Sunday night, that backup contains everything from that profile as of Sunday. Restoring from a full backup is straightforward; you usually only need that one backup set. The downside is that full backups are slow and large. Doing them too frequently consumes storage quickly and can run into backup windows when users are still active. For that reason, full backups are often scheduled less frequently, perhaps weekly, and then combined with more efficient methods in between.

An **incremental backup** copies only the data that has changed since the last backup of any type, usually the last full or the last incremental. Imagine you run a full backup on Sunday, then incremental backups Monday through Saturday. Monday's incremental contains the changes since Sunday's full, Tuesday's incremental contains the changes since Monday's incremental, and so on. This makes each individual backup after the full relatively fast and small, which is great if you need frequent protection but have limited storage or network bandwidth. The trade-off shows up during restores: to restore the state from Thursday, you need the full Sunday backup plus every incremental from Monday through Thursday. If any one of those increments is missing or corrupted, you cannot fully reconstruct the data for that day.

A **differential backup** is a middle ground. It copies all data that has changed since the last full backup. Using the same schedule—full on Sunday, differentials Monday through Saturday—Monday's differential is similar to an incremental: changes since Sunday. However, Tuesday's differential also copies all changes since Sunday, which means it includes Monday's changes plus any new changes on Tuesday. By Thursday, the differential has grown larger, because it includes the whole week's changes. Restoring, however, is easier than with incrementals. To get back to Thursday's state, you only need the full backup from Sunday and the latest differential from Thursday. Storage usage and backup time for each differential increase over the week, but restore complexity decreases, which is often attractive in small environments where you know you will be doing restores yourself and want them as straightforward as possible.

When you see scenario questions, pay attention to what the user cares about. If storage and network usage are major constraints but restore time can be a bit longer, incremental backups are often the right fit. If the priority is faster restores and you have more room for backup data, differentials can be preferred. Full backups alone are rarely practical on their own in ongoing schedules, but they remain essential as anchors for the other methods and are sometimes used by themselves in very small or low-change environments.

Another important dimension is what you are backing up. A **file-level backup** operates at the level of individual files and folders. You choose specific directories or file types, and the software copies those. Windows File History, macOS Time Machine, and many cloud backup tools primarily work this way. They are excellent for protecting user data with reasonable storage efficiency and flexibility. The downside is that if you lose the entire system drive, you still need to reinstall the operating system and applications, configure settings, and then restore the files. That can take significant time in a busy support environment.

An **image-based backup**, often called a system image, captures an entire drive or partition, including the operating system, installed applications, configuration, and data. The backup usually works at the block level, not caring about individual files. This approach is more storage-intensive, but it lets you restore a machine to a known-good state very quickly, which is ideal when the RTO requirement is aggressive or when recreating a particular configuration would be painful. A common pattern in small businesses is to create a clean "golden image" of a workstation right after building it, then periodically update that image or supplement it with file-level backups of the users' data. On the exam, if the scenario emphasizes quickly getting a workstation back "exactly as it was before the failure," an image-based solution is usually the intended answer.

Where to Put Backups: Local, Network, and Cloud

Backing up data to the same drive that holds the original data does not meet the real definition of "backup" in IT. A real backup must live on separate storage so that a single failure does not take out both the original and the copy. Once you accept that, you can compare common backup locations: **local**, **network**, and **cloud**.

Local backups are stored on devices directly attached to the computer or on another internal disk in the same chassis. External USB hard drives and SSDs are the most common example in SOHO environments. They provide fast backups and restores, no Internet dependency, and usually simple setup. Their weakness is that they are vulnerable to the same local risks as the workstation: theft, fire, flood, or certain types of malware. Ransomware in particular is a concern, because if the external drive is always connected, the malware can encrypt it along with the system drive, eliminating your safety net.

Network backups shift the storage to a device elsewhere on the local network, such as a file server or a NAS (Network Attached Storage) appliance. Multiple workstations can back up to the same shared storage, which simplifies management and can allow for more robust hardware with RAID and better power protection. Network backups protect against the failure of an individual workstation or its attached drives, but they are still physically located in the same building or site, so a serious disaster can affect both the original and the backup.

Cloud backups store data in an offsite provider's infrastructure. This category includes dedicated backup services as well as cloud storage tools like OneDrive, Google Drive, and iCloud, especially when they offer version history and restore points. The big advantages are that the data is offsite by default, protected against local physical disasters, and accessible from anywhere with an Internet connection. The trade-offs are dependence on connectivity and provider availability, ongoing subscription costs, and careful consideration of data privacy and compliance. From a security angle, cloud storage with versioning is particularly valuable during ransomware incidents: even if encrypted files sync up to the cloud, you can often roll back to unencrypted earlier versions.

For many small offices, a layered approach is ideal: for example, local image backups for fast bare-metal restores, combined with cloud or offsite backups for long-term protection and disaster recovery. On the exam, pay attention to clues like "concerned about building-wide disasters" or "limited Internet bandwidth" to infer whether cloud or on-premises storage makes more sense.

Schedules, Retention, and the Power of Automation

Once you know the type and location of backups, the next question is, "How often, and for how long?" This connects back to the RPO discussion. If someone only uses their workstation from 9 to 5 and rarely works late, scheduling backups overnight is usually sufficient and avoids competing with daytime work. Some tools support near-continuous or hourly backups, which are appropriate when data changes constantly and the RPO is very tight.

Retention refers to how long you keep each backup. Many backup systems implement a tiered pattern, such as keeping daily backups for a week, weekly backups for a month, and monthly backups for a year. The idea is to balance storage usage against the ability to go back to older versions if needed. In practice, built-in tools like Time Machine or File History handle much of this automatically by pruning older versions when space runs low, but you still need to understand the concept so you can explain to a user why their backup drive eventually fills up and how far back they can realistically restore.

Automation is non-negotiable in professional environments. Relying on users to remember to plug in a drive and click "Back up now" guarantees missed backups. Configuring scheduled jobs that run at defined times, or enabling continuous background backups through cloud agents, greatly increases reliability. From an operational standpoint, you should also make sure backup jobs generate logs or alerts so that failures are visible. Quietly failing backups are one of the most painful situations to discover—typically only after you try to restore and realize nothing usable was captured for months.

Verifying That Backups Are Real

There is a saying in systems administration: "If you haven't tested the restore, you don't have a backup." A file that looks like a backup but cannot be restored successfully is just wasted storage. Verification needs to happen at two levels: confirming that backup jobs ran successfully, and confirming that you can actually restore data from them.

Most backup software generates logs indicating whether jobs completed, how many files were backed up, and whether there were any errors. As an entry-level technician, you may be the one checking these logs periodically or responding to alerts that something failed. This is not busywork; it is the difference between discovering problems while there is still time to fix them and discovering them in the middle of a crisis. If you configure backups for a user or department, build into your routine some regular verification that the jobs are succeeding.

Beyond log checks, you should perform test restores. That might mean restoring a random file from last week's backup into a temporary folder and opening it to confirm it is intact and current, or, in more advanced environments, restoring an entire system image into a virtual machine to verify that it boots. Test restores also teach you the restore procedure itself while the stakes are low, so you are not learning under pressure during an actual incident. Be conscious of the data you use in tests; if it contains sensitive information, you still need to handle the test copies according to your organization's security policies.

Common Recovery Scenarios in the Real World

Eventually something will go wrong, and you will move from backup theory to recovery practice. One of the most frequent scenarios is a user who has deleted or overwritten a file. In that case, you start with the simplest and fastest options: check the Recycle Bin or Trash, and check any built-in version history features, such as Windows' Previous Versions or File History, macOS Time Machine's timeline, or version history in cloud services like OneDrive or Google Drive. If those do not produce the needed file, you move to the backup tool's interface, select an appropriate date, and search for the file there.

A subtle but important skill is choosing the right version. If a user worked on a document Monday through Wednesday and realized on Thursday morning that they ruined it with changes, the "latest" version in the backup might already include the bad edits. You might need to restore Tuesday night's version instead. To avoid making things worse, it is good practice to restore into an alternate location first, such as a temporary directory or the user's desktop under a different name, then compare and copy over what they actually need. Restoring directly over current files without thinking can overwrite good data with older content.

Another scenario is a corrupt user profile or a migration to a new PC. In these situations, you are often concerned with restoring the contents of profile folders—Documents, Desktop, Pictures, Favorites, Downloads, and application data like Outlook PST files or browser profiles. If you have a backup of the old profile, you can restore those directories into the appropriate locations in the new or repaired profile. Pay attention to ownership and permissions, especially in domain environments; files restored under the wrong account may not be accessible until you adjust ACLs.

Security incidents add another layer of complexity. With malware infections, and especially with ransomware, you usually cannot trust the existing operating system installation. The standard workflow is to isolate the system from the network to prevent further spread, perform malware analysis if required, and then either thoroughly clean the system or, more commonly for ransomware and severe compromises, wipe and reinstall the OS from known-good media. Only after you are confident that the system is clean do you restore data from backups. Here, the choice of backup date is critical. If you restore from a backup that was taken after the ransomware began encrypting files, you will simply bring back encrypted or infected data. The correct strategy is to identify a backup from before the infection started and restore from that point. CompTIA loves to test this point by giving you a choice between "most recent backup" and "last known good backup before infection"; the latter is almost always the right answer.

The most dramatic form of recovery is a **bare-metal restore**, where you take a new or completely wiped disk and restore an image to it. Typically, you boot from recovery media—a USB drive or DVD that contains the restore environment—connect the machine to the storage location where the backup image lives (another local disk, a network share, or sometimes the cloud), and then select the image and the target disk. You must be meticulous in choosing the correct destination drive, because the restore will overwrite whatever is there. After the restore completes, you reboot from the restored disk, and in a successful case, the system comes up as it was at the time of the backup. Differences in hardware, especially between very old and very new systems, can sometimes complicate image restores, but in many small-office scenarios where you are restoring to the same machine with a new drive, image-based bare-metal recovery is straightforward and extremely time-saving.

Policies, Documentation, and Communicating with Users

All of this technical work sits inside a larger framework of policies and documentation. Your organization should define what data must be backed up, how often, where it is stored, and how long it is retained. As a technician, you might not write these policies, but you are responsible for implementing them accurately and updating documentation when configurations change. When you set up a backup for a workstation, you should document which folders are included, what schedule is configured, and where the backups land, so that another technician—or you, six months later—can understand the setup quickly during a restore.

Restores themselves should be documented in your ticketing system, including what was restored, from which date or backup set, and whether any data could not be recovered. This creates an audit trail and helps refine backup strategies over time. Just as important is how you talk to users around backup and recovery. If there is no backup, or if the most recent one is old, you need to explain calmly and clearly what that means for their data, without overpromising miraculous recoveries. Conversely, when a backup saves the day, you can use the opportunity to reinforce good practices, such as keeping critical data in backed-up locations rather than on an unprotected local folder. Over time, your reliability in this area builds trust; people learn that when something bad happens to their data, you have a plan, not just a hope.

9.4 Safety Procedures for IT Work

In IT support, safety is not an optional "extra" you add if you have time. It is part of being a professional. Your organization may talk about OSHA, local safety laws, or internal policies, but all of that boils down to the same basic expectation: you do not put people at risk to fix a technical problem, and you do not sacrifice equipment because you were in a hurry or skipped a simple precaution. CompTIA A+ reflects this reality. Many questions will tempt you with answers that sound technically clever but quietly break a safety rule. The goal in this section is to help you instinctively recognize those unsafe shortcuts and replace them with a methodical, safe way of working.

A useful way to think about safety in IT is to put it in three layers. At the core is **personal safety**—avoiding electric shock, physical injury, and long-term strain. Around that is **equipment safety**, keeping components free from static damage, electrical faults, and contamination. Finally, there is **workspace safety**, making sure the environment itself—cables, furniture, airflow, fire risk—is not creating hazards. When you walk up to a desk, server room, or lab bench, you should be quietly scanning for risks in all three layers before you even touch a keyboard.

Electrical safety: respecting the dangerous parts

Although IT work looks tame compared to construction or factory work, the electrical systems you deal with can absolutely hurt or kill someone if handled incorrectly. Every PC that plugs into a wall outlet is connected to mains AC power, typically in the 100–240 volt range depending on the region. Voltage alone does not tell the whole story; what matters is that the building circuit can supply significant current, and human bodies conduct electricity well enough that a shock across the wrong path can disrupt muscles or the heart.

It is important to distinguish between the **low-voltage DC** circuitry on a motherboard and the **high-voltage** side of devices like power supplies, CRT monitors (if you ever encounter them), laser printers, and some UPS units. The logic-level voltages inside a running system—3.3, 5, or 12 volts DC—are not the direct shock problem. The hazard lies upstream, where AC is converted, rectified, and stored. That work is done in components such as large capacitors inside a power supply. Those capacitors can hold a charge even after the system has been shut down and unplugged.

Because of that, a baseline rule in IT support is "always disconnect and verify" before you open anything. In practice, that means you perform an orderly shutdown of the computer through the operating system, wait for it to power down fully, and then **unplug** the power cord from the wall or power strip. Do not rely on just flipping the back switch on the power supply. Once you have unplugged the cord, it is good practice to press the power button on the front of the system for a few seconds. This helps discharge residual energy on the motherboard and can prevent odd behavior during troubleshooting. However, you should understand that this step does not make it safe to open the power supply itself; the high-voltage components inside a PSU can remain charged for quite some time.

For the A+ exam and in real life as an entry-level technician, you should treat the interior of a power supply as off-limits. If a PSU is suspected to be faulty, you replace the entire unit or test it using an appropriate external tool, such as a PSU tester or a multimeter at the connector level, following manufacturer procedures. You do not remove the cover, you do not probe its internal circuit board, and you do not "discharge" capacitors manually. Any answer choice that involves opening a power supply or similar sealed high-voltage device is not just wrong; it violates the expectation that you know your scope and when to escalate to qualified personnel.

Not all of your electrical interaction will be with devices that are turned off. You will often be plugging and unplugging power cords, checking outlets, inspecting power strips, or confirming that a UPS is running. When you are around energized equipment, even at the simple level of a plugged-in power strip, you must enforce a few habits. Your hands should be dry, your tools should have intact insulation, and you should avoid metal jewelry such as bracelets and long necklaces that could accidentally bridge contacts. If a cord or plug appears damaged—exposed copper, cracked insulation, broken ground pin—your role is to take it out of service and report or replace it, not "make it work" temporarily.

This ties directly into **grounding** and **polarity**. Modern power cords and outlets use a three-prong design: hot, neutral, and ground. The round or U-shaped ground pin is a safety feature, providing a path for fault current so that a short circuit will trip a breaker instead of energizing the case of a device. You should never remove the ground pin from a plug, use an adapter that defeats the ground, or file down a plug to "fit" an older outlet. Any suggestion along those lines, whether during an exam question or at work, should immediately trigger a mental red flag. If the outlet does not match the plug, the correct remedy involves a properly installed receptacle or, in some cases, a different device—not improvisation with metal cutters.

There is also a bright line around what an A+ technician does not do. Working inside service panels, modifying building wiring, bypassing interlocks on copiers or other machines, and any activity that exposes bare AC conductors is outside your role. The safe response is to stop, secure the area if necessary, and escalate to facilities or a qualified electrician. Being able to say "no" to that kind of request is part of professional judgment.

ESD: the invisible threat to components

While electrical safety is about protecting people from shock and burns, **electrostatic discharge (ESD)** is about protecting components from microscopic damage. Static electricity is familiar in everyday life: the tiny spark when you touch a doorknob after walking on carpet, or the snap you feel when you pull a sweater off. Those visible or audible discharges are thousands of volts in a very short pulse. Computer components can be damaged by far smaller discharges that you never even feel.

Inside components such as RAM modules, CPUs, and chipset controllers, electrical pathways are measured in nanometers. A brief static discharge can punch through insulators or subtly alter these paths. Sometimes the damage is immediate: the system will not boot with the new RAM you just installed. Often, though, the damage is **latent**. The part appears to work at first but fails weeks later with intermittent crashes or data corruption. Because latent failures are so hard to diagnose and attribute, professional environments take ESD prevention very seriously. The only reliable fix is not to cause the damage in the first place.

An **ESD-safe workstation** is built around the idea of equalizing electrical potential between you, the equipment, and a safe ground. The most visible tools are the **antistatic wrist strap**, the ESD mat, and ESD-safe storage bags. When you use a wrist strap correctly, you fasten the strap snugly against bare skin on your wrist, then attach the other end to a known good ground point. In a typical PC repair scenario, that ground point is an unpainted metal part of the computer case or a designated grounding post. The PC itself must be unplugged from AC power while you do this. The strap is not a shock-protection device; it is a slow bleed-off path for static charge. Wearing a strap while working on live AC circuits is dangerous and should never be done.

The ESD mat extends this concept to the work surface. Components placed on the mat will tend to equalize with it, and if the mat is grounded, the overall system stays at the same potential. Proper use looks like this: you place the unplugged PC on or next to the mat, clip your wrist strap to the mat or case, and work so that your hands frequently touch the case. Think of it as forming a little "bubble" where everything is at the same electrical potential, so there is no incentive for charge to jump from one object to another.

Component handling fits naturally into this picture. Whenever you remove or install RAM, expansion cards, or other circuit boards, handle them by the edges. Avoid touching the gold or tin contacts, IC pins, or any exposed solder points. Do not stack boards on top of each other where pins could scratch traces, and never rest components on a carpeted floor, a metal table without an ESD mat, or on top of a powered device. When you need to set something aside, an **antistatic bag** is the right place. These bags are often metallic-looking or semi-transparent and are specifically designed to dissipate charge. Ordinary plastic bags are insulators and can actually build up static; they are not a substitute.

Environmental factors matter, too. Low humidity environments, such as heated offices in winter, make static buildup more likely. Certain clothing, like wool sweaters and some synthetic fabrics, are notorious for generating charge. Walking long distances on carpeted floors and then reaching directly into an open PC case is a recipe for a damaging discharge. Part of your preparation before working on equipment is to control what you can: use ESD tools, touch the case periodically, minimize unnecessary movement, and avoid clothing that crackles when you move.

On the exam, you will see ESD concepts contrasted with other electrical ideas. For example, a surge protector protects against overvoltage coming from the power line, not static on your body. An electromagnetic pulse (EMP) is a completely different phenomenon, unrelated to the routine static you combat in an office. Being able to pick out the ESD-specific tool or procedure in a list is essential.

Tools, cleaning, and the hidden hazards in routine tasks

Day to day, you will use hand tools and cleaning supplies so often that it is easy to stop thinking about their risks. That complacency is what you want to avoid. A basic screwdriver can bridge two contacts and short out a motherboard if left loose in a case. A can of compressed air, if used incorrectly, can spray freezing liquid or stir up a dust cloud that irritates lungs and eyes. Good habits with tools and cleaners keep both people and hardware safe.

For hand tools, the guiding principle is control. Use tools that are appropriately sized for the fasteners you are working with so that you are not slipping and gouging surfaces. If you are working anywhere near live circuits—perhaps checking voltage at a connector while a system is powered for diagnostics—use tools with insulated handles and avoid contacting more than one conductive point at a time. When you are not actively holding a tool, put it somewhere secure: a magnetic tray, a tool roll, or a clear corner of the bench. Screws, jumpers, and loose metal objects should never be left inside an open chassis.

Cleaning is another area where common sense and a bit of physics help. Dust acts like an insulating blanket inside systems, trapping heat and clogging airflow through fans and heatsinks. Removing dust is a critical maintenance task, but doing it wrong can generate static, damage components, or put debris into people's eyes. **Compressed air** is generally the right tool for blowing dust out of power supply vents, heatsinks, and keyboards. The safe technique is to keep the can upright, use short bursts, and hold fans in place with a finger or a plastic tool so they do not overspin and damage their bearings. You should also be aware that the propellant in these cans is often flammable and very cold when expelled as liquid, so you avoid open flames and never spray it directly on skin.

A common exam trap involves vacuum cleaners. Household vacuums are designed to move a lot of air, but the friction of dust and air moving through plastic hoses can create significant static buildup. Using a normal vacuum inside a computer chassis is a classic way to zap components, even if you never see a spark. The safer alternative is either to use compressed air and let the dust fall into a trash can or onto a disposable surface, or to use a specially designed **ESD-safe vacuum** made for electronics. If you see an answer choice suggesting a regular vacuum on a motherboard or RAM, that is your cue to look for a safer cleaning method.

For stubborn grime—fingerprints on a monitor bezel, sticky residue on a mouse, or oxidation on contacts—**isopropyl alcohol** (ideally 90% or higher) and lint-free cloths or swabs are your friends. Alcohol evaporates quickly and leaves minimal residue, making it suitable for many electronics-related surfaces. Even here, fire safety matters. You should not smoke or have open flames nearby when using flammable solvents or compressed air, and you should use them in well-ventilated areas to avoid breathing concentrated fumes.

Physical safety, lifting, and ergonomics

Not all IT injuries involve electricity or static. Some are much more mundane: strained backs from moving equipment, tripped users from poor cable routing, or repetitive strain from hours at poorly arranged workstations. Part of your value as a technician is your ability to set up and maintain environments that minimize these risks.

Moving equipment is one of the most physically demanding parts of the job. Desktop towers, CRTs (if you still see them), and especially UPS units can be surprisingly heavy. The right lifting technique is simple but non-negotiable. You position yourself close to the load, plant your feet for balance, bend at your knees rather than at your waist, and lift by straightening your legs while keeping the object close to your torso. Avoid twisting while you are lifting or carrying; if you need to turn, pivot your feet instead of rotating your spine with a heavy box in your hands. For very heavy or awkward items, such as large UPS units or servers, do not hesitate to ask for help or use a cart. A minor delay is always preferable to a back injury.

Cable management sits at the intersection of safety and professionalism. Under desks, behind TVs, and in network closets, you will see every possible cable disaster: loops of Ethernet and power cords across walkways, tightly stretched wires hanging from ports, unlabeled tangles that snag feet. Loose cables are not just ugly; they are genuine trip hazards and can stress connectors to the point of failure if they are pulled. A thoughtful technician routes cables along walls or under protective covers, uses ties or Velcro straps to bundle excess length, and labels both ends for easy identification. It takes a bit of extra time, but it greatly reduces accidental unplugging and makes future troubleshooting safer and faster.

Ergonomics may feel slightly outside traditional "tech" topics, yet it shows up both on the job and on the exam. When you set up a user's workstation, you have a chance to prevent discomfort and long-term injury. A well-positioned monitor sits roughly at eye level so that the user's neck stays in a neutral position. The keyboard and mouse should be at a height where the user's elbows are near a 90-degree angle and wrists can stay straight, not bent sharply up or down. A chair that supports the lower back and allows feet to rest flat on the floor or on a footrest contributes to overall posture. Long sessions of typing or mousing with poor ergonomics can contribute to **repetitive strain injury (RSI)**, characterized by pain or numbness in wrists, hands, or shoulders. Encouraging users to take short breaks, stretch, and adjust positions is part of a broader safety culture.

Safe procedures and professional judgment in action

When you combine all of these ideas, a clear pattern emerges: the safest work is the most deliberate. Before you open a case or start disconnecting cables, you pause to think through power, environment, and ESD. You confirm that the system is properly shut down and unplugged, and only then do you press the power button to drain residual charge. You prepare the workspace by clearing clutter, arranging adequate lighting, and securing cables so you are not crawling through a maze. You set up your ESD strap and mat, ground yourself to the case, and move components one at a time, placing them on safe surfaces or in antistatic bags.

As you work, you keep tools under control and small parts corralled so nothing is lost or left behind inside the chassis. If you are asked to hurry or pressured to cut corners—"Just leave it plugged in, it will be fine" or "Can't you just tape that ground pin?"—you rely on your understanding of the risks to push back politely but firmly. You explain that while the shortcut might save a minute now, it creates a much larger risk of injury, data loss, or equipment failure later. That ability to articulate the "why" behind safe procedures is as much a part of your job as knowing which slot a RAM stick goes into.

In many A+ exam scenarios, you will be presented with technically plausible but incomplete solutions. A choice might correctly identify a failed PSU but suggest opening it for repair, or recommend cleaning a dusty system but using a household vacuum. Your task is not just to recognize the technical diagnosis, but also to reject any remedy that bypasses basic safety principles. Over time, this mindset shifts from something you consciously apply for the exam to an automatic filter you bring to every real-world troubleshooting situation, shaping you into a technician that colleagues and users trust not only to fix problems but to do so safely.

9.5 Privacy, Licensing & Policy Compliance

When you start working in IT support, it's easy to think of yourself primarily as a technician: someone who fixes computers, resets passwords, and installs software. From an organization's point of view, though, you are also something else: a trusted gatekeeper. You will routinely see information that most employees never see, you will have access to tools that can bypass normal restrictions, and you will be asked to make quick decisions that have legal, financial, and ethical consequences. This is why the A+ exam spends time on topics like privacy, software licensing, and policy compliance. They are not abstract rules in a handbook; they are the framework that defines what you are allowed to do with the technical power you've been given.

It helps to understand the stakes clearly. A careless click or a "helpful" shortcut can hurt three different parties at once. There is the user, whose personal or financial data might be exposed or misused. There is the organization, which could face data breaches, regulatory investigations, fines, or reputational damage. And then there is you: the person who can be disciplined or fired, and who may find future employers asking why you left your last role. None of this is meant to scare you away from the profession; it is simply the reality that IT support is a position of trust. The good news is that if you learn to see your work through the lenses of privacy, licensing, and policy, you can protect everyone involved while still solving problems efficiently.

Privacy Fundamentals for IT Support

In day-to-day support work, privacy is less about memorizing laws and more about how you behave when you encounter other people's information. Think of it in three dimensions: what you see, what you record, and what you share. Every time you open a user's file to troubleshoot an issue, watch their desktop through a remote session, or scroll through logs and email headers, you are "seeing" things. Every time you update a ticket, take a screenshot, or send a diagnostic email, you are "recording" things. And every time you talk to a coworker about an issue or send logs to a vendor, you are "sharing" things. Good privacy practice is about being deliberate and restrained in all three.

You will encounter different categories of sensitive data, often in very ordinary-looking situations. The most obvious is **personally identifiable information (PII)**—details that can identify a specific individual. This might be something as simple as a user's full name combined with their address, phone number, email, or employee ID. Sometimes it's more sensitive, like a Social Security number, national ID, or date of birth. You may see credit card numbers or bank account details appear in a billing email the user is trying to print. You may open an HR spreadsheet to diagnose an Excel problem and find salary information, performance review notes, or disciplinary comments. Even the business itself has confidential data: customer lists, internal pricing models, and strategic plans that might be sitting in a shared folder when you're troubleshooting a slow file server. None of this looks like a movie-style "data breach" when you encounter it. It just looks like people trying to get their work done—and you, trying to help.

The best way to navigate this is to internalize a few core privacy principles. One is **minimum necessary access**. Just because you can read the entire contents of a document doesn't mean you should. If the user is reporting that "Excel crashes when I click Sort," you do not need to read every row of their HR data; you only need to reproduce and analyze the crash behavior. Another is **need-to-know sharing**. If you must involve a coworker or a vendor to solve an issue, you share only the specific information required for them to help, and only with people who are authorized to see it. A third is keeping **clean documentation**. Tickets, emails, and chat logs should describe the problem clearly without becoming a second repository of highly sensitive content. Finally, you practice **secure handling**: closing confidential documents when you're done, logging out of accounts you've accessed, and never walking away from an unlocked screen full of private data.

Consider a common remote support scenario. A user calls because their payroll software keeps generating an error when they run a report. You initiate a remote session and, before you do anything else, you explain that you're going to be able to see their screen and ask them to close any personal email, unrelated documents, or private windows. This is not just polite; it reduces the chance that you will be exposed to something you shouldn't see. As you work, you focus your attention on the error dialog and the steps that reproduce it. If you need a screenshot to attach to the ticket, you frame it to include only the error and any technical details, not the list of employee names and salaries behind it. If your capture ends up including more than you intended, you crop or redact it before saving or sending it. You avoid comments such as, "Wow, I didn't realize we paid that person so much," because you recognize that whatever you incidentally see is not for you to judge or discuss.

The same mindset applies when you handle devices physically. If someone drops off a laptop that "won't boot," your job is to diagnose the boot issue, not to browse through their pictures once you have it working. When you're asked to fix a smartphone with a broken app, you don't scroll through their messages or photo gallery out of curiosity. Even if the user is sitting there and says, "It's fine, you can go through anything," you are still bound by organizational privacy and security policies. On a corporate device, the company's rules and legal obligations usually take precedence over a user's casual consent.

Sometimes you'll see something that goes beyond an individual privacy concern and looks like a broader problem. Maybe you stumble across an unencrypted spreadsheet containing thousands of customer records on a publicly accessible shared drive. Maybe you see a text document on someone's desktop labeled "passwords" with multiple accounts in plain text. Or perhaps you receive a suspicious phone call from someone claiming to be from an external vendor, insisting they "need" a database export to troubleshoot an issue. In these situations, your responsibility is not to silently fix everything or ignore it because it feels awkward. Instead, you follow your organization's incident or escalation process: you notify your supervisor, security team, or designated privacy contact, and let them decide how to proceed. You do not try to cover it up, you do not start emailing copies of the sensitive file around "for safekeeping," and you definitely do not send data outside the company without formal authorization.

Software Licensing Basics

Privacy deals with how you handle information; licensing deals with how you handle software. In both cases, the central question is similar: just because something is technically possible, is it actually allowed? As a support technician, you are often the one installing, activating, and troubleshooting applications. That means you are also on the front line of making sure those applications are being used within the boundaries set by their creators and by your organization.

At a high level, a **software license** is simply a legal agreement that defines how a piece of software may be used: where it can be installed, how many copies can run at once, who can use it, and for what purposes. When you click "I Agree" under a long end user license agreement (EULA), you are accepting those terms on behalf of your organization. That's one reason many companies have standard procedures and approved software lists: they don't want front-line techs making ad hoc licensing decisions under pressure. Your role is to understand the basics well enough to recognize obvious problems and to follow your internal rules for everything else.

You will see several common license types again and again. An **OEM (Original Equipment Manufacturer)** license is one that comes preinstalled on hardware, such as a copy of Windows that ships with a new PC. These licenses are usually tied to that specific device and cannot be legally transferred to another system when the hardware is retired or replaced. As a technician, you might be tempted to "save money" by taking the product key from an old machine and applying it to a new build, but that typically violates the license. A **retail** or full packaged product license, by contrast, is often purchased separately and may allow transfer to a new device, provided it is removed from the old one and used within the EULA's conditions. When you decommission a workstation that has a retail license installed, you might be allowed to reuse that license on a replacement—if your organization's asset management process and the license terms permit it.

In larger environments, you will likely encounter **volume** or enterprise licenses. Here, the organization purchases the right to install software on a certain number of systems or for a certain number of users, often managed through a central key management system or license server. Your practical responsibility is to use the proper activation method, not to share the volume key outside the company, and to record installations so that license counts stay in sync with reality. Increasingly, you'll also handle **subscription** or **Software as a Service (SaaS)** products, like Microsoft 365 or Adobe Creative Cloud. In those models, the license often follows a user account rather than a device, and access may be controlled through sign-ins and cloud-based administration portals. Installing the desktop client is not enough; you must verify that the user has an active subscription assigned to their account.

On the other end of the spectrum, you will run into "free" software: freeware, trials, shareware, and open source. These can be deceptively tricky. **Freeware** may cost nothing to download, but the license might explicitly prohibit commercial use, or it might include adware or tracking that violates company security policy. **Shareware** or trial versions are meant for temporary evaluation, not long-term production use; deploying a trial product to an entire team and never paying for it is a form of piracy. **Open source** software provides access to the source code under specific licenses; it can be perfectly acceptable in business environments, but those licenses still impose conditions, especially if the organization modifies or redistributes the software. The key idea is that "free to download" does not automatically mean "free to use however we want." When in doubt, you consult documented policy or the people in your organization who handle procurement and licensing, rather than guessing.

Product keys and activations are the mechanisms vendors use to enforce these agreements. A **product key** is usually a unique code associated with a license or set of licenses. **Activation** is the process of validating that key with the vendor's service, ensuring that the number of active installations stays within the purchased limit. Your responsibility is to use only keys that come from authorized internal sources, never from random websites, and to avoid reusing keys in ways that exceed license counts. If a user's software suddenly goes into "unlicensed" mode because the activation failed, you treat it as a potential compliance issue as well as a technical one, and you coordinate with your licensing or asset management team.

From an exam and real-world perspective, what often matters most is your ability to recognize and refuse obvious violations. A manager might say, "We bought one copy of this expensive graphics program; can you just image that machine and clone it to the rest of the team?" The user might insist, "Can you put your copy of Office on my personal laptop? I just need it for a project." A colleague might half-jokingly mention a key generator or cracked version of a tool that "everyone uses, it's fine." In these situations, you are expected to choose policy and law over convenience or social pressure. That means politely explaining that software has to be installed within license limits, declining to deploy unlicensed copies, and pointing them toward legitimate alternatives or to procurement. The fact that it is technically easy to clone a machine or run a keygen is precisely why vendors and employers take these issues seriously.

Policy Compliance in Daily Operations

Privacy and licensing rules do not float in isolation; they are usually embedded in a broader set of organizational policies. These policies translate legal requirements, security standards, and management decisions into concrete rules that apply to your daily work. When the exam talks about "following policy," it is really asking whether you understand that your job is to operate within those rules, even when bending them might look like the fastest way to solve someone's immediate problem.

One of the first policies you'll encounter in most environments is an **acceptable use policy (AUP)**. This defines what users are and are not allowed to do with company systems and networks: for example, prohibiting illegal downloads, offensive content, unapproved software, or using corporate email for certain kinds of personal business. When you troubleshoot a user's machine and see torrent software and pirated movies, or a browser full of inappropriate sites, you are looking at potential AUP violations. Your job is not to act as a moral enforcer on the spot, but neither is it to ignore clear misuse. You follow your organization's procedures, which might include documenting the observation and informing a supervisor or HR, rather than uninstalling things quietly and pretending nothing happened.

Password and access control policies are another area where techs are frequently tested. These policies specify password complexity, expiration, multi-factor authentication, and, importantly, rules against sharing accounts. It is very common for a user to say something like, "I'm new here and my manager is out; can you just log in to the HR system with your account so I can run this report?" or "My coworker is on vacation; can you reset their password and give it to me so I can check their email?" No matter how urgent the situation seems, using your own elevated account to grant someone access, or handing out another person's credentials, is not acceptable. Proper procedure might involve verifying identity, obtaining formal authorization, creating temporary accounts with limited permissions, or escalating to the security team. On the exam, the answer that respects account ownership and identity verification—even if it delays the requested task—is the professional one.

Modern workplaces often rely on **BYOD (Bring Your Own Device)** and mobile device policies, as well as **remote access** policies. These govern when and how personal phones, tablets, and laptops can access corporate email, file shares, or internal applications, and they normally require certain safeguards like encryption, screen locks, and enrollment in a mobile device management (MDM) system. You may have users asking you to "just add my work email to my old Android; I don't want the company's management profile on my new one," or to configure remote desktop access directly to their workstation from home, bypassing the corporate VPN. If policy says that only managed devices can connect, or that remote access must go through a specific VPN client, you follow that policy. You do not open firewall ports on the user's router or install unapproved remote control tools simply because "that's easier."

Data retention and disposal policies connect directly back to earlier chapters on backup and destruction. These rules specify how long certain types of data must be kept—for legal, regulatory, or business reasons—and how that data must be destroyed when it is no longer needed. From your perspective, this means you don't arbitrarily delete old email archives or log files that policy requires to be retained, even if you are trying to free up disk space. It also means you don't quietly keep your own private backup of a user's home folder on a USB drive "just in case," outside of official backup systems. When decommissioning equipment, you follow procedures for wiping or physically destroying drives; you do not take old drives home as souvenirs or leave them in an unsecured drawer.

One of the more challenging aspects of policy compliance is learning to hold your ground under pressure while staying professional. Users—and sometimes managers—will frame their requests in ways that make noncompliance feel almost noble. "If we don't do this now, the project will fail." "The policy is stupid; everyone ignores it." "Just this once; you can trust me." Your task is to separate the emotional framing from the underlying rule. You calmly restate the relevant policy, explain that it exists for reasons like security, legal compliance, or auditability, and then look for alternatives that stay within the rules. That might mean suggesting that the user contact procurement for more licenses, asking your supervisor to consider a formal exception through change management, or showing the user a different approved tool that can solve most of their problem. The key point is that doing something you know violates policy is not part of "good customer service," even if the person asking is higher than you in the org chart.

You will also encounter situations where you witness clear policy violations. Maybe while helping someone with an email issue, you see harassing or discriminatory messages that are obviously out of line. Maybe you notice a shared folder full of cracked software installers. In those cases, you resist the impulse to confront the user angrily or to collect more "evidence" than necessary. You stick to factual observations, document only what your process requires, and follow the designated reporting chain—usually your supervisor, HR, or a security/compliance office. You avoid broadcasting what you saw to colleagues as gossip, and you do not go hunting for more examples. Your goal is to hand the concern to the people whose job it is to investigate, not to become an amateur detective.

When you put all of this together—privacy awareness, licensing discipline, and policy compliance—you get a simple but powerful filter for your daily work: is what I'm about to do allowed by our rules, our agreements, and our users' reasonable expectations of confidentiality? If your answer is not a confident yes, you stop and ask instead of improvising. That might mean checking the software catalog before installing a tool, reviewing the AUP before enabling a new kind of remote access, or asking your supervisor how to handle a file full of PII you weren't expecting to see. Over time, this habit becomes second nature, and it marks the difference between someone who just knows how systems work and someone who can be trusted to operate them responsibly.

9.6 Communication & Professionalism in Support

In day-to-day IT support, users rarely see you swap a power supply or configure a firewall rule. What they do see—and remember—is how you talk to them, how you listen, and whether you follow through on what you say. For most non-technical people, your communication style is the main evidence they have to judge your competence. That is why, in the CompTIA A+ world, so-called "soft skills" are not optional extras; they are core tools of your job, as important as a screwdriver or remote access client. The exam writers know this, which is why so many scenario questions hinge not on which command is correct, but on which response is most professional.

Professional communication in IT support is broader than just speaking politely. It includes the words you choose, the tone of your voice, your body language if you are on-site, and the way you write emails, chat messages, and ticket updates. A rushed "Yeah, that's not our problem" can undo twenty minutes of smart troubleshooting. In contrast, "Let's see what we can do on our side, and if needed I'll involve the team that handles that system" sends a very different message, even if the technical outcome is identical. This chapter focuses on how to build communication habits that help users feel heard and supported, keep your work aligned with policy, and feed cleanly into the documentation, ticketing, and escalation processes you saw earlier.

Professional Communication in Practice

When you think about professional communication, it helps to picture a specific interaction. Imagine walking up to a user's desk after a help desk ticket is assigned to you. They look frustrated and say, "My computer keeps freezing. This thing is useless." In that moment, everything from your greeting to your facial expression shapes how the rest of the interaction will go. A professional technician introduces themselves, establishes a basic connection, and signals that they are there to help. "Hi, I'm Sam from IT. I see you're having trouble with the system freezing—let's take a look and get you back up and running." You have not fixed anything yet, but you have already done something important: you have reduced tension and made it clear you and the user are on the same side.

Word choice matters a lot more than many new technicians realize. Phrases like "You must have done something wrong" or "That's not how you're supposed to use it" may feel efficient, but they shift blame onto the user and make them defensive. A more professional alternative keeps the focus on the problem, not the person: "Let's walk through exactly what happened before it froze so we can figure out what's going on." Technically, you are asking for the same information, yet one version attacks the user while the other invites cooperation. The A+ exam often presents answer choices that are technically accurate but poorly phrased; the correct choice will usually respect the user and avoid blaming language.

The level of technical language you use should track the user's understanding, not your desire to sound knowledgeable. Telling a marketing manager, "It looks like your DHCP lease expired and your NIC didn't renew properly" is not helpful unless you immediately translate it into plain language. A more user-centered version would be, "Your computer lost its network address, so it couldn't talk to the rest of the network. I've renewed that address, and now you should be able to get to your files again." You can still mention the technical term briefly if appropriate, but you anchor it in everyday language. The exam will sometimes test this by giving you choices between jargon-heavy and plain-language responses; assume you are speaking to a non-technical user unless the question specifically says otherwise.

Tone is just as important as content. Sarcasm, even if meant as humor, rarely comes across well in support interactions, especially in written form where the user cannot see your facial expression. A chat message like "Well, that's one way to do it..." can look condescending even if you thought you were being playful. A professional tone avoids sarcasm, avoids slang that can be misinterpreted, and stays calm even when the user is upset. That doesn't mean you must sound robotic. You can be friendly and human while still being careful: "No worries, a lot of people run into this. Here's what we'll do next."

Written communication adds another layer. Emails, ticket notes, and chat logs can be forwarded, audited, and pulled into incident reviews. A message you meant for one coworker may end up in front of a manager or even a legal team. That is why clear language, complete sentences, and basic spelling matter—not because you are being graded on grammar, but because you want your message to be unambiguous. "Fixed it" as a ticket update tells the next technician almost nothing. "Reset user's password, confirmed successful login and email send with user present" gives concrete detail and supports later troubleshooting if the issue returns. When the exam asks which ticket note is most appropriate, look for the one that is specific, neutral, and free of emotional or judgmental language.

Active Listening and Clarifying the Problem

Good troubleshooting starts with good listening. **Active listening** is more than just letting someone talk; it is a deliberate effort to understand what they are saying, including what they may not be articulating clearly. Users often call you when they are stressed or in a hurry, and they may jump around in their explanations: "It was fine this morning, then I got this weird thing, then everything disappeared, and I had that meeting and..." Your job is to slow the conversation down enough that you can extract the technical signal from the emotional noise.

Practically, active listening involves focusing fully on the user instead of half-listening while you type or think ahead to your favorite fix. On the phone, that might mean using short acknowledgments—"Okay," "I see," "Go on"—so the user knows you are still with them. In person, eye contact, a neutral facial expression, and nodding at appropriate times communicate the same thing. CompTIA pays attention to this; in scenario questions, interrupting the user too early or ignoring their description in favor of jumping to your favorite command is often the wrong choice.

Once the user has finished their initial explanation, you move into **clarifying questions**. These are targeted questions that fill in gaps and make vague statements precise. If a user says, "My email doesn't work," you might ask, "What exactly happens when you try to send or receive a message?" or "Did this start today, or has it been happening for a while?" The key is to avoid sounding accusatory. "What did you do before it broke?" puts the user on the defensive, while "What were you working on right before you noticed the issue?" invites useful detail without blame.

After you have gathered information, **paraphrasing** helps confirm that you understood correctly. You restate the problem in your own words and ask for confirmation: "So, just to make sure I have this right: you can open Outlook and read old emails, but any new messages you send just sit in the Outbox and never leave. Is that correct?" If the user says yes, you know you are troubleshooting the right problem. If they say no and correct you, you have just caught a misunderstanding before it wasted time. The A+ exam will often show a technician who immediately starts changing settings after hearing a vague complaint; the better answer usually involves paraphrasing and clarifying first.

Active listening, clarifying questions, and paraphrasing are not just politeness techniques; they tie directly into accurate documentation and efficient use of your time. The more precisely you can define the symptom, the more likely you are to choose an effective troubleshooting path. This also matters when you escalate. A vague escalation note like "User's network is broken" forces the next team to repeat your entire intake process. A note grounded in active listening—"User reports intermittent connection drops over Wi-Fi since yesterday afternoon; wired connection remains stable; issue began after moving to new conference room"—gives the next tier a head start.

Empathy, Emotional Control, and Difficult Customers

Most people do not call IT when everything is fine. They call when they are locked out of their account five minutes before a presentation, or when they think they have just deleted a week's worth of work. It is normal for them to arrive in your queue frustrated, anxious, or even angry. **Empathy**—the ability to recognize and acknowledge what they are feeling—helps you defuse those emotions so you can work together productively. This does not mean you agree with every complaint or accept abuse; it means you signal that you understand the impact the problem is having on them.

A simple, effective pattern here is acknowledge, reassure, then act. Suppose a remote sales representative calls, speaking rapidly and angrily: "My VPN never works! I've been trying for an hour, I keep getting some authentication error, and I have a meeting in 15 minutes. What are you people doing over there?" A purely technical response might be, "What's the exact error code?" That is not wrong, but it ignores the emotional context. A more professional response would be, "I'm sorry you're dealing with this right before a meeting; I know that's stressful. My name is Jordan; I'll work with you on this now. First, can you tell me exactly what message you see when you try to connect?" You have acknowledged the frustration, reassured them that someone is taking ownership, and then moved into the technical step.

It is important to distinguish empathy from joining in on blame. You might be tempted to say, "Yeah, our VPN is terrible" to build rapport, but that undermines trust in your organization and can create problems if the call is reviewed later. A more professional line keeps the focus on the user's experience and the path forward: "I can see this is causing you a real problem; let's see what we can do right now, and if needed I'll get the network team involved." The exam will sometimes include answer choices where the technician criticizes their own IT department in front of the user; however relatable that might feel, it is not considered professional behavior.

When a customer is truly angry, your own emotional control becomes crucial. Raising your voice to match theirs, arguing, or saying, "Calm down" almost always escalates the situation. Staying calm, speaking a little more slowly, and sticking to the acknowledge–reassure–act pattern can gradually bring the temperature down. If a user becomes abusive or threatening, you are not required to tolerate that indefinitely. Professionalism here means following your organization's policies: giving clear warnings if required, ending the interaction if it crosses a line, and involving a supervisor or security if needed. CompTIA expects you to recognize when escalation to a manager is appropriate for behavioral reasons, not just technical ones.

Managing Expectations and Being Honest

Users care about two main things: whether their issue will be fixed, and how long it will take. **Managing expectations** is the process of setting realistic answers to those questions and keeping the user informed as circumstances change. Overpromising is one of the fastest ways to damage trust. Telling a user, "I'll have this fixed in five minutes," when you are not sure, may win you a brief moment of relief, but if the problem turns out to be more complex you now have an even more frustrated user who feels misled.

A better approach is to explain what you will do first and what might happen after that. You might say, "I'll start by checking your network connection; if that doesn't solve it, I may need to escalate this to our network team, which could take longer. I'll keep you updated as we go." This is honest, sets a baseline expectation, and signals that escalation is a normal part of the process, not a failure. You can also tie expectations to known service level agreements (SLAs) without going into policy detail: "Our goal is to restore access within an hour for this type of issue; if it looks like it will take longer, I'll let you know."

Honesty also means admitting when you do not know something yet. Many new technicians worry that saying "I don't know" will make them seem incompetent, but the unprofessional alternative is pretending you know and making guesses on production systems. A professional way to handle this is to pair honesty with a plan: "I'm not sure yet why you're seeing that error, but I'm going to research it and, if needed, check with our senior technician. I'll update you by 3:00 PM." On the exam, answers that admit uncertainty while committing to follow-up and escalation are usually preferred over answers where the technician bluffs or experiments on live data without authorization.

Expectation management continues throughout the interaction. If you initially thought a fix would be quick but then discover it requires a server change that only the systems team can perform, you should update the user rather than hoping they will not notice the delay. "This appears to be an issue on the server side that I don't have access to change. I've escalated it to our systems team, and they will contact you by email once they've made the change. In the meantime, here is a temporary workaround you can use today." That kind of transparency, anchored in process, prevents users from feeling abandoned.

Professionalism, Confidentiality, and Escalation

Communication is a big part of **professionalism**, but not the whole story. Professional behavior also includes showing up on time for appointments, respecting dress codes and safety requirements, and treating users' physical and digital spaces with respect. When you are at a user's desk, you are often in their personal bubble: you can see family photos, private notes, and sometimes sensitive documents on the screen. Professional technicians do not comment on this or poke around out of curiosity. If you need to close windows to work, you might say, "Is it okay if I close these windows while I work on your email client?" That simple question respects both their time and their privacy.

Confidentiality is especially important because you will have access to information other employees may never see. You might open an email client and see messages about medical issues, legal matters, or performance reviews. You may be able to browse network shares with confidential financial data. Professionalism here means accessing only what you need to address the technical problem, avoiding reading content that is irrelevant to your task, and never discussing what you saw with other users. On the A+ exam, any answer choice where the technician reads through personal files "to look for the missing document" or gossips about another user's issue is almost certainly wrong.

Escalation sits at the intersection of professionalism and process. **Escalation** simply means involving someone with more authority, access, or expertise when a problem is outside your scope or cannot be resolved within policy limits. Some new technicians see escalation as a sign of weakness, as if they have failed. In reality, appropriate escalation is a sign of judgment. Knowing when to stop experimenting and bring in the right resource protects the user, the data, and the systems. If you are working on a laptop for an executive and you discover that the issue is related to a server-side email rule you cannot change, the professional move is not to "hack around it," but to say, "This is related to a rule on our email server that I don't have access to change. I'll document what I've found and escalate this to our messaging team. You should receive an update from them by this afternoon."

A good escalation includes the right information for the next tier. At minimum, that means who is affected and how to contact them, what system and symptoms are involved, what steps you have already taken and their results, and any time constraints. "Executive user unable to receive external email since this morning; internal mail works. Verified Outlook profile, tested on OWA, issue persists across devices. Suspect server-side rule preventing external delivery. User has client meetings this afternoon." Compare that to "User email broken," and you can see why the first example is preferred. The A+ objectives expect you to recognize that this level of detail is part of professionalism.

Following the **chain of command** is another aspect of proper escalation. In most organizations, you would not bypass your help desk lead and email the CIO about a routine printer problem, even if you happen to know their address. Escalation usually flows through defined tiers or roles: from front-line technicians to senior techs, from there to specialized teams or managers. When the issue involves safety, legal concerns, or potential policy violations—such as suspected data breaches, harassment, or evidence of illegal activity—you escalate to the appropriate internal party and do not discuss it with other users. Confidential reporting and restricted communication are part of being a trusted IT professional.

Finally, professionalism extends to how you close interactions. Once the technical work is done—whether by you or through escalation—you should take a moment to summarize what was done, confirm that the user is satisfied, and explain any follow-up. "We updated your VPN client and reset your credentials. You're able to connect now, and I've documented the change in your ticket. If you see the same error again, please reference ticket 45231 when you call." That closing moment often shapes the user's lasting impression more than the specific technical steps you took, and it creates a clean handoff if the issue returns later.

9.7 Remote Access Technologies

If you spend any time in a modern support role, you quickly realize that "walking over to the user's desk" is the exception, not the rule. Users work from home, from branch offices, from hotel Wi-Fi, or from networks you've never seen. Yet they still expect you to fix problems, configure settings, and sometimes even train them on new tools. Remote access is how you put your hands on a system that might be hundreds or thousands of miles away, and on the CompTIA A+ exam it is treated not just as a technical skill, but as a professional responsibility that touches security, privacy, and user trust.

A good starting point is to separate two ideas that often get mixed together: remote access for the user and remote access for support. Users might connect to a corporate desktop from home using a VPN and a remote desktop client, or log into a cloud app from their laptop while traveling. That's user-centric remote access. This section, however, focuses on the other side of the screen: the **remote support** tools and workflows you use as a technician to see what the user sees, control their device when appropriate, and do all of that in a way that is secure, authorized, and transparent.

Types of Remote Access Tools from a Support Perspective

Most environments give you a mix of options, and part of your job is recognizing which one fits a particular situation. Even if you don't memorize every product name, you should recognize the main categories and how they behave.

On Windows systems, you will encounter two broad families of built-in tools. The first is **Remote Desktop**, Microsoft's implementation of the Remote Desktop Protocol (RDP). With Remote Desktop, you are essentially logging into the computer as if you were physically at its keyboard, but your session is separate from any local user. In most configurations, when you connect via Remote Desktop, the person sitting at that machine is signed out or locked out of the interactive console, and they can't see what you're doing. This is great when you need to administer a workstation or server after hours, install software, or run scripts without the user present. It is a poor choice when the scenario clearly states that the user must demonstrate an issue or watch what you're doing, which is a favorite trap on the exam.

That second scenario—where you and the user need to share the same session—is where **assistance tools** like Windows **Quick Assist** come in. With Quick Assist, you and the user both see the same desktop. The user remains logged in, and typically they must actively approve the support session, often by entering a code you provide and then clicking an "Allow" or "Share" prompt. This is ideal when you need the user to reproduce an error ("Show me exactly what you click before the application crashes") or when you are training them and want them to see your cursor and follow your steps. Unlike Remote Desktop, these tools are designed around consent and collaboration, so CompTIA will often favor them in scenarios involving user participation.

Not every environment relies solely on OS-native tools. Many help desks standardize on **third-party remote support platforms** such as TeamViewer, AnyDesk, LogMeIn, or enterprise suites from major vendors. The names are less important than their shared capabilities. Typically, they provide a small client the user runs, which then generates a session code or invite link. You, as the technician, enter that code into your console to request a connection. The user must confirm the request, often choosing whether you have view-only access or full control. Most of these tools include integrated chat, file transfer, and automatic logging of connection times and actions. In a corporate setting, policy usually dictates which tool you may use, and this becomes important in exam questions where a user says, "I already have this other remote app installed; can you just use that?" The correct response is almost always to stick with approved, company-managed tools, even if another option might seem quicker.

Graphical desktop sharing is not the only way to manage systems remotely. Especially in server or Linux environments, support often relies on **remote shell** access. On Linux and macOS, **SSH (Secure Shell)** is the standard. When you SSH into a system, you get a command-line session, not a graphical desktop. It is heavily encrypted and uses strong authentication, often with key pairs instead of just passwords. On Windows, you might see **PowerShell Remoting** or other secure shell-like mechanisms that allow you to run commands and scripts on remote machines. From an A+ point of view, you don't need to configure SSH servers or write complex PowerShell scripts, but you should understand that remote administration is not always about moving a mouse on someone else's desktop. Sometimes, especially for batch changes or automation, a remote shell is more efficient and more secure.

A growing amount of remote management happens without any "session" in the classic sense. Many organizations use **web-based management consoles**—part of cloud services, mobile device management (MDM) platforms, or remote monitoring and management (RMM) tools. From a browser, you might see device inventories, patch status, and configuration profiles, and you might be able to push changes like "turn on full disk encryption" or "deploy this app" without ever opening a remote desktop session. Some of these consoles also offer a button to launch remote control when needed, blurring the line between centralized management and one-on-one support. For the exam, recognize that in a managed environment, the "remote access tool" might really be this larger platform, and using it is often preferred to ad-hoc tools because it fits within policy, logging, and change management practices.

Security, Privacy, and Professional Conduct in Remote Sessions

Because remote access gives you powerful control over user systems, security and privacy concerns are always in the foreground. CompTIA consistently rewards answers that show you understand that your first job is to protect users and the organization, not just to fix the computer fast.

Before you even think about connecting, you must **verify the user's identity** using methods your organization has approved. That might mean calling them back on an internal phone number from the directory, checking their employee ID against the ticketing system, or using information stored in HR or identity systems. What you should not do is ask for their password or other sensitive authentication details. A correct answer on the exam will never have you say, "Please tell me your password so I can log in as you." If something truly requires elevated credentials, you either have your own admin account or you follow a secure, documented process to obtain temporary access; you do not shortcut by borrowing user credentials.

Once you are confident you are working with the right person, you shift into consent and communication. A legitimate remote support session should never feel sneaky. The user should understand that you intend to connect, what tool you will use, what they will see on their screen, and what level of control you will have. You might tell them, "I'm going to start a Quick Assist session. You'll see a prompt asking if you want to share your screen. Please read it and click Allow if you're okay with me viewing and controlling your desktop." Many remote tools show a clear banner or notification while the session is active. As a professional, you should prefer tools that provide this visibility, and you should never try to hide your presence or minimize notifications so you can work "in the background" without the user noticing.

Privacy is where many new technicians unintentionally cross lines. When you control someone's computer, you are stepping into their digital workspace—and sometimes into their personal life. Best practice is to touch only what is necessary for the task. If you need to open File Explorer, you focus on the application's installation directory or relevant logs, not the user's "Pictures" or a folder obviously labeled with personal content. If part of troubleshooting requires you to look at something that could be sensitive—browser history, screenshots, or cached documents—you explain why you need to do it and ask before proceeding. In an exam scenario, any option that has you casually browsing their personal files "to see what's there" or reading private email messages "just in case" should be a red flag.

The broader security principle at work here is **least privilege**. Remote tools often let you choose between view-only and full control, or between connecting as a standard user and performing actions as an administrator. When you can, you start with the least powerful mode that will allow you to do the job. If you only need to watch the user recreate a problem, you don't need to take over the mouse. If a task truly requires admin rights, you elevate for that step, perform it, and then drop back down. Some support tools even require the user to explicitly approve elevation to administrator tasks during a session, which further reinforces consent. On the exam, answers that minimize privileges and session duration are usually the right direction.

Remote sessions can also be abused by attackers, which overlaps with the social engineering content you saw earlier. Scammers often call or email users pretending to be "from IT" or "from Microsoft support," then persuade the victim to install a remote access tool or accept a connection. As a real technician, you will spend time undoing the damage from these incidents and educating users. It is common to say, "We will never initiate a remote session with you out of the blue. We only connect after you've opened a ticket or contacted our help desk, and we only use approved tools that show our company name." From a testing perspective, watch for scenarios where the best advice to give a user is that they should never accept unsolicited remote-control requests or install tools at a stranger's direction.

A Professional Remote Support Workflow

To tie the technical pieces together, it helps to walk mentally through a typical support interaction delivered remotely. This is the same mental checklist you'll want to apply when answering scenario questions on the exam.

Imagine a user calls the help desk because a line-of-business application crashes every time they try to run a report. Your first step is **intake and assessment**, which means listening carefully, asking clarifying questions, and deciding whether remote access is appropriate. You might ask, "Is your computer turning on normally?" and "Can you open a browser and reach the company intranet?" If the machine will not power on, or there is no network connectivity at all, a remote session is pointless and you would instead schedule an in-person visit or walk them through hardware checks. The exam will sometimes offer remote access as an option in a situation where it cannot possibly work; recognizing that and choosing a more realistic next step is part of what's being tested.

Once you decide remote support makes sense, you move into **preparation and communication**. You verify the user's identity per policy, confirm that they are on a network where your tools will function (for instance, some tools require VPN access for offsite users), and select the appropriate support tool. If the user needs to demonstrate the error while staying logged in, you choose a session-sharing tool like Quick Assist or a third-party remote assistance client. If it's after hours and you just need to install an update, you might instead use Remote Desktop or an RMM console. You tell the user what to expect: "I'm going to send you a link to our remote support app. Once it opens, it will show a six-digit code. Read that code to me, and then I'll request permission to view your screen."

Establishing the connection often requires guiding the user through several small steps, and this is where your communication skills matter as much as your technical ones. A common friction point with tools like Quick Assist or third-party clients is that the consent dialog might be hidden behind other windows, minimized, or dismissed accidentally. When a user says, "Nothing is happening," your troubleshooting brain should check simple things first: Is their internet connection stable? Is a local firewall blocking the tool? Did they actually click the link you sent, or did their browser block the download? In an exam question, the "best next step" after a failed connection attempt is often something basic like verifying network connectivity or confirming that remote access is enabled in the OS settings, rather than immediately reinstalling the OS or blaming the tool.

Once you are in, you move into **conducting the session**. A good habit is to narrate your actions at a high level: "I'm going to open your application's settings now to check the logging options," or, "I'm going to close this window so I can see the error message behind it." This reassures the user that you are not randomly clicking around. Before closing applications, especially if they might contain unsaved work, you ask: "Do you have any unsaved documents in this program before I close it?" If the fix requires a reboot, you tell the user first, explain what will happen to the remote session, and coordinate with them so they are not surprised when their screen suddenly goes black. If bandwidth is poor and the screen updates slowly, you might disable unnecessary visual effects or ask the user to close video calls and streaming to stabilize the connection.

Throughout the session, you maintain professional boundaries. If the user moves the mouse or types while you are working, you pause and clarify who is in control. Some tools allow you to temporarily release control so the user can perform actions under your observation; this can be a good teaching moment and reduces the risk that they feel disempowered. If at any point the user expresses discomfort—"I don't like that you can see everything on my desktop"—you explain what you are doing, remind them they can end the session at any time, and, if necessary, offer to switch to guided instructions instead of direct control.

When the work is complete, you don't silently disconnect and hang up. The final phase is **closing and documenting**. You confirm the issue is resolved by having the user test: "Please try running that report again and tell me what happens." Once they verify things are working, you tell them explicitly that you are ending the remote session and explain how they can close any remaining windows related to the tool. Only then do you disconnect. Afterward, you update the ticket or documentation system, recording that remote access was used, which tool, at what time, and what changes you made during the session. If you viewed or modified anything sensitive, you note that as well, in line with your organization's policies. CompTIA treats this as part of the job, not an optional courtesy, so expect exam answers that emphasize accurate documentation as the final step.

All of these details—choosing the right tool, verifying identity, obtaining consent, working with least privilege, narrating your actions, and documenting your work—add up to a picture of remote access as more than just a piece of software. It is a way of working that depends on trust, policy, and professionalism every bit as much as it does on technical connectivity.

9.9 Knowledge Check

Question 1: A user calls the help desk to report "weird icons and missing files." What is the FIRST action you should take according to good operational procedures?

A. Create or locate a ticket and begin documenting the interaction
B. Immediately remote into the user's system to look at the issue
C. Ask the user to reboot and call back if the problem continues
D. Search the knowledge base for "weird icons and missing files"

Question 2: In a ticketing system, which field combination is typically used together to determine a ticket's overall priority?

A. Category and subcategory
B. Status and assigned group
C. Asset and configuration item
D. Impact and urgency

Question 3: A ticket shows "Network > Wi-Fi" as its category, and it has been assigned to the desktop support team by mistake. What is the BEST action to take?

A. Resolve the ticket with a note that it is not your team's responsibility
B. Delete the ticket so it can be recreated in the correct queue
C. Reassign the ticket to the appropriate network support queue and update notes
D. Ignore the ticket and wait for a manager to reroute it

Question 4: Which of the following best describes the purpose of a change record in relation to incident tickets?

A. It replaces incident tickets when users report problems
B. It stores hardware inventory like serial numbers and hostnames
C. It tracks individual user contact details and preferences
D. It documents planned system modifications and can be linked to related incidents

Question 5: A junior technician closes a ticket with the note "ran some basic checks, it works now." Why is this inadequate documentation?

A. It is too detailed for managers to read efficiently
B. It lacks specific steps, error codes, and configuration details needed for future analysis
C. It improperly omits the user's password used during testing
D. It fails to include the technician's personal opinion of the user

Question 6: Which ticket note most appropriately balances detail and confidentiality?

A. "Reset user's password to Pa$$w0rd123 and emailed it to them."
B. "User gave me their banking PIN so I could test the website; stored in ticket for reference."
C. "Reset the user's password per policy; user entered new password directly and confirmed successful login."
D. "User is clueless; had to fix their mistake again."

Question 7: An organization's policy states that any action affecting multiple users or production systems must follow change management. Which of the following should be handled as a formal change?

A. Replacing a faulty mouse on a receptionist's PC
B. Changing the screen resolution on a single kiosk
C. Deploying a Windows update to all finance department workstations
D. Assisting one user with installing a local printer driver

Question 8: In the change management workflow, which step focuses on determining what systems and business processes could be affected and what might go wrong?

A. Implementation
B. Impact and risk assessment
C. Documentation and closeout
D. Communication with users

Question 9: A critical security vulnerability is actively being exploited on your VPN servers, and the business is at immediate risk. Which classification of change is MOST appropriate for the patching response?

A. Emergency change
B. Standard change
C. Normal change
D. Unauthorized change

Question 10: A small business cannot afford to lose more than one day of data on its shared file server. Which backup schedule best matches this Recovery Point Objective (RPO)?

A. Nightly backups of the shared data
B. Monthly full backups only
C. Quarterly full backups with no interim backups
D. One full backup per year combined with daily antivirus scans

Question 11: Which backup type copies only the data that has changed since the last full backup, requiring just the latest full and latest backup set to restore?

A. Full
B. Incremental
C. Differential
D. Snapshot

Question 12: A user's hard drive has failed, and they need their entire workstation restored to its exact previous state as quickly as possible. Which backup approach is MOST appropriate?

A. File-level backup of only the Documents folder
B. Weekly full backup plus no other backups
C. Cloud sync of selected spreadsheets
D. Recent image-based (system image) backup of the entire drive

Question 13: Which cleaning method is MOST appropriate for removing dust from inside a desktop PC while minimizing the risk of component damage?

A. Use a household vacuum cleaner directly on the motherboard
B. Wipe components with a wet cloth while the PC is powered on
C. Use a hair dryer on high heat to blow dust out of the case
D. Use compressed air in short bursts while holding fans in place and the system powered off and unplugged

Question 14: A coworker suggests opening a faulty power supply to "look for burnt components." As an A+ technician, how should you respond?

A. Decline and replace the PSU as a unit, since opening it is unsafe and outside your role
B. Open it only if it has been unplugged for at least one minute
C. Proceed as long as you wear an antistatic wrist strap
D. Open it only when the PC is powered on so you can see the fault

Question 15: While working inside a desktop computer, which ESD practice is MOST appropriate?

A. Wear an antistatic wrist strap connected to an unpainted metal part of the unplugged case
B. Wear a wrist strap connected to the building's hot (live) conductor
C. Work on a carpeted floor without any grounding equipment
D. Store RAM modules in regular plastic grocery bags while you work

Question 16: A manager insists that you install a single licensed copy of an expensive application on five different employee computers to "save money." What should you do?

A. Comply, since the manager is responsible for budget decisions
B. Explain that this violates the software license and refer them to procurement for additional licenses
C. Install it but remove the product key from the documentation
D. Share your personal copy of the software to avoid licensing issues

Question 17: A user demands that you log in to the HR system with your elevated account so they can run a report while their own access is pending approval. What is the MOST appropriate response?

A. Agree to help just this once, since the request is urgent
B. Ask them to use another coworker's credentials instead
C. Create a shared account for the department and email everyone the password
D. Decline, explain that policies prohibit sharing elevated access, and escalate the access request through proper channels

Question 18: A user says, "My email is broken," but provides no further details. Which response BEST demonstrates active listening and clarification?

A. "Can you walk me through exactly what happens when you try to send or receive an email, from the beginning?"
B. "You must have done something wrong with your email settings."
C. "Email problems are always the server; I'll just restart it."
D. "I don't need more details; this is a common issue."

ANSWERS

1: Correct Answer: A
Rationale: Good operational procedure starts with creating or finding a ticket so the issue, actions, and communications can be tracked and documented before troubleshooting.

2: Correct Answer: D
Rationale: Impact (how many or what systems are affected) and urgency (how quickly it must be resolved) are combined to set ticket priority in most ITSM systems.

3: Correct Answer: C
Rationale: Proper workflow is to reroute misassigned tickets to the correct queue and add notes, not close, delete, or ignore them.

4: Correct Answer: D
Rationale: A change record documents planned modifications, approvals, timing, and can be linked to incidents for tracking cause and effect.

5: Correct Answer: B
Rationale: Documentation must include concrete steps, findings, and configuration details so another technician can understand and, if needed, repeat or build on the work.

6: Correct Answer: C
Rationale: It records the action and outcome without exposing passwords or other sensitive data, maintaining confidentiality and professionalism.

7: Correct Answer: C
Rationale: Deploying updates to all finance workstations affects multiple users and a critical business function, so it must follow formal change procedures.

8: Correct Answer: B
Rationale: Impact and risk assessment evaluates which systems and processes are affected and what could go wrong before approving or scheduling the change.

9: Correct Answer: A
Rationale: An actively exploited, high-risk vulnerability requires an emergency change, which allows expedited review and implementation.

10: Correct Answer: A
Rationale: An RPO of one day means at most one day of data loss is acceptable; nightly backups meet that requirement.

11: Correct Answer: C
Rationale: Differential backups copy all changes since the last full backup, so restoration needs only the last full and the latest differential set.

12: Correct Answer: D
Rationale: An image-based backup captures the entire system (OS, apps, data) and supports fast bare-metal restore to the previous state.

13: Correct Answer: D
Rationale: Using compressed air on a powered-off, unplugged system and holding fans in place avoids overspin and reduces risk of physical and ESD damage.

14: Correct Answer: A
Rationale: Power supplies contain dangerous stored voltages; A+ technicians should not open them and should replace the entire unit instead.

15: Correct Answer: A
Rationale: Connecting an antistatic wrist strap to bare metal on an unplugged case equalizes potential between you and components, reducing ESD risk.

16: Correct Answer: B
Rationale: Installing software beyond its license terms is piracy; you must follow licensing rules and direct the manager to obtain proper licenses.

17: Correct Answer: D
Rationale: Sharing or misusing elevated credentials violates security policy; you must refuse and route the request through approved access procedures.

18: Correct Answer: A
Rationale: Asking for a step-by-step description shows active listening and gathers the detail needed to diagnose a vague "email is broken" complaint.

ACCESS YOUR EXTRA STUDY MATERIALS

We hope this guide has helped you build a solid understanding of the CompTIA A+ exam objectives and feel more confident in your preparation for both Core 1 and Core 2. While this book provides a strong foundation, effective exam preparation is often reinforced through active practice and structured review. To support your continued progress, additional study tools are available to complement the material covered in this guide.

Here's what's waiting for you:

- **CompTIA A+ Exam Simulator (Core 1 & Core 2)**
  Generate unlimited custom practice exams with a realistic test simulator that mirrors actual exam conditions and helps you build confidence, speed, and accuracy before test day.
- **1,300+ Digital Flashcards**
  Reinforce your understanding of key IT terms, acronyms, and troubleshooting steps with dynamic flashcards that make even short study sessions productive and efficient.
- **Question Bank Download Center**
  Access over 5,000 downloadable, exam-style questions spanning all CompTIA A+ domains. Test your knowledge on paper and strengthen your exam readiness.
- **The SYSTEM-14 Course**
  Master critical exam content in just 14 days with guided flashcard strategies and effective memory techniques.
- **Mindshift Video Program**
  Get insider tips on test-taking strategies, managing exam stress, and staying sharp under pressure—so you walk into the testing center with confidence and a clear plan.

These study tools are available for ongoing use.

To access them, visit the link below and enter the access code when prompted.

tinyurl.com/he-aplus

Your secret code is: **comptiaa1208**

Made in the USA
Monee, IL
08 November 2026

68183978R00144